Media and Communication

Media and Communication

Paddy Scannell

Los Angeles | London | New Delhi
Singapore | Washington DC

First published 2007
Reprinted 2008, 2009, 2010

SAGE Publications Ltd
1 Oliver's Yard
55 City Road
London EC1Y 1SP

SAGE Publications Inc.
2455 Teller Road
Thousand Oaks, California 91320

SAGE Publications India Pvt Ltd
B-1/11 Mohan Cooperative Industrial Area
Mathura Road, New Delhi 110 044
India

SAGE Publications Asia-Pacific Ptc Ltd
33 pekin Street #02-01
Far East Square
Singapore 04763

British Library Cataloguing in Publication data

A catalogue record for this book is available from the British Library

ISBN 978 1 4129 0268 7
ISBN 978 1 4129 0269 4 (pbk)

Library of Congress control number available

Typeset by C&M Digitals (P) Ltd., Chennai, India
Printed in Great Britain by Ashford Colour Press Ltd., Gosport, Hampshire
Printed on paper from sustainable resources

Contents

Acknowledgements

This book is based on teaching courses on media and communication over many years. I have a primary debt of gratitude then to all the students who, each time we went through some version of what follows, understood or didn't understand the point in general, or particular, of what we were talking about, agreed with it or not and by sheer dint of incremental repetition helped me to clarify, at least, what *I* thought we were up to. It has taken me a long time to grasp an elementary point: you only *really* begin to engage with what you teach and see what it's about after many returns to it. When I was younger I used to feel slightly ashamed at repeating the same course with small variations year after year. Now I enjoy finding different perspectives each year and trying out old and new material from different angles. And each time I do this I learn a little more and understand more clearly what I am trying to do and why.

A number of people have read sections of this book as I was working on it and I am grateful to Martin Montgomery, Shaun Moores, Andrew Tolson, Pete Simonson and Bill Schwarz for their comments on particular chapters. I am especially grateful to the four readers of the manuscript for their helpful, detailed responses to it. I have taken note of what all my readers had to say in the final revision of the text. My thanks too, to Maren Hartman who provided me with information about contemporary views of the Frankfurt School in Germany, and to Sarah Crymble for heroic work on the picture search.

I first began teaching the contents of this book with David Cardiff in the early 1980s. David died three years ago at the untimely age of 59. It was always a great pleasure teaching with him. I like to think we were a good double act and that between us we entertained, enthused and informed a generation of students – well, some of them at any rate. This book is for him; an affectionate token of remembrance for a deeply missed colleague, co-author and friend.

Figures

Paul Lazarsfeld © Columbia University

Theodor Adorno © Akademie der Künste, Berlin, Theodor W. Adorno Archiv, Frankfurt am Main, photo by Ilse Mayer-Gehrken

Max Horkheimer © Universitaetsbibliothek Frankfurt am Main, Archivzentrum

Walter Benjamin © Akademie der Künste, Berlin, Walter Benjamin Archiv, Berlin, photo by Joël-Heinzelmann

Bertold Brecht © Academy of Arts/Bertolt-Brecht-Archive

Robert Merton © Columbia University

David Riesman © Jane Reed, Harvard News Office

Elihu Katz © Kyle Cassidy

Frank and Queenie Leavis © Robert Fothergill

Richard Hoggart © David Mark Radford

Harold Innis © Strategic Communication, University of Toronto, Canada

Marshall McLuhan © the Estate Of Marshall McLuhan

Erving Goffman © the American Sociological Association

Harold Garfinkel © Bernard Leach and Manchester Metropolitan University

John Austin © Jean Austin

Paul Grice © Kathleen Grice

Penelope Brown © S.C. Levinson

Stephen Levinson © Inge Doehring

Harvey Sacks © Emanuel A. Schegloff

Jurgen Habermas © Darren McCollester, Getty Images

Hannah Arendt © Jennifer Anna, American Jewish Historical Society

Ian Watt © Stanford University

Introduction

My first concern in writing this book is to provide students who are seriously interested in the study of media and communication with an account of how academic studies of both developed in the course of the last century. Each of the first nine chapters provides an introduction to a key 'moment' in the study of media and communication. The chapters mostly deal with one or two authors, sometimes with a single text, and provide summary accounts of the issues addressed by their work and the new methodologies and concepts that they introduced. Thus, each chapter may serve as the basis of a class or seminar and the end references indicate the readings that underpin it. The website that accompanies the book provides further teaching resources, including summary class notes, a glossary of key terms and selected key texts for each of the first nine chapters.

I had better make clear the limitations of what I have attempted. This book is not in any way an exhaustive review of academic developments in the study of media and communication in the past century. One reader of the draft manuscript described it, not unfairly, as 'a view of the mountain tops'. Many important aspects of the study of media and communication are not included here. The fact that 'media' comes before 'communication' in the title of the book is the clue to what it is about. If it were called *Communication and Media* it would have a different emphasis and weight. I am here primarily concerned with how the academic study of what we now think of as 'the media' developed in the past century. It would be uncontentious, I think, to propose that it had two key historical moments: (1) the development of a sociology of mass communication in the United States over a 20-year period from the mid-1930s to the mid-1950s; and (2) the development of media studies as a branch of Cultural Studies in Britain from the mid-1960s to the end of the 1970s. These two moments are the twin pillars of the book. The first is dealt with in Chapters 1 and 3, while the second is accounted for in Chapters 4 and 8. There is a third important strand involved in both these two constitutive moments; the German intellectual tradition of critical social theory that lies across the borders of philosophy, sociology and history. It came to fruition in the work of the Frankfurt School and, in Chapters 1 and 2, I explore its formative moment in Europe and in exile in the United States in the 1930s. In Chapter 9 I examine a key work by Jürgen Habermas, the leading representative of a post-war, second-generation Frankfurt School.

Between them, these three strands account for more than half the contents of the book. It follows then that alternative developments are largely overlooked. I do not, for instance, account for the important work in the USA of the late James Carey and the approach to communication as ritual which he advocated as an antidote to the dominant 'effects tradition' whose origins I trace. Nor have attempted to follow through either of the two 'moments' that define this book's architecture. I have tried to trace, in each case, the development of a formative moment in the study of the media: what it was initially concerned with, and why and how. In each case there is an identifiable point in time when innovation and discovery give way to consolidation and dissemination. I have been concerned with the former and not the latter. So I do not consider how mass communication studies expanded through American universities from the 1950s to the present and the key role of Wilbur Schramm and his contemporaries in this process. Nor do I deal with the expansion of media studies in Britain from the 1980s onwards, nor its remarkable diffusion since then as a cadet branch of global cultural studies.

Moreover, since each moment defined the study of then new media (radio in the 1930s, television in the 1970s) in particular ways, many other important aspects of their study are thereby excluded. I do not deal with the media industries of radio, television and the press, nor their economic and political underpinnings which are, of course, crucial to their institutional formation and development. And so the political economy of media, the sociology of news, not to mention institutional histories of the press and broadcasting are all passed over in silence because they were not focal concerns of the American sociology of mass communication at the University of Columbia in the 1930s nor of British Media Studies at Birmingham in the 1970s. In the first case, the new medium of radio was treated as a social question, and in the second case, the new medium of television was treated as a cultural question. Why this was so and with what consequences are a core concern of the book as a whole.

The book's title proposes that the question of the media is intimately linked to the question of communication. However, this was not so in either of the moments that established them as objects of academic enquiry. The sociology of mass communication in the USA in the 1930s and 1940s and British media studies in the 1970s were more concerned with the social and cultural impact and effect of then new media (radio in pre-war America: television in 1970s Britain). Thus my title has something of an advocatory intent. I want to argue that the question of communication has not yet been properly addressed in the study of the media and that it is, or should be, quite central to their study if we are at all concerned with how they work for viewers, listeners and readers. This book is the first in a trilogy and one of its functions is to serve as an introduction to the next two books in which the question of communication and media will be a core concern. By way of preparation for the work that follows I have included, in this volume, accounts of what I take to be key developments in the study of communication in different academic fields in the second half of the last century. They are outlined in Chapters 6 and 7 which go together. These two chapters have a somewhat different function to most of the others and are written in a plainer exegetical style, with less biographical and historical detail. A fuller historical analysis of the developments outlined in them will be offered in the final volume of this trilogy.

In the course of writing this book I have become more and more fascinated by the historiographical issues it has posed and particularly the relationship between the academic work of writing history (historiography) and history itself. Although for teaching purposes, each chapter can be treated as a stand-alone topic, there is a strong, unfolding narrative from one chapter to the next as they progress.

The chapters are arranged chronologically, though several overlap, and deal mainly, as indicated in the subheadings, with academic developments in the United States and Britain, while further strands trace developments in Canada and Germany (though in the latter case the emphasis is on the impact of Critical Theory in the USA and the UK rather than Germany itself). The last chapter is the clue to the whole book and in it I examine the issues at stake in writing the histories of academic fields before proceeding to explicate the historical narrative threaded through all that precedes it. I aim to account for what the study of mass media was concerned with in its historical development and why it had those concerns, thereby justifying my claim that the question of communication was not central to the study of media in the twentieth century.

I do not want here to anticipate my conclusions, but I should like to make a couple of points about what I have *not* tried to do. I have not attempted to write a history of ideas, nor have I attempted a comparative history of academic developments in Britain and America. The history of the formation of academic fields is a particular kind of historical writing that poses particular problems. I have sought to emphasize the work, the labour that goes into the production of academic texts, particularly those that are later found to have had a defining role in the establishment of an academic field. I have tried to show how academic texts get written, the hidden histories of their production. I do this especially in Chapters 3 and 8 where I reconstruct the life histories of two famous texts (*Personal Influence* by Elihu Katz and Paul Lazarsfeld (1955), and 'Encoding/Decoding' by Stuart Hall (1980)) and how they came to be, in the end, written as published. I apply the same method to the study of radio and television programmes in the next volume. The aim is to make visible the hidden labour of production, whether of books or articles produced by academics working in universities or of the output produced by broadcasters working in, for instance, the BBC. The explanation and justification of this method, which discloses the care-structure of humanly made things, are a matter for the next two books. It has the effect, I hope, when applied to academic work, of making clear that academic 'texts' (like anything else) have life histories; that the history of their making is about the institutional working lives of those who made them and that this is what goes into the final products which never simply 'happen' as if they fell like manna from the skies. Histories of ideas (and academic writing generally) tend to idealize texts-as-published that seem to have appeared from nowhere to float and circulate in an airy inter-textual world. My aim is to show something of the effort involved in coming up with what eventually gets to publication, to show academics at work, how things get to be written (and sometimes not). The point of this is not just to provide descriptive institutional or biographical background; it is to account for the form and content of the realized end-product as determined by the hidden life and the unseen labour (the effort, the care) that produced it as such. That has been the basis of all my work on radio and television and I continue with that approach in the volume that follows this one. Here I have applied it to academic institutions and the labour process of intellectual production.

This book is not, then, a history of ideas. Nor a comparative history either. I am not really after comparisons between the USA and Britain, for instance, though I am concerned with the connections and differences between North America and Europe, the new world and the old. North America means Canada as well as the USA and in Chapter 5 I examine the distinctively Canadian work of Harold Innis who pioneered the historical study of technologies of communication. It is not an incidental bit of biographical detail to note that Innis was Canadian. The experience of the United States as a powerful next-door neighbour shaped his thinking and his work. I *am* interested in the core distinction between the old world and the new – Europe and North America. The USA and Canada were colonized by European settlers escaping from the old world for one reason or another to find a new life in a new world. There is an umbilical connection between Europe and North America that persists to this day and the tensions between the two continents is something of a subterranean stream that runs through the chapters that follow. But the key reason I disclaim an interest in comparative history is that I treat developments in North America and Europe as responses to the same single, unitary historical process of world modernization. All particular histories – whether of individuals, institutions or nation-states – are determined by history itself. But what that could possibly mean is a matter to be explored progressively in all three volumes. In the next volume I examine the work of broadcasting in the history-making process, and in the final volume I return to the relationship between the academic discipline of historiography and the time horizons of human history.

The primary obligation which the author of a textbook must acknowledge to his/her readers is that of providing a fair, balanced, reasonable and reliable account of the authors and issues under review and this I have tried to do. It is not my business to impose my views on the matters to hand, or to dish out praise and blame. That said, it does not follow that I agree with everything in the accounts that I offer here. I have my own views on these matters and I intend to pursue them more fully in the books that follow this. Writing *Media and Communication* has fulfilled a number of purposes, not the least of which has been the process of self-clarification it entailed and readers will gradually find something of the author in the text that follows. Working through the thematic concerns of this book has been, for me, a way of settling accounts with the intellectual traditions that defined the field in which I began to work some 40 years ago. In that respect its serves as a necessary clearing of ground before turning to my own particular concerns and ways of thinking in this book's two companions.

The next book in the trilogy is called *Television and the Meaning of 'Live'* and extends the work begun in *Radio, Television and Modern Life*, published in 1996. That in turn was the product of the foundational historical study of broadcasting that I wrote with my late friend and colleague, David Cardiff. The key thing I learnt from that study concerned the relationship between the production process in radio and television and its final products – the programmes as broadcast – and I have carried forward that concern in all my subsequent work on broadcasting. The question of communication lies at the heart of the production process, if it is the case, as I take it to be, that programmes are made *for* audiences. How to communicate with their audiences, how to make programmes that work for them, was and remains a crucial question for people making programmes for absent listeners and viewers. One key aim of this book is to provide introductory accounts to what I regard as adequate approaches to thinking about communication that have, over the years, come to inform my own work on the output of radio and television. Those accounts are set out in Chapters 6 and 7. The concluding part of Chapter 7 makes explicit the lines of enquiry that I and others have pursued in our work on the communicative ethos of radio and television. It emerges from the development of a pragmatics of language outlined in the main part of the chapter and the sociology of interaction as examined in the preceding chapter, and serves as an introduction to *Television and the Meaning of 'Live'*.

Inside any academic book there is always, I suspect, at least one more book, struggling to get out since it is bound to raise more questions than it could possibly answer. The final book in this trilogy, *Love and Communication*, serves as a commentary and reflection on the two that precede it. It allows me to identify my own preferred approach to the study of communication and media, to supply reasons and justifications for it and, from that position, to engage in a critical discussion with other approaches to their study. It has taken me a long time to be clear about my own way of thinking and why I would advocate it and how I would defend it as a relevant contribution to thinking about matters of concern to all of us interested in the question of communication as it shows up in all 'new' media as they have entered into the life of modern societies from the nineteenth to the twenty-first centuries. I defer that discussion to my final book. Here I will simply identify and offer a preliminary definition of my own 'take' on media and communication. I would call it, for want of a better word, phenomenological and I would define it as an effort at an understanding of the world uncluttered by the usual academic baggage. This is intended not as a frivolous but an exact description of what I mean by phenomenology and what I aspire to in my own thinking and writing.

PART I

The masses

Mass communication

Lazarsfeld, Adorno, Merton
USA, 1930s and 1940s

Sociology and communication

The great, defining period of American sociology spanned the decades immediately before and after the Second World War, from the mid-1930s through to the mid-1950s. It was a period of continuing innovation and exploration both in terms of methodology and subject matter for a new academic discipline whose question concerned the nature of social life. It was appropriate that American universities should take the lead in systematic investigation of a question that in some respects appeared to be if not peculiar at least particularly appropriate to America itself. The new world was more evidently a social invention and a political experiment than the more historically deep-rooted old world from which so many millions had emigrated in search of a new and better life. America had less historical baggage than Europe. The West had only finally been 'settled' by the end of the nineteenth century and something of the 'new frontier' mentality pervaded American progressive thought in the early decades of the twentieth century and its concern with the 'great society' – the practical realization of the American dream; the hopes and aspirations of the huddled masses who had arrived on its Eastern shores believing in it as the new-found land of opportunity.

Thus, a range of questions about the nature of the social – what *is* a society? What are the bonds between people? What regulates individual behaviours? How should they live together *as* a community? How is community created? What is the relationship between the self and others? How do they communicate? – were never, in the American context, simply academic questions. Nor were they retrospective. They were about the present and the future. The relationship between individual and 'group' in a city like Chicago – the fastest growing city in the world in the late nineteenth century, with a rich and teeming mix of newly arrived peoples of diverse ethnicities, languages, religions and beliefs – presented itself as an immediate and pressing issue, there on its doorstep, for the university's Department of Sociology, the first in the United States, founded in 1899. Urban Studies was pioneered in Chicago and, along with this, the question of communication. In an urban world in flux, without established traditions and customs – in which nothing was familiar or given and everything had to be invented, in which individuals encountered each other daily as strangers – questions of how people related to each other (how they inter-acted, how they communicated) had something of the force of a naturally 'found' object of sociological enquiry. Communication was both the problem and the solution to social psychology's basic question: the link between individuals (the psychological) and groups (the social). Social psychology and urban studies developed early in Chicago and formed the core of the Department's research and teaching, giving it a distinctive sociological agenda and identity as the 'Chicago School' (Abbott, 1999).

Paul Lazarsfeld

The study of communication at Chicago dealt with it in psychological and sociological terms, focusing on individual and small (or primary) group interactions in immediate, face-to-face situations. It was not concerned with the study of *mediated* communication. That development took place elsewhere in the 1930s at Columbia University, NY, where the then 'new' media of mass communication began to be systematically investigated. Chicago's research style was based on ethnographic fieldwork, with researchers immersing themselves as participant observers in the cultures that they studied. Although data were gathered and facts found, they were always to be understood *in situ*, in terms of their particular location or ecology (a key Chicago concept); the specificity of context was always critical in the Chicago School. This approach was overshadowed in the 1930s by the rise of Columbia and the growth of opinion polling and market research (ibid.: 205–10). *In situ* studies of individuals and small groups in local social settings (real people in real places) were displaced by decontextualized data collection of attitudes, opinions and

beliefs to serve as evidence for strategic or policy decisions by businesses, advertisers, broadcasters or politicians. Here what mattered was the evidential reliability of the information that had been gathered and the logic of the inferences that could be drawn from it for administrative purposes. Chicago, one might over-simply say, pioneered qualitative methods of social investigation while Columbia took the lead in quantitative social science research whose results were guaranteed by their statistical reliability and the internal logic of the relationship between data variables. The leader in this field of research was Paul F. Lazarsfeld (1901–76), an Austrian émigré, who settled in the United States in the early 1930s and made a fundamental contribution to establishing sociology as an empirical social science.

Lazarsfeld's early career

Lazarsfeld was born in Vienna in 1901 of Jewish parents. His father was a lawyer, his mother an Adlerian psychoanalyst, and both were fervent socialists. He studied maths and physics at university and wrote his doctoral thesis on a mathematical aspect of Einstein's gravitational theory.[1] He was, like many of his contemporaries, fascinated by politics and psychoanalysis and began post-doctoral work with Karl and Charlotte Buhler who had established an Institute of Psychology at the University of Vienna. In what was then a strikingly novel arrangement, Lazarsfeld suggested to the Buhlers that he should establish a financially independent unit that did commercial contract research, attached to but not part of the university. The idea was to do surveys for local industries (herein lies the origin of market research) to raise enough money to pay Lazarsfeld and his co-workers (whom the Buhlers were unable to support from university resources) and any surplus would be applied to socio-psychological studies. Lazarsfeld and his young, enthusiastic co-workers did not merely gather and analyse data for their clients, they re-interpreted their initially simple commercial tasks to produce more subtle, socially revealing information:

> When a laundry wanted to know why more housewives did not make use of its services, they set out to discover on what occasions housewives sent their laundry to be done outside the house. As a result, the firm learned to watch for occasions such as births, deaths, weddings and the like. Studying the purchase of different kinds of food, they made a profile of the 'proletarian' consumer as compared to the middle class consumer. When Radio Vienna wanted to know what radio programs people preferred, they made a social class profile of tastes for light versus heavy music. (Schramm, 1997: 48)

The last study would turn out to be the precursor of Lazarsfeld's later detailed work on the American radio industry.

In the early 1930s, Lazarsfeld and two colleagues, Marie Jahoda (his first wife) and Hans Zeisel, made a study of the impact of unemployment in a small Austrian mill-town, Marienthal, where most of the adult male population was out of work. A key (and typically Lazarsfeldian) question for the research team concerned the

---

1 These biographical details are mainly compiled from Coleman (1980), Wiggershaus (1994) and Schramm (1997). See also Lazarsfeld's own intellectual memoir in Fleming and Bailyn (1969: 270–338). For a wide-ranging collection of essays on many aspects of Lazarsfeld's life and career, see Merton et al. (1979). See Peters and Simonson (2004: 84–7). Douglas (2004: 126–39) offers an excellent character sketch of Lazarsfeld and his work in Austria and the USA. David Morrison, who did his PhD on Lazarsfeld, is the best and most detailed guide to Lazarsfeld's life and work in Austria and the United States. See Morrison (1998: 1–120) and *passim*.

political effect of unemployment: did it radicalize individuals or make them more apathetic? The answer, regrettably, was that unemployment seemed to have the latter effect. The report was published in 1933 at the precise moment that Hitler came to power. It was immediately repressed and not republished in German until 1960 and not in English until 1971. But the Buhlers thought it important and sent Lazarsfeld to report his findings at the International Congress of Psychology at Hamburg. There he impressed the European representative of the Rockefeller Foundation who was attending the conference and was offered a one-year travelling fellowship to America. In October 1933, Lazarsfeld arrived in New York.

Following up on contacts he had made at Hamburg, Lazarsfeld quickly got in touch with Robert Lynd, a recently appointed Professor of Sociology at Columbia University. Lynd and his wife Helen had published, in 1929, a widely reviewed and highly praised survey of changing patterns of work and leisure in America social life.[2] In *Middletown* (1929) the Lynds attempted an anthropology of everyday life in the American town of Muncie, Indiana (Robert Lynd's home state). It was a study of a community in transition, comparing the ways of life in the city a generation or so earlier at the turn of the century, with new patterns of work and leisure emerging at the time of the study. The community study methods used by the Lynds were employed by Lazarsfeld and his associates in their survey of Marienthal. Lynd was to be, in Schramm's words, Lazarsfeld's 'guardian angel' in America, helping him get started and finally establishing him at Columbia.

Within months of arriving in the USA, there was a fascist coup in Austria and Lazarsfeld decided to remain in the USA. Lynd found him a job at the University of Newark, New Jersey, supervising student relief provided by a New Deal organization, the National Youth Administration. Soon Lazarsfeld had persuaded the President of Newark that he needed a research centre which he proceeded to set up on the same principles as the institute he had invented at the University of Vienna. He got a career-making break when the opportunity to head a major research project into radio came his way, at Lynd's suggestion, funded by the Rockefeller Foundation and initially in association with Hadley Cantril of Princeton and Frank Stanton, director of research at the Columbia Broadcasting System (CBS). The project got off to a rocky start and was finally stabilized when Princeton withdrew and Lazarsfeld transferred to New York where, again through Lynd's good offices, what had started as the Princeton Radio Project in association with the Newark Research Centre, finally emerged from its chrysalis as the project of the Columbia Office of Radio Research, expanded and renamed, a few years later, as the Bureau of Applied Social Research at Columbia.

---

2 *Middletown* was much admired by F.R. Leavis at Cambridge, UK, who regarded it as a key contemporary analaysis of the impact of 'mass civilization' on older more traditional ways of life. See Chapter 4.

Much has been written about this famous research centre that Lazarsfeld founded and ran for many years. It was the prototype of the university-based organization for large-scale social research that was subsequently taken as a model by many other universities in the USA and abroad. The independent research institute, hosted by a university but funded by income generated from projects commissioned by industry and government, was Lazarsfeld's first enduring creation. His second, crucial contribution was to the then emergent discipline of sociology. More than anyone else, Lazarsfeld gave it its methodology. He pioneered techniques and rationales for both quantitative and qualitative research methods. These were worked out and applied in three new areas of sociological enquiry: opinion polling, voting behaviours and market research. Third, Lazarsfeld was committed to research as a collective collaborative endeavour: the roll call of those who worked with him on one project or another includes some of the most distinguished names in American sociology and European social theory in those days: Theodor Adorno, Robert Merton, Elihu Katz, David Riesman, and Bernard Berelson. Lazarsfeld's style was not that of the lone scholar. On the contrary, as Merton notes, he was happiest as the initiator and organizer of collaborative enquiries, as his many co-authored publications indicate. I propose to explore the development of the study of mass communication in America through the work of Lazarsfeld himself, some of his key collaborative projects and some of the important work produced by his associates, friends and colleagues. Two topics will be examined in a little detail in this chapter: the radio project sponsored by the Rockefeller Foundation; and relations between Lazarsfeld and the Frankfurt Institute of Social Research. In Chapter 3 I will continue with accounts of the work of Robert Merton and his collaborations with Lazarsfeld and, finally, the Decatur project which was eventually published as *Personal Influence* – a work that set the seal on the American effects tradition of mass communication research.

The radio project and the Institute of Social Research

In 1941, the Institute of Social Research, based in Morningside, New York City, published a special issue of its journal, *Studies in Philosophy and Social Science,* on the sociology of communication.[3] It was the outcome of collaboration between the Institute and Columbia's Office of Radio Research. In the preface to the issue, the Director of the Institute, Max Horkheimer, acknowledged his particular gratitude to Paul Lazarsfeld and expressed his great satisfaction that,

---

3 This is the first publication in English in which, as far as I know, communication is named as a distinctive sub-branch of sociology.

in collaboration with him, some of the Institute's ideas had been applied for the first time to specifically American subject matter and introduced into the American methodological debate. The Institute of Social Research, now attached to Columbia University, had begun its life in the mid-1920s as an endowed, independently-funded research centre attached to the University of Frankfurt. Horkheimer and most of his colleagues were German Jews and, when Hitler came to power, the Institute's assets had already been prudently transferred abroad. A new home for the Institute was sought and eventually found in New York, where most of its leading members eventually made their way. Its affiliation with Columbia was due, as was Lazarsfeld's, to Robert Lynd who regarded the work of the Institute as reinforcing the kind of social research that he, and the Department of Sociology at Columbia, stood for. The combination of a burgeoning sociology department at Columbia with Lazarsfeld and the Frankfurt Institute was, as many commentators have noted, one of the entirely unintended yet felicitous outcomes of the diaspora of intellectuals from Germany, Austria and central Europe precipitated by the tyranny of Hitler. Both parties (Americans and Europeans) had a common interest, though from different perspectives, in the study of contemporary social life. These differences emerged in the course of the work on the Princeton Radio Project, some of whose first fruits were published in the special issue of the Institute's now anglicized journal, originally the *Zeitschrift für Sozialforschung (ZfS)*, that dealt with what Horkheimer in the Preface called the 'problems of mass communication'.

Collaboration between Lazarsfeld and the Institute preceded its arrival in the United States. It had begun in the early 1930s when Horkheimer had contacted the Vienna Economic and Psychological Research Group, which Lazarsfeld had founded, to carry out fieldwork on young workers in Austria. Horkheimer, when he arrived in New York, used Institute funds to support the impecunious little team of researchers that Lazarsfeld had taken on at Newark. Professor Lynd, our 'mutual and respected friend', as Horkheimer put it in a letter, had suggested that he might invite Lazarsfeld to spend some of his time in New York working with the Institute, an offer that was warmly and gladly accepted. Lazarsfeld and his assistants – especially Herta Herzog who had worked with him in Vienna and would become his second wife – advised the Institute on questions of methodology and assisted in the technical analysis of empirical data (Wiggershaus, 1994: 167–8). When Lazarsfeld began in 1937 to draw up his plans for the big two-year radio project,[4] he conceived of it as concentrating on four major themes: radio and reading, music, news and politics. It was natural enough for Lazarsfeld to suggest to Horkheimer (to whom by now he owed several favours) that he might invite Theodor (Teddy) Wiesengrund to leave Oxford,

---

4 It had a huge grant of $67,000 from the Rockefeller Foundation and Lazarsfeld was on the princely salary of $6000 a year (Wiggershaus, 1994: 239).

where he was currently studying, to join the Institute in the USA and head up research into the impact of radio on music.

Wiesengrund was glad to accept. He was pursuing, in desultory fashion, a PhD at Oxford that was going nowhere. He was a jealous admirer of Horkheimer and he was deeply knowledgeable about music, having studied composition with Schoenberg and written a sociological interpretation of Jazz in *ZfS* (in 1936) under the nom de plume of Hektor Rottweiler. Horkheimer, for his part, admired Teddy's aggressiveness, his 'maliciously sharp eye for existing conditions' (Wiggershaus, 1994: 162). It was he as much as anyone who put the teeth into the Institute's critical, theoretical approach to the analysis of contemporary social life. When it became renowned later in the century as the 'Frankfurt School' its fame was largely on account of its *Critical* Theory. When Wiesengrund arrived in America, he dropped his father's name and assumed that of his Italian mother. It is thus as Theodor Adorno that he is now known as a leading cultural critic of the last century.

Theodor Adorno

The relationship on the radio project that developed between Adorno and Lazarsfeld did not turn out to be a marriage of like minds. Even before he arrived, Horkheimer cautioned Adorno to watch his language, especially in the inaugural lecture he would be expected to give at the Institute when he arrived. In particular, he should 'not say a word that could be interpreted politically'. Expressions such as 'materialism' (Marxist theory) were to be avoided at all costs, and he should 'try to speak as simply as possible. Complexity here is always suspect' (Jäger 2004: 101). In his own account of his time in America, Adorno emphatically states that he considered himself European through and through, 'from the first to the last day abroad'. He refused to 'adjust' (though he did change his name):

> 'Adjustment' was still a magic word, particularly for those who came from Europe as a persecuted people, of whom it was expected that they would prove themselves in the new land not to be so haughty as to insist stubbornly on remaining what they had been before. (Adorno, 1966: 338)

Lazarsfeld, in Adorno's eyes, had adjusted only too well to the USA, while Lazarsfeld remarked, to American colleagues, after a week of working with him, that Adorno 'looks exactly as you would imagine a very absent-minded German professor, and he behaves so foreign that I feel like a member of the Mayflower Society' (Wiggershaus, 1994: 241). On the other hand, as he would often say of himself when speaking publicly, 'You can tell from my accent that I didn't come over with the *Mayflower*.' Lazarsfeld always looked and sounded like a European intellectual, but he quickly and easily adjusted to and accepted the economic and political workings of America, as well as to its institutional academic life. He adjusted to the American way of life and is regarded to this day by American sociologists as one of the key figures in the intellectual formation and history of their discipline. Adorno, however, remained an exotic hothouse plant from another country to which he returned at the end of the war.

The differences between Adorno and Lazarsfeld are doubtless, at one level, matters of personality and temperament, but they are also historically determinate responses to 'the shock of the new' which every newcomer experiences in the New World. The question of the relationship between the individual and the social – a core disciplinary concern in sociology – has a different weight and meaning in America and Europe, since the defining terms themselves ('individual' and 'social') have different textures of relevance and significance. The question of mass communication (of mass culture as it was called on both sides of the Atlantic in the 1930s) was common ground for a European research institute, grounded in the German intellectual tradition, grafted onto the leading American sociology department of that time, but the meanings of 'mass' and 'masses' had different resonances. The creative tension that resulted from the application of American and German ideas and approaches to the study of the new mass medium of radio was something that Lazarsfeld himself grappled with and tried to resolve. It shows up in the lead article he wrote for the special issue of the Institute's journal called 'Administrative and Critical Communication Research' (Lazarsfeld, 1941) – a seminal text for the historical study of the development of the field in twentieth-century America.

Adorno, in the memoir he wrote of his time in America, could not recall whether he or Lazarsfeld coined the phrase 'administrative research' to describe the activities of the Office of Radio Research at Columbia University. Either way, he was simply astonished at a practically oriented kind of science with which he was entirely unfamiliar when he arrived in the USA to take up his new post:

> At Lazarsfeld's suggestion, I went from room to room and spoke with colleagues, heard words like 'Likes and Dislikes Study', 'success or failure of a program', of which at first I could make very little. But this much I did understand: that it was concerned with the collection of data, which were supposed to benefit the planning departments in the field of the mass media, whether in industry itself or in the cultural advisory boards and similar bodies. For the first time I saw 'administrative research' before me. (Adorno, 1969: 342)

'Administrative research' was not, for Adorno or Horkheimer, a term of endearment, yet it was clearly appropriate to describe the kind of research undertaken by Lazarsfeld since his Vienna days. In his essay on the two approaches, Lazarsfeld begins by defining administrative research as academic work in the service of external public or private agencies. He sets out the techniques he had developed for collecting and analysing information about attitudes to the mass media, notably radio, print and film. The new mass audiences were the primary object of enquiry. The audiences for all major radio programmes had been carefully measured and established first in terms of their composition (age, sex, income) and then in terms of their preferences – their likes and dislikes. Adorno had been astounded by the Lazarsfeld–Stanton programme analyser, developed to discover, from moment to moment, how audiences responded to what they were listening to. Little Annie, as it was affectionately known at CBS where it was installed, was a primitive poly-graph that could record and tabulate the responses of a room full of people listen-ing to a particular programme. At pre-selected moments, signalled by a light, they were asked to indicate by pressing a red or green button on their chair, whether they did or did not like what they were hearing at that moment. It provided a pro-file of changing audience responses in the course of an individual radio pro-gramme or a movie and could be used to test them in advance of transmission or release and adjust their structure and content in accordance with measured audi-ence preferences (Douglas, 2004: 137–9; Schramm, 1997: 55). This was but one in a whole battery of techniques developed by Lazarsfeld and his colleagues to mea-sure responses to the outputs of the modern media of mass communication. The new media might be used to sell goods, or to raise intellectual standards or to pro-mote an understanding of government policies. In any case, it was the task of research to facilitate such uses by providing the users with evidence of how their messages had been received and responded to (or not). Thus communications research came to focus on a small, standard set of problems: Who are the people exposed to different media? What do they like? What are the effects of different methods of presentation? (Lazarsfeld, [1941] 2004: 169).

Lazarsfeld noted a number of objections to such research. Those who paid for it, the corporate or government sponsors, might feel they did not get value for money – why not rely on intuition? That argument was briskly dismissed. Empirical research, if done honestly and competently, provided otherwise unavailable sound evidence of consumer responses that could be reliably used as a basis for executive decisions. Two other criticisms were more substantial. The first, a liberal academic critique, came from his friend and colleague Robert Lynd who, in *Knowledge for What?*, argued vigorously against purely commercial market research in favour of applying its methods to pressing public and political issues (race relations, for instance). Lynd was not hostile to administrative research as such, he simply wanted it to be used for purposes more worthy than profit (Lynd, 1939). The third objection was the most telling, since it attacked the very assumption that issues such as attitudes and opinions could be analysed as isolated social variables without considering the total historical situation in which such research and what it investigated were situated:

Modern media of mass communication have become such complex instruments that whenever they are used they do much more to people than those who administer them mean them to do, and they may have a momentum of their own which leaves the administrative agencies much less choice than they believe they have. The idea of *critical research* is posed against the practice of administrative research, requiring that, prior and in addition to whatever special purpose is to be served, the general role of our media of communication in the present social system should be studied. (Lazarsfeld, [1941] 2004: 169. Original emphases)

Lazarsfeld attributes the concept of critical research to Max Horkheimer and distinguishes it from administrative research in two respects. First, it aspired to a general theory of prevailing contemporary social trends that could be brought to bear on any particular research problem. Second, it presumed a set of basic human values against which to appraise such trends and their effects. The prevailing economic trend, so the critical argument goes, is towards the centralization and concentration of ownership in the hands of fewer and fewer large organizations in competition with each other for mass markets. The manipulation of large masses of people by the business world has come to permeate our whole culture. Everything is promoted. We live more and more in an 'advertising culture'. Such trends impair basic values in human life. In the face of this, critical research demands that we seek for the truth and try to act upon it while refusing to adjust (conform) to the present situation as if it were inescapable. The critical analyst of modern media of communication will ask: 'How are these media organized and controlled? How in their institutional set-up is the trend towards centralization, standardization and promotional pressure expressed? In what form, however disguised, are they threatening human values?' (Lazarsfeld, in Peters and Simonson, 2004: 170).

Lazarsfeld considers one or two instances of critical interpretations of audience responses. His first, very obviously from Adorno, concerns laughter. When people laugh, in the cinema, at out-of-date fashions and the funny clothes of yesteryear worn by people in old newsreels, could this not be seen as the malicious revenge of present-day audiences who are thereby compensating for their own conformity to fashion?[5] For Lazarsfeld, the question is, how could such a critical

---

5 The application of psychoanalytic theory to contemporary social phenomena was *de rigueur* among the members of the Institute some of whose leading members were practising analysts (Erich Fromm) while others were in analysis (Horkheimer, for a while). Audience laughter, in this particular case, is understood (via psychoanalytic theory) as a displacement mechanism whereby self-contempt is transferred from oneself in the present to others in the past. One of Lazarsfeld's most pointed objections to such thinking (typical of Adorno) is its refusal to consider any alternative interpretation or explanation other than its own.

perception be tested? What are the appropriate research methods to investigate it? He saw no easy answer. Moreover, Lazarsfeld noted, the critical approach concentrates on negative interpretations rather than fact-finding or constructive suggestions. How could it be accommodated within his own kind of administrative research? In his final paragraph he reflects that he wrote the essay 'for the purpose of clarifying some of the difficulties he experienced in formulating what critical social research consists in' (Lazarsfeld, 1941: 16).[6] Those difficulties had come to include the problem of working with Adorno.

Lazarsfeld had begun with high hopes. He had written to 'Dr Wiesengrund' in Oxford setting out his initial intentions for the musical section of the radio project.[7] It was to be the hunting ground, so to speak, for the 'European approach'. That for Lazarsfeld meant two things. He expected Adorno to be more theoretical and less optimistic about radio as an instrument of social progress. A critical, theoretical stance was expected from the start but, and this was heavily emphasized, it should be anchored in actual fieldwork and empirical research. He invited Adorno to send a list of what he took to be the key issues. Adorno replied that his theoretical attitude did not preclude empirical research. To his six-page letter he added a 16-page draft of 'Questions and Theses' that sketched in a 'dialectical theory of broadcasting' while criticizing actually existing radio output for inhibiting its immanent progressive tendencies. Lazarsfeld, somewhat taken aback, replied:

> I agree with you also that such an approach needs a theoretical analysis first, and might have to start definitely by an analysis of radio production. It is exactly as a stronghold of theoretical analysis preceding any research that I am looking forward to your coming. On the other hand, we shall have to understand that you have to end up finally with actual research among listeners. (Wiggershaus, 1994: 239)

On has arrival, Adorno did get stuck into actual research. He studied listeners' letters to CBS, conducted interviews (feeling very pleased with his efforts as he tried this, for him, quite novel research method) and talked to people working in the radio industry. He worked all this into a 160-page memorandum on 'Music in Radio' which he wrote in the early summer of 1938. Lazarsfeld was appalled when he read it. It was 'definitely below the standards of intellectual cleanliness, discipline and responsibility which have to be requested from anyone active in academic work'. He went on to make three major critical points. Adorno never

---

6 Previous citations for Lazarsfeld's essay have been taken from the slightly abridged reprint of it (the last paragraph is missing, for instance) in Peters and Simonson (2004) which is more readily accessible than the original.

7 All details in this paragraph are from Wiggershaus (1994: 238–43).

considered any alternatives to his own views and as a result, much of what he wrote was either wrong or unfounded or biased. He did not know very much about empirical research work, yet he wrote as if were an authority on it. Finally and *ad hominem*, 'You attack other people as fetishist, neurotic and sloppy but you show yourself the same traits very clearly.' In sum, 'It is as if you would give us with your right hand the gift of your ideas [which Lazarsfeld appreciated] and would take them away with your left hand by the lack of discipline in your presentation.' Adorno reacted defensively. He felt that his work was quite empirical and that he was doing what Lazarsfeld had asked of him. In truth, the differences between the two men on the task Lazarsfeld had set – how to widen the appeal of good music on radio – were irreconcilable. Lazarsfeld's empirical pragmatic approach was instinctively reformist and fitted well with prevailing social and political currents of thought in America. Adorno's theoretical position was that, under actually existing conditions, not just in the radio industry but in the wider economic and political context, the question itself was meaningless and therefore irremediable (ibid.: 243). In the summer of 1940, Adorno's association with the Princeton radio research project was finally terminated.

I will return, in the next chapter, to Adorno's views on music's plight in the contemporary world. Here I have dwelt upon the difficulties in his working relationship with Lazarsfeld not for its biographical interest (which is considerable) but in order to make explicit some important differences between American and European social thought, taking Lazarsfeld as an assimilated European American and Adorno as a non-assimilated European in America. The fact that the former remained in America for the rest of his life and that the latter returned to Germany as soon as something like normality was restored was not just a matter of individual life choices but indicates the play of much larger historical forces upon individuals and their lives. Lazarsfeld quickly became 'American' while Adorno refused to adjust. In the former case, this involved, professionally, adapting to 'new' American modes of thought. In the latter case, it involved precisely a refusal to do that and to remain loyal to 'old' European ways of thinking.

However difficult it may be to achieve precision in appealing to such categories, they are unavoidable and the similarities and differences between American and European modes of social thought are a theme that runs through this book. My indispensable point of reference for this and its companion chapter is called *Mass Communication and American Social Thought: Key Texts, 1919–1968* (Peters and Simonson, 2004). The editors note, in their Introduction, that 'to organise a reader on national lines somehow seems narrow, problematic or politically retrograde'. Fortunately, such anxieties did not deter them, and they have produced a superbly organized historical resource for students of the field of communication. They have not hesitated to invoke 'American social thought' as a meaningful category, and I have no hesitation in using it to identify a historically immanent structure of thinking that *is* American and, by way of contrast, other

(Canadian, British, German, European) structures of thinking in comparison with which its distinctiveness is disclosed.

Radio and the psychology of panic

A simple but crucial fact should be noted about the work on the mass media undertaken or initiated by Lazarsfeld and his colleagues. It is *not* about the mass media themselves: not their economic underpinnings, their political regulation, their institutional organization or their production methods – all that is overlooked. The focus of attention is exclusively on the audiences of the mass media. Most typically, the research is concerned with their *effects* on audiences and the American sociology of mass communication would later, and somewhat dismissively, be labelled the effects tradition. It was, as we shall see, rather more than just that, but it *was* focused almost wholly on the side of consumption and not of production. Wilbur Schramm recounts a nice story that Lazarsfeld used to tell against himself. In the late 1930s, Iowa State College (now a university) had commissioned from the Office of Radio Research a study of the impact of its campus-based radio station, then perhaps the leading educational radio station in the country. The college wanted to know what its audience was and what it thought of the station's output. Lazarsfeld decided to deliver the final report himself. He was met at the railway station by the president of the college and driven through the college's new and extensive campus, with Lazarsfeld making polite and suitable comments, including his amazement at the tall steel tower with a large mast that dominated the landscape. 'Oh, so you have a broadcasting station,' he exclaimed, only to realize with instant embarrassment that of course they had and he was there to deliver a report on it.[8] Later, reflecting on his *faux pas*, Lazarsfeld came to the conclusion that 'radio as a medium was simply not *real* to him. The programs, the people sitting around their radios listening, the survey interviews – all these were real, but he did not actually connect the tower and the radio station with them' (Schramm, 1997: 18–19. Original emphasis).

It is, as we shall see in the next chapter, a decisive feature of the new 'culture industries' that the immediate relationship between cultural performers, performance and audiences – characteristic of older, live performing arts (most notably music and drama) – is transmogrified into one between producers, product and consumers. The social relations of the live performing arts are split in two by the mass media: there is no direct immediate link between what were later to be called the moments of encoding (production) and decoding

---

8 The Iowa radio station (WOI) is discussed in Lazarsfeld (1940: 116–17).

(consumption).[9] The study of the fractured determinate *mediated* relationship between cultural production and consumption is at the heart of the problem posed by the new mass media of communication as they appear at different times in the course of the twentieth century; radio and cinema in the 1930s, television in the 1950s. This fractured communicative relationship is reproduced in the academic field that emerges to study it. Research tends to focus *either* on the side of production *or* on the side of consumption but seldom on both. My immediate task is to consider why it should be that, in the case of research at Columbia, the audience is constituted as the natural object of study for a sociology of mass communication. To understand this, we must first explore *how* it was studied and *why*.

One of the earliest studies undertaken as part of the Princeton Radio Project was by Hadley Cantril of Princeton, assisted by Hazel Gaudet and Herta Herzog, into the notorious Orson Welles's broadcast in the fall of 1938.[10] On 30 October, the Mercury Theater broadcast, on the CBS network, an adaptation for radio of H. G. Wells' *War of the Worlds*. At the start and finish of the program it was made quite clear that it *was* only a play; 'a holiday offering', the Mercury Theater's 'own radio version of dressing up in a sheet and jumping out of a bush saying Boo!'. 'Remember', said Orson Welles, right at the end, 'the terrible lesson you learned tonight. That grinning, glowing, globular invader of your living room is an inhabitant of the pumpkin patch, and if your doorbell rings and nobody's there, that was no Martian ... it's Halloween' (Cantril, et al., 1940: 42–3). However, Welles and his fellow actors succeeded so well in putting the wind up the programme's estimated 6 million listeners that many actually took to the road in panic to flee the terror of the invading Martians. At least a million audience members were seriously frightened or disturbed. If a radio programme could be mistaken for an invasion from Mars that produced mass panic, it presented Lazarsfeld[11] and his colleagues with a perfect opportunity to explore the power and impact of this new mass medium of communication.

---

9 See Chapter 8 for a full discussion of the 'encoding–decoding' model developed by Stuart Hall.

10 See Heyer (2005) for an historical study of Orson Welles and radio and pp. 46–114 for his most notorious broadcast. The original grant from the Rockefeller Foundation was not sufficient to cover the research on the programme. Extra funding was provided by a special grant from the General Educational Board.

11 Lazarsfeld was very much involved, behind the scenes, in the study of *War of the Worlds*, as Cantril makes clear in his Foreword: 'He has not only given [me] innumerable suggestions for analysis and interpretation, but he has, with his rigorous and ingenious methodological help, provided an invaluable intellectual experience. Because of his insistence, the study has been revised many times, each revision bringing out new information hidden in the statistics and case studies' (Cantril et al., 1940: xiii–xiv). Though Cantril is the author of the study, Lazarsfeld was influential in shaping its approach to and interpretation of the event.

The book's sub-title is 'A study in the psychology of panic', and the Preface describes it as an investigation of 'mass behavior' and 'the psychology of the common man of our times'. The radio audience is 'the most modern type of social group'. It is unlike the readerships of newspapers or the audiences for the movies. Radio is the medium *par excellence* for informing all segments of a population of current happenings. It combines the inherent characteristics of contemporaneousness, availability, personal appeal and ubiquity. Of 32 million American households, 27.5 million had a radio set. Radio makes possible the largest grouping of people (as its listeners) ever known. It is a complex social phenomenon with the potential to reveal something of the social psychology[12] of contemporary Americans (ibid.: vii–x). As such, it requires a complex battery of techniques to investigate it. These included the study of the composition of the audience for the programme (its profile in terms of income, age and sex) which was not large in relation to the total available audience at the time on that particular night. Most Americans were listening on another network to Charlie McCarthy (a ventriloquist act), the most popular weekly show on radio at the time, against which Orson Welles and the Mercury Theater were distinctly minority fare. Next, immediate reactions to the programme were sought in the study of the surge of calls it precipitated both on general telephone lines and to radio and police stations in particular. Both CBS and the Mercury Theater received huge mail bags about the programme and these were studied for their responses (in both cases overwhelmingly supportive of the broadcast). Press coverage in the days that followed was carefully weighed and measured.

But the hub of the matter was, what created the panic? Why were so many deceived? And how? The dramatic techniques used in the programme and the wider historical context at the time were both important considerations. Although the programme at the start and finish is clearly presented as a play performed by actors (and Orson Welles was well known by then), the techniques it used were startlingly innovative. The narrative frame for Wells's story was transposed to radio itself. The play starts as an ordinary night on American radio. Dance music is on air when it is suddenly interrupted by an emergency news flash of a strange object, a meteor most probably, crash landing near Trenton, New Jersey. Normal service resumes only to be interrupted again by another news flash and a report from the scene of the crash. Thereafter the rest of the play unfolds as if it were a news story, using all the then very new techniques

---

12 The assumed point of view in this and other studies of radio undertaken at Columbia is that of 'social psychology'. What this means is everywhere assumed in the literature and nowhere explained. It seems to mean the effects of others (the primary or peer group, the crowd) on the individual. This was the object domain of the symbolic interactionists at Chicago. At Columbia, it is the effects of mass communication on individual behaviours. The concept of 'mass' tends to be applied to the processes of production, not consumption. What it means exactly is, again, largely taken as read. In American usage, 'mass' tends to be equated with the urban crowd. In European usage, it tends to mean the urban proletariat.

of radio news reportage; these included on-the-spot eye-witness reports and interviews, comments and interpretations from experts and authorities (in this case, astronomers) and finally and most unnervingly, a national emergency statement, live-to-air, from the Secretary of State. The programme created a powerful aura of narrative realism through its combination of radio news techniques with apparently real-live people (experts, politicians and ordinary folk as eye-witnesses – all played by actors) and actual real live places (not only Trenton, but other places, including the actual numbers of American routes and highways).[13] Crucially, by the time of the broadcast, American listeners had become accustomed to the interruption of the normal radio schedules by flash news announcements from the trouble-spots of Europe. These had been pioneered by the CBS network earlier that year, when Hitler annexed Austria. The Munich crisis, only weeks before the broadcast, had deepened the gathering crisis and the European slide towards war now appeared inevitable. All this immeasurably heightened the effect of the programme and what Cantril (or is it Lazarsfeld here?) calls its *Stimmung* (the experienced mood of the occasion). Finally, and most critically, those who panicked were more than likely either (1) to have tuned in after the programme began or (2) to have been tuned in but not paying attention at the start and in either case (3) to have stopped listening before the programme ended. For all the reasons suggested above, if you hadn't spotted or didn't know that what you were listening to was, as a matter of fact, only a play, then what you were hearing, if you weren't paying careful attention, might well appear only too believable and thereby precipitate panic behaviour.

These objective determinants of individual behaviours are described in careful, fascinating detail in the main body of the book, but are largely overlooked in the final review and interpretation of the first great media-induced event. There the emphasis is on the psychology of individual listeners, already arranged in different typologies derived from detailed interviews with 135 people of whom 100 were known to have been upset by the programme. The interviewees were all from or around New Jersey, mainly for financial reasons, but partly because that was where the Martians had supposedly landed and hence the programme's events were likely to be of more immediate concern for folk from New Jersey than New Mexico. Herta Herzog was closely involved in the preparation of the interview schedule and in the analysis of the results. Chapter VIII, which describes representative individual case studies, was written by her. In trying to distinguish between those who were disturbed by the programme and those who weren't, 'critical ability' was identified as a key factor and that was linked to level of education and economic status. What made some people more

---

13 Against all these effects of realism, the time of the narrative was spectacularly condensed in the time of its telling. Events unfolded at an absurdly rapid rate, as many listeners noted. The Martians landed and were caught up in full-scale battles with the American military, fully and magically deployed against them, in minutes.

'suggestible' and others less so depended on whether they possessed adequate standards of judgement that enabled them to distinguish between reliable and unreliable sources of information.

In sum, objective factors are overlooked in the study and the psychology of panic is treated subjectively in terms of the susceptibility or not of individuals depending on character type, education, religious beliefs, income and job security. The immediate historic situation – the European war crisis – is acknowledged but discounted, and the crucial question of the role of radio itself and its communicative techniques is entirely ignored. Chapter III, which examines the production methods of the programme (for me, the most fascinating chapter in the book) is called ''It didn't sound like a play': How the stimulus was experienced'. Radio is merely 'the stimulus'. The study is of the response. In the final analysis, stimulus–response theory is applied to the whole event which is thus treated essentially in psychological, rather than sociological terms. Radio is a powerful medium with a direct and immediate effect on individual behaviours. This is a worry:

> Our study of the common man of our times has shown us that his ability to orient himself appropriately in critical situations will be increased if he can be taught to adopt an attitude of readiness to question the interpretations he hears ... If scepticism and knowledge are to be spread more widely among common men, they must be provided more extensive educational opportunities ... and be less harassed by the emotional insecurities which stem from underprivileged environments.' (Cantril et al., 1940: 205)

So, if it is the case that the new mass media have a direct effect on individual behaviours, then it is the responsibility of those with the critical ability to judge rightly and correctly to educate the common man, who lacks education and discrimination, and bring him to a critical view of the media and the ways in which they inform us. This was the intelligentsia's 'progressive' view of the masses not only in America but in Europe in the 1930s and which led to an emphasis, on both sides of the Atlantic, on the need for 'media education'.

Print and radio

That concern permeates the first major published study of the Office of Radio Research written by Lazarsfeld himself. *Radio and the Printed Page* is subtitled 'An introduction to the study of radio and its role in the communication of ideas'. It is not only a methodological primer and a comparative study of print and radio as means of communicating *serious* ideas; it is an introduction to the *study of radio*, staking out a new domain of enquiry and the terms of engagement with it. For this, if for no other reason, it is of great interest, but it is also a book of considerable charm, written with an engaging clarity (Lazarsfeld, unlike so many sociologists, is always readable) and containing a wealth of historical data about reading and listening in the historical circumstances of America in the late 1930s. Susan Douglas laments that *Radio and the Printed Page* and, indeed, all the work of Lazarsfeld and his colleagues are rarely glanced at today, even where media studies is taught. They moulder on the shelves, providing faded snapshots of a bygone audience – and antiquated research methods – that few today care to dust off. Yet, taken as a whole, the body of work produced at Columbia on the new mass medium of radio provides, as Douglas rightly claims, a 'fascinating portrait of a society and many of its subcultures coming to terms with a revolutionary technology' (2004: 140). There is a striking freshness to the engagement of Lazarsfeld and his colleagues with something they all felt to be very new and very important and very imperfectly understood. That effort at understanding is something that still radiates from the pages of *Radio and the Printed Page* and its concerted effort 'to determine which people, under what conditions, and for the sake of what gratification choose radio or print as a source of communication for comparable subject matter' (Lazarsfeld, 1940: 154).

Lazarsfeld emphasizes that his comparative study is based on the relationship between broad statistical studies drawing on a mass of data, and small detailed case studies placed in the frame of reference provided by the statistical data (ibid.: xvi). Quantitative and qualitative methods are indispensable and intertwined. A central concern is with what listening to radio means to people (ibid.: 55). There are three, linked methods of enquiry: (1) the analysis of programme content; (2) the differential analysis of audiences; and (3) 'gratification studies'. In the first place, some systematic typology of programmes must be established between, say, music and talk programmes. Since this is a study of radio as a medium for the communication of ideas, music on radio is bracketed and the study focuses on talk programmes and, within these, those that are 'serious' and those that are not. The notion of serious listening is derived from that of serious reading. The first chapter is called 'The importance of being earnest', an importance that is assumed rather than justified. The question is whether radio can be a 'serious' medium like the book or broadsheet newspaper. Serious readers listen to serious radio programmes. They turn out to have high status occupations and to be well off and well educated. Examples of serious reading are not offered (there is no need), but examples of serious listening include the *University of Chicago Round Table, America's Town Meeting of the Air*[14] and

---

14 Both programmes were admired by Talks producers working in the BBC at that time and their formats were adapted for British public service broadcasting. *Chicago Round Table* was used twice. The London Talks Department produced a regular round table discussion in the studio called *Men Talking*, while in the BBC North Region, in Manchester, the programme became a 'Socratic discussion' in the radio studio between three regular speakers. *Town Meeting of the Air* was also taken up by Manchester where it became *Public Inquiry*, in which local issues were discussed in a public hall before a large, invited audience (Scannell and Cardiff, 1991: 168–9, 351).

Americans All – Immigrants All,[15] a series put out by the Federal Office of Education. All three programmes had two characteristics: they attracted small, elite audiences and no sponsorship. They were 'sustaining' programmes put on by the networks at little cost, as public service fillers, in those slots in the schedule for which there was no advertising revenue.

People of low income, educational and cultural attainment did not, it was found, listen to serious radio broadcasts, although the lower down the social scale you went, the more people listened to radio and the higher you went, the less. The problem thus became how to reach the mass of the listening population, who did not listen to serious discussion on radio of matters of high importance and urgency (the book was published in 1940 when Europe was already at war though the USA was not). To deal with that, one must first know what the mass actually do like listening to if radio is to become what, at the time of reporting it most clearly was not – 'a tool for mass education' (ibid.: 48). Leaving aside entertainment programmes and fictional series and serials (since these were not about the communication of ideas), Lazarsfeld was left with a bundle of what he called 'service programs' after serious 'public affairs' and 'straight education' programmes had been taken out of the reckoning. These he classified as 'home economics', 'self-improvement', 'hobbies and special interests', 'true-life dramas', and general knowledge and popular knowledge programmes. What is the difference between serious and service programmes? The former have a more detached, objective character, while the latter have a more personal appeal as forms of self-improvement for those who feel the need to supplement their knowledge or compensate for their sense of educational or cultural inadequacy (Lazarsfeld, 1940: 8).

The most popular genre in the bundle was the general knowledge quiz programme, and a case study of the audience appeal of the highly successful *Professor Quiz* programme was undertaken. The programme was regarded as informative and educational by its audience of low achievers, though not by Lazarsfeld or Herta Herzog who did the research and wrote the analysis of it. Herzog pioneered the gratifications approach to the study of broadcast programmes. One of her most important studies was of the female audience for day-time radio serials (soap operas), published in the special number on the Sociology of Communication in *Studies in Philosophy and Social Science*

---

15 For an excellent history of this programme, in the context of radio and the politics of race in the 1930s and 1940s, see Savage (1999: 21–72), which also includes fascinating studies of the *Chicago Round Table* and *Town Meeting of the Air* as public forums for the discussion of 'race relations' on radio (ibid.: 194–245).

discussed above.[16] The gratifications approach is not concerned with what radio does to listeners, but with what listeners do with radio. It sets aside assumptions of powerful 'effects' and regards radio as an ordinary resource for listeners who use it for entertainment, relaxation, and so on. Herzog was the first to study popular radio and what it meant for non-elite female audiences. She pioneered the technique of extended, open-ended interviews with individual listeners in order to explore in detail their likes and dislikes and what radio meant for them. When feminist media studies in the 1980s began to apply such questions to television soap operas, Herzog was rediscovered as an ancestral voice mentioned in the footnotes. But whereas 1980s feminism sought to validate the ordinary pleasures of television for ordinary women, that was not Herzog's approach.

Herzog has an unerring ear for the telling detail and in all her writings the actual responses of listeners to the programmes they like or dislike remain vividly revealing to this day. She is, however, not exactly a sympathetic analyst of the feelings and attitudes of those who talk to her. She was into socialism and psychoanalysis from her Vienna days and her analyses of listeners to day-time serials or *Professor Quiz* is based, as Liebes points out, on Freudian psychoanalytic theory (Liebes, 2003: 40). The gratifications that listeners derive from *Professor Quiz* are interpreted as an outlet for the resentment of the uneducated against those who are more educated (Lazarsfeld, 1940: 89) while, at the same time, relieving them of guilt about their indolence and failure to better themselves (ibid.: 84). This judgemental attitude bears comparison with Adorno's interpretation of laughter in the cinema. But such judgements must be understood more as symptomatic than diagnostic of their times. They reveal something of the general outlook of the 1930s generation of intellectuals – right or left, progressive or reactionary – in Europe and North America.

'Progress', Lazarsfeld declared, 'is the result of efforts originated by small, advanced groups and gradually accepted by the population' (ibid.: 94) and, so defined, *Radio and the Printed Page* is a progressive text. It was meant as a serious response to the criticisms of administrative research raised by Robert Lynd's *Knowledge for What?* It provided information relevant to 'that question which is uppermost in the minds of many intelligent citizens: what will radio do to society?' (Lazarsfeld, 1940: 133) by providing those concerned with mass education with an analysis of the conditions under which the 'masses'[17] would

---

16 'On borrowed experience. An analysis of listening to daytime sketches' (Herzog, 1941) is reprinted in full in Peters and Simonson (2004: 139–56). For a critical discussion of this now classic article and a companion piece published in *Radio Research 1942–3* (Herzog, 1944), see Liebes (2003: 39–53). Susan Douglas lavishes praise on Herzog and describes her *Professor Quiz* study as 'nothing short of brilliant' (2004: 144–8).

17 While Horkheimer and Adorno had no qualms in writing of the masses, it is an expression infrequently and gingerly used by Lazarsfeld in scare quotes.

or would not expose themselves to education by radio. Since it was apparent that they overwhelmingly avoided such exposure, some now obvious but then fundamental suggestions were made about how educative radio might be made accessible to the ordinary mass of listeners. It was useless for upper-class people to try and enforce their educational standards over the radio since they were rejected by lower-class people, because they were not adjusted to their point of view. The masses were researched and written up not to condemn them but to make available their point of view as a contribution to social planning, which cannot work *de haut en bas* but must begin with an understanding of the attitudes of those whom the planners seek to improve. A more nuanced assessment of Lazarsfeld's work here and more generally is called for than simplistic denunciations of it as administrative research that serves the commercial interests of the media industry, thereby reproducing the existing economic and political power system. From start to finish, *Radio and the Printed Page* was intended to elevate the study of the mass media 'beyond the mere routine of hand-to-mouth commercial research' (Lazarsfeld, 1940: 114).

References

Abbott, A. (1999) *Department and Discipline: Chicago Sociology at One Hundred.* Chicago: University of Chicago Press.

Adorno, T. (1969) 'Scientific experiences of a European scholar in America', in D. Fleming and B. Baileyn (eds), *The Intellectual Migration: Europe and America 1930–1960.* Cambridge, MA: Harvard University Press, pp. 338–70.

Cantril, H., Gaudet, H. and Herzog, H. (1940) *The Invasion from Mars: A Study in the Psychology of Panic.* Princeton, NJ: Princeton University Press.

Coleman, J.S. (1980) 'Paul F. Lazarsfeld: the substance and style of his work', in R.K. Merton and M.W. Riley (eds), *Sociological Traditions from Generation to Generation.* New Jersey: Ablex Publishing Corporation, pp. 153–75.

Douglas, S. (2004) *Listening In: Radio and the American Imagination.* Minneapolis, MN: University of Minnesota Press.

Fleming, D. and Bailyn, B. (1969) *The Intellectual Migration: Europe and America 1930–1960.* Cambridge, MA: Harvard University Press.

Herzog, H. (1941) 'On borrowed experience: an analysis of listening to daytime sketches', *Studies in Philosophy and Social Science,* IX(1): 65–95.

Herzog, H. (1944) 'What do we really know about daytime serial listeners?' in P.F. Lazarsfeld and F.N. Stanton (eds), *Radio Research 1942–3.* New York: Duell, Pearce and Sloan, pp. 3–33.

Heyer, P. (2005) *The Medium and the Magician: Orson Welles, the Radio Years, 1934–1952.* Lanham, MD: Rowman and Littlefield.

Jäger, L. (2004) *Adorno.* New Haven, CT: Yale University Press.

Lazarsfeld, P. (1940) *Radio and the Printed Page.* New York: Duell, Sloan and Pearce.

Lazarsfeld, P. (1941) 'Remarks on administrative and critical communications research', *Studies in Philosophy and Social Science,* IX(1): 3–20.

Liebes, T. (2003) 'Herzog's 'On borrowed experience'. Its place in the debate over the active audience', in E. Katz et al. (eds), *Canonic Texts in Media Research.* Cambridge: Polity Press, pp. 39–54.

Lynd, R. (1939) *Knowledge for What? The Place of Social Science in American Culture.* Princeton, NJ: Princeton University Press.

Lynd, R. and Lynd, H. (1929) *Middletown: A Study in American Culture.* London: Constable.

Merton, R.K., Coleman, J.S. and Rossi, P.H. (1979) *Qualitative and Quantitative Research. Papers in Honour of Paul F. Lazarsfeld.* New York: Free Press.

Morrison, D.E. (1998) *The Search for a Method: Focus Groups and the Development of Mass Communication Research.* Luton: Luton University Press.

Peters, J.D. and Simonson, P. (eds) (2004) *Mass Communication and American Social Thought: Key Texts, 1919–1968.* Lanham, MD: Rowman and Littlefield.

Savage, B.D. (1999) *Broadcasting Freedom: Radio, War and the Politics of Race, 1938–1948.* Chapel Hill, NC: University of North Carolina Press.

Scannell, P. and Cardiff, D. (1991) *A Social History of British Broadcasting.* Oxford: Blackwell.

Schramm, W. (1997) *The Beginnings of Communication Study in America: A Personal Memoir,* ed. S.H. Chafee and E.M. Rogers. Thousand Oaks, CA: Sage.

Wiggershaus, R. (1994) *The Frankfurt School.* Cambridge: Polity Press.

Mass culture

Horkheimer, Adorno, Brecht, Benjamin
Germany/USA, 1930s and 1940s

The social question

We have already encountered the Frankfurt Institute for Social Research in
America. In this chapter I will consider its European intellectual roots and, in
particular, the critical components of its approach to the study of contemporary
society. But first, I must consider why and in what way society presented itself as
an object of academic enquiry in Germany after the Great War. I have suggested
reasons for the appearance of sociology as an object domain in American universities. For over three centuries people had migrated from Europe to America. In the
seventeeth and eighteenth centuries, they left the old world to escape from religious and political persecution (the two being often inseparable) and in the new
world they sought to create communities in which they were free to live without fear according to their beliefs and practices. Later in the nineteenth century,
mass migrations from Europe were prompted less by ideological and more by
economic factors. The poor of Europe migrated to America as the land of opportunity and advancement for individuals and their families. America and Europe
thus stood in a complicated relationship in which the new world offered political,
religious and economic freedoms variously denied in the countries of the old
world. One way or another, freedom was (and remains) America's *raison d'être*;
the reason for being there in the first place and the cornerstone of the forms
of organized social life created there. America as 'the great society' was, in
the first place, a European dream of freedom, given flesh and substance as a
political reality in a written constitution which created, on a newly colonized
continent far from old Europe, the first wholly deliberate, invented, meant-and-
intended, modern nation–state; the creation and achievement, as Hannah
Arendt emphasizes, of free men in free association with each other (Arendt

[1963] 1990).[1] The meaning of modernity, rough-hew it how we may, is intimately linked to America for it is the first truly modern society. At the start of the twentieth century, it was on the cusp of becoming so. American sociology, from the start, was engaged with the study of a society in the process of discovering how to become a society.

In nineteenth-century Europe, 'society' was everywhere a given, notwithstanding the earthquake of the French Revolution. Its political and social institutions were many centuries-old and relations between individuals and different status groups were defined by long tradition, custom and law. The driver of societal modernization, factory capitalism, encountered stubborn resistance to the toil and hardship it created. Working conditions in the mines, steel, wool and cotton mills were brutal, dirty, dangerous and unhealthy, while the subsistence wage was barely enough to live on. The 'social question' in nineteenth-century Europe became, as Arendt points out, the question of the impoverished masses.[2] In Britain, the immiseration of the urban proletariat (child labour, in particular) was a national scandal by the 1840s, vividly described in the industrial novels of the time (notably *Hard Times*) and by Friedrich Engels in his classic account of *The Condition of the Working Class in England,* published in 1845. Deportation or emigration to the far corners of the Empire was a partial and immediate reaction in Britain. Elsewhere in Europe the huddled masses left for America. But this was no solution to the structural problem posed for European societies by the emergence of the urban masses, particularly as they began to organize their labour power to squeeze concessions from the factory owners and to demand political rights. The question of the masses became inseparable from economic conflict and political struggle. Marx was the first and greatest analyst of societal modernization which he naturally understood in

---

1 Though based of course, like ancient Athens, on slavery. If the injustice of the impoverished masses defined 'the social question' in Europe, the annihilation of the indigenous people of America by incoming Europeans and the kidnapped African slaves they brought with them to provide the labour that would build the new world defined the double injustice on which the new society was built.

2 Arendt ([1963] 1990: 59–114). She argues that since the eighteenth century, 'the social question' has been a euphemism for poverty. It acquired a quite new significance in France when the Parisian poor rose in support of the Revolution, 'inspired it, drove it onward, and eventually sent it to its doom' (ibid.: 60). Poverty, driven by hunger, has always provoked spontaneous riots in demand of bread. In Paris, the masses demanded bread and freedom, and poverty was politicised. The poor no longer rose only for the satisfaction of immediate need, but for the structural transformation of society. Poverty thus ceased to be a natural fact about which nothing could humanly be done and became a historical fact that demanded a human resolution. The politicization of the impoverished masses, sparked by the French Revolution, haunted Europe throughout the nineteenth century with the fear of revolutionary terror as the social question of poverty transmogrified into the political threat of the masses for the settled parts of European society.

terms of the profound restructuring of social relations precipitated by the revolution in manufacturing that he encountered, as a political refugee, in England. Factory capitalism and mass production redefined the fault-lines of social relations: no longer lord and peasant bound to each other (in principle, at least) by ancient mutual ties and obligations, but masters and men bound to each other only by the wage bargain and in conflict over the surplus value extracted by the capitalist from the workforce whose labour he mercilessly exploited. The social relations of modern societies, redefined in terms of capital and labour, were intrinsically antagonistic and unjust. The just redistribution of the social surplus, created by labour but expropriated from it, could only be achieved, in Marx's view, by political revolution.

Max Horkheimer

At the start of the twentieth century, then, 'the social question' had very different meanings in Europe and America. In both cases, it centred on the masses, but whereas in Europe the question presented itself in economic and political terms, in America, it presented itself instead as a *social* question (the forms of urban social life *in the making* by newly arrived economic immigrants) to be treated as such by a new academic field of enquiry in a great, teeming city such as Chicago – itself newly re-made after the devastating fire of 1874. However, an Institute for *Social* Research set up in Frankfurt, in the immediate aftermath of a hugely destructive European war, naturally took the social question to be that of the economic and political fate of the masses whose poverty and exploitation were keenly, and personally, felt by its founding members.[3] Critical theory never represented a clearly stated and defined theoretical hypothesis or position that Horkheimer and his colleagues sought to prove or defend. Rather, it indicated a shared critical attitude to contemporary

---

3 Felix Weil, who provided the funding for the Institute, and Max Horkheimer, its administrative and intellectual leader, were both the sons of very wealthy men and most members of the Institute came from well-to-do families. Horkheimer's father was a millionaire industrialist and his son had a highly privileged, cosseted upbringing. Horkheimer was expected, as his father's heir, to take over the business and he worked, for a while as a junior manager in one of the factories. It was clear, however, that the young Horkheimer was quite unsuited for a life in business (he also fell in love, to the family's horror, with a secretary eight years older than himself) and he was allowed to pursue an academic career. His personal, unpublished writings, in his late adolescence and early adulthood, are full of expressions of indignation at the social injustice of the profound inequality between rich and poor, the 'total inhumanity' of the capitalist system and 'the urgent necessity for change' (Wiggershaus, 1994: 49. See pp. 41–52 for a biographical sketch of the young Horkheimer).

social life which members of the Institute thought of as fundamentally contradictory and antagonistic. Negative criticism had a positive aim and purpose. The task of intellectuals was to contribute to the emancipation and liberation of the masses, by identifying those forces in society that worked against their true human interests. For Horkheimer and his colleagues – as for their contemporary, Georg Lukács – the fate of the masses was the fate of society as a whole and their emancipation was the realization of a free and just society in the interests of all. In this commitment to human emancipation, the members of the Frankfurt School thought of themselves as, and indeed were, the heirs of the eighteenth-century *Aufklärung* (Enlightenment) and the great German intellectual tradition on which they drew to formulate their critique of the contemporary world. In time, though, it would seem that the tradition which nourished them was exhausted and that Enlightenment had turned against itself. Modern rationality, Adorno and Horkheimer would argue in *Dialectic of Enlightenment*, was based on lies and the systematic deception of the masses.

Critical theory and the masses

It was Horkheimer who coined the term 'critical theory'. He first used the term (in English) to define the work of the Institute in his Preface to the special issue of *Studies in Philosophy and Social Science* on the Sociology of Communication, published in 1941. He explained what he meant by 'the conception of critical social research' later in the issue in his 'Notes on Institute Activities'. In the first place, generalizing concepts (such as 'the masses') remain mere abstractions unless understood in their particular historical situation and circumstances:

> The proper meaning of 'masses', for example cannot be derived through an essentially quantitative analysis … Proper methodological usage must recognize that the masses are basically different at different stages of the socio-historical process and that their function in society is essentially determined by that of other social strata as well as by the peculiar social and economic mechanisms that produce and perpetuate the masses. (Horkheimer, 1941: 121–2)

Any single generalized concept, in theoretical analysis, is to be understood as a concrete element in a given social configuration and, as such, related to the whole of the historical process of which it is an indissoluble part. Such analysis is essentially critical in character, for it recognizes and seeks to account for the discrepancy between the professed values of a society and its actual workings:

> The media of public communication – radio, press and film – for instance, constantly profess their adherence to the individual's ultimate value and his inalienable freedom, but they operate in such a way that they tend to forswear such values by fettering the individual to prescribed attitudes, thoughts and buying habits. (Ibid.: 122)

A properly critical theory presupposes certain identifiable, fundamental values to which historical societies are committed and for which they may be justly criticized if they fail, in actual practice, to defend and realize them. The primary theoretical task was to develop an analysis of the workings of society as a whole in order to account for its failure to deliver in practice the values it professed.

That task was underlined by Horkheimer in his inaugural address, on 24 January 1931, on the occasion of his appointment to a chair in Social Philosophy and the Directorship of the Institute. His speech dealt with the current condition of social philosophy and the task of an institute dedicated to social research. The German philosophical tradition, beginning with Hegel, had seen individuals as part of the social whole, although that totality was indifferent to the fate of individuals. In the course of the nineteenth century, as Marx had clearly foreseen, the progressive development of industry, technology and science seemed to promise an end to material scarcity and thereby the arbitrary, unequal and unfair distribution of the material means of existence between rich and poor. Mass production promised the abolition of poverty for the masses. That hope had not yet been realized. The Institute would seek to combine a materialist (Marxist) theory with empirical studies of contemporary economic relations between workers and employers.[4] The central issue today, Horkheimer argued, was 'the question of the connections between the economic life of society, the psychic formation of individuals and changes taking place in the cultural sphere' (Wiggershaus, 1994: 38). In the years that followed, the transformations taking place in contemporary cultural life would become increasingly important for Horkheimer and Adorno.

The role of culture is one of the great themes of this history, and it first emerges as a critical issue for social theory in the work of Adorno and Horkheimer. In trying to think of society-as-a-whole, it appeared that it had three structural elements: economic, political and cultural forms of life. If now it seems obvious that a society *as* a totality is a complex formation of these three elements, that was something that had, in the first place, to be discovered. In the early twentieth century the importance of the cultural formation of modern societies was far less evident than it is today, for the cultural turn in social thought is a product of the second half of the last century. As we have seen, the social question of modernization in the nineteenth century was centred on economic relations, the antagonisms to which they gave rise and political struggles to overcome them. It had seemed, for a moment, in the immediate aftermath of the First World War, as if a political victory had been won in Russia when Lenin seized political power and established state socialism on behalf of the masses.

---

4 It was the implementation of the project announced here that first brought Horkheimer and Lazarsfeld (then in Vienna) in contact with each other a year or so later.

In the revolutionary year of 1918, it was widely anticipated that the overthrow of the monarchy in Russia would provoke revolutions elsewhere in Europe. In Germany, England and Italy it seemed, for a moment at least, as if deep industrial unrest might give rise to spontaneous revolutions from below and the capture of state power by the masses. But in each country, though in different ways, the moment came and went. A decade later the failure of the revolutionary potential of the masses was something that required urgent attention from a materialist social theory. Brute force and oppression would not do as an explanation.[5] It began to look as if the springs of revolutionary action were unbent by the false enchantments, the siren songs, of mass culture.

'Culture' is, according to Raymond Williams, one of the most difficult words in the English language and his attempts to grapple with its meaning is a central theme of Chapter 4, in which I trace British responses to 'the social question'. The task, as Williams well knew, is always to understand the historical significance of words if we are to grasp their meaning; that is, we must consider how it is, and when, that words readjust their meaning and usage in response to all the 'innumerable and unforeseeable demands that the world makes on language'.[6] Old words acquire new meaning as they adjust to new historical circumstances. In the interwar period, the meaning of 'culture' was put in question by a fundamental shift in the capitalist mode of production that destabilized its established association with the European tradition in the arts, literature and music. Consumer capitalism was decisively established in Europe and North America in the 1920s and 1930s when mass markets were created for a whole new range of domestic and leisure consumer goods. Intimately linked to this was the wide social penetration of new electronic forms of communication (telephone and radio) and of 'mass' entertainment (cinema and the record industry). 'Mass culture' became another key concern for contemporary intellectuals engaged with the question of the masses.

One of the aims of this book is to understand historically the formation of academic disciplines, their characteristic concerns and conceptual frameworks. The work of the Frankfurt School was almost wholly unknown in its most creative, productive period, in exile in America. It only became widely known and read some 30 or 40 years later as it was translated into English and absorbed

---

5 Antonio Gramsci's analysis of the Italian case was the most brilliant interpretation of this crux for contemporary Marxism. Gramsci (1891–1937), the leader of the Italian Communist Party, was imprisoned when Mussolini came to power and in his posthumously published *Prison Notebooks* worked out his understanding of the historical forces that 'blocked' the revolutionary potential of the post-war moment. The Notebooks achieved legendary status amongst the New Left when they were translated into English in 1971.

6 A phrase I've taken from Austin (1964: 73).

into the critical literature of a latter-day concern with the study of media and culture. A critique of mass culture, developed in the 1930s, was read quite unhistorically in the 1970s and rejected for its elitism and cultural pessimism. The astonishing originality of that critique in comparison with anything else on offer at the time (or since) was, as John Durham Peters (2003) has pointed out, largely ignored. Salvaging that originality is not without its difficulties, for the key text in which the critique of mass communication and culture is elaborated quite deliberately refuses to offer any coherent, systematic or reasoned account of its position. 'The culture industry: enlightenment as mass deception' is the title of a chapter in *Dialectic of Enlightenment* written by Adorno and Horkheimer in Los Angeles (the home of Hollywood) in the early 1940s far from, but pervasively aware of, the total war engulfing Europe. It was precisely this moment that presented them, as émigré German Jewish intellectuals, with the cruellest of historical ironies; namely, that in Europe reason had turned against itself and darkness had eclipsed enlightenment. But before turning to how this theme was elaborated in *Dialectic of Enlightenment* and, in particular, their critique of what they called the culture industry, some preparatory exegesis is required of Horkheimer and Adorno's key sources of inspiration. I will briefly outline, in turn, Karl Marx's concepts of alienation and commodity fetishism, Max Weber's concept of instrumental reason and Georg Lukács's concept of the reification of consciousness. All were crucial to the thinking of Horkheimer and Adorno and underpin their remarkable analysis of mass culture to which I will return after this brief excursus.

Alienation and commodity fetishism

The legacy of Karl Marx (1818–83) is difficult to assess today, partly because of the collapse of Communism in Russia and Eastern Europe and partly because of the not unconnected collapse – for the time being – of western academic Marxism which, in its various revisions, also drew inspiration from him. Marx's genius, however, transcends what his political and intellectual heirs have made – or failed to make – of him. He was the first and greatest critical analyst of the historical engine of societal modernization, factory capitalism, the theme of his life's work that culminated in his unfinished masterpiece *Capital*, the first volume of which was published in 1867. Marx came to the study of economic life after studying philosophy, religion and politics. In his early, unpublished writings, he focused on the nature of labour under factory capitalism, arguing that in such conditions the worker was necessarily *alienated* from his work which no longer expressed or fulfilled his own humanity or his human relations with others. In a resonant passage, Marx considers what non-alienated labour might be like, what it would be to produce *humanly*:

(1) In my production I would have objectified the specific character of my individuality and for that reason I would both have enjoyed the expression of my own individual life during my activity and also, in contemplating the object, I would experience an individual pleasure, I would experience my personality as an objective sensuously perceptible power beyond all shadow of doubt. (2) In your use or enjoyment of my product I would have the immediate satisfaction and knowledge that in my labour I had gratified a human need, i.e. that I had objectified human nature and hence had procured an object corresponding to the needs of another human being. (3) I would have acted for you as the mediator between you and the species, thus I would be acknowledged by you as the complement of your own being, as an essential part of yourself. I would thus know myself to be confirmed both in your thoughts and your love. (4) In the individual expression of my own life I would have brought about the immediate expression of your life, and so in my individual activity I would have directly confirmed and realized my authentic nature, my human, communal nature. (Marx, 1992: 277–8)

Our natural humanity is essentially social and communal and expressed in the basic human activity of making things. Humanly made things are the expression and the embodiment of a set of social relations between the maker, the product and those for whom the product is made. In the social relations of production the product expresses and confirms the character of that relationship as a shared and common humanity. 'Our productions would be as many mirrors from which our natures shine forth' (ibid.: 177).

The nature of labour, in capitalist production, destroys its human social character. Under factory capitalism, 'the devaluation of the human world grows in direct proportion to the increase in value of the world of things. Labour not only produces commodities; it also produces itself and other workers as a commodity and it does so in the same proportion in which it produces commodities in general' (ibid.: 323–4). Alienated labour shows up first in the fact that the labourer, even before he starts to work has already sold himself for a wage. As such, the worker has already commodified himself both in terms of selling himself for money and, in so doing, becoming a mere instrument of the will of the capitalist. In the labour process, the labourer is alienated from his labour because he has no control over the terms or conditions of work. He does not set the length of the working day, or when or where he will work. He does not control the process of production, he merely performs pre-allocated tasks. There is no 'job satisfaction', no pleasure in making something and supervising all aspects of that process to ensure that the thing is made as one would wish, thereby becoming an expression of oneself. Finally, the product is not in any sense the property of the worker. It belongs to the capitalist who sells it at a profit which he pockets for himself. Thus, alienated labour indicates the commodification of the very conditions of labour: of the labourer himself, of the labour process and of the product of that process. Labour no longer expresses the character of human life as essentially social. Rather, it is the denial of social existence. It confirms the relations of production as essentially antagonistic. The interests of the capitalist are directly opposed to those of the worker. It is not a relationship of mutuality in which each benefits the other. It is a relationship based on exploitation and domination in which human beings are *necessarily* in conflict with each other.

The study of contemporary economic life that Marx began in the *Economic and Philosophical Manuscripts* was fully developed many years later in the first volume of *Capital*. Here Marx took as his starting point, not the character of labour but its end product, the commodity. He sought to show the extent to which commodities expressed even as they concealed the decline of the social world and the rising value of the world of things. The key to the book is contained in the celebrated chapter on 'The fetishism of the commodity and its secret' (Marx, 1976: 163–77). What is its secret? It is that it hides the character of the human effort and energy that went into making it. A commodity could be defined as the objectification of 'dead labour' – all the invisible work that went into its manufacture. This is scarcely an original perception. What is original to Marx is the analysis of the precise character of the labour power that is concealed by commodities. What they conceal is the exploitative character of that labour. The rate of exploitation can be measured by the rate of surplus value (loosely, profit). Surplus value is created in the production process, but realized in exchange. All societies make things for human use. As such, manufactured things have use value which is essentially social. But commodities also have exchange value which is independent of their use value. Exchange value (loosely, price) is realized in exchange against money. Money is 'pure value', 'the commodity of commodities'. It is the absolute measure of all exchange values. Thus, in commodity exchange things enter into relationship with other things and social relations are entirely absent. Yet it is here that surplus value is realized. It is here, in other words, that the rate of exploitation is hidden. For, according to Marx, the value of the commodity (the price at which it exchanges) is the realization of all the labour that went into it. But the labourer does not of course receive back the full value of his labour that is realized in exchange. The gap between what the capitalist pockets as profit (surplus value) and the labourer pockets as his wage discloses the rate of exploitation. It is this that is hidden in the commodity; that is created in the labour process and realized in exchange.

'So far', Marx observes with heavy irony, 'no chemist has ever discovered exchange value either in a pearl or diamond' (ibid.: 177). The value of a commodity is not a material property of the thing. This is the riddle of the commodity form. 'Value does not have its description branded on its forehead; it rather transforms every product of labour into a social hieroglyphic.' Marx's immense labour in *Capital* is to decode this social hieroglyph and, in so doing, solve the riddle of the *fetishism* of commodities. A fetish is an object endowed with magical properties; a charm, say, that you might purchase to protect yourself from harm or misfortune. Fetishism is the worship of things with supposedly magical properties. Marx thinks that commodities are fetish objects, especially money. The magic of money is the riddle of the commodity fetish (ibid.: 187). The fetishism of commodities is (literally) the *object*ification of the social relations of production into relationships between things. This process displaces and devalues human social life, for when commodities realize their value *as* commodities in exchange with the money commodity, they do so at the expense of all those who made the commodity but who have no control whatsoever over the objects of their labour and who derive little benefit from it other than a 'living wage'. Commodity fetishism indicates the commodification of the social relations of production. If labour is – as Marx thought – the expression of our common human nature, then the fate of labour under capitalist conditions indicates the falling value of social life and the rising value of the life of things.

Instrumental reason

Two central concerns in the sociology of Max Weber (1864–1920) were the growing *rationalization of society* and the corresponding *disenchantment of the world*. Weber, writing at the end of the nineteenth century, perceived that social life was increasingly organized on the basis of a particular kind of rationality, *Zweckrationalität* or purposive rationality. This kind of rationality underpinned the organisation of contemporary economic and political life: the modern business enterprise and the modern nation–state. What drives modern economic and political institutions is the pursuit of *technical efficiency*. The aim of the capitalist business is the maximization of profit. How best to achieve that end is a purely technical question, a question of technique or method, of finding the most effective (efficient) means of realizing profit. It is a strictly rational matter of calculating the relation of means to ends. This is what Weber means by purposive rationality. It is the logic of this way of thinking (the rational calculation of means to ends) that he regards as the dominant form of rationality in modern societies, its 'inner logic', as it were.

What are the implications of this kind of rationality? Weber noted that it could be emphasized in two different ways. On the one hand, you might prioritize means over ends (*means*-oriented rationality). On the other, you might prioritize ends over means (*ends*-oriented rationality). Weber called the latter *substantive* rationality and the former, *formal* rationality.[7] Substantive rationality

---

7 Weber (1964: 184–212). See also the lengthy introduction (ibid.: 3–86) by Talcott Parsons who translated Weber's *Grundriss der Sozialökonomik*.

is concerned with ends. It expresses a *telos* (a goal or purpose). That telos may be profit in the case of the business organisation or it might be some welfare policy (increasing child allowance, say) for a government in power. What is the basis upon which agreement is reached over social goals or aims? Weber observed that in modern societies there are many different, competing substantive rationalities. The substantive aims of the worker and the substantive aims of the capitalist are not only different but opposed to each other, and so it is in respect of many important issues: abortion, for instance. Thus there was no overriding substantive rationality (no shared 'world-view') to modern societies. They were not underpinned by a general agreement about the aims or purposes of their existence. The resolution of substantive differences between individual or social groups was increasingly a matter to be decided through political or legal processes.

Faced with what might be called social incoherence at the level of substantive rationality, formal rationality (or technical efficiency) achieved greater significance, increasingly becoming an end in itself. The logic of technical efficiency underpinned modern bureaucracies. Weber produced a penetrating analysis of the organisation of non-manual labour whose concern was, in various forms, with political or economic administration. If Marx analysed the labour process in the factory, thereby revealing the *modus operandi*, the inner logic, of the economic organisation of modern life, Weber analysed the workings of the office, thereby revealing the *modus operandi* of the state, the political organisation of modern life. The state has the monopoly of legitimate violence (the army, the police) with which it crushes internal rebellion within its territorial borders and resists external threats from foreign powers (Weber, 1964: 156). Its power to defend life and property within its territorial limits is the basis of its legitimacy. Its continuing existence depends upon a permanent administrative apparatus (or bureaucracy) that collects taxes and administers the legislation enacted by the state.

Modern bureaucracies have consistent, methodically prepared and precisely executed relations of command and obedience. They are hierarchies of power, with a chain of command that works from top to bottom, in which all know their place in the organization, what they can and cannot do and with what consequences. They are systems of 'organized inequality' that compel conformity via sanctions that are available against those who, for whatever reason, fail to conform. These relations of subordination are subject to strict internal differentiation: a complex division of duties, tasks and responsibilities. The regulation of the system is calculated in relation to considerations of cost and efficiency and is spelled out in written documents. The efficient working of bureaucratic organizations depends on a rationally calculated division of labour. The work of subordinates is subject to continuous monitoring and assessment from above. Every aspect of the organisation is compartmentalized, departmentalized and governed by particular rules. Bureaucracies are *impersonal* – one of their defining characteristics. They operate 'without regard for particular persons and situations'. They do not take personal considerations into account in any aspect of their work. This impersonality is principled. It abolishes favouritism, nepotism and bribery – in short, what were regarded as corruption in older systems of administration which modern bureaucracies are designed to replace. Those who work in bureaucracies are not the personal servants or property of those who appoint them. Appointments are based on merit, not on personal considerations of friendship, kinship or gain. Even those who hold high office, do so on the same principle. The post held is separable, in principle and practice, from the person who holds it. Anyone can be sacked for failing to meet the requirements of the post.

Bureaucratic forms of organisation come to dominate all aspects of modern institutional life. It is precisely their technical efficiency – their capacity to impose administrative order on the complexities of the world – that establishes them decisively and irreversibly, as the dominant institutional means of co-ordination and control in modern societies. Weber writes of bureaucracies as complex mechanisms that remain in 'good working order' like a well-running machine. The modern world is an increasingly *administered* world, a calculating, mechanized, technical-rational world. What cannot be rationally calculated is of no significance.

In the administered world what is excluded from rational consideration are all aspects of personal life: emotions, feelings and all non-rational elements. All those things that do not readily succumb to administration and rational calculation tend be eliminated. This is one aspect of what Weber thought of as the *disenchantment* of the modern world; the loss of the possibility of enchantment or magic. This process was a direct consequence of Enlightenment thinking which was resolutely hostile to religion and dismissed it as the embodiment of the irrational. The secularization of the world meant, in effect, the de-sacralization of the world of nature and of human experience; a loss of the sense of the sacred. Pre-modern thought had a sense of the world as a live and living thing, an attitude that was expressed in a belief in the gods, in the spirit of place, in an animistic attitude to nature. Modern scientific thinking sees the world as dead matter, mere stuff whose chemical and physical properties can be analysed, described and classified. The loss of a sense of enchantment points to a decline in a natural religious or poetic attitude to the world. Modern societies gain in knowledge in direct proportion to the loss of their capacity to experience or understand the world.

In a celebrated passage at the end of his most famous work, *The Protestant Ethic and the Spirit of Capitalism*, Weber describes the modern world as 'an iron cage'. He had attempted, in the preceding pages, to trace the development of the whole tremendous modern economic order from the spirit of worldly asceticism in certain Protestant religious sects in seventeenth-century Europe:

Today the spirit of religious asceticism – whether finally, who knows? – has escaped from the cage. But victorious capitalism, since it rests on mechanical foundations, needs its support no longer. The rosy blush of its laughing heir, the Enlightenment, seems also to be irretrievably fading ... No-one knows who will live in this cage in the future, or whether at the end of this tremendous development there will be a great rebirth of old ideas and ideals or, if neither, mechanized petrification, embellished with a sort of convulsive self-importance. For, of the last stage of this cultural development, it might well be truly said: 'Specialists without spirit, sensualists without heart; this nullity imagines that it has attained a level of civilization never before achieved'. (Weber, [1930] 1971: 181–2)

The reification of consciousness

In a brilliant essay called 'Reification and the consciousness of the proletariat', written in 1923, Georg Lukács (1885–1971) attempted a synthesis of the ideas of Marx and Weber outlined above. Reification (from Latin *res*, a thing) literally means 'thing-ification'. It redefines the process of commodification that Marx had analysed. Lukács begins with Marx's analysis of the fetishism of commodities but, whereas Marx had confined his analysis to the relations of economic production, Lukács pushes beyond this to the radical question: How far does the character of commodity exchange affect the whole outer and inner life of modern societies? It seemed, to Lukács, that the commodity structure had come to penetrate society in all its aspects and to reconstruct it in its own image. The commodity was now 'the universal category of society as a whole'. Lukács follows Marx closely, acutely inferring the alienation of labour[8] from his reading of *Capital*. He then proceeds to graft on to Marx's analysis of the labour process, Weber's analysis of instrumental (technical) rationality, arguing that the analysis of bureaucratic reason applies just as much to the management of a factory as an office. The commodification process (Marx) and instrumental rationality (Weber) achieved a ruthless synthesis in the new 'scientific management' which developed in the USA at the beginning of the twentieth century. Its leading exponent, the pioneer of industrial psychology, was Fredrick Winslow Taylor. In *Principles of Scientific Management*, which he wrote in 1911, Taylor describes how he increased the efficiency of the workforce in the Bethlehem Steel Company in Pittsburgh. A basic part of the work process was the job of shifting the raw pig-iron from the yard to the blast furnaces for refining into steel. A 'pig' of iron weighed about 92 pounds and Taylor found that their handlers

---

8 Marx's early writings, in which alienated labour is fully analyzed, were not published until the early 1930s.

shifted about 12.5 tons of iron each day. After careful observation, in which individual workers were timed with a stop-watch in the performance of their work (a 'time and motion study'), Taylor calculated that 'a first class pig-iron handler' ought to be capable of moving about 48 tons a day, and described in detail how this was, in fact, achieved.[9] Lukács comments:

> With the modern 'psychological' analysis of the work-process (in Taylorism) this rational mechanization extends right into the worker's 'soul'; even his psychological attributes are separated from his total personality and placed in opposition to it so as to facilitate their integration into specialized rational systems and their reduction to statistically viable concepts. (1983: 88)

The increasing rationalization of the work process – scientific management in the service of increasing technical efficiency and, of course, profit – fragments the labour process and the labourer to an extent that was unknown in Marx's time. As this mechanized rationality comes to dominate production – in its other form in the 1920s, it was known as 'Fordism' (assembly line mass-production of automobiles) – Lukács claims that 'the fate of the worker becomes the fate of society as a whole'. That fate is definitive reification, a process which has now colonized consciousness or thought itself.

So what is reified thinking? It is fragmented thought, the product and expression of a fragmented subjectivity. The division of labour in the name of technical efficiency affects all forms of work; not just manual labour but intellectual labour as well. It is not just the worker by hand whose 'soul' (or very being) is reified by Taylorism; it is also the worker by brain whose mental activity is both fragmented and alienated along the same lines. As an example of definitive reification, in this respect, Lukács offers us the example of the modern journalist who suppresses his own subjectivity in exchange for a wage. What the journalist writes is not self-expression. He is, indeed, required to suppress his own opinions and attitudes. He must write in the house-style of the newspaper he works for. He must achieve 'objectivity' in his writing and write as if he had no convictions of his own (Lukács, 1983: 100).

The reification of thought itself is characterized by increasing specialization and a corresponding preoccupation with purely technical issues. Taylorism exemplifies that tendency identified by Weber, namely, the dominance of means-oriented reason over ends-oriented reason. The consequence of this is, perhaps, Lukacs's most penetrating insight. It is the destruction of any possibility of understanding life or the world *as a whole*:

---

9 For a full account of Taylorism, see Harry Braverman's excellent and highly readable book, *Labour and Monopoly Capitalism* (1974), whose sub-title ('The degradation of work in the twentieth century') clearly indicates its main theme; a theme that is explored in relation to work in the factory and the office.

The specialization of skills leads to the destruction of every image of the whole ... The more highly developed it [knowledge] becomes and the more scientific, the more it will become a formally closed system of partial laws. It [knowledge] will then find that the world lying beyond its confines and in particular the material base which it is its task to understand, *its own concrete underlying reality* lies, methodologically and in principle, *beyond its grasp*. (Lukács, 1983: 103–4. Original emphases)

Weber's distinction between formal and substantive reason – his perception that there was no agreement over questions of human aims and purposes – pointed to the moral incoherence of the modern world. Lukács drew the inevitable conclusion. The meaningfulness of the world – its moral significance – could not be comprehended. The original project of the Enlightenment – human emancipation through the achievement of the good society – was both a political *and* a moral project. Reason in the service of justice and freedom was ultimately a moral concern. But the modern world was morally incoherent. It was characterized by a rationality of means and an irrationality of ends. It is fundamentally irrational (it violates basic norms of justice) if the whole system of economic production whereby the material needs of society's members are met is harnessed to the enrichment of the few and the exploitation and deprivation of the many. Thus it might be said that modern society is characterized by the rationality of its parts and the irrationality of the whole. Or, as Herbert Marcuse put it much later:

All thinking that does not testify to an awareness of the radical falsity of the established forms of life is faulty thinking ... No way of thinking can claim a monopoly of understanding, but no way of thinking seems authentic which does not recognize that these two propositions are meaningful descriptions of our situation: 'The whole is the truth', and 'the whole is false'. ([1960] 1978: 450–1)

Dialectic of Enlightenment

The critical tradition I have briefly sketched above was absorbed into the bloodstream of the thinking of the leading members of the Frankfurt School. It showed how enlightened self-interest became transformed into instrumental reason which, concerned with the most efficient means in the pursuit of irrational ends, turned into powerful means of economic exploitation and political domination. For Adorno and Horkheimer, the fading of the Enlightenment that Weber had noted was now complete. The chilly logic of an increasingly administered world stripped it of meaning and significance, while commodity fetishism conjured up its pseudo re-enchantment. Marx and Weber had analysed the totalizing logic of domination in modern economic and political life – monopoly capitalism and the nation–state. Critical theory completed the picture by showing how the logic of domination had penetrated cultural life and, thus, how the whole social formation (the totality of organized economic, political and cultural life) appeared as an objective force, a power over and above and against the interests of individual human beings. Lukács's synthesis of Marx and Weber was particularly important for it posed their most immediate dilemma as Adorno and Horkheimer turned to the task of writing *Dialectic of Enlightenment*. If modern consciousness was reified, how could they express their thoughts when thought itself had become a commodity 'and language the means of promoting that commodity'?

> When examining its own guilty conscience, thought has to forgo not only the affirmative use of scientific and everyday conceptual language, but just as much that of the opposition. There is no longer any available form of linguistic expression which has not tended toward accommodation to dominant currents of thought; and what a devalued language does not do automatically is proficiently executed by societal mechanisms. (Adorno and Horkheimer, [1944] 1979: xii)

The freedom to think for oneself and not to be dominated by the externally imposed beliefs, values or ideas of others was perhaps the basic tenet of the eighteenth-century Enlightenment, or so Kant claimed, in his famous short essay on the question 'What is Enlightenment? '*Sapere aude!*' he wrote (borrowing a phrase from Horace) in answer to himself. 'Have the courage to use your own reason' – that is the motto of Enlightenment' (Kant, [1784] 1995: 1). Two centuries later it now seemed that the application of human reason led slowly but surely to the first truly global, fully technological war as the culmination of the world-historical process of modernization. Horkheimer made this explicit in an essay on 'The end of reason' written in 1941:

> Locke once wrote, 'the word reason in the English language has different significations; sometimes it is taken for true and clear principles; sometimes for clear and fair deductions from those principles; and sometimes for the cause, and particularly the final cause'. He appended four degrees of reason: discovering truths, regularly and methodically ordering them, perceiving their connections, and drawing the right conclusion. Apart from the final cause, these functions today are still held to be rational. Reason in this sense is as indispensable in the modern technique of war as it has always been in the conduct of business. Its features can be summarised as the optimum adaptation of means to ends, thinking as an energy-conserving operation. It is a pragmatic instrument oriented to expediency, cold and sober ... When even the dictators of today appeal to reason, they mean they possess the most tanks. They were rational enough to build them; others should be rational enough to yield to them. ([1941] 1978: 28)

The Second World War was the end of reason in a double sense: it was the final outcome of what began as the European Enlightenment centuries earlier. It was also the end of hope in the promise of reason to which the Enlightenment thinkers were committed. Thus the *dialectic* of Enlightenment was the inner contradiction of the very idea of Enlightenment and the historical working out of that contradiction in the slow inexorable progress towards the apocalyptic moment of a global war.

Neither Adorno nor Horkheimer were against Enlightenment and what it stood for. They were 'wholly convinced' that 'social freedom is inseparable from enlightened thought' ([1944] 1986: xiii). The task they set themselves was to explore 'the self-destruction of Enlightenment' in order to redeem its original hope and promise. But this could not be done systematically, for systematic thinking was the basis of the logic of domination. Implicit in modern thought, from the start, was a totalizing drive to mastery, control and domination. 'Enlightenment is totalitarian' (ibid.: 6). Totalizing thought gave birth to totalitarian economic and political systems and, eventually, total war. Modern societies *as* totalities proclaimed the systematic domination of social life over individual lives. Modern thought, hailed at first as the means for the liberation of individuals, turned out to be, in the twentieth century, the means of their systematic domination 'from above'. To try and come up with some alternative system of thought or programme for the organisation and management of society, would simply be to remain within the cage from which Horkheimer and Adorno sought to escape. Their anti-systematic thinking was intentionally fragmentary and elusive. Their style was a protest against the commodification of thought and language. It was fuelled by two predominant feelings that rarely find expression in academic writing: anger and disgust.

Their anger was mobilized on behalf of the masses and their disgust was with the moral shoddiness of the deception perpetrated on them. In an essay written some years later, Adorno reflected on what he and Horkheimer had been trying to say in *Dialectic of Enlightenment*. In the original drafts, they had written of 'mass culture' but had deliberately replaced this with the phrase 'the culture industry', because they feared that mass culture might be interpreted by readers as meaning something like 'popular culture', a culture; *of* the masses. But the culture industry had nothing to do with popular culture, a culture produced by the people for their own enjoyment. It was external to the mass of the people, part of the logic of their domination. It 'integrates its consumers from above' (Adorno, 1992: 85):

> In so far as the culture industry arouses a feeling of well-being that the world is precisely in that order suggested by the culture industry, the substitute gratification which it prepares for human beings cheats them out of the same happiness which it deceitfully projects. The total effect of the culture industry is one of anti-enlightenment, in which, as Horkheimer and I have noted, enlightenment, that is the progressive technical domination of nature, becomes mass deception

and is turned into a means for fettering consciousness. It impedes the development of autonomous, independent individuals who judge and decide con-
sciously for themselves. (Adorno, 1992: 91–2)

Art and culture have been penetrated by the techniques and methods of industrial mass production. By the culture *industry,* Adorno and Horkheimer meant
in the first place the commodification of art forms which now succumbed to the
production methods and sales techniques of mass-production. They used the
term more generally to cover a range of overlapping developments between
the wars that saw the decisive gearing of production towards 'mass consumption'; everything from mass-produced cars to domestic appliances. And a crucial
part of this whole complex process was the development of 'mass culture' characterized particularly by the rise of mass circulation daily newspapers, radio,
cinema (Hollywood), photography (especially in connection with advertising and
mass circulation magazines) and the 'music industry' (the growth of the record
business). The lubricant of these interlocking developments was the emerging
advertising industry whose job it was to market and 'sell' the new products of a
capitalist market newly geared towards individual consumers.

The methods of mass production are geared to the manufacture of a uniform
and indefinitely repeatable product. Every vinyl gramophone record is the same
as every other. Mass production was geared to standardization and uniformity. 'It
imposes the stamp of sameness on everything' and thereby destroys difference
and individuality. It homogenized everything. Mass culture made everything in
its own likeness and thus tended towards the liquidation of individuality. It
undermined the independence of individual taste and judgement. Everyone was
dished up the same bill of fare – the same movies and radio programmes, the
same records, the same 'stars' – and none could escape. Resistance was impossible.
All succumbed to the same fate. When millions, for instance, went to 'the
pictures' week in, week out (as they did in the 1930s and 1940s), it seemed as
if whole populations had fallen victim to the false enchantments of the movie
industry. In a capitalist society, dominated by the work ethic, 'free time'
appeared as the marginal surplus left over after the long hours of the working
week. It seemed like a residual moment in which individuals were genuinely
free to pursue their own interests, no longer compelled, by dull economic necessity, to work for and at the bidding of the industrial firm, or large organisation. But
free time, colonized by mass consumption, turned into its opposite. People 'worked'
at their free time (in pursuit of hobbies, or on mass-produced holidays). There was
a strong degree of compulsory behaviour in this. Individuals were not free in any
genuine sense; not free, that is, to realize their own, particular interests as the
expression of their individuality. Rather, everyone now did the same thing:
bought the same records, watched the same movies, admired the same 'stars'.
It was a compulsion to conformity of opinion and taste and judgement on a massive scale. It was also a compulsion to spend and consume time and money.

'Amusement under late capitalism is the prolongation of work' (Adorno and Horkheimer, [1944] 1986: 137).

The pleasures on offer were not real pleasures. In the first place, they were unsatisfying because they were undemanding. They required no thought or effort. They were easily and quickly consumed – the 3-minute music record, for instance. Everything has been done in advance for the consumer, and everything is the same. All popular songs have the same beat. All movies have the same storyline. The adventure movie has its predictable action-man hero, the romance its predictable heroine. There is no choice on offer; no significant difference; no departure from the norms created by the industry and imposed on the mass of consumers from above. It 'perpetually cheats its consumers of what it perpetually promises' (ibid.: 139). The culture industry promises to satisfy sexual desire, for instance, but does no more than titillate. 'The mass production of the sexual automatically achieves its repression' (ibid.: 140). It might promise entertainment and amusement, but 'it makes laughter the instrument of the fraud practised on happiness' (ibid.: 140).

For critical theory, happiness was the rational kernel of freedom and justice, the promissory note of a good and just society. The deepest deception of the culture industry was its false promise of freedom and happiness. The penetration of art and culture by the methods, techniques and aims of mass production was the means whereby the masses were finally bought off by and 'made safe' for capitalism. In the immediate aftermath of the First World War, it had seemed for a moment as if the inherent antagonisms of the relations between capital and labour must give rise to revolution. By the end of the 1930s that possibility had vanished. And one key reason for this was that mass culture provided false satisfactions and pleasures for the masses – 'euphoria in unhappiness' – and thereby integrated them 'from above' into an unjust and unfree society from which there was no longer any escape because the possibility of resistance had finally been overcome. The mass of ordinary people were cynically manipulated, and their subordination secured at the price of a bit of entertainment.

But it was not only, or even primarily, the masses who suffered in the merciless glare of the light of reason. Nature, animals and women are all seen as the irrational victims of *male* rationality and its irresistible drive to world domination, the proof of which was all around in the global war then convulsing the earth as men went about their killing business.[10] In the long tradition of European

---

10 On these themes see especially 'Man and animal' (Adorno and Horkheimer, [1944] 1981: 245–55) which appears in 'Notes and Drafts' at the end of the book and consists of all the fragments that could not be worked into the main body of the text. The domination of nature is a key theme of Horkheimer's most important individual work, *Eclipse of Reason* ([1947] 2004, see pp. 63–86). Originally presented as a series of lectures at Columbia in 1946, this text (written in English) was intended as a companion to *Dialectic of Enlightenment* (written in German) and lucidly recapitulates and elaborates its central themes. Adorno and Horkheimer both wrote in English with great fluency and clarity.

thought animals were less than men because they were irrational and hence they had no soul. 'Reason, mercilessly advancing, belongs to man. The animal, from which he draws his bloody conclusion, knows only irrational terror and the urge to make an escape from which he is cut off' (ibid.: 245). The irrationality of animals permits every abuse of them, culminating in 'the unrelenting exploitation of the animal kingdom in our own days' and their use for scientific purposes, a barbarism that finds its ultimate, paradoxical expression in the laboratory experiments of behavioural psychology. It is paradoxical because, in order to understand the soul (the psyche) of free and rational man, the behaviour of trapped, irrational animals in cages is studied. But perhaps their cages disclose the unconscious truth of the situation of those who study them.

Rational man feels no concern for irrational animals. Western civilization has left this to women who have no personal responsibility for that civilization:

> It is man who has to go out into an unfriendly world, who has to struggle and produce. Woman is not a being in her own right, a subject. She produces nothing but looks after those who do; she is a living monument to a long-vanished era when the domestic economy was self-contained. The division of labour, imposed on her by man brought her little that was worthwhile. She became the embodiment of the biological function, the image of nature, the subjugation of which constituted that civilisation's title to fame. For millennia men dreamed of acquiring absolute mastery over nature, of converting the cosmos into one immense hunting-ground. It was to this that the idea of man was geared in a male-dominated society. This was the significance of reason, his proudest boast. Woman was weaker and smaller. Between her and man there was a difference she could not bridge – a difference imposed by nature, the most humiliating that can exist in a male-dominated society. Where the mastery of nature is the true goal, biological inferiority remains a glaring stigma, the weakness imprinted by nature as a key stimulus to aggression. (Adorno and Horkheimer, [1944] 1986: 248)

Male aggression towards women is built into the fabric of Western culture and religion. In its long history, women have been idealized and demonized, worshipped and reviled. Female rage against male domination and aggression took the form of the Furies in ancient mythology. Today it takes the form of endless nagging whereby the contemporary woman 'takes revenge in her own home for the misery inflicted upon her sex from time immemorial' (ibid.: 249). The writings of the Marquis de Sade are taken as the embodiment of Kant's definition of Enlightenment as reason freed from the tutelage of another. De Sade's most infamous texts – *Juliette* and *120 Days of Sodom* – are read as the unbridled play of male sexuality and its unrestrained urge to domination. One of the libertines in *Juliette* declares, when a girl he is torturing breaks into tears: 'That's how I like women ... if only I could reduce them all to such a state with a single word' (ibid.: 111). The strong despise the weak and take pleasure in their humiliation and suffering. The hatred for woman that represents her as intellectually and physically inferior, and bearing the brand of domination on her forehead, is equally that of hatred for Jews (ibid.: 112). It is scarcely necessary to point out that Adorno and Horkheimer themselves – strangers in a strange land, in forced exile in America – could not but see their own condition as one of the ultimate ironies and betrayals of Enlightenment thinking. Anti-Semitism is a key theme in *Dialectic of Enlightenment*. The Jews' homelessness and powerlessness made them vulnerable, while their refusal to adjust and insistence on their difference provoked rage.

The work of art in the age of mechanical reproduction

If the methods and techniques of mass production had penetrated culture, what were the consequences for the work of art? Did art succumb to commodification? Could it resist fetishization? These questions were intensely discussed in a celebrated exchange of views between Adorno and Walter Benjamin some years before *Dialectic of Enlightenment* was written. In the mid-1930s Benjamin wrote an essay on 'The work of art in the age of mechanical reproduction' that argued for a progressive interpretation of the industrialization of culture. Adorno replied with a powerful analysis of the impact of mass production on music. It is not a question of who was right or who 'won' this debate, nor even which viewpoint is preferable. My aim is not to adjudicate on its outcome, but rather to consider the complexity of the issues it raised about the social and political role of art and its enduring relevance, for it was the return of this question in very different circumstances four decades later that prompted the resurrection in the 1970s of the texts discussed here.[11] We must understand how and why the question of art and politics mattered at the time. Far from being of merely academic interest, the issues that concerned Benjamin and Adorno were compelling ones that intimately and fatefully touched their lives in different ways.

Since the beginning of societal modernization, art had been in retreat. Industrialization and urbanization drove it from the centres of modern life and expelled it to the margins where it found refuge in Nature, a powerful inspiration for Wordsworth and Romantic art, poetry and music in general. In modern conditions, art was simply useless. It might well be a thing of beauty and a joy forever, but so what? It was neither use nor ornament in the utilitarian logic that defined the new and hard times of factory capitalism. There was no place

---

11 Many of the key works of the Frankfurt School and other notable figures of 'Western Marxism' past and present were translated into English for the first time and published by *New Left Review* in the 1970s.

for art in the grim struggle of the war of all against all by which men lived their daily lives, encapsulated in the brutal philosophy of Jonas Chuzzlewit: 'Do other men, for they would do you'. Thus art was compelled to make a virtue of necessity and accept its pointlessness, conceded in the late nineteenth-century slogan 'Art for art's sake'. Art and the artist now stood aloof from the struggle for existence and proclaimed the transcendent timeless values of truth and beauty as, at best, a consolation for contemporary life whose desolateness was a key theme of early twentieth-century modernism, memorably expressed in its most famous poem *The Wasteland*. The English comic magazine *Punch* published a cartoon in the late 1920s which George Orwell picked out as pinpointing contemporary artistic attitudes. An elderly aunt is asking her nephew (who is an author) what he is writing about. 'My dear aunt', the intolerable youth crushingly replies, 'One doesn't write *about* anything. One just writes' (Orwell [1940] 1968).

That attitude, and this was Orwell's point, was put under increasing strain in the aftermath of the Wall Street crash of 1929 and the global economic recession that defined the politics of the 1930s in Europe and North America. Large-scale unemployment on both sides of the Atlantic raised again the question of the masses and demanded immediate political action: the New Deal in America, Fascism in continental Europe and muddled inertia in Britain. In the 1930s, 'society' was everywhere politicized in that most political of decades. Art could no longer stand aloof in face of the prolonged economic and political crisis and the question of political commitment for the artist was intensely debated throughout Europe and the United States. It would no longer do just to write: one must engage with and write about the pressing issues of the day. In the Soviet Union, writers and intellectuals were called upon to be 'engineers of the soul': to throw themselves wholeheartedly behind the new Communist society and produce artistic representations of the men and women of the new Russia. A whole new genre of 'socialist realism' in art and literature came into being to celebrate the achievements of the socialist revolution. In Britain, the intellectuals marched sharply to the left. They were deeply concerned with the prolonged social fall-out of the economic crisis that created long-term unemployment in the industrial heartlands of the United Kingdom. They espoused new popular movements: for peace, for the republican cause in the Spanish civil war (Hynes, 1966). In the USA, intellectuals became enthusiastic recruits to the New Deal administration and made films, photographed, and wrote about the impact of the Depression and the heroic efforts of the New Deal to counter it (Stott, 1986). It was this situation – the rise of Fascism, the impact of mass production on art and culture, the accompanying new forms of art and entertainment (film, photography, radio, and gramophone records) – that Walter Benjamin addressed in his essay on 'The work of art in the age of mechanical reproduction' (Benjamin, 1973b).

The central thesis of Benjamin's essay is that in modern conditions, art has lost its *aura*, which is destroyed by mechanical reproduction (or mass production). This loss underscores the disenchantment of the contemporary world but Benjamin's attitude to this is without nostalgia. *Aura* means 'breeze' in Latin. It is used as a metaphor for the subtle emanation things give off as the mark of their distinctiveness. In European painting, for instance, the aura of sanctity is represented by a halo around the saint's head, or a subtle glow around the figure of the Madonna. For Benjamin, art is invested with and surrounded by aura, a halo of significance that distinguishes it from non-auratic, everyday things. In modern societies art proclaims itself as art by its *uniqueness* and *distance* from daily life and its affairs – the two key marks of auratic art. There is only one Mona Lisa, for instance, and its significance as art is caught up to a considerable extent in its status as a unique and singular thing. Art is also marked by its distance from everyday life, retreating into the museum, the gallery, the theatre, or the concert hall.

Walter Benjamin

In pre-modern times, this was not the case. Art was embedded in the very fabric of society. It embodied and expressed a society's most intimate values and beliefs, its sense of its history and place in the world. As such, what we now call art had a very different function then, and was closely linked to religion, magic, and ritual. In a beautiful essay called 'The Storyteller', Benjamin reflects on the decline of storytelling in modern societies, displaced on the one hand by the novel and on the other, by the newspaper (Benjamin, 1973a). The former testifies to the collapse of tradition, the latter the extent to which experience has been displaced by information. Storytelling, Benjamin argues, is at the heart of traditional societies. It embodies and expresses the tradition; indeed, it *is* the tradition. The authenticity of the tradition (its living quality, its aliveness, its *aura*) is preserved in the practice of storytelling. But modern, secular rationality destroys tradition, ritual, magic, and religious beliefs. Enlightenment invented a new thing, *art*, which it invested with an invented tradition – creativity, genius, beauty – to stand as timeless reminders of the human spirit. The aura of, let us call it, 'Gallery Art' (which is what we mean by art in modern times) is a secular mystique, and the 'worship' of great art is a secular ritual practised largely by the European bourgeoisie and their intellectuals.

Mass production destroys art's aura because it destroys its twin characteristics of uniqueness and distance. Photography and cinema multiply the image *ad infinitum*. There may be one Mona Lisa, but there are umpteen photographic reproductions of it in all sorts of contexts, including the downright vulgar. At the same time, mass reproduction destroys the *distance* of the art object. No longer the unique original to which we all must go in reverence if we wish to see it, it is pried from its shell. It goes out into the world, where it circulates in many forms. It comes to us. The sense of reverence for the auratic art object is shattered. In the concert hall or at the art gallery we display our reverence by our concentrated and silent attentiveness to the performance or exhibition. But the mass publics for new forms of mass culture take a more relaxed attitude. They do not have to concentrate on the auratic experience. They can watch in a state of distraction. They can listen to music on the radio or gramophone and do other things at the same time.

What are the implications of the destruction of aura? For Benjamin, it is the *democratization* of art. What was once for the select few is now available for the many. Modern technologies of visual reproduction (Benjamin had in mind photography and cinema in particular) can become art forms for the millions. Moreover, they bring about transformations in how we perceive reality, offering us new perspectives on the world. The camera is deeply enmeshed in the web of reality. It can go to places that were hitherto inaccessible to most of us. Movement can be speeded up and slowed down to reveal the beauty of things not available to ordinary perception; the moment, say, of the impact of a drop of water. The cinematic close-up creates a new kind of intimacy in public, allowing millions access to the human face that was formerly reserved as a look shared only by lovers or by parent and child. In all this, what Benjamin calls the 'theology of art' – its ritual or cult value as a thing of beauty and a joy forever – is put in question. Mass reproduction destroys the unique authenticity of the original work, which can no longer be worshipped as such. 'The total function of art is reversed. Instead of being based on ritual, it begins to be based on another practice – politics' (Benjamin, 1973b: 226).

Unlike Adorno and Horkheimer, Benjamin still believed in the revolutionary potential of the masses. His views on the relationship between the masses and new modes of production were spelled out in a 1934 lecture he gave in Paris to the Institute for the Study of Fascism and published three years later as 'The author as producer'. Here Benjamin argued that the revolutionary potential of new technologies depended on the role in the production process of the intellectual, who must align himself with the masses. It is no use invoking the autonomy of the poet, his freedom to write whatever he pleases (Benjamin, 1978: 255). Art is not about *self*-expression: the author must serve the interests of the people. In new 'mass' forms of writing such as newspapers, there is a greater opportunity for readers to play an active part rather than being mere consumers. They can write letters and influence editorial opinion. In the new post-revolutionary Russian cinema, Benjamin points out, ordinary Russians are used instead of actors to portray ordinary people. Thus, new forms of mass communication may transform consumers into active participants and therein lies a new relationship between producers, products, and audiences. Not the worship of the author (as genius) or of the work (as truth and beauty) by an adoring audience, but a more equal and collaborative relationship in which the author aligns himself with the audience (the masses), takes their point of view, and gives it expression in his work.

This was the kind of theatre to which Bertolt Brecht was committed. For Brecht, the dominant theatrical tradition – the whole commercial business, or 'apparatus' of theatre – served primarily to confirm middle-class audiences in their good opinion of themselves. It did nothing to make them confront contemporary reality or question their own social attitudes and values. Brecht thought of this kind of theatre as 'culinary consumption' – pleasant, bland food dished up for bourgeois audiences who wanted nothing more than a comforting, self-affirming, emotional theatrical experience. He, by contrast, wanted to create theatre for new non-bourgeois audiences who did not ordinarily go to the theatre. He wanted a theatre that a working-class audience would enjoy, where they would feel at ease and not constrained to be 'on their best behaviour'. Going to the theatre could be fun. It could also be a learning experience, inviting audiences to think about the contemporary world and their position in it. It should therefore be *realistic* in a double sense: in respect of what is actu-

Bertold Brecht

ally going on in the world, and how this affects those for whom the tale is told (working-class audiences). To do this, Brecht argued, the new theatre must employ new techniques and methods: 'Reality changes; to represent it the means of representation must change too. Nothing arises from nothing; the new springs from the old, but that is just what makes it new' (Brecht, 1978: 110). In all this, the aim was to achieve a new kind of involvement for a new kind of audience. Not the cosy, self-affirming emotional involvement that bourgeois theatre offered its audiences, but active, conscious political involvement: a theatre that would make people think, that might change their attitudes, that could play a part in social change rather than merely re-affirming the existing order.

Brecht's ideas about theatre underlie much of Benjamin's thinking in both essays under discussion here. In 'The author as producer', Benjamin makes explicit the links between his ideas and Brechtian theatre (1978: 261–2, 265–7). He also makes clear that he is discussing the role of art in relation to class struggle. The instruments of production are in the hands of the enemy – the newspaper, for instance, 'belongs to capital' (ibid.: 259). The new technologies have no revolution-ary potential in themselves but are put to reactionary use in reactionary hands. Consider the case of 'art' photography: 'It is unable to say anything of a power sta-tion or a cable factory other than this: what a beautiful world! ... It has succeeded in making even abject poverty, by recording it in a fashionably perfected manner, into an object of enjoyment' (ibid.: 262–3). This is what Adorno meant by 'the bar-barism of perfection' (see below): technically perfect images dished up for culinary consumption, that aestheticize the world and thereby close off the possibility of any critical perspective on a less-than-perfect reality. In 'The author as producer', Benjamin calls on intellectuals to work within existing cultural institutions to sub-vert their functions. They must change their practices and use the new instru-ments of communication for politically progressive purposes, to make them work in the interest of the masses rather than against them: 'Technical progress is for the author as producer the foundation of his political progress' (ibid.: 263).

In 'The work of art in the age of mechanical reproduction', Benjamin takes a less explicitly political line. He no longer calls on intellectuals to change the apparatuses of cultural production from within. Rather, he sees the technologies of mass cul-tural production as having an intrinsic emancipatory potential. By transforming the scale of cultural production and distribution, he argues, they play a democratizing role, bringing culture to the millions and shattering the aura of culture as some-thing for 'the happy few'. And by transforming the nature of perception, they offer new perspectives on contemporary reality that were hitherto unavailable. In 'The author as producer', Benjamin had argued that photography when put to modish use, had a flatly reactionary social function. In 'The work of art in the age of mechanical reproduction', the camera *per se* can change perceptions of reality. Do technologies themselves change the world or is it a question of how they are put to use by human beings? 'The question of technology' is the theme of Chapter 5 in this book. Here I wish only to note that it is raised by Benjamin but in contradic-tory ways. The key point at issue in both essays concerns the potential use of mass media and the contemporary arts for progressive political purposes.

Brecht was a member of the German Communist Party and his work had an explicit propagandist intention. Benjamin was never a Communist although he was, like so many of his contemporaries, fascinated by the Russian experiment. He had visited Moscow in 1926 to see it for himself, though his reasons for going there were as much to do with the Communist theatre director, artist and teacher, Asja Lacis, with whom he had fallen in love two years earlier (Wiggershaus, 1994: 89). It was through Lacis that Benjamin met Brecht in the late 1920s and became a close friend. Benjamin, the most subtle and allusive of writers, admired Brecht for his *plumpes Denken*, his 'crude thinking' that got directly to the heart of the matter. When Hitler came to power, Benjamin fled to Paris where he remained, in spite of pressing invitations from Horkheimer and Adorno to join them in America. When the Nazis invaded France in 1940, he fled south, hoping to escape into neutral Spain. He was turned back at the border and committed suicide, believing he would soon be arrested, on 26 September in the little border town of Port Bou where he is buried. After 1933, Brecht led a nomadic life in Denmark, Sweden and Finland, finally arriving in America in 1941, where he joined the Los Angeles community of Germans in exile, re-affirmed his dislike of Adorno and tried his hand (unsuccessfully) as a Hollywood scriptwriter. In 1946, he was summoned before Senator Joe McCarthy's Committee on Un-American Activities that would have compelled him to confirm or deny that he was a Communist and to name others he knew to be Communists. He left America immediately but, whereas Adorno and Horkheimer returned to the Western side of post-war partitioned Germany, Brecht eventually settled in the Communist East where he established a national theatre, the famous Berliner Ensemble.

These brief biographical notes should suffice to make it clear that the issues at stake in the writings of these men were never merely academic matters. They were central to their lives, their concerns and their fates. Benjamin was never wholly convinced of the Socialist alternative to the existing economic and political order but he was quite sure of where he stood on Fascism, against which the political aim of both his essays was directed. Fascism creates *fake aura* by appropriating mass culture for ritual purposes:

> Fascism sees its salvation in giving the masses not their right, but instead a chance to express themselves. The masses have a right to change property relations. Fascism seeks to allow them expression while preserving property. The logical result of Fascism is the introduction of aesthetics into political life. The violation of the masses, whom Fascism, with its *Führer* cult, forces to its knees, has its counterpart in the violation of an apparatus which is pressed into the production of ritual values. (Benjamin, 1973b: 243)

Fascism recruits the masses to politics, not to mobilize them for social change, but to allow them to express themselves, 'to let off steam'. This is why Fascism aestheticizes politics. It transforms politics into theatre, a spectacle in which participants can participate directly in political life but cannot effect change. It does this through the fake aura of the mass rally with its ritual pomp and pageantry, and the cult of *Führer*-worship which is given charismatic expression on such occasions. The forms of mass culture (cinema, radio) are harnessed to the purposes of propaganda and the cult of the mass event. All this leads to one thing: war. Against the aestheticization of politics by Fascism, socialism responds by politicizing art. That was the objective of Brechtian theatre, and the final point of Benjamin's essay.

The fetishization of music

Benjamin sent a copy of 'The work of art in the age of mechanical reproduction' to Adorno for comment. He hoped Adorno would publish it in the Institute's journal. Adorno, however, disliked some of Benjamin's key arguments and especially the influence of Brecht, as he made clear in an exchange of letters (in Taylor, 1980). The essay was published in the *Zeitschrift für Sozialforschung* (1936) but edited and toned down by Horkheimer in New York. A preface, invoking Marx, was cut out altogether (Taylor, 1980: 106). Adorno took issue with Benjamin's critique of auratic art at length in an essay 'On the fetish character in music and the regression of listening' (Adorno, [1938] 1978a) which put forward a detailed counter-argument to the case for mass culture that Benjamin had advanced. Adorno's Italian mother was an accomplished singer and music was central to his family life from his earliest years. He studied philosophy and musical theory at Frankfurt and, on graduating, went to Vienna to study composition under the tutelage of Alban Berg and Arnold Schönberg and the piano with Eduard Steuermann. In his 20s, Adorno wanted to be a composer. In his 30s, he turned to social philosophy and the Institute. His writings on music make up about a third of his total published work and today he is read less as a cultural critic and more as a theorist of music and aesthetics (Huhn, 2005). In the 1930s, he was one of the very first to attempt a sociology of music, to theorize the social roots of music and its relationship with the society and culture of which it was a part. That was the underlying concern of his reply to Benjamin in which he attacked the impact of industrialized music on contemporary musical life. The mass-produced music of the present day consolidated the fateful separation of music into two distinct categories: the serious and the popular, which began in the late eighteenth century. Mozart was the last composer who effortlessly combined both elements in his music. This splitting of the serious and the popular into 'high' and 'low' art was crippling for both. In his letter to Benjamin commenting in pungent detail on his essay, Adorno wrote that it would be romantic to sacrifice one (high art) for the other (mass culture). The art work and cinema are both 'torn halves of an integral freedom, to which, however, they do not add up' (Taylor, 1980: 123).

Two related technical developments at the end of the nineteenth century – the phonogram recording and wireless radio transmission – had an enormous impact on every aspect of musical life in the early twentieth century. Before the gramophone and the radio, music was overwhelmingly a live art in which the performance itself was central to its experience. It was thus a social activity, involving players and audience in the production and experience of the musical event. But the record and the radio shattered the immediate social relations of musical life by their destruction of the performed event. Music now had two separate and unconnected moments: the moment of production (the recording, the radio transmission) and the moment of consumption (listening via radio or the gramophone). What connected these two moments was the musical 'product'. These two new social technologies of sound had the effect, Adorno argued, of reifying music. It was not simply that music was reified as a marketable commodity-thing in the form of a gramophone record. It was fetishized in all sorts of ways that combined to conceal the fate of music in modern times, namely, the loss of its social, sociable character and with that, the accompanying possibility of true musical pleasure. The first part of Adorno's essay explores the many ways in which contemporary music exhibits its fetish character in its production, performance and consumption, all of which bear the stigmata of reification 'for all contemporary musical life is dominated by the commodity form, and the last pre-capitalist residues have been eliminated' (Adorno, [1938] 1978a: 278).

The fetishization of performance shows up in various ways. First, there is the worship of 'the beautiful voice'. Then there is the fetishization of the great composer or conductor, particularly the latter. Finally, there is the notion of the authentic performance, a tendency greatly enhanced by the professionalization of music-playing and the notion of the 'definitive' recording. The fetishization of authenticity (the great voice, the great performance, the great conductor) is an aspect of a total standardization and conformity that allows no place for imperfection. The professionalization of music (itself an accelerated consequence of new technologies) devalues all other musics, which are now relegated to the inferior status of 'amateur' performance. In a telling phrase taken from his piano teacher, Eduard Steuermann, Adorno wrote of 'the barbarism of perfection', which he regarded as definitive reification:

> The new fetish is the flawlessly functioning, metallically brilliant apparatus as such, in which all the cogwheels mesh so perfectly that not the slightest hole remains open for the meaning of the whole. Perfect, immaculate performance in the latest style preserves the work at the price of its definitive reification. It presents itself as complete from the very first note. The performance sounds like its own phonograph record. (ibid.: 284)

Technical perfection is barbarous because it is inhuman. Its flawless, mechanical brilliance excludes the element of human fallibility (the less than perfect performance on less than perfect instruments) and its human charm.

> If one dares even in conversation to assert that it is just as possible to make beautiful music with a moderately good voice as it is on a moderately good piano, one will immediately find oneself faced with a situation of hostility and aversion whose emotional roots go far deeper than the occasion. (ibid.: 277).

Amateur music, in all its social, sociable aspects is devalued by the professionalization of performance and the charm of, say, a child's stumbling performance in a school concert loses its own special magic. The spontaneous character of live performance is eliminated in the recording studio and in its end product, the definitively reified performance, fixed forever as such on disc. Risk and failure are removed. So too the unique, individual quality of the live performance. 'The liquidation of the individual is the real signature of the new musical situation' (ibid.: 276).

The stylization of production means its standardization into something like an assembly-line sound. Adorno detected Fordism in the standard 3-minute recorded hit number. The standardization of music meant its transformation into 'easy listening', something that was instantly and effortlessly consumed, epitomized by the catchy tune or refrain and the standardized rhythm of four beats to the bar. All this loses sight of the intrinsic pleasure of music, which is in performance. It has regressed to an isolated pleasure for an isolated listener, who fetishizes the act of listening but loses sight of that which is listened to. This shows, Adorno argued, in the peculiar obsessions of equipment freaks who fetishize *sound* as an abstract thing independent of what is being played. Adorno pointed to radio hams as an instance of this process. We might point to hi-fi freaks and the fetishization of perfect acoustics. It also shows in the phenomenon of the fan who knows everything there is to know about the fetishized object, who writes to radio stations demanding more airtime for the object-fetish, and who is lost in fake ecstasy at live performances. In all such ways the fan is in thrall to the 'star' fetish object.

Yet no one *really* listens to music any more, Adorno argued. More music is available on a daily basis than was ever possible in earlier times. In fact, thanks to the music industry, it is almost impossible to escape from music nowadays. But the more there is, the less people listen. The reification of music is indicative of music's regression from a worldly, social pleasure to an inner state of mind, a matter of subjective taste ('I know what I like'). Reified music is, first and last, in the head of the isolated, individual consumer of music. Adorno saw all these aspects of reified, fetishized music as indicative of the *regression* of listening. This term, taken from Freudian psychoanalysis, means a reversion to an earlier child-like state. For Adorno, the experience of music had lost its rational, adult character. 'Regressive listeners behave like children. Again and again and with stubborn malice, they demand the one dish they have once been served with' (Adorno, [1938] 1978a: 290). The reification of music produces a kind of mass infantilism in listening publics who no longer listen any more. What is thus lost is the possibility of resistance or criticism, and beyond that, the possibility of *autonomous art*: art as the expression of human autonomy, independence and freedom.

Adorno believed in the redemptive possibility of autonomous art which obeyed its own laws. The Enlightenment was predicated on the play of thought of the autonomous (self-regulating) individual, free from heteronomous constraint (the tutelage of another). Autonomous art is thus the free expression of a self-determining, creative 'author' who produces the art work. More crucially, this integral artistic freedom is embodied in the autonomy of the form and content of the art work itself. Art, in other words, obeys its own laws. As such, it stands in opposition to mass culture, which is governed by heteronymous (external) regulatory factors, most obviously the profit motive and the law of the market. The heteronomy of mass culture reveals itself in the search for mass audiences. In order to reach large and diverse audiences the form and content of cultural products must be simple, accessible, and easy to understand. Thus, the *forms* of mass culture are determined by external pressures. It follows that the autonomy of art, if it is to be true to itself, must reveal itself in forms and content that resist the pull of heteronymous forces. Adorno accepted and defended autonomous art as 'difficult'. It was meant to be. That was how it resisted easy culinary consumption. Benjamin might defend the 'distracted attention' of mass audiences, but Adorno would have none of it. The concentration demanded by modern art was the mark of its negation of the culture market.

In their exchange of letters on his essay, Benjamin tactfully conceded, 'I have tried to articulate positive moments as clearly as you managed to articulate negative ones' (Taylor, 1980: 140). But Adorno rejected the political stance of Benjamin and Brecht. Adorno, for his part, was disturbed by the presence of Brechtian motifs in the essay, the casual transfer of magical aura to the autonomous work of art and the assignation to it of a counter-revolutionary function. Art for art's sake, he declared, was in need of defence and rescue from 'the united front which exists against it from Brecht to the [Communist] Youth Movement' (ibid.: 122). Years later he elaborated his criticism of political commitment in art. Against Sartre, Lukács and Brecht, all of whom, in different ways, defended the position that writers should be politically 'engaged' and express this commitment in their works, Adorno argued that commitment can too quickly lapse into propaganda (Adorno, [1962] 1978). When it does so, it has betrayed its own cause and commitment, namely, truth. That for Adorno was the sticking point. He defended to the last the autonomous work of art for its stance against its betrayal by contemporary economic and political life. If it offered few pleasures, if its appeal was limited it was, nevertheless, true to itself. Its negativity exposed the essentially negative character of dominant forms of economic, political and cultural life even as they thought of themselves as affirmative.

References

Adorno, T. ([1938] 1978a) 'On the fetish character in music and the regression of listening', in A. Arato and E. Gebhardt (eds), *The Essential Frankfurt School Reader*. Oxford: Blackwell, pp. 270–99.

Adorno, T. ([1962] 1978b) 'Commitment', in A. Arato and E. Gebhardt (eds), *The Essential Frankfurt School Reader*. Oxford: Blackwell, pp. 300–18.

Adorno, T. (1992) 'Culture industry reconsidered', in J.M. Bernstein (ed.), *The Culture Industry: Selected Essays on Mass Culture*. London: Routledge, pp. 85–92.

Adorno, T. and Horkheimer, M. ([1944] 1986) *Dialectic of Enlightenment*. London: Verso.

Arendt, H. ([1963] 1990) *On Revolution*. Harmondsworth: Penguin Books.

Austin, J.L. (1964) *Sense and Sensibilia*. Oxford: Oxford University Press.

Benjamin, W. ([1936a] 1973a) 'The storyteller', in H. Arendt (ed.), *Illuminations*. London: Fontana, pp. 83–110.

Benjamin, W. ([1936b] 1973b) 'The work of art in the age of mechanical reproduction', in H. Arendt (ed.), *Illuminations*. London: Fontana, pp. 219–54.

Benjamin, W. ([1937] 1978) 'The author as producer', in A. Arato and E. Gebhardt (eds), *The Essential Frankfurt School Reader*. Oxford: Blackwell, pp. 254–69.

Braverman, H. (1974) *Labor and Monopoly Capitalism: The Degradation of Work in the Twentieth Century*. New York: Monthly Review Press.

Brecht, B. (1978) *Brecht on Theatre,* trans. and ed. J. Willet. New York and London: Hill and Wang, Eyre Methuen.

Gramsci, A. (1971) *The Prison Notebooks*. London: Lawrence and Wishart.

Horkheimer, M. (1941a) 'Notes on Institute activities', *Studies in Philosophy and Social Science,* IX(1): 121–3.

Horkheimer, M. ([1941b] 1978) 'The end of reason', in A. Arato and E. Gebhardt (eds), *The Essential Frankfurt School Reader*. Oxford: Blackwell, pp. 26–48.

Horkheimer, M. ([1947] 2004) *Eclipse of Reason*. London and New York: Continuum.

Huhn, T. (2005) *The Cambridge Companion to Adorno*. Cambridge: Cambridge University Press.

Hynes, S. (1966) *The Auden Generation: Literature and Politics in England in the 1930s*. London: Faber and Faber.

Jäger, L. (2004) *Adorno: A Political Biography*. New Haven, CT: Yale University Press.

Kant, E. ([1784] 1995) 'What is Enlightenment?' in I. Kramnick (ed.), *The Portable Enlightenment Reader*. Harmondsworth: Penguin Books, pp. 1–7.

Lukács, G. ([1922] 1983) 'Reification and the consciousness of the proletariat', in *History and Class Consciousness*. London: Merlin Press, pp. 83–222.

Marcuse, H. ([1960] 1978) 'A note on dialectic', in A. Arato and E. Gebhardt (eds), *The Essential Frankfurt School Reader*. Oxford: Blackwell, pp. 444–51.

Marx, K. (1976) *Capital: A Critique of Political Economy, Vol. 1*. Harmondsworth: Penguin Books.

Marx, K. (1992) *Early Writings*. Harmondsworth: Penguin Classics.

New Left Review (1977) *Western Marxism: A Critical Reader*. London: New Left Books.

Orwell, G. (1940) 'Inside the whale', in *The Collected Essays: Journalism and Letters of George Orwell*. Vol. 1 (1968). London: Secker and Warburg, pp. 506–15.

Peters, J.D. (2003) 'The subtlety of Horkheimer and Adorno: reading "the Culture Industry"', in E. Katz et al. (eds), *Canonic Texts in Media Research*. Cambridge: Polity Press, pp. 58–73.

Stott, W. (1986) *Documentary Expression and Thirties America*. Chicago: University of Chicago Press.

Taylor, R. (ed.) (1980) *Aesthetics and Politics*. London: Verso.

Weber, M. ([1930] 1971) *The Protestant Ethic and the Spirit of Capitalism*. London: Unwin University Books.

Weber, M. (1964) *Theory of Social and Economic Organization*. New York: The Free Press.

Wiggershaus, R. (1994) *The Frankfurt School*. Cambridge: Polity Press.

The end of the masses

Merton, Lazarsfeld, Riesman, Katz
USA, 1940s and 1950s

Robert Merton

Robert Merton (1910–2003) is, along with Talcott Parsons, perhaps the most influential American sociologist of his generation. Merton's parents were immigrant Russian Jews who settled in Philadelphia. He was born Meyer Schkolnik and changed in his teens to Robert Merlin; a name chosen because the young Schkolnik wanted to be a magician like his idol, Ehrich Weiss, the son of an immigrant rabbi, who had metamorphosed into the legendary Harry Houdini. When that fancy passed, Merton seemed a more appropriately 'adjusted' name for an aspirant American intellectual. His doctoral thesis was a work of historical sociology: *Science, Technology and Society in 17th Century England*. He was a leading member in a brilliant group of post-doctoral students at Harvard in the mid-1930s clustered around Talcott Parsons who made his name with the publication in 1937 of *Structures of Social Action*. Like Parsons, Merton was steeped in European sociology: Marx, Weber and Durkheim were all important sources of inspiration. Parsons translated

Robert Merton

Weber from German, Merton translated Durkheim from French to make European sociology available to American academic (and British) readers. Along with Parsons, Merton was the leading exponent of structural functionalism which became, through them, the dominant theoretical underpinning of American sociology until its challenge by Marxist and other structuralisms in the 1970s. Merton's engagement with the sociology of mass communication was but one moment in a long, distinguished academic career. It was an important moment, however, and it was prompted by two factors: the war in Europe and his association with Paul Lazarsfeld, which began when he joined Columbia in 1941. His key work was a case study of a marathon live-to-air radio broadcast by the immensely popular singer, Kate Smith, to promote the sale of government war bonds.

Mass persuasion

The initial idea for the study came, unsurprisingly, from Lazarsfeld who saw it as yet another opportunity to study the impact of the new medium of radio by focusing on a single programme which clearly had an immediate and powerful impact on its audience. Just as the study of Orson Welles's *Invasion from Mars* broadcast was, in itself, a 'media event' which raised questions about the social psychology of mass panic, so too the Kate Smith broadcast was another spectacular media event that raised questions about the social psychology of mass persuasion. Smith was the most popular radio singer of her day. At the time of the broadcast she was in her late 30s. She was tall and fat and plain.[1] She was no glamour icon, but she was very widely liked and admired. She had a natural, untrained contralto voice and by 1932 was earning $7,500 a week as the star of the *Swanee Revue*, a radio vaudeville show. In 1938, she recorded Irving Berlin's 'God Bless America' which achieved instant status as a popular national anthem. The following year she was invited to the White House to perform this, and other numbers, at a presidential banquet for King George VI and Queen Elizabeth on their first state visit to America. President Roosevelt introduced Kate Smith to their majesties as 'one of our greatest singers', adding, it is said, 'This is Kate Smith. This is America.' By the outbreak of war she was already regarded as 'the embodiment of the homey American virtues'.[2]

During the war, Smith had two regular programmes: a 15-minute daytime slot on Wednesday afternoons called *Kate Smith Speaks* in which she read out letters sent in to her, adding her own comments on them and on current issues of concern to ordinary listeners – child labour, war, families and discrimination against workers over 40. It was the top daytime show on radio with an audience of ten million regular listeners for which she earned $5,000 a week. This supplemented the evening prime time *Kate Smith Hour* broadcast by CBS between 8 and 9 p.m. which had begun in 1938 and ran until 1945. For this, she earned

---

1 'More than half the respondents in the study of the broadcast spontaneously alluded to Kate Smith's physical appearance: she is described as a large, stout woman who neither possesses nor makes any apparent effort to achieve sexual allure ... In affectionate summary, "she's just fat, plain Kate Smith"' (Merton, 2004: 146–7).

2 This is according to the *New York Times*, cited in the biography of Kate Smith by Richard K. Hayes (1995: 67), from which most details in this and the next paragraph are taken.

$12,500 a week. She was revered in Tin Pan Alley as the number one hit-maker of the 1930s and 1940s. Her shows advertised cigars, automobiles, coffee, cake flour, baking powder, shaker salt, Jell-O and Postum, a breakfast cereal (I believe).[3]

It was in this context that Smith was asked by CBS to take part in an all-day campaign to persuade Americans to buy government war bonds. The sale of bonds was an important means whereby the government raised money to finance the war through voluntary individual and corporate contributions rather than increasing general taxation. By the end of 1945, the War Finance Committee had sold security bonds to the value of $185.7 billion, purchased by over 85 million Americans. War bonds were promoted by continuous government or corporate advertising, supported by periodical intensive drives to boost sales. The first drive began on 30 November 1942. The third began in early September 1943 with a target of $15 billion in a month. It was launched on the evening of 8 September with a rousing address to the nation by President Roosevelt on network radio. Two weeks later CBS ran its own war bond drive with Kate Smith appealing directly to listeners to buy the new Series E savings bond.[4] This was Smith and CBS's third radio war bond drive, but this time it was made into an unprecedented 18-hour marathon with Smith broadcasting live roughly every 15 minutes without a break. As a result of her efforts, listeners wrote in or phoned to pledge the purchase of bonds to the value of nearly $40 million. It seemed to prove the power of radio to persuade the masses.

It also proved the persuasive powers of Paul Lazarsfeld who had drawn the initially reluctant Merton into the activities of the Radio Research Office. Peter Simonson has given us a fascinating account of the beginnings of the Lazarsfeld–Merton relationship and, more particularly, the distinctive contribution made by Robert Merton to the development of the study of mass communication. Merton was appointed an Associate Professor at Columbia at the same time as Lazarsfeld. He arrived as 'a lone scholar who worked in library and study and had little taste for "applied" research of any kind'. Yet, as he put it many years later looking back on their long friendship, Lazarsfeld had 'ways of drawing others into the vortex of his ideas, commitments, passions and visions'. He introduced Merton to Little Annie, the CBS polygraph, and got him interested in the interpretation of the data it generated via follow-up interviews. Merton was critical of the interview techniques he saw, was urged by Lazarsfeld to have a go himself and thus found himself drawn into pioneering

---

3 I am informed, by John Durham Peters, that Postum is, in fact, a grain-based hot drink, taken as a substitute for coffee. Coffee-lovers shudder at the mention of it. He quite likes it.

4 Information on war bonds in this paragraph is taken from the Digital Scriptorium of Duke University: http://scriptorium.lib.dukes.edu/adaccess/warbonds.html

the methodology of the focused interview, the precursor of today's ubiquitous focus group research.[5]

Those methods provided the basic empirical underpinnings of the Kate Smith study which was based on three sets of inter-related data: (1) a content analysis of the Kate Smith broadcasts; (2) 'intensive focused interviews' with 100 people who listened to the broadcasts; and (3) polling interviews with a cross-section of about a thousand people. The content analysis showed the 'objective' character of the broadcasts to which listeners responded; the intensive interviews revealed how the process of persuasion worked while the extensive (polling) interviews provided a cross-check on the interpretation of the intensive interview material. Methodologically the study is a classic in the literature of the sociology of mass communication, a 'neglected jewel' as Simonson aptly calls it in his Introduction to the new (2004) edition of *Mass Persuasion*. Having set out his methodological stall, Merton moves on to the temporal structure of the broadcast which he characterizes as 'an outstanding event', in relation to which listeners clearly felt themselves to be witnesses or even participants in a very special occasion (Merton, [1946] 2004: 24). Only when the broadcast was considered as a whole, as having a structured temporal unity, could its effect on the behaviours of listeners be understood, particularly the compulsion to carry on listening right through the day to which many of those interviewed testified: 'We never left her that day. We stood by her side. I didn't go out all day, except to go shopping. Even then, I was anxious to get back and listen' (ibid.: 27).

Merton attributes this compulsion to the 'tyranny of radio' though today we would regard it, I think, as evidence of the compelling power of the event as much as the medium in which it is realized. The fact that Smith was committed, like a marathon runner, to keep on going to the end was a crucial aspect of the event's cumulative, compelling power for listeners: 'It built you up as she went along'. It was not, Merton argues, an exercise in propaganda, but in persuasion; the difference being that the former is more of a one-way and the latter a two-way system of communication. Persuasion has a more interactive character: it is more like conversation. Thus, in the course of the event, what Smith said was carefully attuned both to the changing time of day and the responses of listeners who had phoned in to the station to make their pledge. It was an indirect radio phone-in in which:

> the usual radio monologue became something of a conversation. The essence of a two-way conversation is that what each says is modified by what the other has just said or by what one anticipates the other will say in return ...: the marathon permitted Smith to achieve the appearance, and in part the reality, of a conversation. (ibid.: 39)

---

5 All details in this paragraph are from Simonson (2004). For further discussion of the 'focused interview' technique, see Merton ([1946] 2004: 14).

In the thematic analysis of the content of Smith's broadcasts a pie-chart shows that about 50 per cent of the content of what Smith said addressed the theme of war-time sacrifice as it affected all Americans; those in the forces, civilians and Kate Smith herself. The rest of the pie chart shows five different aspects of the ways in which the call to sacrifice was thematized in terms of collective participation in the war effort, in terms of families sundered by war and in terms of surpassing the sums achieved in the two previous CBS radio drives in which Smith had partici-pated. These themes were clearly content- and action-oriented. The other two themes were different: the 'personal theme' and the 'facilitation theme' were rela-tional and medium-oriented aspects of Smith's radio appeals. The personal theme underlined the conversational character of the event. Although this was a huge appeal for a massive collective effort, Smith's talks emphasized the direct intimate you-and-I – 'You and I might send this [war drive] right over the top' – which invoked a direct and immediate response in her listeners: 'She was speaking straight to me', 'You'd think she was a personal friend. I feel she's talking to me' (ibid.: 61). This sense of an intimate rapport between broadcaster and listener was underpinned by the 'facilitation theme' in which Smith repeatedly stressed that the phone was the easiest way to make a pledge and that the station's lines were open and ready. Many listeners went to the phone in the hope of speaking to Smith herself. The phone not only made the purchase of bonds easier, it seemed to sus-tain the personal link with Smith that was felt by many of her listeners for whom 'the telephone afforded the simulacrum of personal contact' (ibid.: 69).

This leads to the central theme of the study. What was it about the broadcast that made is so persuasive? The answer seemed to lie in the personality of Smith herself, whose outstanding characteristic was deemed, by listeners, to be 'sincerity'. But what does this mean in the immediate context of a wartime broadcast that aimed to sell war bonds, and the wider context of a society that is experienced as exploitative and manipulative?

> The enormous importance ascribed to her [Kate Smith's] integrity reflected our subjects' conviction based on experience and magnified by consequent anxiety, that they are often the subject of exploitation, manipulation and control by others who have their own private interests at heart. The emphasis on this theme reflects a social disorder – 'anomie'[6] is the sociological term – in which common values have been submerged in the welter of private interests seeking satisfaction

---

6 A key concept from the French sociologist, Emile Durkheim, whose writings were an important influence on Merton's thinking (cf. Merton, 1938). *Anomie* is derived from Greek *nomos* (law) with the privative a- prefix. It thus means something like the absence of laws, rules or, in sociological terms, norms. It is taken by Durkheim and Merton, whose usage of the concept made it familiar in Anglo-American sociology, to indicate the collapse of traditional values (norms) in conditions of societal modernization. Contemporary America is anomic, as Merton makes clear in this passage, because it has no agreed and accepted value-system to regulate the conduct of social life.

by virtually any means which are effective. It is a product of a society in which 'salesmanship' – in the sense of selling through deft pretense of concern with the other fellow – has run riot. Only against this background of skepticism and distrust stemming from a prevalently manipulative society were we able to interpret our subjects' magnified 'will to believe' in a public figure who is thought to incarnate the virtues of sincerity, integrity, good fellowship and altruism. (ibid.: 10–11)

This effect is all the more paradoxical since Smith is patently 'selling' something, is reading from a script and is known to be extremely rich, unlike most if not all of her listeners? Why does she *not* appear to be part of that process of 'exploitation, manipulation and control' which, Merton claims, is the common experience of her listening public?

In a celebrated section of the book, Merton interprets contemporary America as characterized by pseudo-*Gemeinschaft*. If *Gemeinschaft*[7] stands for a genuine community of values, pseudo-*Gemeinschaft* is its negation: 'the feigning of personal concern with the other fellow', as Merton puts it, 'in order to get the better of him'. Urban Americans live in a climate of reciprocal distrust. Anomie, pseudo-*Gemeinschaft* and cynicism are the psychological effects of a society which, focused on capital and the market, tends to instrumentalize human relationships:

> In such a society, as Marx long since indicated, and as Durkheim and Simmel came to see, there are few dependable ties between each man and others. In such a society 'men will tend to look at every relationship through a tradesman's eyes. They will tend more and more to picture natural objects as commodities and look at personal relationships from a mercenary point of view. In this process those much-discussed psychological phenomena, self-estrangement and dehumanization, will develop and a type of man is born for whom a tree is not a tree but timber'.[8] As codes regulating this money-centered behavior decay, there develops acute distrust of the dependability and sincerity of the other. Society is experienced as an arena for rival frauds. There is little belief in the disinterestedness of human conduct. (Merton, [1946] 2004: 143)

Literary theory has come up with the useful concept of narrative *excess*: points at which a novel or film exceeds the limits of its genre, overflows its own banks, as

---

7 *Gemeinschaft* is usually linked, in the sociological literature, with *Gesellschaft*. The terms were used contrastively by Ferdinand Tönnies (1855–1936) to distinguish between traditional, close and homogeneous communities, based on face-to-face relations of presence in which all knew their place (*Gemeinschaft*) and modern industrialized urban societies characterized by anonymous, impersonal, mobile heterogeneous social groupings (*Gesellschaft*). This strongly normative distinction fits well with Weber's interpretation of the rationalization process at the heart of societal modernization.

8 Merton is quoting from Karl Mannheim, *Man and Society in an Age of Reconstruction* (1940: 19) (New York: Harcourt, Brace & Co).

it were, and generates an excess, a superfluity of meaning. Something like this seems to happen in Merton's study. We start with a seemingly simple thing, a radio broadcast, a popular singer, a successful war-bond drive and end up with a general indictment of contemporary America. How do we get from one to the other? Merton provides an explanation in the final chapter of his book, 'A technical problem and moral dilemma'. What is the problem and what is the dilemma?

It is possible to treat the research topic – Kate Smith's broadcast – as a purely methodological or technical problem. That, Merton suggests, is how the producers of the broadcast treated it. Those who wrote her scripts were concerned with techniques for the effective management of the emotions of listeners in order to persuade them to buy war bonds. Their goal was technical efficiency, the means to their persuasive end. From the perspective of the practitioners of propaganda, success (effectiveness) 'is measured solely by the number of people who can be brought to the desired frame of action or the desired frame of mind' (ibid.: 185). The fact that the broadcast broke new records in the sale of bonds proved the success of the persuasive techniques applied in the broadcast. But this is to apply 'narrowly technical and amoral criteria' which express a manipulative attitude to man and society (ibid.). The broadcasters are criticized for appealing to mass emotions and exploiting mass anxieties while ignoring the underlying economic rationale for war bonds as an anti inflationary regulatory device. They manipulate the masses, rather than informing them. They fail to reflect on the ethical implications of their applied techniques.

But the same criticism applies equally, though the point is seldom made, to the social scientist. The notion that science is disinterested and thereby indifferent or neutral to values is 'specious and delusory'. Social science research is not a value-free activity. It is not merely naïve to think so; it is an abdication of moral responsibility, for the crux of the matter is that the initial formulation of the scientific investigation is conditioned by the implied values of the scientist. These should be made explicit. It was inconceivable for Merton that the study of a singular radio broadcast should be a purely technical, methodological exercise. It had an unavoidable moral dimension to it concerning the role of citizens and the nature of action in a mass democratic society in a time of crisis. The study of this does not permit 'the convenient splitting of our personality into the technician and the citizen selves' (ibid.: 175). Thus, in the concluding chapter, Merton reiterates and unites the distinction, drawn by Lazarsfeld, between administrative and critical research.

Even Adorno acknowledged that there was a difference between exploitative and benevolent administrative research, a distinction that Lazarsfeld had made. The former contributed to the manipulation of the masses, the latter aspired to their improvement (Adorno, [1945] 2004: 211). Lazarsfeld, as we have seen, never thought of the work of the Office of Radio Research as engaged in what he called mere hand-to-mouth commercial research. In his essay on critical and administrative research he had emphasized, drawing on Horkheimer, that a central strand of critical research was concerned with fundamental human values as the moral basis for the evaluation of human social praxis.[9] Human praxis, moreover, must always be understood as shaped by the wider historical social structure in which any and all thought and action are situated. This was common ground for Merton whose thinking was permeated by European 'classic' sociology. It is not enough to note that Marx, Weber, Durkheim, Simmel and Mannheim are all points of reference in Merton's text. The critical texture of European social thought is absorbed, re-interpreted and combined with a new empirical American approach to social phenomena. It is this that remains so distinctive, fresh and original about Merton's *Mass Persuasion*. What is at stake, in both sociological cultures, is the same: the shock of the new, the effort at understanding a world in flux, characterized by rapid, continuing change, the long historical process, that we are still living through today, of world modernization. Sociology is perhaps *the* discipline that has this as its object. It must try to understand immediate, local, concrete social phenomena *and* see in them the significance of the world-transforming process of societal modernization. That is how Merton understood his study of Kate Smith's radio marathon.

The relevance of the study of mass communication

A year or so after the publication of *Mass Persuasion,* Merton agreed to revise for publication the rather fragmentary notes of a paper that Lazarsfeld had recently presented at a colloquium on the communication of ideas. When he got it back, Lazarsfeld found that his ideas had been put into fluent English and occasionally enriched by reference to classical writers he had never heard of. He also found that Merton had added a four-page section called 'Some Social Functions of the Mass Media' containing a set of entirely new ideas.[10] It therefore seemed only right that the piece should appear as a jointly authored endeavour and as such it duly appeared in *The Communication of Ideas* (1948), edited by Lyndon Bryson. 'Mass communication, popular taste and organised social action' is, perhaps, a rather clunky title but it was, in effect, the final considered synthesis of the work of two of America's most influential sociologists on the topic of mass communication. Although the two men remained life-long friends, they both moved away from research into mass communication in the 1950s and each pursued diverging paths of sociological enquiry. Their joint essay stands as an impressive summary of the collaborative relationship between two colleagues and two defining pathways of American mass communication research – the empirical and the critical – which between them they helped to define.

---

9 Praxis: the unity of theory and practice, thought and action, in Marxist social theory.
10 Lazarsfeld (1975: 52–3), quoted in Simonson and Weimann (2003: 17).

They begin with the relevance of the question of communication in post-war America. They note a widespread interest in the role of film, print and radio in contemporary society, which is reflected in the current flurry of academic conferences, books and articles on these topics. A common theme is anxiety about the ubiquity and power of the mass media. One participant in the symposium that Lazarsfeld attended had suggested that 'the power of radio can be compared only with the power of the atomic bomb'. But for Lazarsfeld and Merton, that was to misunderstand how power worked in contemporary America. It no longer depended, as in Hitler's Germany, on organized violence and mass coercion. More subtle forms of social control were now at work that operated on the soul rather than the body:

> Increasingly the chief power groups, among which organised business occupies the most spectacular place, have come to adopt techniques for manipulating mass publics through propaganda in place of more direct means of control. Industrial organizations no longer compel eight year old children to attend the machines for fourteen hours a day; they engage in elaborate programs of 'public relations'. They place large and impressive advertisements in the newspapers of the nation; they sponsor numerous radio programs; on the advice of public relations counsellors they organize prize contests, establish welfare foundations and support worthy causes. Economic power seems to have reduced direct exploitation and turned to a subtler type of psychological exploitation, achieved largely by disseminating propaganda through the mass media. (Lazarsfeld and Merton, [1948] 2004: 231)

Mass persuasion has replaced older and harsher direct methods of mass intimidation and coercion and the mass media are the agencies of new and softer forms of indirect social control. The media have created what we might call a pseudo public sphere.[11] They 'have taken on the job of rendering mass publics conformative to the social and economic *status quo*' (ibid.: 231).

I confess my astonishment when I first read this. I had avoided reading American mass communication sociology for at least 30 years because I thought it was boring uncritical 'mindless' empiricism. That was the received wisdom in Britain when I first began teaching 'media studies' in the mid-1970s. So completely did I buy this line that it was with considerable reluctance that I recently forced myself to start reading the now forgotten sociological literature on the media that was produced in America some 60 or 70 years ago. I did so

---

11 'Pseudo' is a word rarely used today but common in 1940s and 1950s America and Britain. It is used to indicate something as fake, phoney or false. Simonson has an illuminating note on its recurrence in the literature (Merton, 2004: xxxii, n.34). Thus we find pseudo-acts (Merton), pseudo-events (Daniel Boorstin, later) and from Adorno, pseudo-individualization and pseudo-experience.

only for the sake of writing this book, whose historical aim and scope evidently meant I could not omit the early and, as I now see it, foundational work of American sociology. It was little short of a revelation to find, when at last I applied myself to it, that the literature was altogether more seriously engaging and important (and readable) than I had ever supposed. American colleagues have begun the process of redeeming and revaluing their lost inheritance. In their essay on critical research at Columbia, taking the Lazarsfeld/Merton essay as the focal text, Peter Simonson and Gabriel Wiemann argue that it suffered symbolic annihilation in the USA and Britain in the 1970s and 1980s at the hands of apologists for born-again critical cultural studies seeking to stake out the emerging field of media studies (2003: 15). Why that happened and what we can learn today from American mass communication sociology and its complex interaction with the tradition of European social theory are matters I will return to on another occasion. For the moment I simply note that for many years I laboured under the delusion that critical social theory began with the Frankfurt School and only really got going in the 1970s when the economic and social status quo came under fire in the fall-out from the cultural 'revolution' of the late 1960s. Hence my astonishment at Lazarsfeld and Merton's critique of the media as soft disciplinary agents of the economic and social status quo in post-war America. It anticipates themes that would appear many years later, as if freshly minted, in the writings of Stuart Hall, Michel Foucault and others.

As the title indicates, there are three major themes to the essay: the social role of the media, their impact on popular taste and their potential for progressive social action. The last is a résumé of earlier work discussed above – Lazarsfeld on the educative potential of radio, Merton on its persuasive power. If the media are to be used for progressive social and political purposes – for educational reform or to promote non-discriminatory race relations – it is necessary to understand how they work. Three distinctively Mertonian concepts are introduced and summarily discussed: (1) monopolization; (2) canalization and; (3) supplementation. In the first place, the media monopolize the definition of the issue to the exclusion of countervailing arguments and alternative interpretative frames (the dominant ideology thesis[12] in all but name). Second, they work to channel rather than transform existing social attitudes. Finally, they do not work alone. 'Nazism did not attain its brief moment of hegemony by capturing the mass media of communication.' They played an ancillary role, supplementing the use of organized violence, organized distribution of rewards for conformity and organized centres of local indoctrination (Lazarsfeld and Merton [1948] 2004: 240). The last point is crucial. Mass media have proved most effective, as in the Soviet Union, 'in local centers of organized face to face contact'. Direct contact and interpersonal discussion are key supplements to the

---

12 On the dominant ideology thesis, see Chapter 8, pp. 202–3.

workings of the media. This would later be taken up by Elihu Katz and worked into a major thesis about the importance of *Personal Influence*.

The central section of the paper deals briefly with popular taste. It is, in Simonson and Wiemann's view, the least interesting and original part of the article and contains, as they note, some jarringly condescending remarks about women listeners to radio soap operas,[13] some commonplace assumptions about declining cultural tastes and some unexamined attitudes about the role of progressive intellectuals in defining cultural standards. The most original part of the paper is, as Lazarsfeld noted, the four-page supplement on the social function of the mass media that Merton inserted into his lecture notes. Here Merton highlights three functions of the mass media that merit, in his view, further research: status conferral, the enforcement of social norms and, finally, their narcotizing dysfunction. In the first place, the media function as agents of legitimization by conferring status on public issues, persons, organizations and social movements. If they are acknowledged and taken up by the media, they are important and if not, then they are not. Second, the media enforce prevailing social attitudes and values by the negative publicity they bestow on deviations from the norm, thereby closing the gap between private attitudes and public morality as many people in the public eye, politicians especially, have found to their cost. If these are positive functions, the narcotizing effect of the media is their negative dysfunction. They induce political apathy in mass audiences by creating the illusion of participation in the democratic process while in fact undermining it. From reading the papers and listening to the news on radio, the individual comes to believe that he knows what's going on. He *is* concerned. He *is* informed. But this is 'to mistake *knowing* about problems of the day for *doing* something about them'. A vicarious sphere of public opinion (a pseudo-public sphere[14]) is formed that displaces action and participation in the democratic decision-making process.

Many of the concerns that would resurface two or three generations later, re-incarnated as Media Studies, can be found in American mass communication

---

13 The oppression of women by men in everyday life would soon be raised by the women's movement which took off in the United States in the late 1950s and rapidly spread throughout the world. Their marginalization in academic life is disturbingly apparent in many ways in the working lives and literature under review. You would not realize, for instance, from the text itself that almost all the interviews upon which *Mass Persuasion* relied and depended were undertaken by women, nor that the vast majority of those interviewed were women listeners (these points are tactfully noted in Simonson's introduction). The profoundly *gendered* character of Kate Smith's broadcast and especially her communicative style, though touched on, are simply not recognized as perhaps a crucial component of its success with an overwhelmingly female audience.

14 Merton does not use this phrase which I have coined in order to flag up the similarities between the analysis of public life developed by Riesman and Merton in mid-century America and that of Jürgen Habermas who established the importance of 'the public sphere' in modern democratic politics. See Chapter 9 for a full discussion of Habermas.

sociology of the 1930s and 1940s and in summary form in this key essay by two of its leading figures. Structures of media ownership and control? The dominant ideology? Legitimization of the existing economic and social order? Active audiences? All these matters that seemed to be discovered as if for the first time in the 1970s can be found in the research and writings of Paul Lazarsfeld and Robert Merton and their contemporaries. They can be summarized as a concern with the question of social control and its structural transformation, in which the media play a crucial part, from older, harder and more direct forms of domination to newer, softer and more indirect methods of disciplining the masses. America in the mid-century appeared to be increasingly conformist and as such, increasingly alarming to contemporary progressive intellectuals. This was the central theme of a book that came out a couple of years later and which turned out to be the single most widely read work of sociology, ever.

The lonely crowd

David Riesman

In 1950, David Riesman published *The Lonely Crowd* whose sub-title was 'A study of the changing American character'. It was one of those rare academic books that reached beyond the confines of the university to become a 'must read' for all who wanted to keep up with the currents of contemporary thought. It became a best-seller when issued as a paperback by Doubleday Anchor in 1953, going through several new editions and innumerable re-prints. Fifty years down the line it has sold 1.4 million copies, making it the best-selling sociology text to date. It is an unusual book, written by an unusual sociologist. Riesman (1909–2002) was born into an elite Philadelphia family and enjoyed a privileged upbringing and education. He read law at Harvard and on graduating served as clerk to the Supreme Court for some years before turning to sociology in the late 1930s. He became a Professor of Social Science at the University of Chicago (1948–59) before moving back to Harvard where he remained for the rest of his working life. If American sociology at the time was mainly preoccupied with establishing itself on a positivist, scientific footing, Riesman, like Merton, took a broader, more European view of sociology's task as critical and interpretative. The writings of Marx, Weber and Durkheim all figure significantly in his narrative, and Freud was an important influence. One of the readers of the draft manuscript of the book, acknowledged in the Preface, was Erich Fromm, a psychoanalyst and leading member of the

Frankfurt School who had emigrated to the USA in 1934 and who was, for a while, Riesman's personal analyst. The psycho-pathology of everyday life in contemporary America is a central theme of *The Lonely Crowd*.

It is, in essence, an historical morality play in three acts.[15] Riesman begins with pre-modern societies as a contrastive back-drop to the central themes of his drama; namely the transformation from classic early modern to contemporary American society. Each social order (traditional; early modern; contemporary) produces (requires) a certain kind of individual, or character-type, the structure of whose personality is oriented in a certain direction: the *tradition*-directed, the *inner*-directed and the *other*-directed individual.[16] These terms quickly passed into common usage:

> Half a century ago, you might hear people in cocktail parties saying: Are you inner-directed? Is he other-directed? Do we know anybody who is tradition-directed? When these words swam into public consciousness, they became a new way to classify humanity. Some of us may not have entirely understood this system when we used it, but as self-conscious, pseudo-intellectual gossip it flowered for years. (Fulford, 2001)

Underpinning these distinctions is a set of assumptions about the nature of the relationship between individual and society, one of sociology's fundamental themes. For Riesman:

> the link between character and society … is to be found in the way in which society ensures some degree of conformity from the individuals who make it up. In each society, such a mode of ensuring conformity is built into the child, and then either encouraged or frustrated in later adult experience … While individuals and societies may live well enough – if rather boringly – without creativity, it is not likely that they can live without some mode of conformity – even be it one of rebellion.

The cardinal assumption – never challenged, always a given – is that society exists as an external force that imposes itself upon individuals compelling their

---

15 Riesman's three-act drama has a historical narrative structure that bears comparison with Jürgen Habermas's account of *The Structural Transformation of the Public Sphere* (see Chapter 9), written a little later in the very different context of post-war Germany. Though the authors frame and interpret their dramas differently, there is a shared concern with the transformations of modernity and the roles therein of politics and the media. Both tell the story of the emergence of modernity from an immemorial, pre-modern past and then go on to argue that the classic early modern era has been transformed in the mid-twentieth century, with this difference: for Habermas, the transformation is a regression to pre-modern forms of public life, for Riesman (though heavily qualified), it is a progression to post-modern forms of private life.

16 These are universal types or 'in Max Weber's sense, "ideal types", that is, constructions necessary for analytic work' (Riesman, [1950] 1976: 243).

conformity to 'group norms'. How is this achieved? Through the socialization of individuals, which begins at birth and is 'built into the child' by its parents. Here was a potent rationalization of the founding assumption that drew on current psychoanalytic theory for support:

> In order that any society may function well, its members must acquire the kind of character which makes them *want* to act in the way they *have* to act as members of the society … They have to *desire* what is objectively *necessary* for them to do. *Outer force* is replaced by *inner compulsion*, and by the particular kind of human energy which is channelled into character traits. (Fromm, 1944: 380. Original emphases. Cited in Riesman, [1950] 1976: 5)

The socialization of individuals, then, is a disciplinary process which tames unruly souls and bends them to the requirements of society. Freudian-inspired psycho-analytic theory was seen, at the time, as a powerful explanation of the means whereby the functional adjustment of individuals to the social order was achieved in early childhood as a process of internalizing external norms without recourse to physical violence.

Different societies at different times demand different 'modes of conformity'. Riesman's historical narrative draws the line between modernity and all previous history. Family and clan-oriented traditional ways of life have existed everywhere for most of history. They may be miserable affairs, 'ridden with anxiety, sadism and disease' (Riesman, [1950] 1976: 12), but they do not deny individual difference. These, however, are determined by birth, sex and status and individuals can rarely, if ever, move out of their pre-allocated life-roles. Social misfits – those who might later have been innovators or rebels – find a role for themselves as shamans or sorcerers, while the monasteries absorb other 'characterological mutations', a task performed today by universities. *Gemeinschaft* societies are all alike, whether in Europe, India, Africa or China: they depend on kith and kin loyalties, are slow to change and are bound together in a tight web of values, to which all unquestioningly subscribe.

Never mind how accurate or true this is. It serves as a foil to highlight the European revolution of the sixteenth and seventeenth centuries which heralded the decisive break with tradition and custom and ushered in the modern era of the inner-directed individual. Societal modernization presupposes the splintering of tradition and the new individual freedoms and life-defining courses of action that this affords. These possibilities are situated within changes in population growth and the rise of industrial capitalism and its vastly expanded mode of mass production. How are individuals to regulate themselves in a world no longer in the swaddling bands of custom and tradition and characterized by unceasing change? They must be self-regulating via the inner mechanism of their 'psychological gyroscope' that is set spinning within them by their parents. The gyroscope metaphor indicates that the inner-directed individual, once set in motion, does not swerve from his chosen pathway. His inner compulsions keep him on course.[17] The sociological source of this character type is, as Riesman acknowledges, Max Weber's famous interpretation of the connections between the Protestant ethic of seventeenth-century Europe and the rise of capitalism.[18] This by now old, early-modern, middle-class type is figured in the banker, the tradesman, the entrepreneur, the engineer.

However, on the cusp of the mid-twentieth century a new post-modern type[19] begins to appear: the other-directed individual who takes his norms not from his own inner compulsions but from external social pressures, the 'primary group norms' of those he encounters in his daily life. Riesman stresses that this is a very recent development, a newly emerging social phenomenon that is not restricted to, but is most advanced in, the USA. The 'new' middle-class type is figured in the bureaucrat, the salaried employee in the large firm. What produces conformity in this kind of individual is not some inner self-regulating device, but the values and attitudes of others: 'either those known to him or those with whom he is indirectly acquainted, through friends and through the mass media' (ibid.: 21). The post-modern individual, unlike his rugged go-it-alone modern predecessor, is exceptionally sensitive to others: he is shallower, freer with his money, friendlier, less certain of himself, more dependent on the approval of others (ibid.: 19).

Summing up the structural differences between the three types, Riesman identifies the different emotional control mechanisms that regulate their behaviours.

---

17 The character types, throughout the text, are generically male. I have not attempted to correct this now incorrect manner of writing. Riesman has some important insights about the privatization of experience for women that anticipate the concerns of Betty Friedan's *The Feminine Mystique*.

18 Riesman ([1950] 1976: 18). Though Riesman emphasizes that he does not conceive of the inner-directed individual simply as a non-conformist Protestant, the way that he writes of this type throughout the book suggests that he is indeed an American WASP (White Anglo-Saxon Protestant). *Die protestantische Ethik und der Geist des Kapitalismus* was translated into English by Talcott Parsons, then Tutor in Economics at Harvard, in 1930.

19 Not a term used by Riesman and I use it as a deliberate anachronism. Postmodernism is not generally named and recognized as such by European academics until the 1980s (cf. Chapter 8). I will argue in the concluding chapter of this book that the historical supercession of modernity begins to show up in the 1950s, accelerated by the world-shattering event of the Second World War. Riesman's study, based on perceived changes in post-war America is, I think, one of the earliest to identify and grapple with the transformation of modernity and its consequences for individuals in the figure of the other-directed 'new' (post-modern) man.

In traditional societies individuals are *shamed* into conformity. The inner-directed individual is controlled by feelings of personal *guilt*, while the other-directed individual experiences a vague *anxiety* when not fitting in with the rest. His self-regulatory equipment is not a gyroscope but an inbuilt radar system with which he constantly scans the environment to detect potential disturbances to his sense of self (ibid.: 24–5). This transformation of the structure of the self, in Riesman's account, is first an adjustment to the changing nature and experience of work and the workplace and second, to the growing priority of leisure in people's lives. The nineteenth-century workplace (typically the factory) had a clear managerial hierarchy of authority and status, was governed by impersonal relationships between masters and men and driven by a concern with the management of the technical, productive aspects of the work process. Life was work-determined and most people had little surplus income or free time at their disposal. The mid-twentieth century workplace (typically, the office) has a flatter hierarchic structure, is less command-driven and more concerned with people management and good working relationships in the workplace. There is more time and money available to spend on something hitherto reserved for the rich and privileged – namely, leisure – as more free time becomes more available for more and more people.[20] Relationships, at work and play, are now defined by *sociability*.

The rise of sociability is the manifest sign of the new people-minded social type. Other-directed individuals are less the products of their parents than their peer groups. These stand 'midway between the individual and the messages which flow from the mass media' (ibid.: 84). In traditional societies, communal 'chimney-corner media' articulate the culture's oral traditions, myths, legends and songs via bards and storytellers (ibid.: 85–7). In early modern societies, the dominant medium is print. The inner-directed man, open to 'reason' via print, tends to develop a character structure that drives him to work long hours and shun leisure and laxity. Print serves up narratives of the battle of life and appropriate future role models for the solitary, reading child caught in the small pool of light cast by his reading lamp or candle. *Pilgrim's Progress, Robinson Crusoe* and *Poor Richard's Progress* (chosen, Riesman notes, by Weber as a typical inspirational text that embodies the Protestant ethic) all aim to fire the ambition of

---

20 Thorstein Veblen had noted the emergence of what he called the 'leisure class' in America at the start of the twentieth century. The new rich were given over to a culture of conspicuous consumption which, in the United States, served rather to encourage than (as in France, say) enrage the masses. Their lifestyle was something to be actively pursued rather than passively envied. In the 1950s, it appeared within reach of ordinary Americans.

inner-directed youth. Biographies provide heroic role models.[21] In contrast with the solitary inner-directed child-reader of earlier generations:

> we have the group of kids today, lying on the floor, reading and trading comics and preferences among comics or listening to 'The Lone Ranger'.[22] When reading and listening are not communal in fact they are apt to be so in feeling; one is almost always conscious of the brooding omnipresence of the peer group. (ibid.: 99)

The chapter is headed by an extract from an interview with a 12-year-old girl who, when asked by her interviewers whether she would like to be able to fly like Superman, self-consciously replies: 'I would like to be able to fly if everybody else did, but otherwise it would be kind of conspicuous' (Wolfe and Fiske, 1949). Such are the anxieties of the contemporary, peer-group-oriented child. It is not good to stand out alone in the lonely crowd.

The first part of the book considers the structural transformation of the American soul; the second part, its political implications. Riesman detects a number of shifts in American politics that he links to changes in economic life and corresponding transformations in the social typologies of individuals. As the economy shifts from production to consumption, there are corresponding shifts from the politics of *indignation* to the politics of *tolerance* as the *moralizing* inner-directed individual begins to be displaced by the other-directed *inside-dopester* (an oddly inelegant term in an otherwise elegantly written book). Nineteenth-century American politics was faction-ridden and partisan. It was a politics of protest or position in which individuals or factions sought to protect or advance their interests and

---

21 Leo Lowenthal's 'excellent' study of 'Biographies in popular magazines' (1944), as Riesman notes later, shows a clear shift away from popular biographies of captains of industry, leading politicians and 'serious' artists and writers which dominate this sector of the book market at the start of the twentieth century, to the life-stories of entertainers and the stars of the new mass media which increasingly predominate as the mid-century is reached (Riesman, [1950] 1976: 209). This is in accordance with Riesman's thesis of the transition from inner- to outer-directed individuals and from work- and production-oriented values to leisure- and consumption-oriented values. Lowenthal is another key member of the Frankfurt School who fled Germany in 1934 (for brief biographical details, see Wiggershaus, 1994: 64–6). It was he who introduced Erich Fromm to the Institute in the 1920s.

22 At the time of writing (1950) television had not yet quite become the dominant everyday medium in the lives of children. There were many moral panics, in the adult world of the 1940s and 1950s, about the harmful effect of comics on the young. Now they are nostalgically recuperated by Hollywood as innocent family entertainment, from Superman, Batman and Spiderman (icons of the 1940s) to the computer-generated, twenty-first-century Incredibles.

beliefs. It was fired by *moral* indignation: a boisterous, fractious public arena full of opinionated individuals who wanted to change the world in line with their own vision of things and be damned with what anyone else might think. The emollient politics of mid-twentieth-century America require far greater attention to what others, with their different beliefs and opinions, might think. The new politics is underpinned by tolerance. Moral certainties, and the clash of values that they generate, have faded. What now matters is to know what's going on, to be in the know (to have the inside 'dope'), in the complex game of power politics. Less idealistic and more realistic, mid-century American politics in the aftermath of a global war fought simultaneously in Europe, the Pacific and the Far East, has a breadth and scope that was simply unimaginable in the narrower and more parochial politics of the preceding century. By 1950, many people, not just experts, 'have become accustomed to thinking in world-political terms, and cross-cultural terms, such as were hardly to be found amid the ethnocentrisms ... of even a generation ago' (Riesman [1950] 1976: 185–6).

This ability to recognize and accept the otherness of people is powerfully augmented by the mass media who are tutors in political tolerance for other-directed individuals. A key reason for this is that the media themselves have a stake in tolerance. First, they aspire to address very large audiences whom it is not in their interests to antagonize. Their style, like that of the new politics, is emollient. Their manner is sociable and sincere. Sincerity is a defining characteristic of post-war American society with its emphasis on tolerance, sociability and friendliness. If sincerity is a virtue, its vice is cynicism to which it appears as the antidote. Pre-war America had a long streak of hard-boiled cynical mistrust running through it.[23] If inner-directed individuals are engaged, in the first place, in the pursuit of their own economic interests, why should they trust the motives and intentions of others? Are not the glad-handing, seemingly friendly styles of the sales pitch in the ads or the boss in the work place or the politician on the campaign trail, all really just thinly veiled forms of manipulation? The question of whether or not the new communicative styles in contemporary popular culture and politics are *genuine* becomes a crucial issue. Eisenhower was admired as a presidential candidate because he was seen as sincere, and popular singers of the day – Dinah Shore, Kate Smith and, above all, Frank Sinatra – were idolized for the sincerity of their voice and delivery:

> While it is clear that people want to personalise their relationships to their heroes of consumption and that their yearning for sincerity is a grim reminder of how little they can trust themselves or others in daily life, it is less clear just what

---

23 The 'hard-boiled' crime novels of the inter-war period and Film Noir may be taken as exemplifying this attitude.

it is that they find 'sincere' in a singer or other performer. One element may be the apparent freedom of the entertainer to express emotions that others cannot or dare not express. Again, sincerity means performance in a style which is not aggressive or cynical, which may even be defenceless, as the question-answering or press-conference technique of some politicians appears to be. The performer puts himself at the mercy of both his audience and his emotions. Thus sincerity on the side of the performer evokes the audience's tolerance for him: it would not be fair to be too critical of the person who has left himself wide open and extended the glad hand of friendliness. (Riesman [1950] 1976: 194)

In the first half of the last century, intellectuals in Europe and North America were worried about the manipulation of helpless individuals by anonymous and invisible social, political, economic and cultural forces. Cynicism or scepticism towards 'the social', and anxiety on behalf of vulnerable individuality was their natural stance. Riesman detects an important shift from suspicion to trust of others in 1950s America in which it becomes crucial that displays of friendliness and sociability (indicative of more open and relaxed relations between individuals) are experienced as non-manipulative and non-exploitative. The crux of the new style of sociable relations is whether they are phoney and false or genuine and true: sincerity becomes the litmus test that distinguishes between inauthentic and authentic communication.[24]

The Lonely Crowd is remarkable for the breadth of its historical vision and the range of its non-sociological references. The present is considered both in terms of its past and, crucially, its future. One of the book's most original features is its attempt to identify the emerging social, cultural and political forms of a

---

24 I have traced these developments in Britain, as they show up on radio from the mid-1930s to the mid-1950s. The orientation of radio to sociable forms of address and interaction with its audiences is marked by the BBC's discovery of 'ordinary people' as a new source and subject of entertainment. The key programme was a little series called *Harry Hopeful* produced by BBC North Region (Manchester) in 1935–6: the ancestral source of all subsequent studio-based programmes in which ordinary people performed, in various ways, being themselves in public, in interaction with the programme's host, for the entertainment of a live studio audience and absent listeners or viewers. The theme of sincerity, fascinatingly, shows up on British radio at exactly the same time and in exactly the same way as on American radio. One of the 'hits' of BBC wartime radio was a series called *Sincerely Yours, Vera Lynn*. Lynn, 'the forces' sweetheart', was the most popular British singer of the day. Kate Smith's biographer notes that Vera Lynn was known in the USA as the English Kate Smith, while Smith was known in Britain as the American Vera Lynn (Hayes, 1995: 57). For their many fans, sincerity was felt to be the hallmark of their personality and style of singing. For discussions of these programmes and of sociability, sincerity and authenticity as defining characteristics of broadcasting's 'communicative ethos', see Scannell (1996: 22–57, 58–74, 93–116).

society in the process of shifting decisively from scarcity to abundance, from work to leisure, and from local rural 'knowable communities' (Smallville, USA) to the unknowable urban environments of cities (Metropolis, USA) whose inhabitants are numbered in millions. What appears first in America begins to show up a decade or so later in Europe and elsewhere in the world, and increasingly, in the last years of the twentieth century. Continuous growth in manufacturing production and technological innovation, rising living standards for individuals, growing margins of disposable income and time are all indicative of a fundamental shift from subsistence economies and the dull compulsions of necessity, to economies of abundance and a world of greater individual choice and freedom. This transformation, the long-term, historic promise of modernity, becomes a global reality in the course of the second half of the twentieth century. It begins in the United States of America and David Riesman is its prophet.

The two-step flow of communication

The emerging sociology of communication in the USA was concerned with the effects of new mass media on 'atomized' individuals.[25] In this relationship, the media were taken as the sociological object with the individual as their psychological subject. It was an asymmetric relationship in which powerful social forces worked on vulnerable, isolated individuals: the media were active; their recipients, passive. It was further assumed that the media were instruments of propaganda or persuasion that sought to change or at least influence behaviours, attitudes and beliefs. They were agencies for moulding public opinion. Early case studies of the effects of radio (the then dominant 'new' technology of communication) presupposed all this. The studies of mass panic and of mass persuasion are the earliest case studies of what we now think of as 'media events', in which broadcast radio programmes clearly had a direct, immediate and observable effect on their audiences. People *did* panic and they did phone in and buy bonds as a result of the broadcasts. But other research conducted at the time began to challenge the 'powerful effects' thesis that underpinned initial assumptions about the mass media. A

---

25 The *atomized* individual is a revealing phrase. The first half of the twentieth century might well be labelled the atomic age. Atomic physics was the name of the scientific game after Einstein's famous theory of energy in 1905. Thereafter the race was on to discover how to split the atom and release its energy. It culminated in the Manhattan Project and the successful detonation of the atom bomb by nuclear fission (a chain reaction) in the 1940s. To think of individuals as atoms and small groups as 'molecular' is one indication of the appliance of science in contemporary sociology. More importantly, the key sociological concept of 'effects' was thought in terms of scientific causality. Positivism is embedded in the vocabulary of early twentieth-century American sociology.

ground-breaking study of voting behaviours proved to be highly influential in this respect and a fine example of the range of Lazarsfeld's interests and the breadth of his contribution to American sociology. The famous 'two-step' flow model of information diffusion emerged from the study of voting behaviours in Eyrie County, Ohio, in the run-up to the presidential election of 1940.

The People's Choice was a pioneering investigation into 'How the voter makes up his mind in a presidential campaign', the sub-title of the book published in 1944 by Lazarsfeld with the assistance of two young colleagues, Bernard Berelson and Helen Gaudet. It is a sociological classic, conceptually elegant and tightly focused, that established an important object domain (voting behaviour in the democratic election process) and its methodology. The object of enquiry was not the results of elections but how individuals decided how they would cast their vote; it was a study of 'opinion in the making', a *dynamic* investigation of the process whereby individuals made up their minds about how to exercise their democratic right. This could not be treated as a snap decision that could be captured by a one-off snap-shot survey. Lazarsfeld developed the *panel method* in order to monitor how, in the weeks leading up to Election Day, individuals finally made up their minds. A representative panel of 600 voters was chosen in advance and interviewed repeatedly about their voting intentions. Of course, the vast majority had decided how they would vote from the start, and did not swerve from their initial decision. As Lazarsfeld notes, individual voting behaviours are largely predictable because they are pre-determined by a range of social factors: 'the poor, urban residents and the Catholics are more likely to vote the Democratic ticket while the well-to-do, the Protestants and the rural dwellers are more frequently found in the Republican camp' (Lazarsfeld et al. [1944] 1968: xxviii). What the study honed in on was the much smaller percentage of those who (1) initially intended to vote against the party they normally supported or (2) were undecided how they would vote (the don't knows) or (3) did not intend to vote, at all. In these three cases it might be possible to identify the factors that led people either to change or make up their minds. It is now conventional wisdom that these three categories – the swing voters, the undecided and the apathetic – hold the key to any election and are targeted relentlessly by the candidates or parties in marginal constituencies. Lazarsfeld was the first to establish their crucial importance. The panel method tracked intentions over time and finally checked them against actual courses of action on voting day. Thus what could finally be established were how the don't knows, the swing voters and those who hadn't intended to vote did in fact act. It then became a question of what factors influenced their voting behaviours one way or the other. And here the cardinal importance of personal influence quickly became apparent.

The deviants (who voted against the grain), the undecided (who were not sure how they would vote) and the apathetic (who weren't sure that they would vote) all frequently mentioned, in follow-up interviews, that other people influenced their final decision: family members, friends and acquaintances – 'I've heard fellows talk at the plant ... I hear men talk at the shop ... My husband heard that talked about at work ...' (ibid.: 153). It became apparent that some people were *opinion leaders*. They were more interested in the election, had followed it in the papers and on the radio. They had formed their views and were articulate about them. It would be wrong to suppose, Lazarsfeld and his team discovered, that there was a vertical social hierarchy at play in this. Opinion leaders were not confined, as might be thought, to the well off or well educated. There were 'horizontal opinion leaders' in different social strata and social communities. Opinion leaders in a variety of settings could be seen as intervening intermediaries between the media (as sources of political information and propaganda) and individuals; hence a *two-step* flow of communication from the media to interested individuals and from them to family, friends and acquaintances. It looked as if 'ideas often flow *from* radio and print *to* the opinion leaders and *from* them to the less active sections of the population' (ibid.: 151). 'The nature of personal influence' was the title of the last chapter of the book. It was the most striking discovery of the investigation into the opinion-forming process and cried out for further, more detailed investigation.

The Decatur study

The role of opinion leaders in the 'two-step flow' of media-disseminated ideas and information was followed up immediately. The first thing to determine was, as always, where to do it. The choice of place was determined by its size and that in turn was determined by costs. It would have to be somewhere in the mid-West because it had less 'sectional peculiarities' than other parts of the country (Katz and Lazarsfeld, 1955: 335). It would have to have a population of no more than about 60,000 if one in 20 households were to be selected for survey, with 800 as the maximum that could be handled in terms of administrative costs. Bernard Berelson, who had worked on the Eyrie County survey, was responsible for finding, via a complex process of statistical analysis, the most representative town from an initial list of nearly 30. In the end, Decatur, Illinois, appeared closest to the mark and it became the site of an ambitious, wide-ranging study of the opinion-forming process in a representative mid-West American town.

The next task was the design of the survey. It would focus exclusively on women (no reasons for this are given) and on four aspects of their daily lives in which their attitudes, opinions and decisions might be influenced, one way or another, by other women. These were household shopping, fashion, current affairs and going to the movies. Each of these was to be investigated separately and each has a separate chapter in the book that eventually resulted from the Decatur study. The aim of the initial survey was not so much to discover individual attitudes to shopping and so on but rather instances in which the interviewees were influenced in these matters by someone else. If, for instance, it turned out that a woman had recently bought a new breakfast cereal, she would be questioned to find out why she had switched brands and whether it was on the suggestion or recommendation of another (whose name would be noted). The second key stage was to contact and interview these 'influentials' or opinion leaders in order to discover what influenced them and how they exerted their influence on others. In order to construct a typology of influencers and influencees, three key variables were developed for analysis: status, lifecycle position and gregariousness. A cluster of indices was developed as a robust indicator of what each of these terms meant. Thus status was determined by three indices: rent and education, occupation of breadwinner, and the interviewer's intuitive rating. Lifecycle position was determined by age, marital status and number (and age) of children. Gregariousness, perhaps the most interesting of the variables, was originally to be analysed by five or six indicators but these were reduced to two: number of friends, number of organizations. The detailed planning of the project began in the fall of 1944 and the fieldwork was started in the spring of 1945.

The implementation of the study was in the hands of C. Wright Mills, who oversaw all the fieldwork. Jeanette Green trained and supervised the field staff who descended on Decatur and did the interviews. A number of people produced first drafts that synthesized the massive quantities of data thereby generated. Early analyses of the marketing and movie materials were produced by Leila Sussmann and Patricia Kendall, while David Gleicher, Peter Rossi and Leo Srole produced drafts respectively on the characteristics of opinion leaders, the impact of personal influence and the consumption of popular fiction. But at some point in the process of analysing and writing up the data there was a major difference of opinion and a parting of the ways between C. Wright Mills and Lazarsfeld and the project was, for the time being, shelved. Some years later Lazarsfeld asked his post-doctoral student Elihu Katz[26] to take another look at the Decatur material and see if anything could be done with it. The

Elihu Katz

---

26 At the time of writing, 50 years after the publication of *Personal Influence*, Elihu Katz remains active in the field of mass communication research with a string of important co-authored publications to his name in the last half-century. He remains, as Peters puts it, 'the leading researcher of his generation', as interested now as then in the abiding question of the impact of the mass media. Sonia Livingstone's authoritative review of Katz's work and influence includes a complete list of his published books and a selective bibliography of his major articles (Livingstone, 2003).

---

result was *Personal Influence* published in 1955; ten years after the primary data were gathered in Decatur.

Personal Influence

The book, as finally published, falls into two parts. Part one offers 'a new focus for the study of mass media effects', namely the part played by people (Katz and Lazarsfeld, 1955: 15–133) while part two reports on 'the flow of everyday influence in a mid-western community' (ibid.: 137–324). The first part of the book is a synthesis of Katz's doctoral thesis on small groups and the interpersonal networks that sustain them while the second is a summary and discussion of the Decatur study. In a brisk introductory *tour d'horizon* all previous work in the field is situated in relation to the present study which is thereby positioned as the culmination of all that has gone before.

> All communications research aims at the study of effect. From the earliest theorizing on this subject to the most contemporary empirical research, there is, essentially, only one underlying problem – though it may not always be explicit – and that is, 'what can the media "do"?' (ibid.: 18)

While the mass media doubtless have a variety of possible effects on society, the sponsoring agencies of mass communications research have been particularly interested in just one kind of effect which has thus received almost exclusive attention, namely the impact of campaigns – to influence votes, to sell soap, to reduce [race] prejudice. Research has focused on 'how, and under what conditions, mass media "campaigns" (rather specific, short-run efforts) succeed in influencing opinions and attitudes' (ibid.: 18–19).

The initial hypothesis underlying research into 'effects' was of a one-way, one-step flow of communication in which the omnipotent media sent forth their messages and the atomized masses waited to receive them. But as this model was examined, it became apparent that there were a number of 'intervening variables' between the media and the masses in the communication process. Four in particular were soon identified: (1) the degree of exposure to media; (2) the characteristics of different media (print or radio, for instance); (3) the form and content of media products; and, finally, (4) the attitudes and predispositions of media audiences. The most recently discovered variable, and the object of the present study, was 'the newly accented variable of interpersonal relations'. Research, it seemed, had 'greatly underestimated the extent to which an individual's social attachments to other people, and the character of the opinions and activities which he shares with them, will influence his response to the mass media' (ibid.: 25). The social environment (the life-world) and the network of inter-personal relationships, in which individuals are always and everywhere embedded, emerge as crucial intervening factors that affect their uptake of media. This, as we have seen, was the final discovery of the Eyrie County study of uncertain or undecided voters in the 1940 election campaign and what the subsequent Decatur study was intended to explore.

Personal Influence is all about interpersonal relationships and 'the discovery of "people"', the title of a subsection of the introductory chapter called 'Between Media and Mass'. If Lazarsfeld, it is tempting to suggest, thought of individuals as sociological variables or as statistical data, Katz thought of them as people because he came from another branch of sociology that had discovered the 'primary group' as an important object of study. Interpersonal communication was an emerging field of enquiry in post-war American sociology that examined the network of personal relationships in which individuals were embedded within larger social institutions and organizations.[27] The newly developed technique of sociometrics, for instance, asked school children to say who they would like to sit next to in the classroom. From these data a picture emerged of friendship networks, social 'isolates' (whom no-one chose) and 'stars' beside whom everyone wanted to sit – the social dynamics, in short, of a small interpersonal group in the institutional context of the classroom. But mass communications research was predicated on the non-existence, or at best, the irrelevance of inter-personal relations:

> Consider the imagery associated with the notion of mass in the phrase *mass production, mass communication, mass society* of the city. In each case, the idea of the mass is associated with the newly 'independent', newly individuated, citizen of the modern industrial age and, at the same time, for all his individualism, the person who is subject to the remote controls of institutions from which he and the myriads of his 'unorganised' fellows feel far removed. The individual who comes to mind – and the one whom researchers seem to have had in their minds – is a worker attuned to individualistic economic incentives in the competitive race for maximising gain; an anonymous urban dweller trying to 'keep up' with anonymous Joneses; a radio listener shut in his room with a self-sufficient supply of the world outside. (ibid.: 40)

This atomized individual – Poe's 'Man in the Crowd', the urban mass man of the jostling big-city streets – turns out to be a figment of the sociological imagination. When studied *in situ*, he turns out to be embedded in a dense network

---

27 See Katz and Lazarsfeld (1955: 46, n.3) for the origins of the study of groups. Sociometrics was pioneered by Jacob Moreno.

of interpersonal relations: or rather, when *she* (mass woman) is studied – for the Decatur material is exclusively about female interpersonal relations and their dynamics in a small American city in the 1940s.

It is a study of gregariousness, and we should note the ambiguities of this word whose Latin root (*grex, gregis*) means a flock of sheep. On the one hand, then, gregariousness ('associating in flocks and herds': *Chambers*) has the negative implications of the 'herd mentality'. On the other hand, it means more positively 'a fondness for the company of others' and it is this that shines through the Decatur material. It is a pioneering study of the *sociable* character of everyday life in mid-twentieth-century America. A richly patterned quilt-work of relations within and between younger and older, married and unmarried women of differing socio-economic status emerges from the data. When it comes to movie-going, it's the young single girls across all status levels who are the influentials, but in the matter of choosing breakfast cereals, the mothers of young families are opinion leaders. High status women are more informed about public affairs because they have more time for it: their lives are less taken up with household drudgery than their less well-off contemporaries. Fashion, like movie-going, is more determined than the others by life-cycle position: young, single girls across all status levels are the fashion influentials and, unsurprisingly, fashion opinion leaders are highly gregarious. However, while there are less fashion opinion leaders (as might be expected) among low-status young women, it turns out that there are just as many middle-status fashion leaders as there are high-status opinion leaders and this is in spite of the fact that a significantly greater proportion of high-status women have a high interest in fashion compared to middle-status women. Why the discrepancy? Why are there not proportionately more opinion leaders among young, rich, single women? An intriguing answer is suggested: they simply talk less about fashion. They *are* the fashion, and perhaps it's not fashionable to talk about it (ibid.: 266).

Thus the role of personal influence in the formation of people's tastes, attitudes, purchases and media consumption is convincingly established: it is an 'almost invisible, certainly inconspicuous, form of leadership at the person-to-person level of ordinary, intimate, informal, everyday contact' (ibid.: 138). It is 'casually exercised, sometimes unwittingly and unbeknown, within the smallest grouping of friends, family members and neighbours' (ibid.). But what has happened to the original question, namely the impact of the mass media on individuals? By the end of the book it has almost disappeared only to be resumed, briefly, in the penultimate chapter on the original two-step flow hypothesis which precipitated the Decatur study. It turns out that opinion leaders across all four areas of enquiry are more highly exposed to the mass media than the non-leaders (ibid.: 312). But this gross finding needs further refinement. Thus, it turns out that 'local' media are more significant for movie and marketing opinion leaders while cosmopolitan media matter more for opinion leaders in fashion and public affairs who need 'to keep up with "big-city" fashions and world wide news' (ibid.: 315). The fact of greater media exposure, however, does not necessarily indicate greater influence and, in fact, it is only in the case of fashion that the media appear to have more influence than other more immediate factors. Opinion leaders, just as much as those whom they influence, are likely to base their tastes, opinions and purchases on personal contacts and to 'use' the media only in a supplementary way. The 'uses and gratifications' of the media, though peripheral to the concerns of the book, is noted as a potential topic for further research, and a substantive addendum on 'gregariousness, anxiety and the consumption of popular fiction' (ibid.: 377–80) is included, for its intrinsic interest, as a pointer in this direction.

In many ways, *Personal Influence* seemed to resolve the tensions in the study of mass communication at Columbia that preceded it. At the time, and subsequently, it was read as showing that anxieties about the power of the media to manipulate the attitudes and choices of individuals were largely groundless. Nor were those individuals the isolated atoms in the lonely crowd as sociologists had supposed. By the early 1950s the masses were disappearing and in their place 'people' were found to be alive and well, enjoying a richly textured sociable existence embedded in local interpersonal networks of families, friends and acquaintances at home and work. No need to worry, then. Critical theorists of media power appeared disproved by empirical, administrative research. Within the academic field of mass communication sociology there was little new work after the publication of *Personal Influence*. Indeed, four years later, Bernard Berelson, one of the pioneers of the field, proclaimed it to be dead or, at least, withering away. The great ideas that gave the field of communication research so much vitality 10 and 20 years earlier were now, in his view, largely worn out and no new ideas had emerged in their place (Berelson, 1959, in Peters and Simonson, 2004: 445). The respondents to Berelson, in the same issue of *Public Opinion Quarterly* did not gainsay his claim. Nor does the material published after 1955 selected by Peters and Simonson (2004) for inclusion in their historical survey of American mass communication research. There are one or two important individual studies (notably Horton and Wohl's 1956 widely cited analysis of television viewing as 'para-social interaction) and C. Wright Mills's robust defence of the mass society thesis in *The Power Elite* (1956). But there are no new directions, new theories, or new debates. Rather, a second generation, led by Wilbur Schramm at Stanford, was busily consolidating and routinizing mass communication teaching and research within the university. Meanwhile, as we will see in Chapter 6, the study of communication in America was growing new wings elsewhere as the work of Erving Goffman took flight in the 1950s.

References

Adorno, T. ([1945] 2004) 'A social critique of radio music', in J.D. Peters and P. Simonson (eds), *Mass Communication and American Social Thought*. Lanham, MD: Rowman and Littlefield, pp. 210–15.

Berelson, B. ([1959] 2004) 'The state of communication research', in J.D. Peters and P. Simonson (eds), *Mass Communication and American Social Thought*. Lanham, MD: Rowman and Littlefield, pp. 440–5.

Fulford, R. (2001) 'The lonely crowd', *The National Post*, 3 July 2001. Available at: http//www.robertfulford.com/LonelyCrowd.html/

Hayes, R.K. (1995) *Kate Smith*. Jefferson, NC: McFarland and Co.

Horton, D. and Wohl, R. ([1956] 2004) 'Mass communication and para-social interaction: observations on intimacy at a distance', in J.D. Peters and P. Simonson (eds), *Mass Communication and American Social Thought*. Lanham, MD: Rowman and Littlefield, pp. 373–87.

Katz, E. and Lazarsfeld, P. (1955) *Personal Influence: The Part Played by People in the Flow of Mass Communications*. Glencoe, IL: The Free Press.

Lazarsfeld, P., Berelson, B. and Gaudet, H. ([1944] 1968) *The People's Choice*. New York: Columbia University Press.

Lazarsfeld, P. and Merton, R.K. ([1948] 2004) 'Mass communication, popular taste and organised social action', in J.D. Peters and P. Simonson (eds), *Mass Communication and American Social Thought*. Lanham, MD: Rowman and Littlefield, pp. 230–41.

Livingstone, S. (2003) 'The work of Elihu Katz: conceptualizing media effects in context', in J. Corner, P. Schlesinger and R. Silverstone (eds). *The International Handbook of Media Research*. London: Routledge.

Lowenthal, L. ([1944] 2004) 'Biographies in popular magazines', in J.D. Peters and P. Simonson, (eds), *Mass Communication and American Social Thought*. Lanham, MD: Rowman and Littlefield, pp. 188–205.

Merton, R.K. (1938) 'Social structure and anomie', *American Sociological Review*, 3(5): 672–82.

Merton, R.K. ([1946] 2004) *Mass Persuasion*, edited and with an Introduction by P. Simonson. New York: Howard Fertig.

Mills, C. Wright ([1956] 2000) *The Power Elite*. New York: Oxford University Press.

Riesman, D. ([1950] 1976) *The Lonely Crowd*. New Haven, CT: Yale University Press.

Scannell, P. (1996) *Radio, Television and Modern Life*. Oxford: Blackwell.

Simonson, P. (2004) 'The serendipity of Merton's communications research', *International Journal of Public Opinion Research*, 17(3): 277–97.

Simonson, P. and Weimann, G. (2003) 'Critical research at Columbia: Lazarsfeld's and Merton's "Mass communication, popular taste and organised social action"', in E. Katz et al. (eds), *Canonic Texts in Media Research*. Cambridge: Polity Press, pp. 12–38.

Wolfe, K.M. and Fiske, M. (1949) 'The children talk about comics', in P. Lazarsfeld and F. Stanton (eds), *Communications Research, 1948–1949*. New York: Harper, pp. 20–36.

PART II

Everyday life

Culture and communication

4

Leavis, Hoggart, Williams
England, 1930s–1950s

The absent social question

1968 was the moment of the *cultural* revolution in Europe, led by middle-class students rather than the working class. Its exemplary occurrence was in France, but in Britain too the students revolted against 'the reactionary and mystifying culture inculcated in universities and colleges' while at the same time seeking an alliance with the working class and struggling against imperialism. The analyst of this moment was Perry Anderson the 29-year-old editor of *New Left Review* who, in an astonishing essay, published in *Student Power* (produced by the NLR collective), examined historically 'The components of the national culture'. Britain, he argued, the most conservative major European society, had a culture in its own image and likeness, inert and mediocre, which served to inhibit any possibility of revolutionary change. A political analysis therefore of this culture was a necessary preliminary to that necessary revolution. The Left in the 1950s had accepted an anthropological definition of culture, taking *The Uses of Literacy* by Richard Hoggart as its guide. Raymond Williams had written the essential socialist account of *Culture and Society*, but neither had attempted a total, synthesizing analysis of all the disciplines whose concern was, one way or another, with man and society – the essential axes of all social and political action. The disciplines 'obviously' relevant to such an analysis were 'history, sociology, anthropology, economics, political theory, philosophy, aesthetics, literary criticism, psychology and psychoanalysis'. Anderson undertook to review and critique them all in order to lay bare the intellectual ataraxy (numbness) at the heart of British life and culture.

But first Anderson set out his overall thesis. The stultified character of British life was due in large part to the absence of any coherent critical social analysis of it. Britain, alone of all the major European countries, had failed to develop a sociology of itself. Other countries had produced a structural analysis of the social totality; Germany had Weber, France had Durkheim, Italy had Pareto (and

America had Parsons, we might add). Britain had no such comparable figure.[1] What then was 'the sociology of no sociology'? How to account for this failure? The explanation lay with the historical formation of the British bourgeoisie and its failure to challenge the landed aristocracy, the traditional British ruling class:

> The British bourgeoisie from the outset renounced its intellectual birthright. It refused ever to put society as a whole in question. A deep, instinctive aversion to the very category of the totality marks its entire trajectory. It never had to recast society as a whole in a concrete historical practice. It consequently never had to rethink society as a whole in abstract, theoretical reflection. Empirical, piecemeal intellectual disciplines corresponded to humble, circumscribed social action … The category of the totality was renounced by the British bourgeoisie in its acceptance of a comfortable, but secondary station within the hierarchy of early Victorian capitalism. (Anderson, 1969: 228)

The bourgeois intelligentsia that came to dominate British intellectual life in the course of the nineteenth century was a tightly-knit network of men, connected to each other by interest, friendship and marriage, who constituted what Noel Annan (1955) dubbed an 'intellectual aristocracy' that was part of, not apart from, the dominant social order. Britain thus failed to produce, from within, a *critical* intelligentsia. Nor did it import one. The United States was host in the inter-war years to radical émigré intellectuals from Europe who produced a stringent critical analysis of American society. Britain, by contrast, hosted an influx of reactionary intellectuals who had migrated to its shores in the same inter-war era. These 'White émigrés', as Anderson called them,[2] captured almost every sector of British intellectual life in the inter-war period. According to Anderson (1969: 230) by the mid-century, foreigners had taken over the academy (see Table 4.1).

The émigrés who pitched up in Britain were all fleeing countries prone to continuing, violent turmoil. Britain, for them, epitomized the very opposite of their own experience: tradition, continuity and order. They extolled the virtues of the peaceable British way of life, flattered the susceptibilities of their host and were rewarded by institutional recognition and social acceptance. Only two sectors in Anderson's little list had failed to succumb to foreign invasion: Economics and Literary Criticism. But though Maynard Keynes dominated Economics, it

---

1 The first British sociologist to work out a distinctive analysis of society was Anthony Giddens who achieved international recognition in the 1980s. His key book is *The Constitution of Society* (Giddens, 1984).

2 The civil war in Russia (1919–22), that followed the seizure of power by Lenin, was fought between the Reds (Communists) and Whites (defenders of the old Tsarist regime) and thus, depending on your viewpoint, between progressive (red) and reactionary (white) forces.

Table 4.1 Foreigners in British intellectual life (Anderson, 1969: 230)

Name	Discipline	Country of origin
Ludwig Wittgenstein	Philosophy	Austria
Bronislaw Malinowski	Anthropology	Poland
Lewis Namier	History	Poland
Karl Popper	Social theory	Austria
Isaiah Berlin	Political theory	Russia
Ernst Gombrich	Aesthetics	Austria
Hans-Jürgen Eysenck	Psychology	Germany
Melanie Klein	Psychoanalysis	Austria

had nevertheless been infiltrated by expatriates: Nicolas Kaldor from Hungary and Piero Sraffa from Italy. The only sector to sustain its native independence was Literary Criticism, dominated without challenge by the lonely, intransigent figure of Frank Leavis, an English don at Downing College, Cambridge. It was here that a concern with the social totality, suppressed everywhere else in the desolate landscape of British intellectual life, found an unlikely home.

English and the masses

Anderson's thesis is an extraordinary mixture of brilliance and absurdity. It is evidently written by someone who was very young, very clever and very self-confident. However much one may dislike and disagree with the kind of programmatic history Anderson favoured (and it provoked Edward Thompson to fury),[3] the essay posed the crucial question of the symptomatic absence of any available coherent theoretical analysis of British society as a whole. That absence was deeply felt in the pivotal moment of cultural crisis in post-war British society. It prompted the search for such a theory as the basis of the study of culture in the aptly named Centre for Contemporary Cultural Studies at the University of

---

3 Edward Thompson was the leading English, Socialist historian at that time. His masterpiece, *The Making of the English Working Class* (Thompson, 1962), was a landmark work that opened up a new approach to historical enquiry, what Thompson himself called 'history from below' (see Sharpe, 1992 for an overview). The thrust of Thompson's heroic narrative of the formation of the English working class is that it was active in its own making. It was not merely the determinate product of abstract historical forces operating on it from without. In a nutshell, Thompson put human agency back into the historical analysis of class. He was bitterly opposed to the structuralist analysis of historical, social processes favoured by Anderson and the notorious 'Pope' of structuralist Marxism, Louis Althusser. For Thompson's polemics against both Anderson and Althusser, see respectively 'The peculiarities of the English' and 'The poverty of Theory' (Thompson, 1978): they are both hugely entertaining. For Anderson on Thompson, see Anderson (1980).

Birmingham, under the directorship of Stuart Hall in the following decade. That moment, the moment of Cultural Studies, is the theme of Chapter 8. Here I am concerned with the aetiology of 'the social question' in Britain and why it should have been addressed by literary criticism. To answer that, we must first consider the factors that led to the establishment of the study of English within the British educational system in the early twentieth century.

Today the teaching of English in schools is part of the core National Curriculum, and a respectable and popular choice of study at university. Both the ancient universities, Oxford and Cambridge, have well-established English faculties. At the beginning of the last century it was taught in neither. Nor was it an accepted component of the curriculum in the recently established national system of education. As Brian Doyle has shown, in his excellent study of the origins and development of 'English', the guiding impulse from the start was the amelioration of social tensions in a deeply divided class society. He also shows how the teaching of English in nineteenth-century elementary schools was a low status, caring activity performed by women. As the status of English gradually rose in the educational system, it was taken over by men so that as it became a profession, it also became masculine (Doyle, 1989: 69–93). The demand to place English at the centre of the educational system crystallized at the end of the nineteenth century with the formation of a lobby group, the English Association, who saw it as an essential humanizing element in the training of the young. Hitherto, the teaching of English had been largely concerned with inculcating literacy in working-class children. It was defined by the dominant utilitarian ethos of nineteenth-century Britain in which some basic education for all was seen as increasingly necessary for the efficient functioning of the economy. Capitalism needed a functionally literate factory workforce.

The utilitarian approach to education was savagely caricatured in the brilliant opening scene of *Hard Times* ('The Murder of the Innocents') in which Mr Gradgrind (who has made a fortune in the wholesale hardware trade) exhorts the newly appointed schoolmaster, Mr McChoakumchild, to the task of stuffing full of facts his classroom of nameless, numbered pupils:

> Now what I want is Facts. Teach these boys and girls nothing but Facts. Facts alone are wanted in life. Plant nothing else, and root out everything else. You can only form the minds of reasoning animals upon Facts: nothing else will be of any service to them. This is the principle on which I bring up my own children, and this is the principle on which I bring up these children. Stick to Facts, Sir!

Pressure for some leavening of this cheerless approach to the education of children grew in the late nineteenth century. A key figure was the educationalist Matthew Arnold, whose father, Tom, had been a famous headmaster of Rugby, one of the leading English public (i.e. private, fee-paying) schools. Arnold belonged to that intellectual aristocracy whose ramified interconnections were traced by

Noel Annan. He led the demand for the study of English literature not only in the public schools but in the national educational system put in place by the Education Act of 1870. There was a prudent politics to his concern. His most famous publication, *Culture and Anarchy*, addressed the antagonisms of a class-divided society and argued that without the spiritual nourishment of a humane culture, social anarchy would ensue.

The old, aristocratic English educational system was based on the ancient literatures of Greece and Rome which were flogged into generations of school-boys in the great public schools and a crop of more recent establishments. The cause of English literature was promoted by the English Association as a more relevant and less painful modern alternative to the classics. Its moment came in the immediate aftermath of the First World War which killed one in ten of the male population. The war, A.J.P. Taylor has argued, merged for the first time (and irreversibly) the history of the English state and the history of the English people: 'the mass of the people became, for the first time, active citizens whose lives were shaped by orders from above' (Taylor, 1975: 26). As it came to an end, working-class militancy in Britain, as elsewhere, seemed to threaten the internal peace of the kingdom even as a conclusion was finally being reached to the interminable slaughter of the disenfranchised millions in the killing fields of Europe. The condition of the masses became an immediate priority of the government, since 'the modern community could not work without some cooperation from the masses and the war in particular had made their active cooperation essential in factories as in the trenches' (ibid.: 231). As a necessary concession to the masses, formal democracy was finally granted (after centuries of struggle and bloodshed) to all adult males aged 21 and over and all women aged 30 and over by the 1918 Representation of the People Act. In the same year, a new Education Act established a fully national, salaried teaching system and raised the school-leaving age from 12 to 14 years.

In these circumstances the English Association, led by Sir Henry Newbolt, renewed its lobbying on behalf of 'a liberal education for the whole people based on the masterpieces of English literature'. In a keynote speech to the Association, Newbolt set out its guiding concerns. It was no longer possible to maintain 'that our native culture must always remain in great part the possession and influence of a single class or a small minority'. To the contrary, he believed that:

> [T]he national culture should be, and in good time may be, the tradition and inheritance of all British men and women who care to receive it. I put before you no hope of securing a general equality in wealth or health, in intellect or physique or in any other of the circumstances of a varying world; but I ask you to hope with me for a national fellowship in which it shall be possible for everyone to forget the existence of classes and to find a personal interest in each other's circumstances and events. (Newbolt, 1928: 9–10)

Here, then, was the case for English as the core component of a national culture; as the means whereby material class-based inequalities might be wished away through a new equality of cultural opportunity for all – a deeply political de-politicization of culture. This was the guiding spirit of the report on *The Teaching of English in England*, drawn up by a committee chaired by Newbolt and presented in 1921 to H.A.L. Fisher, President of the Board of Education, who had brought the 1918 Education Bill to the House of Commons.[4] The report argued that English literature must be central to the new *national* educational system that the Act had created:

> the common right to it, the common discipline and enjoyment of it, the common possession of the tastes and associations connected with it, would form a new element of national unity, linking together the mental life of all classes by experiences which have hitherto been the privilege of a limited section. (Newbolt, 1921, quoted in Doyle, 1989: 48–9)

The study of English would provide the basis of a common culture that transcended class differences and unified them in a shared national cultural identity. In so doing, it might alleviate the then real threat of working-class revolt. As George Sampson, author of *English for the English* (1921), put it: 'Deny to working class children any common share in the immaterial and presently they will grow into the men who demand with menaces a communism of the material' (Doyle, 1981: 11).[5]

Mass civilization

Every new academic subject taught in schools needs a syllabus and curriculum and these depend not only on agreed authors and works and suitable textbooks but also, in support, a cumulative body of research and knowledge about the subject, the provision of which is one of the functions of the universities. What was required, in the first place, was the staking out of the territorial boundaries of the new discipline. What was Literature and what was not (and why)? If any one person could be said to have done this it was F.R. Leavis in the English Faculty at Cambridge. In

---

4 See Doyle (1989: 41–68) for a full discussion of the Report and its impact.

5 Sampson was a member of the Newbolt Committee. The passage quoted by Doyle (see n.4) is from the Preface (added in 1926) to *English for the English,* published by Cambridge University Press. Doyle's article – 'Some uses of English: Denys Thompson and the development of English in secondary schools – was written at the Centre for Contemporary Cultural Studies and published as one of their famous 'Stencilled Occasional Papers'. The historical study of English education was an important strand of the Centre's work introduced by the historian, Richard Johnson, when he joined Stuart Hall as a lecturer at the Centre in the mid-1970s.

his working lifetime, as Anderson rightly observes, he simply dominated the new discipline whose boundaries he defined and whose intellectual agenda he set.

It is crucial to note that Leavis was always concerned with *modern* literature. He was no medievalist, no advocate of the teaching of Anglo-Saxon grammar as the gateway to the somewhat austere pleasures of Old English poetry. His most famous literary publication was *The Great Tradition* which 'not dogmatically but deliberately' named those authors and their works that defined the canonical tradition of the modern English novel. The tradition, according to Leavis, began with Jane Austen, ended with Henry James and Joseph Conrad and notoriously excluded the greatest of all English novelists, Charles Dickens. He and D.H. Lawrence were later admitted to the canon. What distinguished the authors chosen by Leavis as embodying the tradition, what made it *great*, was their moral seriousness. All the writers, in different ways exhibited a moral intelligence in their engagement with the life and times of the society to which they belonged and about which they wrote. Leavis's preference, in the novel at least, was for narrative realism. The fictional life-worlds of the novels of, say, George Eliott (who, for Leavis, was *the*

Frank and Queenie Leavis

English novelist), were engaged social commentaries on England in the mid-nineteenth century. *Middlemarch* and *Daniel Deronda*, her two greatest achievements, were incomparable studies of the damaged lives of men and women, entangled in the snares of class-based British society. But social realism was not the primary focus of Leavis's concern. The touchstone for him, why literature *really* mattered, was the life-affirming quality of the writing, of the compellingly created, fully realized fictional worlds in which characters of real moral complexity encountered and coped (or not) with the perplexities and difficulties of modern life. The life-affirming power of modern literature was what justified its claim to be taken seriously; to be thought about, discussed, argued over and defended against its enemies.

That was the other aspect of Leavis's work, for English literature and what it stood for, as he conceived it, had many enemies, not the least of which was the irresistible rise of 'mass civilization'. In the 1930s, Leavis and his wife, Queenie, were the most outspoken critics of the new mass culture and its begetter, factory-based mass production. The Leavisite critique of mass culture became, as Anderson argued, the displaced site of a critique of modern society as a whole.

I have examined the ways in which the 'social question' was raised in American and German social thought at exactly the same time. In each case the question was raised in an emerging academic discipline tailored to that question: sociology. American sociology at Columbia was permeated by scientific positivism and German social theory at Frankfurt was permeated by idealist philosophy and the critical tradition. England at that time produced nothing remotely like either of them. In the absence of anything resembling sociology, the British critique of modern society was forged by the new academic discipline of English Studies because, as defined by the Leavises, the literature itself was forged in response to the dialectics of Enlightenment and modernity (though that is not how either of them would ever have put it). Modern literature – poetry and the novel – in its form and content was an engaged, continuing response to the experience of modernity. There to be found in the texts was a serious, critical engagement with societal modernization and at the same time a redemptive resistance to it, an alternative hope summed up, for the Leavises, in a single word: 'life'.

If literature was life-affirming, mass civilization was life-denying. Literature had, for the Leavises, the same function as autonomous art for Adorno. It was the lonely site of resistance to the dominant forms of contemporary cultural life. But the English interpretation of this function stood the German on its head. For the members of the Institute for Social Theory, autonomous art had a negative function in the face of affirmative culture.[6] For the Leavises, literature had an affirmative function in the face of negative culture. This function was made explicit as part of the pedagogics of English in schools. It was not just enough to teach the young to experience good literature. They must also develop a discriminatory intelligence that could distinguish good from bad. Both the Leavises had studied mass culture. Queenie did a famous study of the popular novel, *Fiction and the Reading Public,* while Frank did his PhD (then a very new thing at Cambridge and regarded with deep suspicion by the old guard) on 'Journalism and Literature: A Historical Study of the Relations between them in England' (McKillop, 1995: 71). The clearest general statement of the 'desperate plight of culture today' is in 'Mass civilization and minority culture', a pamphlet hastily put together and published in 1930. It argued that the heritage of European culture[7] was beyond the grasp of the great majority of people and could only be adequately understood by a small, educated minority upon whom its continuing existence depended. The opinions and tastes of the masses were formed by newspapers, which were the products of a machine civilization.

Machine civilization produces a catastrophic levelling down and standardization of taste and thereby destroys discrimination and judgement. This change

---

6 'The affirmative character of culture' was worked out and analysed by Herbert Marcuse in an essay of that title published in *ZfS* in 1937 (Marcuse, [1937] 1968: 88–133).

7 It is not just English texts and authors, but the works of 'Dante, Shakespeare, Donne, Baudelaire and Conrad' that Leavis chooses to exemplify the greatness of the European literary canon (see Leavis, [1930] 1978: 144).

had been better observed and analysed in the USA than in Britain. A key text that the Leavises used in support of their general thesis was *Middletown* (1929), the just published classic study of social and cultural change in the mid-west town of Muncie, Illinois, by Robert and Helen Lynd.[8] It was pointless blaming America and Americans for mass production and mass culture. No-one in Britain, least of all those who blamed it all on the USA, proposed to abandon 'the processes consequent upon the machine – greater efficiency, better salesmanship, and more mass-production and standardization' (Leavis, [1930] 1978: 147).

'Mass civilization and minority culture' is neither well written nor well thought out. It is a hastily assembled patchwork of quotations strung together from a variety of sources that the Leavises had quarried from their historical research on the press and the popular novel. The subsequent textbook for use in schools, *Culture and Environment*, that Leavis produced almost immediately with his ex-student and faithful acolyte, Denys Thompson,[9] sets out the Leavisite case against contemporary culture much more clearly and cogently. There the consequences of mass production – standardization and uniformity of products – are acknowledged as not necessarily bad. Power machinery had many advantages over older, harder manual toil. The baneful consequences of machine civilization showed less in the manufacture of material goods and more in the new forms of mass culture and entertainment – the press and popular fiction, which both the Leavises had studied, but also in cinema and radio. All offered satisfaction at the lowest level, providing the most immediate pleasures for the least amount of effort. Mass culture undermined the standards of discriminatory taste that teachers of English were trying to inculcate in the young. It was the responsibility of teachers to get children to see through the environment (the life-world) in which they lived and to understand how inadequate it was. It was essential to train critical awareness of the cultural environment of contemporary life and the vicarious pleasures of what Leavis and Thompson dubbed 'substitute living' (1932: 99–103). But, literature aside, where was an alternative, authentic life to be found? The answer was 'the organic community', for which literary education could only be, at best, a substitute:

> What we have lost is the organic community with the living culture it embodied. Folk-songs, folk-dances, Cotswold cottages and handicraft products are signs and expressions of something more: an art of life, a way of living, ordered and patterned, involving social arts, codes of intercourse and a responsive adjustment, growing out of immemorial experience, to the natural environment and the rhythm of the year. (ibid.: 2)

---

8 *Middletown* is 'a remarkable work of anthropology' (Leavis, [1930] 1978: 146). It was the most highly recommended text in the essential reading list appended to *Culture and Environment*: 'an indispensable book which should be in all libraries' (Leavis and Thompson, 1932: 147).

9 On Thompson, see Doyle, (1981). McKillop, Leavis's biographer, notes that Queenie did a lot of unacknowledged work on *Culture and Environment*.

This culture was within living memory and still lingered on, here and there, in remote pockets of the country, as a reminder of an art of living that had now perished. Leavis was no fool. He did not for a moment imagine that any of this could be revived. Indeed, folk revivals (Morris dancing, real ale, country fayres, etc.) were definitively inauthentic because they were no more than isolated fragments of what once was a living, relational totality of involvements; an organic community, a *whole* way of life. The key perception is of culture as *an art of life, a way of living* that was preserved through speech. 'The cultivation of *the art of speech* was as essential to the old popular culture that in local variations existed throughout the country as song, dance and handicrafts' (ibid.: emphasis added). Adorno and Horkheimer were deeply aware of the commodification of language. Leavis grieved for a lost art of conversation – the living medium of ordinary social life through which a living culture is expressed and sustained. This was the core of a redefinition of culture that would be taken up and elaborated by the next generation of university teachers of English Literature.

Leavis is now deeply unfashionable and his once famous books on poetry and the novel, read by every student of English literature, are today out of print. But he commanded his field for two generations because of the moral power of his critique of contemporary life. He knew perfectly well that no amount of folk revivals and efforts at fake community (Merton's pseudo-*Gemeinschaft*) could breathe life into what he mourned for; older forms of sociable life which embodied and expressed an art (a dignity) of living that industrialization and urbanization had killed off without putting anything remotely adequate in its place. There is an often desperate tone to Leavis's writings about literature and mass culture because *both* are substitutes for authentic life and experience – the former a best, the latter a worst, alternative to life itself as an art. This perception is not expressed with the theoretical elegance of the German critical tradition, but it is similar in many respects. The critique of English utilitarianism that Leavis took over from Matthew Arnold is essentially the same as Weber's critique of instrumental reason and Leavis would doubtless have agreed, had he known of it, with Weber's perception of the disenchanted modern world as an iron cage. What Leavis lacked was any political analysis of the current plight of British society and culture such as the Institute for Social Research fashioned from Marx, Weber and Lukács. But Leavis saw something that Adorno and Horkheimer missed: the question of culture was not so much an aesthetic but a moral matter that was linked not to art in the first place but to life itself, an art of life.[10] This was the hidden pearl, the essential connection, in the

---

10 The German contemporary whom Leavis most resembles is Martin Heidegger. Both are temperamentally conservative thinkers. Both mourn the passing of traditional rural, communal, handicraft ways of life. Heidegger is as exercised by 'The question of technology' as Leavis is by machine civilization and for the same fundamental reason. The deepest connection between them is a shared concern with the question of existence (life). Heidegger's *Existenz* philosophy, worked out in *Sein und Zeit* (Being and Time) and published in 1927, articulates what remains incommunicable in Leavis's stubborn faith in 'life' as the authentic, experiential touchstone of our 'being-in-the-world' (Heidegger, [1927] 1962; Dreyfus, 1991).

Leavisite social critique of contemporary culture. It was this that was taken up and explored in new ways after the Second World War by his successors in the 1950s, Richard Hoggart and Raymond Williams. Both were his protégés, but both challenged the Leavisite specification of modern culture in essentially literary terms. They reworked the meaning of culture to make visible its social and political implications. In particular, they exposed the extent to which questions of class underpinned the 'question of culture'. Was not all culture the product and property of the upper and middle classes? What of working-class culture?

The uses of literacy

To speak of working-class culture was something of an oxymoron, for it was the culture of no culture, if that meant a self-produced, coherent body of art and literature – and that was the dominant definition of culture in Britain and elsewhere in the 1950s. Hoggart and Williams both came from working-class backgrounds. Both did well at school and went on to university (a very unusual thing for working-class children) where they studied English Literature. Even more unusually they went on to become English lecturers, teaching not only in their universities (Hull and Cambridge) but also to adults in the WEA (Workers' Educational Association). Both men absorbed that moral seriousness with which the study of literature was invested by Leavis, but they brought to it a new understanding and a fresh perspective shaped by their own lives and experience. Between them they redefined 'the question of culture' as it was understood in post-war Britain. Both took up Leavis's essential definition of culture as an art of life, a way of living as the basis of their re-working of the meaning of 'culture', but each did so in their own and somewhat different terms. Each published a book in the 1950s that had an immediate and widespread impact. The first was *The Uses of Literacy* by Richard Hoggart.

The original title was *The Abuses of Literacy*, which more accurately described its central thesis – the debilitating impact of tabloid journalism and pulp fiction on working-class readers – but the publisher did not like it and so it was changed. It is a book that was written back-to-front: the second part was written first and the first part was subsequently added by way of contextualizing the original concerns of the book. Those concerns were with the impact of mass culture on the newly literate masses. The book was prompted by Hoggart's experience of teaching literature in WEA classes at Hull in the aftermath of the Second World War and the gap between what he was teaching and the lives of those he taught. Modern literature was the product of an educated social stratum: it was written and read by members of the same social class and spoke to their essential shared concerns. The novel, as it developed in the eighteenth century, was the new literary genre of a new social class which explored the changing dynamics of money, sex and power in the intimate sphere of family life. In the nineteenth century, the historical novel moved on to the larger question of the relationship between this new way of life and the public world of war and politics. In all this there was no fundamental lack of fit between the concerns of the genre and the lives of those who produced and consumed it. But for working-class readers there was a huge chasm between the life-worlds of the literature that would supposedly enrich their lives and their own world of experience. It was this gap, this lack of fit between what was taught and the lives and experience of those who were taught it that prompted the cultural turn in the 1950s exemplified in the writings of Richard Hoggart and Raymond Williams. The question of class is the social question at the heart of the rethinking of culture that they undertook – class, culture and society.

In Britain especially, class is a term used in two distinct yet related ways. On the one hand, as a social question, it concerns the long historic relationship going back many centuries between the crown and church and lords and commons – the richly layered, hierarchic structure of British society – which gradually morphed into relations between the common people (the lower class), the bourgeoisie (the middle class) and the aristocracy (the upper class). Overlaid on this, in the course of the nineteenth century, was the rise of urban factory capitalism and the creation of a new economic relation between capitalists and workers, masters and men. The English Working Class (EWC), with whom Hoggart and Williams were both concerned, was forged in the convulsive developments of the nineteenth century. To speak of the working class in the 1950s was to invoke the people who still lived in those parts of the country where the industrial revolution took hold a century earlier. It meant those who still worked in the primary industries of nineteenth-century factory capitalism: coal (the basic energy source that fuelled the economic revolution) and steel (from which ships, railroads and locomotives, the new transport infrastructure, were built). It meant those who still worked in the cotton and woollen mills of Lancashire and Yorkshire. It meant the North as the historic heartland of industrial factory capitalism and the urban working class. The history of this class was one of unrelenting struggle against exploitation in the workplace and the miseries of primary poverty. Its self-understanding and definition were not forged in the creation of a culture of leisure but in the struggle to maintain an always precarious grip on existence itself. Its experience was one of deprivation: subsistence wages, meagre diet, poor housing, shoddy clothes, ill-health and a shortened life span.

By the 1950s, this had begun to change. It is instructive to compare the condition of the EWC in that decade with its condition in the 1930s. The 1930s as a decade were defined by the crisis in the American economy of 1929 whose social and political consequences in Europe led, within ten years, to a global war. The 1930s was defined by the politics of poverty on both continents as many millions of people, thrown out of work by the down-turn in the economy, were reduced to near starvation. The immediate consequences of mass poverty were chronicled on both sides of the Atlantic by well-meaning middle-class intellectuals. The documentary movement used the new technologies of communication (photography, film and radio) to record the impact of the Depression on individual lives and to publicize their suffering. The two classic texts of the 1930s about poverty and the masses were *The Road to Wigan Pier* by George Orwell ([1937] 1965) and *Let Us Now Praise Famous Men* by James Agee and Walker Evans ([1939] 1975). The former chronicled the wretched living conditions of the working classes in the North of England (Wigan is in Lancashire) while the latter paid tribute to the endurance of the rural poor, the share croppers reduced to penury by drought in the Dust Bowl. In both cases, members of the educated elite investigated the circumstances of the poor in order to make visible their suffering. It was a politics of pity motivated by indignation or compassion that made public the circumstances of people for whom culture had no meaning, for their lives were beneath culture.

The Second World War immediately resolved the problem of poverty in Britain and the United States. Unemployment melted away as each country turned to a full-scale war economy. For the masses working in the factories pouring out the planes, ships, tanks, guns and munitions for the fighting fronts on land, sea and air, the war provided a newfound economic security and a rising standard of living. Although Britain experienced a short sharp economic crisis in the late 1940s, the 1950s was a period of continuing growth. Living standards continued to rise while post-war politics created a system of welfare that provided free education and medical care for all and a raft of measures to ensure social security in the case of sickness or unemployment. There was no return to the chronic insecurities of the 1930s. This then was the situation in which the question of culture took on a quite new significance. Now that the masses had a marginal surplus of disposable time and money for the pursuits of leisure, how could they be guided to use these precious assets well? In the 1930s, the Leavises had tried to provide training in schools to help the young see through the tawdry triviality of the new forms of mass culture. In the 1950s, this question confronted Hoggart and others as they taught grown men and women attending their evening classes put on by the Workers Educational Association:

> We were very interested ... by the fact that our pupils came and usually they learned about 'classical' literature in almost the Leavisite sense, but they *lived* in another world ... They lived in the world of newspapers and magazines and radio (not television at the time) and pop songs. There was a side interest in making sense of that among many extramural tutors. We did learn a great deal from the whole *Scrutiny* and Leavis group. (Hoggart, [1957] 1992: 382)

Richard Hoggart

Hoggart wanted to write another textbook exposing the shallowness of the new mass culture (Part two of the book) and was much influenced in his approach by Q.D Leavis's *Fiction and the Reading Public*. But there was, he felt, too much of a gap between Leavis and her understanding of what mass fiction might mean to its readers, too much of a 'peg in the nose' attitude both towards the fiction itself and its reading public (Hoggart, in Corner, 1991). It was to remedy this gap that Hoggart wrote an introductory first part which put in context the lives and circumstances of working-class consumers of post-war mass culture and it was this that made the book and its author famous. It is difficult today to understand what was so remarkable, at the time, about *The Uses of Literacy*. It was truly a ground-breaking book for it was the first written by a member of the English working class about the ordinary everyday life and culture of working-class people living in the towns and cities of the north of England. Much had been written in fiction and non-fiction going back to the 1840s about the industrial working class. But all of it was written by outsiders, by men and sometimes women of good will from other classes concerned with the fate of the poor, and almost all of it presented the working class as passive, suffering victims in need of help. The EWC, before the 1950s, was always spoken for. It had yet to speak for itself. Richard Hoggart's account of ordinary daily lives and experience of working people in the towns and cities of northern England had the force of revelation when first published in 1957.

The culture of everyday life

The Uses of Literacy was an account of the lives of the majority. Two important minority groups – those who were active in working-class politics and those who were interested in self-improvement (both of whom tended to go to WEA classes) – were noted and set aside. The majority of working-class people were neither politically active nor earnest seekers after knowledge and it was their way of life that Hoggart sought to capture. Leavis had mourned the loss of an art of conversation and a way of living then almost extinct whose marginal existence he saw still surviving in the rural countryside and the communal culture of the village. Hoggart found elements of this in the everyday lives of the urban Northern working class. He begins with overheard conversations in public places to show that the 'oral tradition' lives on in working-class speech. He notes its down-to-earth humour, its proverbial and formal character that links it to older, pre-industrial patterns of social relations.

Conversational fragments that show the idioms of working-class speech are invoked with great effect throughout the first part of the book in order to 'let the subaltern speak'. Working-class culture is not shallow and depthless. It is rooted in experience that extends back through generations, and this experience (which I will come to shortly) is preserved in idioms of speech that express a common collective attitude to the world. The roles of women and men (and the formal character of that relationship), marriage, family and children are all deftly located in a home-based way of life. The working-class home is lovingly described, so too the working-class street and neighbourhood with the pub and corner-shop. And all this begins to disclose 'the 'real' world of people' ([1957] 1992: 102–31). We have seen the discovery of 'people' in Katz and Lazarsfeld's *Personal Influence*. At exactly the same time, but in a very different idiom, real people are discovered in *The Uses of Literacy*. These two landmark studies of the mid-1950s, one American and one British, both testify to a profound sea-change in the contemporary post-war world which I will examine in detail in the last chapter of this book. They both bear witness to the passing of the time of the masses and the emergence of the time of everyday life.

The everyday world of working-class life is 'carved out under the shadow of giant abstractions' in which the masses 'are asked to respond to "the needs of the state" and "the needs of society", to study "good citizenship" and to have in mind "the common good"' (ibid.: 104). But these are externally imposed abstractions: 'If we want to capture something of the essence of working-class life in a phrase, we must say that it is the "dense and concrete life", a life whose main stress is on the intimate, the sensory, the detailed, and the personal' (ibid.). It is a life that is lived in the present, from day to day. Fate and luck determine the future. Meanwhile, it's best to be cheerful, to take things as they come and enjoy what life has to offer. In a wonderful chapter Hoggart invokes the pleasures of 'the full rich life':

> Life goes on from day to day and from week to week: the seasons turn over, marked by the great festivals regarded as holidays or bean feasts, and by an occasional special event – a wedding in the family, a charabanc trip, a funeral, a cup-tie. There is bound to be some planning: a twelve-week Christmas club for presents and extras, perhaps a club for Whitsuntide clothes paid in advance,[11] and, after that, saving for a holiday in some cases. But in general the striking feature

---

11 It was customary to buy new 'best clothes' for children each year at Whitsuntide (the feast of Pentecost which follows six weeks after Easter Sunday). On the morning of Whit Sunday little boys and girls would be dressed up in their finest and paraded round to friends and relatives who would present them with small gifts of money (Hoggart, [1957] 1992: 32). This extra expenditure, like that of Christmas, was prudently anticipated by paying a small weekly amount to the local department store months in advance – a small reminder that every penny mattered in the family budget. It is impossible today to understand what these things meant: how much it mattered and what pride there was in turning out one's children properly dressed. 'Keeping up appearances' and being 'respectable' were the visible outward signs that the family was doing all right, that it hadn't gone under, that it could do more than make ends meet (just).

is the unplanned nature of life, the moment-to-moment meeting of troubles or taking of pleasure; schemes are mostly short-term. (Hoggart, [1957] 1992: 134–5)

The routines of day-to-day life serve as the backdrop to 'specific acts of baroque living', set-aside moments of celebration and carnival when life is enjoyed to the full:

> Most working-class pleasures tend to be mass-pleasures, over-crowded and sprawling. Everyone wants to have fun at the same time, since most factory buzzers blow within an hour of each other. Special occasions – a wedding, a trip to the pantomime, a visit to the fair, a charabanc outing – assume this, and assume also that a really special splendour and glitter must be displayed. (ibid.: 145)

A vivid sketch of a day's outing to the seaside exemplifies the occasional baroque enjoyments of working-class life.

In the politicized climate of Cultural Studies in the 1970s there was a tendency to be a bit condescending towards *The Uses of Literacy*: it was genuflected towards as a canonical text and then criticized for not being theoretical or critical or political enough. Some thought it too sentimental and romantic about its subject. But such criticisms fail to acknowledge its innovatory re-specification of culture. It is tempting to call it an anthropological or ethnographic approach, but that would be to make it more 'academic' than it was. It was a narrative from within the culture of which it told, not an account from without by an intrepid academic ethnographer of native culture. It was a vivid, fresh, earthy, engaged and engaging account that unobtrusively loosened the proprietary grip of the educated elites on culture by redefining it as a way of life rooted in everyday life and experience. Nor did Hoggart overlook the political implications of this way of life. The key chapter to the whole book is called '"Them" and "Us"' (ibid.: 72–101). Who are 'They'?

> 'They' are 'the people at the top', 'the higher-ups', the people who give you your dole, call you up, tell you to go to war, fine you, made you split the family in the thirties to avoid a reduction in the Means Test allowance, 'get yer in the end', 'aren't really to be trusted', 'talk posh', 'are all twisters really', 'never tell yer owt' (about a relative in hospital), 'clap yer in clink', 'will do yer down if they can', 'summons yer', 'are all in a click (clique) together', treat yer like muck'. (ibid.: 72–3)

'They' are the agents of the official culture that looms over and above working-class life; the doctors, teachers, vicars, policemen and magistrates who boss you about and tell you what to do. They are 'the vast apparatus of authority' as it intrudes on working-class life. It is as unaccountable, implacable and arbitrary as Fate. It would be quite unjust to treat the account of the culture of the apolitical majority as itself apolitical. Hoggart makes it crystal clear that this is the subordinate culture of a subaltern social class; a ghetto culture with a ghetto mentality. The working classes live in neighbourhoods that are separate and isolated from other classes who live elsewhere, not in the back-to-back terraced housing of the inner city but in the semi-detached and detached houses with gardens in the leafy suburbs. The attitude to life of the urban working class came from long experience and bitter memory of deprivation and poverty. It was a resilient, stoic culture shaped by economic exploitation and the social domination of other classes. It was a genuinely shared, communal culture in which people created, of necessity, collective forms of mutual support and help to see them through lean times and to provide some insurance and protection against the vagaries of fate.

By the mid-1950s life was looking better than it had ever been in the past. Unemployment was low and there was real economic security, rising wages and a better standard of living. George Orwell (who had a very sensitive nose) had scandalized Left Book Club readers in the 1930s by declaring in *The Road to Wigan Pier* that the working classes *smell*. Hoggart notes that in the 1950s 'we no longer hear about the sheer stink of a working class crowd' ([1957] 1992: 172). Housing with electricity, hot and cold water, a bathroom and lavatory were post-war novelties for many. Cars, washing machines and television sets were much prized and purchased in instalments on 'the never-never' (because you *never* stop paying) or, in the case of TV sets, rented. The novel phenomenon of post-war working-class 'affluence' engaged the attention of sociologists (Goldthorpe, 1969) and provoked harrumphing noises from predictable quarters about working-class 'materialism' and their tendency to waste money on stupid things (why did they need television sets and cars?). But as Hoggart points out, such things were desired not from a greed for possessions, but because without them life was a hard and constant fight simply 'to keep your head above water' spiritually as well as economically.

Culture and society

'E's bright. E's got brains.' Hoggart notes how this was said admiringly by the families and friends of clever working-class boys. In a chapter shot through with personal experience he discusses the 'uprooted and the anxious', those who move up the educational ladder from grammar school to university and perhaps a PhD. As they climb, they leave behind their cultural heritage. They move from one class to another. It is hard today to convey a sense of the sheer awfulness of class in Britain 50 years ago. It was not primarily about money and inequalities of economic wealth. It was about the sound of your voice, the things you ate (and the way you ate), your clothes, your 'taste' (or lack of it), the school you'd been to (the old school tie), and so on and so forth. It was about a thousand small things that subtly marked out class boundaries, and the petty snobberies, anxieties and hatreds that policed them. It was, as Hoggart's discussion of Them and Us made plain, a deeply authoritarian and hierarchical society in which the higher orders looked down on the lower orders and expected them to look up to 'their betters' and behave themselves. If they did not, they would of course be made to. Richard Hoggart and Raymond Williams both clearly had brains and moved up the ladder of opportunity. Both as a consequence experienced the peculiarly haunted experience of being displaced persons in their own society.

Williams perhaps more than Hoggart. He went the extra mile. Hoggart moved from Leeds to Hull, another Yorkshire city with a strong local sense of identity and a solid working-class population. He did not really move away. But Williams moved from the Welsh borders where his father was a railway signalman to Cambridge University and a fellowship at Jesus College, where he remained for his working life. He did not feel put down by the university itself but he did by the sort of people he encountered in Cambridge teashops:

> I was not oppressed by the university, but the teashop, acting as if it were one of the older and more respectable departments, was a different matter. Here was culture, not in any sense I knew, but in a special sense: the outward and emphatically visible sign of a special kind of people, cultivated people. They were not, the great majority of them, particularly learned; they practised few arts, but they had it, and they showed you they had it. They are still there, I suppose, still showing it, though even they must be hearing rude noises from outside, from a few scholars and writers they call – how comforting a label it is! – angry young men.[12] As a matter of fact there is no need to be rude. It is simply that if that is culture, we don't want it; we have seen other people living. (Williams, 1989: 5)

The raw, uncomfortable tone, the palpable 'them and us' attitude that marks this autobiographical passage in an essay called 'Culture is ordinary' first published in 1958, still resonates in the writing 50 years later. Williams described

---

12 A catch-phrase at the time of writing for a number of writers in the early 1950s (they were not in any sense a movement) who reacted to what Williams here precisely describes; the suffocating smugness and condescension of social class in contemporary Britain. John Osborne's play *Look Back in Anger* (1956) gave it a name, while Kingsley Amis's *Lucky Jim* (1954), a novel about a young lecturer in History at a provincial university, can be read as an extended darkly funny gloss on what Williams here describes.

himself, in *The Long Revolution*, as one of 'the awkward squad', those who through education moved up the rungs of post-war British society and who were much discussed at the time as a distinctive new social type. 'Many people have told us that the reason for our interest in class is that we are frustrated to find that educational mobility is not quite social mobility; that however far we have gone we still find an older system above us' (Williams, 1962: 348). To which Williams replies, 'I have never felt that I wanted to go on climbing, resentful of old barriers in my way: where else is there to go, but into my own life?' (ibid.). The ways of thinking about class in mid-century Britain were, he notes, exceptionally uncertain and confused, but it was an unavoidable issue that permeated all aspects of social life at the time. It is *the* issue that underlies everything that Williams wrote then. For *Culture and Society*, his defining work, read culture and class.

We have seen that the origins of English Literature, in schools and universities, were intimately connected with the politics of class in nineteenth-century Britain. It was proposed as a solution to the manifest tensions of a class-divided society in the hope that a redistribution of the common cultural heritage might assuage demands from below for economic redistribution. Thus the political project of English Literature was conceived as a means of avoiding social anarchy and class war (a fitfully real possibility throughout the nineteenth and early twentieth centuries). That of course was concealed in the implementation of the project. The literary heritage was presented as above politics. It was a culture of no politics. It was Raymond Williams' great achievement to set the record straight and to make the essential reconnection of culture with politics and class. The question of culture in a class society could not be other than political and Williams traced with exemplary skill its long, historical formation from the late eighteenth century to the mid-twentieth century.

He begins, in the brief Introduction, by linking the word 'culture' to four other keywords: industry, democracy, class and art. Taken together, these are the essential economic, political, social and cultural components of the common life, language and experience, the *whole* way of life of the British people as it develops and changes in and through time. The starting point is the period of revolution in the late eighteenth century; the political revolutions in America and France, and the beginnings of the Industrial Revolution in Britain with the rise of factory capitalism and mass production and the long struggle for a democratic society. Williams was the first to see the essential interconnectedness of economic, political, social and cultural developments and the first to try and hold them together in an extended historical analysis that focused on the literary culture in Britain from the nineteenth to the mid-twentieth century. But why should literature be the lens through which to view the development of a whole social formation? Because, as Williams so patiently reminds us, it was a literature that was at all points deeply engaged with the political, economic and social pressures of the times in which and for which and about which it was written. Today these things show up in the media and that is why they are studied as the registers of economic, political, and cultural processes in play through our own societies and throughout the world. But the age of the media in its fully developed formation goes back no more than 50 years or so to the exact time in which Williams wrote *Culture and Society*. Before then, the arts and literature were one of the best and most revealing contemporary registers of the changing play of those historical processes in their own and present times.

If this now appears to be an elementary truth, it is only because the long and careful narrative of *Culture and Society* showed it to be so. The Romantic poets are exemplary. Wordsworth does not appear, in Williams' accounts, as the wandering poet of Lakeland daffodils; Blake is not communing with angels at the bottom of his garden; Coleridge is not the druggy poet of Xanadu; Shelley and Byron are not a scapegrace pair of celebrity aristos on the run, and poor John Keats did not just die tragically young. All are shown to have been profoundly affected by the American and French Revolutions, by the industrial 'turn' and its impact on urban and rural life and by the changing character of social relations in an emerging 'class' society (the language of 'class' appeared in their lifetime as part of a new vocabulary to capture immense contemporary social change). All are shown not only to have engaged with these things in their poetry, but to have understood the very point and purpose of poetry (what it meant to *be* a poet) as a critique of a society that was declaring poetry and poets to be irrelevant to the business of modern Britain. The marginalization of art and literature in a rapidly industrialized society was a powerful indicator of the disenchantment of the world. A masterly chapter on that very theme provides a critical review of John Stuart Mill's writings on Jeremy Bentham (one of the founders of the new Utilitarianism) and Samuel Taylor Coleridge. It is a brilliant essay in miniature that shows the real complexities of economic change and its impact on contemporary society and ways of thinking all embodied in the person of Mill himself and worked through in his life and writings.

The developing relations between literature, politics and an industrialized, class-based society are traced through the course of the nineteenth century: a study of the 'industrial' novels of the 1840s by Charles Dickens (*Hard Times*), Benjamin Disraeli (*Sybil*) and Elizabeth Gaskell (*Mary Barton, North and South*) shows the extent of the gulf between the 'two nations' thematized in *Sybil* (rich and poor; North and South) and the wretched condition of the newly created urban proletariat in the north of England (*Mary Barton* is set in Manchester, the capital of the cotton industry and *Hard Times* in Coketown, the figurative setting of any sooty industrial town in Lancashire or Yorkshire). A key chapter follows on Matthew Arnold who was the first to propose culture as a political solution to social conflict in Victorian Britain. The title of William's book, *Culture and Society* echoes Arnold's *Culture and Anarchy* although their politics are radically different.

Arnold thought of intellectuals as a free-floating force for good outside the barren clash between three great social classes; upper class 'barbarians', middle-class 'philistines' and the lower-class 'populace', the 'playful giant' who is

> beginning to assert and put into practice an Englishman's right to do what he likes; his right to march where he likes, meet where he likes, enter where he likes, hoot as he likes, threaten as he likes, smash as he likes. All this, I say, tends to anarchy. (quoted in Williams, 1958: 132).

Fear of the masses was a motive force behind *Culture and Anarchy*, written in direct response to large-scale working-class protests against the rejection of the Reform Bill of 1866 and the so-called Hyde Park Riots in the summer of that year.[13] But Arnold's polemic was more than a knee-jerk response to the apparent threat of social disorder. It was he, more than any other nineteenth-century writer in the tradition of thinking that Williams traces, who made the connection between 'culture' and 'society', who saw it in political terms, who advanced culture as a solution to social conflict and who argued for the state as the central agency for the propagation of a common national culture through a national system of education. Such arguments not only led a generation or so later, via the English Association, to English as a core subject in the National Curriculum for schools and as a new subject for study at university. It also provided the justification for political interventions on the terrain of culture that led, for instance, to the regulation by the state of radio broadcasting in the early twentieth century as a public service in the national interest.

The end of the masses

There were two important influences on Williams as he wrote *Culture and Society* and both receive extended consideration in the third section of the book that deals with '20th century opinions'. They were Marxism and the literary criticism of F.R. Leavis. Williams explains why and how they mattered for him

---

13 On 29 June 1866, the Reform League, demanding the extension of the vote to property-less working men, organized a march to Hyde Park where it intended to hold a mass rally calling for electoral reform. The park was then regarded as exclusive to the middle and upper classes and the Home Secretary ordered it to be closed. The march re-routed to Trafalgar Square but some of the protesters broke away, tore down the railings to the park and proceeded to trample on the flower beds. Several days of modest insurrection on such lines aroused wide-spread middle-class fears of a real (French) revolution from below in which the bourgeoisie and not just the flowers would be trampled underfoot.

in the essay 'Culture is ordinary' that was published at the same time as his book. The essay appeared in an appropriately titled collection of essays called *Convictions* (Mackenzie, 1958) and is an important personal, autobiographical gloss on the core concerns of *Culture and Society* and its author. The irreducible conviction is of the ordinariness of culture. This means that it is and must be non-exclusive. It cannot be the birthright only of privileged social sectors. A democratic vision of culture is essential. It follows that it cannot be restricted to special privileged kinds of things and practices as if they and they alone were the expressive embodiments of 'culture'. Thus there is no case for reserving its definition as exclusive to the arts and literature. Culture pervades all human artefacts and practices. And this is why it is necessary to think of culture as a way of life. The emphasis falls on a *whole* way of life, which is to underline its unity and how that is achieved in 'a knowable community'. This is the vision of culture that pervades all Williams' writing and from which he never swerved. It is an ideal which serves as the measure of 'actually existing' culture as traced historically through all the elements of modern British society (economic, political and social) as it developed from the late eighteenth century.

If Marxism and the teaching of F.R. Leavis are the two acknowledged sources of inspiration in the difficult understanding of culture that Williams was reaching for, ultimately he agreed with neither. He agreed with 'the Marxists' that 'a culture must finally be understood in relation to its underlying system of production' (1958: 7), but that was about as far as he went. The 'Marxism' that Williams had in mind (as manifest in the section on 'Marxism and Culture' in *Culture and Society*, 1958: 258–75) was based mainly on the writings of the British Left in the 1930s. Williams himself had briefly joined the British Communist Party in the late 1940s but soon parted company with it and refused to describe himself as Marxist until the late 1960s. While accepting the essential argument of Marx himself about the determining character of the modern, capitalist economy, and while acknowledging that the bourgeois culture to which it gave rise was indeed dominant and linked to economic and political power, he simply refused to accept some basic tenets of (bourgeois) Marxist intellectuals that went along with this. First, in his perception, they spoke too easily and condescendingly of 'the masses' and as if they had at the same time the right to speak and act on their behalf – the intellectuals as the vanguard of the masses. Second, he refused their view (the other side of the same coin) that the only culture to speak of was in fact the culture of the bourgeoisie. The masses were, in this view, beneath culture. This was a mistake that everyone, from conservatives to Marxists, seemed to make:

> There is a distinct working-class way of life, which I for one value – not only because I was bred in it, for I now, in certain respects, live differently. I think this way of life, with its emphasis on neighbourhood, mutual obligation, and common

betterment, as expressed in the great working-class political and industrial institutions, is in fact the best basis for any future English society. As for the arts and learning, they are in a real sense a national inheritance which is, or should be, available to everyone. So when the Marxists say we are living in a dying culture, and that the masses are ignorant, I have to ask them where on earth they have lived. A dying culture and ignorant masses are not what I have known and see. (Williams, [1958b] 1989: 8)

Richard Hoggart's *The Uses of Literacy* perfectly complements the work of Raymond Williams with its vivid accounts of a distinct working-class way of life, rooted in time and place. But Williams had a deeper sense of the historic importance of working-class political and economic institutions (the Labour Party; trade unions; the Co-operative, Building and Mutual Benefit Societies) as creating and sustaining the everyday life of the majority, and argued this in the conclusions to *Culture and Society*.

The irreducible thing that Williams learnt from Leavis was 'about the real relations between art and experience' and here the emphasis falls on *experience* as the validating category of culture as a way of life; culture as lived experience, the experience of life itself. It was this that Leavis found in, for instance, the tradition of the English novel; an engaged concern with the experiences of ordinary men and women as they tried to deal with and manage their lives and relationships in the fictional (yet recognizably English) life-worlds they inhabited. Novels *were* about life, the experience of living. To read them was to learn (to experience) something of that; the business of day-to-day life imaginatively situated in fictional but recognizable social settings. Williams was first and last a teacher of English Literature in the same university as Leavis, and most of the many books he wrote were about literature. That aspect of his working life is outwith my concerns here, but should not be forgotten. Williams never ceased to believe in the importance of teaching Literature that he learnt from Leavis. What he did part company with was the Leavisite critique of mass civilization and minority culture. From a very different starting point Leavis ended up in the same position as the Marxists whom he despised. He was in denial of machine civilization and mass production, the sheer ugliness and squalor of the towns and cities of the Industrial Revolution. The 'organic community' of an older, rural way of life had been destroyed by the monstrous juggernaut of societal modernization and its disastrous mass civilization. To which Williams replies:

For one thing I knew this: at home we were glad of the Industrial Revolution, and of its consequent social and political change. True, we lived in a beautiful farming valley, and the valleys beyond the limestone we could see were all ugly. But there was one gift that was overriding, one gift which at any price we would take, the gift of power that is everything to men who have worked with their hands. It was slow in coming to us, in all its effects, but steam power, the petrol engine, electricity, these and their host of products in commodities and services we took as quickly as we could get them and were glad. I have seen all these things being used, and I have seen the things they replaced. I will not listen to any acid listing of them – you know the sneer you can get into plumbing, baby Austins,[14] aspirin, contraceptives, canned food.[15] But I say to these Pharisees: dirty water, an earth bucket, a four mile walk each way to work, headaches, broken women, hunger and monotony of diet. The working people, in town and country alike, will not listen (and I support them) to any account of our society which supposes that these things are not progress: not just mechanical, external progress, but a real service of life. Moreover, in these new conditions, there is more real freedom to dispose of our lives, more real personal grasp where it matters, more real say. Any account of our culture which implicitly or explicitly denies the value of an industrial society is really irrelevant; not in a million years would you make us give up this power. (Williams, [1958b] 1989: 10)

The power and passion of the writing so evident here are absent from, but underneath everything in the two books that elaborate the essential perception so remarkably and unequivocally stated in this passage: the long revolution was a force for the good, 'a real service of life'. It brought real, unarguable benefits for the mass of the population. It created new conditions of life that raised them out of poverty and the mere dependency of subsistence living defined by immediate need. It gave them a marginal surplus of disposable time and money for the purchase of goods that freed them from toil and that offered new ways of enjoying their new-found leisure. This was the new way of life in post-war Britain. It was the beginning of the realization of the full meaning of democracy, and in that beginning was the end of the masses.

'There are in fact no masses; there are only ways of seeing other people as masses.' No sentence in the famous concluding chapter of *Culture and Society* has been more frequently cited than this ([1958a] 1962: 289). It pins down the

---

14 One of the first British mass-manufactured small and affordable family cars.

15 He is almost certainly thinking of George Orwell in *The Road to Wigan Pier*: 'Whole sections of the working class who have been plundered of all they really need are being compensated, in part, by cheap luxuries which mitigate the surface of life. It is quite likely that fish-and-chips, art-silk stockings, tinned salmon, cut-price chocolate, the movies, the radio, strong tea and the foot-ball pools have between them averted revolution' (Orwell, [1937] 1965: 90–1). This line of argument (there at exactly the same time in Horkheimer and Adorno's critique of the new culture industries and in Marcuse's influential concept of 'affirmative culture') that the masses are 'bought off' and made safe for capitalism by the ground-bait of 'cheap luxuries' is the sneering Pharisaic way of thinking that Williams so vehemently rejects. See his chapter on Orwell in *Culture and Society*, especially pp. 278–9.

essential change in perception that is at the heart of the new structure of thinking in the pivotal post-war decade of the 1950s. We have seen the discovery of 'people' in *Personal Influence* and *The Uses of Literacy*, and here it is again as a key proposition in the final review and critique of the tradition so meticulously traced and discussed over the span of 150 years. We will encounter it yet again in the American post-war sociology of Erving Goffman. The discovery of 'people'–ordinary people with their ordinary language and their ordinary lives – is the most distinctive and characteristic perception in the post-war world of Europe and North America; in their societies at large and in the specialist academic fields of sociology, literature, history and philosophy. It is the effect of a long historical process that finally delivers a modest abundance to the working majorities of the advanced economies and gives them, as Williams saw, more real freedom in the disposal of their lives. That is the new culture of everyday life. It is a differentiated culture in which people are free for the first time to explore and realize their own individual difference, the things that interest them, their own and particular concerns. As they do so, the hitherto undifferentiated life of the masses noiselessly fades away.

Culture and communication

'Culture and communication' is the emphasis in the final chapter of *Culture and Society* which is a summary review and critique of the tradition mapped out in all that precedes it. In most of that tradition the masses are spoken of and spoken for. Now, in post-war Britain, their lives and circumstances have a measure of economic independence and thereby a measure of real freedom and choice. In such circumstances, they also begin to have 'more say'. They are no longer to be ventriloquized by others who think they know better. For Williams, the moment of writing *Culture and Society* was one in which the promise of political democracy, for which the working class had fought for a century and a half, might at last begin to be realized in a truly democratic culture. The final effort of the book is to consider what that would entail and how it might be actualized and here, in the end, a new topic is broached; the question of communication. It is raised as the question of 'mass communication' and follows immediately on from the celebrated section on 'mass and masses' where those terms were interrogated and rejected. And so it follows that the critical issue is whether or not it is appropriate to think of all the new technologies of communication, especially the 'new media' of sound broadcasting, cinema and television, under the rubric of *mass* communication. *Personal Influence* had begun to question the validity of defining communication in 'mass' terms but did not push through to a critical engagement with that question. It is, given Williams' critique of the concept of the masses, necessarily where he begins. In line with his vigorous defence of the benefits of industrial capitalism for the mass of the people, Williams refuses to sneer at the media as the *mass* media. 'The new means of communication represent a major technical advance ... they are all things that need to be valued' (Williams, [1958a] 1962: 290). To begin to do so he needed to jettison the baggage that went with the term 'mass communication', but in trying to go beyond that, Williams was very much out there on his own.

It is worth emphasizing this point. Both *Culture and Society* and *The Long Revolution* are curiously difficult to read. It is partly a question of their uncertain tone and voice, matters to which Williams himself was always delicately sensitive. Who were his readers? To whom did he think he was speaking and in what tone of voice? The conclusion to *Culture and Society* reads very much like someone in conversation with himself and it was of course very much an effort at self-clarification, at working through some difficult, perplexing issues, and the perplexity shows in the writing. At the same time there is an effort at reaching out to, well, what or who exactly? To an imagined community of readers, I think, who might engage with the effort at thinking in which Williams himself was caught up. There was no available shared vocabulary or frame of thought upon which to draw. There was certainly no existing academic community of interest then as there is now for the study of culture, communication and media. He was neither a Leavisite nor (at that time) a Marxist.[16] He was, in his own account, a member of the awkward squad, socially and intellectually out of place in post-war British society. And yet he had a vision of something else, a better way of living: 'The struggle for democracy is a struggle for the recognition of equality of being, or it is nothing' ([1958a] 1962: 323). He saw the possibility of a genuinely common culture now that material well-being had been secured for the majority of people, however unevenly and marginally in many instances, and he saw communication as a crucial means to its realisation.

---

16 Williams's politics are in some respects very simple, in other respects extraordinarily complex. He believed, all his life, in the organized working-class movement and its politics (as distinct from the Labour Party and its politics). He was a life-long Socialist (but what that meant was complicated) and a founding member of the New Left whose beginnings in 1959 can be dated by the first issue of *New Left Review*, of which he was a founding editor. The development of the New Left in the 1960s, of new varieties of 'continental' Marxism (mainly from France) and Williams' own position in the swirling factionalism of the British Left from that time until his death in 1989 – all this is a deeply tangled and contested history. Various groups sought to claim him as their patron saint, but Williams was always resolutely his own man, and resisted all attempts to make him a totemic figure in support of any particular political cause or theoretical position. To get a sense of his politics it is best to read him in his own words: 'You're a Marxist aren't you?' written in 1975 and other essays published by New Left Books shortly after his death provide a fitting introduction to his thinking about politics (Williams, [1958b] 1989).

The move from mass communication to 'communication and community' is particularly difficult to grasp. Williams is strongly aware of all the obstacles in the way, and of all the objections to be made about actually existing social relations and ways of thinking about community. 'Any real theory of communication is a theory of community ... [but] it is very difficult to think clearly about this because the pattern of our thinking about community is, normally, dominative' (ibid.: 303). The meaning of 'community' is elusive. It is not a nostalgic hankering for the valleys of his childhood, and is grounded in the ideal of 'active mutual responsibility' which is more to be found in the working-class tradition than the middle-class tradition of individual service. A good community, a living culture, will encourage the contribution of each and all 'to the advance of consciousness which is the common need' (ibid.: 320):

> Wherever we have started from we need to listen to others who started from a different position. We need to consider every attachment, every value, with our whole attention; for we do not know the future, we can never be certain of what may enrich it; we can only, now, listen to and consider whatever may be offered and take up what we can. (ibid.: 320–1)

The common culture is something like a collective open-ended conversation with an emphasis on the willingness to listen rather than speak in the first place, but how could that be achieved?

A couple of years after the publication of *Culture and Society*, Williams gave a public lecture on 'Communications and Community' which provides a clear and helpful gloss on the issues rather more obscurely under consideration in the book. He starts with the observation that it is impossible to discuss communication or culture without coming up against the question of power and goes on to consider the play of power in three different forms of institutionalized communication: authoritarian, paternal and commercial. Authoritarian institutions of communication are to be found in many countries notably, though Williams does not actually say so, the Soviet bloc. In Britain, the paternal and commercial systems, represented on one hand by the BBC and on the other by the daily press and the then very new system of commercial television, are dominant. There is a fourth alternative, a democratic system of communication, which does not yet exist but is essential if the present paternal/commercial system is to be surpassed. Communication is something that belongs to the whole society and depends on the maximum participation by individuals in the society. But for that to happen 'we have to think of ways which would disperse the control of communications and truly open the channels of participation' (Williams, [1961] 1989: 30). It is partly about making the means of expression available to people so that they can express themselves. Today PCs, the Internet, digital cameras and the blogosphere facilitate this: in the 1960s, Williams saw the typewriter and paint brushes as the means to self-expression. But individual ownership of the means of production is impossible in the case of newspapers, radio, television or film production. So Williams advocates the creation of public trusts which would give all kinds of independent producers access to the means of artistic and cultural production. This general policy of decentralization, within public ownership where necessary, would ensure that the creative producers (not advertisers, or capitalist owners) were in control of the production process and its end products.[17]

At the heart of Williams' concern with communication is the conviction that it is not a secondary matter. In complex modern societies, with an advanced transport and communication infrastructure, communication comes to the fore as a matter of primary concern for it is a primary means to any such society's own self-recognition and self-understanding. The relations between people in a society – how they regard each other, what things they think important, what things they choose to stress, what things they choose to omit – can be most clearly and easily seen by looking at their language and their formal communication systems. Religious institutions, institutions of information, sometimes of command, institutions of persuasion, institutions of art – all these communication systems and in much the same way are right at the centre of what it feels to be a member of a complex modern society:

> We cannot think of it as marginal; or as something that happens after reality has occurred. Because it is through our communication systems that the reality of ourselves, the reality of our society, forms and is interpreted ... How people speak to each other, what conventions they have as to what is important and what is not, how they express these in institutions by which they keep in touch: these things are central. They are central to individuals and central to society. Of course in a complicated society like ours, it is very easy to lose sight of this, and to discuss the press, or television, or broadcasting, as an isolated thing ... [I]n the end, we are looking at the communication systems not just to make points against them, but to see in a new way what sort of relationships we have in this complicated society, which way these relationships are going, what is their possible future. (Williams, [1961] 1989: 22–3)

The lecture is a call for a theory of communication in order to have some idea of how it relates to community and to society, some idea of what kinds of communication systems we now have and what they tell us about our society and its future direction. And this entails a process of necessary theoretical abstraction

---

17 This argument was set out in much more detail in *Britain in the Sixties: Communications*, published a little later (Williams, 1962).

without which the concrete, the immediate detail, remains for ever a close-up scene which you cannot really interpret and you cannot really change (ibid.: 20). In 'Culture is ordinary', Williams declared: 'I believe the central problem of our society, in the coming half century, is the use of our new resources to make a good common culture' (ibid.: 10). Those resources that the post-war abundant economy had begun to provide included new means of communication through which to make good the common culture. While fully aware of all the dangers and obstacles in the way of its realization, especially the suffocating realities of social class, what shines through the conclusions to *Culture and Society* is its hope for the future and its faith in the possibility of the full realization of the meaning of democracy, a true equality of being for all members of society. For that to happen, something like true communication between people is necessary: a willingness to listen and to learn from others in open conversation. Communication is the means and end of a genuinely common culture.

References

Agee, J. and Evans, W. ([1939] 1975) *Let Us Now Praise Famous Men*. London: Peter Evans.

Anderson, P. (1969) 'Components of the national culture', in A. Cockburn and R. Blackburn (eds) *Student Power*. Harmondsworth: Penguin Special in association with New Left Review, pp. 214–84.

Anderson, P. (1980) *Arguments within English Marxism*. London: Verso.

Annan, N. (1955) 'The intellectual anstocracy', in J.H. Plumb (ed.), *Studies in Social History*. London: Longmans.

Corner, J. (1991) 'Studying culture: reflections and assessments: an interview with Richard Hoggart', *Media Culture and Society*, 13(2): 137–52 (reprinted in the 1992 edition of *The Uses of Literacy*).

Doyle, B. (1981) 'Some uses of English: Denys Thompson and the development of English in secondary schools', *Stencilled Occasional Paper 64*. Birmingham: Centre for Contemporary Cultural Studies, the University of Birmingham.

Doyle, B. (1989) *English and Englishness*. London: Routledge.

Dreyfus, H.L. (1991) *Being-in-the-World*. Cambridge, MA: The MIT Press.

Giddens, A. (1984) *The Constitution of Society*. Cambridge: Polity Press.

Goldthorpe, J.H. (1969) *The Affluent Worker in the Class Structure*. Cambridge: Cambridge University Press.

Heidegger, M. ([1927] 1962) *Being and Time*. Oxford: Blackwell.

Hoggart, R. ([1957] 1992) *The Uses of Literacy*. Harmondsworth: Penguin Books.

Leavis, F.R. ([1930] 1978) 'Mass civilization and minority culture', in *Education and the University: A Sketch for an English School*. Cambridge: Cambridge University Press.

Leavis, F.R. ([1948] 1966) *The Great Tradition*. Harmondsworth: Penguin Books.

Leavis, F.R. and Thompson, D. (1932) *Culture and Environment*. London: Chatto and Windus.

Leavis, Q.D. ([1932] 2000) *Fiction and the Reading Public*. London: Pimlico.

Lynd, R. and Lynd, H. (1929) *Middletown: A Study in American Culture*. London: Constable.

Mackenzie, N. (ed.) (1958) *Convictions*. London: McGibbon and Gee.

Marcuse, H. ([1937] 1968) 'The affirmative character of culture', in H. Marcuse, *Negations*. London: Allen Lane, pp. 88–133.

McKillop, I. (1995) *F.R. Leavis: A Life in Criticism*. Harmondsworth: Penguin Books.

Newbolt, Sir H. (1928) 'The idea of an English Association', in *The English Association*. Pamphlet No. 70. Oxford: Oxford University Press.

Orwell, G. ([1937] 1965) *The Road to Wigan Pier*. London: Heinneman Education.

Sampson, G. (1921) *English for the English*. Cambridge: Cambridge University Press.

Sharpe, J. (1992) 'History from below', in P. Burke (ed.), *New Perspectives in Historical Writing*. Cambridge: Polity press.

Taylor, A.J.P. (1975) *English History, 1914–1945*. Harmondsworth: Pelican Books.

Thompson, E.P. (1962) *The Making of the English Working Class*. Harmondsworth: Pelican Books.

Thompson, E.P. (1978) *The Poverty of Theory*. London: Merlin Press.

Williams, R. ([1958a] 1962) *Culture and Society*. Harmondsworth: Penguin Books.

Williams, R. ([1958b] 1989) *Resources of Hope*. London: Verso.

Williams, R. ([1961] 1989) *The Long Revolution*. Harmondsworth: Penguin Books

Williams, R. (1962) *Britain in the Sixties: Communications*. Harmondsworth: Penguin Books.

Communication and technology

Innis, McLuhan
Canada, 1950s–1960s

In the late 1940s, Harold Adams Innis, a Canadian economic historian, developed a distinctive approach to technologies of communication. His ideas were taken up, extended and popularized by a younger colleague at the University of Toronto, Marshall McLuhan, who achieved international fame in the 1960s. The issue of technologies of communication is embedded in the larger 'question concerning technology' (Heidegger, [1949] 1978). Technology is, in a basic sense, as old as mankind, when understood as an applied practice, especially in the form of mechanical appliances that serve some practical human end. Modern technology is usually understood as the application of power machinery to production; steam power in the nineteenth century, electrical and atomic power in the twentieth century. Technological take-off is triggered by the transition from craft production (dependent on human input) to mass production and reproduction in which the process appears to be dominated by machines; an early example being the transition from the hand-press to the steam-press in the nineteenth century and the emergence of the modern daily newspaper industry. The question of modern technology is intimately linked to industrialization and mass production. Its relevance to the study of communication began to emerge from

Harold Innis

Harold Innis's early work on the history of Canada's economic staples in the nineteenth century; fur, fishing and timber.

History and communication

Innis's doctoral thesis was a historical geography of the Canadian Pacific railroad that linked the country's western and eastern seaboards. In the course of his studies, Innis discovered that the railroad overlaid the routes of the old fur trade and this led to his engagement with the staples of the Canadian economy in the eighteenth and nineteenth centuries; not just fur, but also fish, timber and wood pulp. Innis's major work of economic history was his brilliant, definitive study of *The Fur Trade in Canada* (1930) which adumbrated some of the key themes of his later historical work on communication. What drove the Canadian economy, Innis argued, were not purely indigenous factors. The fur trade of the eighteenth and nineteenth centuries was driven by fashion in Europe, with Canada providing the pelts of beavers for the felt hat trade in France and England. At issue was the political geography of space. Canada was geographically and politically peripheral to Europe and the United States. Innis's study was, in part, a challenge to the then well-known and still influential 'frontier hypothesis' of Frederick Jackson Turner who, in a famous paper on 'The significance of the frontier' presented to the American Historical Association in 1893, had argued against the then prevailing interpretation of American history as largely determined by its Eastern seaboard and Europe. Arguing for a historically situated geography, which emphasized the role of the common people as much as political elites, Turner claimed that the expansion westward was decisive in shaping American history. The frontier spirit of self-reliance, independence and self-governing local communities forged the unique character of American democracy (Breisach, 1994: 313–15).

As a Canadian, looking at the United States across the 49th parallel, Innis cast a cold eye on the isolationist and self-gratifying implications of the Turner thesis which placed 'the source of inspiration and action not at the centre but at the periphery of Western culture'. As James Carey, the best and most sympathetic commentator on Innis, puts it:

> Every frontier, in short, has a back tier. The 'back tier' interest was determined by the extent to which the frontier products strengthened its economy, supplemented rather than competed with its products, and enhanced its strategic position. The first back tier was Europe, and to that extent North American economic and communications development was part of the trajectory of European history. The development of [North America] was decisively determined by the policies and struggles of European capitals. The consequences of those policies and struggles were outlined in [Innis's] studies of staples: fur, fish, timber and so on. With the gradual decline of the influence of Europe, the back tier shifted to the North American metropolitan centres – both Canadian and American – but effective control shifted toward New York and Washington relative to both Canadian and American frontiers. (1992: 151)

A pivotal study of paper manufacture began to bring together the key themes that would turn Innis, in his later years, to a full-scale engagement with communication.

In this study, Innis discovered the true Canadian double bind (ibid.: 159). The United States imported the raw materials of printing from its neighbour. It then exported back into Canada the finished products; newspapers, books, magazines and, above all, advertising. In the spirit of free trade the United States imported Canadian raw goods and, in the name of freedom of information, transformed them into cultural commodities which it then exported back to its peripheral neighbour. Implicated in this, Carey argues (ibid.: 151), was the germ of the 'media imperialism' thesis whereby America exerted a cultural hegemony through the export of commodities that embodied the American 'good life' and through the global circulation of its cultural goods (film, television, popular music).

Carey's study of Innis shows how his detailed historical work on Canada began to converge on the economic and political implications of transport and communication. A growing concern with the management and control of space, the political and economic geography of power, would lead to the works for which he is best known outside of Canadian studies; the book-length study of *Empire and Communication* (1950) and the posthumous collection of essays called *The Bias of Communication* (1951). Both adopt a distinctively oracular mode of expression, and show a fondness for sweeping generalizations asserted as flat statements of apparent fact. The kind of history that they represent, though recognized and accepted then, has long since fallen out of fashion with little chance, today, of a comeback. 'Empire' and 'civilization' – keywords in Innis's writings – were part of the lexicon of historians half a century ago. The rise and fall of empires (or civilizations or cultures) were ways of trying to grapple with 'universal' or 'world history'. This venerable project had its origins in the philosophy of Hegel, in whose cosmic vision, the history of the world was an as yet unfinished process whereby *Geist* (the Universal Spirit of Humanity) struggled to achieve its self-realization. In this world-historical process, civilizations achieved a certain degree of development (self-realization) only to be undermined by internal contradictions leading to their supercession by another civilization , which resolved those contradictions only to generate new contradictions which, of course, give rise to further conflict and so on. It was a secular narrative of History as Progress that, for Hegel, was completed by the creation of the Prussian State. Marx produced a famous variation on the Hegelian dialectic in which history would finally resolve all its contradictions when world communism was established.

In the first half of the last century the project of writing universal history was still influential in Europe and America, the best-known example being Arnold Toynbee's massive multi-volume *Study of History* (1934–39) which essayed a history of the world initially in terms of the rise and fall of civilizations and, later, of religions. In his introduction to *Empire and Communication* Innis positioned himself in this tradition: 'Spengler, Toynbee, Kroeber, Sorokin and others have produced works designed to throw light on the causes of the rise and fall of civilizations,[1] which have

---

1 For a brief, clear summary of this moment in twentieth-century historiography, see Breisach (1994: 394–403).

reflected an intense interest in the possible future of our own civilization ... [I am] concerned not only with civilisation but also with empire' (Innis, 1950: 1).

Toynbee's 'bias toward religion' led him, in Innis's view, to neglect problems of space, administration and law (Innis, 1951: 34). These factors, crucial to understanding the real workings of enduring forms of empire and civilization, were very largely dependent on efficient communication (Innis, 1950: 3–7).

The essays collected in *The Bias of Communication* are largely summaries, with variations, of *Empire and Communication*. 'Minerva's owl', the first chapter of *The Bias of Communication*, gets from the ancient empires of Babylon and Mesopotamia to the Industrial Revolution and the *Communist Manifesto* in just over 20 pages. 'The problem of Space', an essay of similar length, covers the same vast time span and hops about all over the place from the Near East to the United States. It is hard, now, to read this kind of writing. It no longer seems like *real* history, especially when compared with the rich detail and specificity of the earlier studies of the fur trade and the cod industry, which were based on a wealth of primary historical data and first-hand experience.[2] The studies in communication on the other hand were based wholly on secondary sources. They are best seen as a kind of 'overview' of history whose abstract and general character is rooted in the concrete particularities of the earlier work. They have, moreover, a particular politics. As R.W. Winks puts it, in his Foreword to the 1969 edition of *The Fur Trade in Canada*:

> The last seven years of his life saw a notable change in his scholarly interests. Devoted to Canada and to Canadian history, worried that Canada's survival as a separate political entity on the North American continent was threatened by the wave of popular or mass culture sweeping in from the United States, Innis turned more and more to broad questions relating to communications, language and time-space relations. (Innis [1930] 1999: xxvii)

Today, a number of adjustments are necessary in order to appreciate the originality and power of Innis's innovative historical approach to communication.

The bias of communication

A fundamental constraint on the scope of human actions is imposed by the temporal and spatial characteristics of our available resources for movement and communication with each other. What are the implications of such constraints for the character of human societies? What if a society like that only has speech

---

2 In 1924, Innis bought a canoe (the original means of transport for getting the furs to the Hudson Bay Company) and paddled up the remote Mackenzie River in northern Canada to observe for himself the last surviving region of the fur trade.

as its available means of communication? Innis's answer was that such societies are necessarily spatially (geographically) small in scale. They may be nomadic or pastoral (they may move about or remain in one place) but, since their shared spoken language is what makes them what they are and holds them together, the size of their community is restricted by its face-to-face character. The group's social memory – its knowledge in the present of 'how and what and when' to do things as derived from past practices – is orally transmitted in a spoken tradition that is passed on from one generation to the next.

Systems of writing, Innis argued, developed as means of coordinating and controlling human activities across extended time and space. Writing is a system of record: a way of putting things down so that information can be transmitted through space over great distances, and preserved through time as a record of what was said and done. Innis draws attention to the different materials used for writing, and the ways they affect the scope and character and purposes of the messages they record. Messages carved with a chisel on heavy, durable materials – such as slate, granite or marble – have a monumental character that endures through deep, or slow time. Messages written on light-weight materials such as papyrus or paper (invented in China and available in Europe, via the Moors, from the thirteenth century) are portable and easily carried over great distances.

Different media, using different materials, have different consequences for the control of time and space. Innis called this the *bias* of communication. He noted the importance of written technologies for the establishment and maintenance of empires – the creation of power blocs spread over great distances and preserved through many generations. Writing, in its primary functions, has always been linked to religious, political and economic power. Wherever writing has established itself, it has immediately produced a fundamental distinction between the lettered and the unlettered, the educated and uneducated. To have the skills of reading and writing is a passport to individual self-advancement. Literacy gives rise to educated elites (in the past, they were priests; today they are academics) that gravitate to the centres of power.

Thus, for Innis, the most basic historical distinction in terms of communication is between oral and literate cultures. It is set out clearly enough in *Empire and Civilisation* in the successive chapters on Greek civilization and the Roman Empire. The civilization of the Greeks is underpinned by the 'oral tradition', while Roman imperialism is underpinned by writing. This distinction is strongly normative. Oral cultures are praised for their power and vitality, their freshness and elasticity, in contrast with 'the dead hand of the written tradition' that threatens to destroy the spirit of Western man (Innis, 1950: 70). It is scarcely possible, we are told, for generations disciplined in the written and printed tradition to appreciate the oral tradition (ibid.: 8–9). The vitality and energy of the Greek city–state 'reflects the power of the spoken word'. Socrates' attack on writing in the *Phaedrus* is approvingly cited.[3] The cut and thrust of open debate in the Athenian *agora* and in face-to-face philosophic discussion are instances of the power and persistence of oral culture as is the importance, in Greek civilization, of music, poetry and theatre.

Greek culture was, of course, permeated by writing, but not dominated by it. In particular, the simplicity and flexibility of the Greek alphabet (an enduring contribution to the preservation and dissemination of knowledge in its widest sense) checked the tendency for writing systems to become 'monopolies of knowledge' controlled by highly specialized professions, the priests and scribes who manage the production of texts and the education necessary for them to be understood (ibid.: 79). The domination of writing was checked by the Greek preference for open discussion and argument which was possible only within the small-scale political geography of the city–state. Rome, too, began as a city–state but, as its empire grew, its civilized, civic, republican culture was superseded by the rise of the emperors and the concentration of imperial power in their hands. Roman imperial rule was massively centralized, legalized, bureaucratized and militarized. And all this was, of necessity, underpinned by efficient means of transport and communication. The codification of law, the development of administrative records, the maintenance of military links between the imperial centre and its far-flung outposts, all depended on roads and ships, on parchment, papyrus and writing; the technological staples of transport and communication.

Innis, then, proposed a novel thesis about world history and the transformations of empires and civilizations. The formation of stable societies, which endured in time over many generations, was in part determined by their available forms of transport and communication. The movement of *Geist* in history was replaced by the movement of goods and peoples, ideas and information. Transport and its technologies were always emphasized by Innis, from the use of the horse and chariot in battle in ancient Babylon to the use of dogs and sleds in nineteenth-century-Canada.[4] The mobility of people, of messages and goods was always driven by material economic and political considerations which, at the most general level, were concerned with the management of time and space. While time and space are intricately and integrally interconnected, they are separated out by different technologies of communication with a bias towards one or the other. Media technologies tend to create monopolies of knowledge and power. Time-biased media tend to underpin religious power, and space-biased media underpin political power. The materiality of the medium through which communication takes place and information is recorded, stored and circulated, must always be attended to in

---

3 For a fascinating discussion of Socrates' famous attack on writing, see Peters (1999: 36–51).

4 In summer, the furs were moved to market by river transport but in winter, with the rivers frozen, dogs and sleds were used. Winter was the best time to kill beaver since their coats were then much glossier, and so more valuable, than their summer coats.

the first place, not its contents. The most fundamental line of division, in respect of communication in world history, was the result of technologies of writing, which split the world into non-literate and literate cultures.

Innis had encountered non-literate cultures at first hand since the indigenous peoples of Canada were an important part of his study of the fur trade. The Indians, in their contact with the frontier whites from Europe, were drawn into their business. With guns to replace their spears they became efficient killers of beaver, and with the money they earned, they purchased commodities and the alien culture that went with them. Innis regarded the arrival of the Europeans as a disaster for the indigenous peoples of North America and their ways of life. For Innis, the difference between oral and written cultures – which in McLuhan and later authors is reduced to a textual distinction – was a live, historical reality. Within the long world historic development and circulation of systems of writing and their materials, the most decisive event was the invention of printing. Any new technology creates disturbances in the existing culture:

> The effect of the discovery of printing was evident in the savage religious wars of the sixteenth and seventeenth centuries. Application of power to communication industries [i.e. the shift from the hand-press to the steam-powered press] hastened the consolidation of vernaculars, the rise of nationalism, revolution, and new outbreaks of savagery in the twentieth century. (Innis, 1951: 29)

Modern western civilization is profoundly disrupted and disruptive. It is obsessed with the noise and speed of space and indifferent to the slow and silent music of time. It has shattered the delicate sensory balance of eye and ear. Innis, who was wounded at Vimy Ridge in the First World War and deeply appalled by the Second World War, noted grimly that 'stability which characterised certain periods in earlier civilisations is not the obvious character of this civilisation. Each civilisation has its own methods of suicide' (Innis, 1951: 141).

Gutenberg's galaxy

Harold Innis suffered that peculiarly ironic fate of being eclipsed by an admirer whose fame (or notoriety) overshadowed him. His key concerns and ideas were taken up and transformed by Marshall McLuhan, a fellow Canadian who, in his lifetime, became perhaps the first academic media celebrity. And appropriately so, for it was McLuhan who ushered in the age of *the media,* a term and an object of enquiry that he established, and whose prophet he became. Innis and McLuhan are of different generations and, in respect of their common concern, inhabited different worlds of communication. Innis's working life stretched from the 1920s to the end of the 1940s, McLuhan's from the 1950s to the end of the 1970s. Their lives overlapped at the point where Innis's was coming to an end and McLuhan's career was beginning to get in gear. Innis had been concerned almost wholly with oral and written forms of communication. He carved world history into pre- and post-literate eras. In the era of European history since the fall of the Roman Empire he drew a dividing line between pre-sixteenth-century manuscript culture and the print culture of modern Europe that culminated in the development of the steam-powered printing press in the nineteenth century and the spread of daily newspapers. For Innis, 'new media' meant cinema and radio and he paid them scant attention. Television had only just appeared on the horizon. McLuhan was the first to engage with the global significance of the then very new medium. He saw himself as the interpreter of a new age of communication; from the first age of oral cultures to the second age of written and print cultures to the beginnings of the third age of global, electronic communication.

Marshall McLuhan

It is hard for us today to realize that the familiar communicative infrastructure of the world that we inhabit extends back in time not much more than half a century. The wired home, with all its plug-in electric goods and appliances, began in the 1930s and then only for affluent urban dwellers. In Britain, before the Second World War, most urban households were wired only for low power lighting (large parts of the countryside were still without electricity) and the only electric appliance in the great majority of homes was the radio set that either plugged into a light socket or ran on wet-cell batteries that needed periodically to be recharged. Not until after the war, with the long economic upturn of Western economies, did most households begin to acquire the diversity and range of electric goods that we all take for granted today. Electric washing machines (and driers), fridges, cookers and television sets began to be common possessions in the 1950s.[5] The newly wired post-war world found its John the Baptist in the engagingly eccentric personality of Marshall McLuhan, whose two linked books, *The Gutenberg Galaxy* (1962) and its sequel, *Understanding Media (1964)*, made him internationally famous not just in the academic world, but also in the worlds of business and media.

McLuhan thought of *The Gutenberg Galaxy* as 'a footnote to the observations of Innis on the subject of the psychic and social consequences, first of writing and

---

5 McLuhan was not fond of labour-saving devices in the home and only purchased a vacuum cleaner in the early 1950s to stop his wife borrowing a neighbour's. He hated cars and avoided driving as much as possible (Marchand, 1998: 178, 86).

then of printing' (McLuhan, 1964: ix). It is a book that defies description and summary. It consists very largely of lengthy quotations from nearly 200 authors surrounded by McLuhan's own thoughts which sometimes connected with the cited text and sometimes not. McLuhan was an avid but hasty reader. In the 1950s, he read, on average, five books a day and his method of dealing with them was to start at page 69 and scan it and the table of contents. If they contained useful information or ideas, then it was probably worth reading. He would then go through, reading only the right-hand pages because all books were too long and repetitious (Marchand, 1998: 138, 164–5). He copied down relevant quotations onto index cards and filed them away. To put together *The Gutenberg Galaxy* he spent three months rummaging through 20 years of accumulated index cards and annotating them with his own ideas. The book, which is 280 pages long, lacks the usual academic organization and structure. It is broken down into 261 sections each headed by an epigrammatic summary, which might or might not have a direct bearing on what followed. One Toronto reviewer described it as 'the writing of a mad jackdaw'. There was, however, a method in it, and a clue to how to read it was provided after the Table of Contents:

> The present book develops a mosaic or field approach to its problems. Such a mosaic image of numerous data and quotations in evidence offers the only practical means of revealing causal operations in history. The alternative procedure would be to offer a series of views of fixed relationships in pictorial space. Thus the galaxy or constellation of events upon which the present study concentrates is itself a mosaic of perpetually interacting forms that have undergone kaleidoscopic transformations – particularly in our own time. (McLuhan, 1962: 1)

The arrangement of the book – its mosaic or field approach – was its message. It was a meditation on and a critique of the impact of the phonetic alphabet and writing on Western culture particularly after their enormous valorization by Gutenberg's invention of printing with movable type in the late fifteenth century. McLuhan affirmed and elaborated Innis's normative distinction between oral and literate cultures. The spoken word addressed not just the ear, but all the senses simultaneously. Speech was necessarily situated in a field, a rich mosaic of interacting elements, that was all at once intimate and involving. Alphabetic writing decomposed the unity and wholeness of speech. It analytically deconstructed the sounds of words into their minimal component parts and represented each one by a sign or letter. Letters (the signs of sounds) are laid out, from left to right in linear sequences of words and sentences that move across and down the written or printed page. The noisy sensory plurality and richness of speech and oral cultures were reduced to a silent monopoly of the eye. The analytic, ordered sequential character of the Greek and Roman alphabets embodied and encouraged rational, logical, sequential thought and thereby transformed the souls and the societies of Western civilizations. Writing and print encouraged a detached, silent, individualistic and visual orientation to the world.

The discovery of perspective in Renaissance painting depended on a privileged point of view which fixed and displayed the correctly proportioned (i.e. rational) relationship between objects in the same two-dimensional visual field. To obtain this 'proper' perspective, the viewer must stand back and view from a distance. Involvement and engagement – the characteristics of speech and oral cultures – are displaced by the objective, detached and distant contemplative gaze that perspectival painting demands. The rationalization of space in painting coincides with the birth of printing and expresses its characteristic world-view (McLuhan, 1962: 125–8). The mosaic technique deployed by McLuhan is a formal device that he uses to avoid the trap of one-dimensional, abced-minded thinking[6] that is characteristic of Western alphabetic man. *The Gutenberg Galaxy* can be thought of as an avant-garde text designed to escape the limits of equitone prose and linear narrative. In Europe, Umberto Eco and Roland Barthes denounced the tyranny of closed texts which start somewhere and end somewhere, and praised the virtues of open texts which avoided any movement towards narrative closure.[7] *The Gutenberg Galaxy* is just such an open text which the reader can begin anywhere, going forwards or backwards at will. It is a shifting, mazy collideorscope (kaleidoscope) of ideas and bits of information designed to puzzle, amuse, inform, infuriate or illuminate. It is a 'writerly' text (Barthes, 1975) that demands the active engagement of its reader and resists passive consumption. 'My consumers, are they not my producers?' McLuhan asks, with a one-liner filleted from *Finnegan's Wake*, at the very end of the book.

Speech and writing are the basic communicative resources of academics who, after all, make a living (or try to) from both. McLuhan wonderfully embodied the contradictions between orality and literacy. He had an immoderate love of talk and was unstoppable once started. He was an indefatigable collector of puns, aphorisms and jokes, which he filed for use in his lectures and innumerable public speaking engagements. He enchanted student audiences. At heart, he was an ideas man, a producer of a never-ending flow of insights packaged as one-liners that, at best, were illuminating and brilliant and, at worst, absurd or outrageous. The story is told of the occasion when, still largely unknown, he was invited to present his ideas to the Sociology Department at the University of Chicago in the early 1950s. The audience included Robert Merton, then the doyen of social-scientific mass communication research in the United States. By

---

6 A Joycean pun from *Finnegan's Wake* that McLuhan often used to indicate the literal, sequential, one-thing-at-a-time, absent-minded mentality induced by the alphabet (cf. McLuhan, 1962: 152).

7 See Eco (1989) and Barthes (1975, 1977). James Joyce's *Ulysses* and *Finnegan's Wake* (fruitful sources of inspiration for McLuhan) were paradigm 'open' texts.

the time McLuhan finished, Merton was purple with indignation. He immediately launched into a cross-examination of everything McLuhan had said. Quite unfazed, McLuhan interrupted him: 'You don't like these ideas? I got others' (Marchand, 1998: 142). He was blessedly indifferent to whether he was right or wrong and was never intimidated by facts. He refused to pass critical judgement on the things he wrote about. He avoided debate and argument and, as with Merton, when directly challenged on an idea or fact would simply sidestep by offering another.

The medium is the message

The Gutenberg Galaxy ends thus:

> The new electric galaxy of events has already moved deeply into Gutenberg's galaxy [bringing] trauma and tension to every living person ... Familiar institutions and associations seem at times menacing and malignant. These multiple transformations, which are the normal consequence of introducing new media into any society, need special study and will be the subject of another volume on *Understanding Media* In the world of our time.

The study of the age of print was a herald to the study of the electronic galaxy of contemporary mid-century America. At his publisher's insistence, and to his own annoyance, there was less quotation and more McLuhan in *Understanding Media*. It is less radical, in its form and presentation, than its predecessor, and quite uncluttered with academic apparatuses and jargon. It is addressed more to a general readership than the academic community which, on the whole, reacted with that special mix of envy and malice that it reserves for those who achieve popular success (cf. Meyrowitz, 2003: 201–5). *Understanding Media* sold 100,000 copies and became a must-read for all those who wanted to be in the know. McLuhan became an instant celebrity. He appeared on television on both sides of the Atlantic, gave seminars to the business leaders of corporate America, was interviewed at length for *Playboy* and had a spot appearance, as himself, in Woody Allen's *Annie Hall*. In the new age of cool, McLuhan had become, virtually overnight, the hottest of marketable properties. He was rumoured to command $5,000 a time for his lecturing appearances and, for the first time in his life, needed an accountant to handle his tax returns.

McLuhan is probably the only academic in this academic text to have made it into every dictionary of quotations. He is remembered now for a handful of memorable aphorisms that have achieved proverbial status: 'the global village', 'hot' and 'cool' media and above all, 'the medium is the message' – a defining concept for *Understanding Media*. It is a book which, like its prequel, only needs dipping into, yet it remains important for the handful of really good ideas it offers. The first of which is to think of media as 'the extensions of man', the book's sub-title. This phrase is not a McLuhan original. He picked it up from Edward Hall's, *The Silent Language*, and ran with it. All media may be thought of as tools that extend the range and scope, not only of human activity in time and space but, more crucially, of one or more of our bodily faculties and senses. Clothing extends our skin, the telephone our ear and television our eyes and ears. As such, they not only alter the scale and scope of human activity, but also disturb the existing balance between the senses. If Innis felt we lived in a space-dominated culture, McLuhan felt we lived in a visual culture in which the eye dominated the ear and other senses (especially touch). He insisted that, in trying to understand the effect of media on our senses, we should focus on their formal properties, not their content. The electric light bulb is a classic example. It is pure information. It has no content or, rather, its content is whatever it illuminates. It serves simply to expand the scope of human activity on a colossal scale, but is quite indifferent to whatever particular activity it casts its light upon. It is a medium without a message.

McLuhan was the first analyst of *the* media. It is in his writings that they are first taken together as interrelated technologies that come together to create media societies. A generally positive reviewer of the draft of a 'media' curriculum, written by McLuhan for use in high schools, noted in his comments that 'the term "media" was not in the average teacher's vocabulary and would need to be explained clearly' (Gordon, 1997, cited in Meyrowitz, 2003: 206) Even his critics, at the time, acknowledged that McLuhan had discovered and named something new. As Hans Fredrik Dahl puts it:

> [T]he aggregation of disparate media of communication (newspapers, newsreels, radio, television) into a synthetic whole – 'the media' – is a very recent phenomenon, perhaps coinciding with the rise of television in the early 1960s as *the* dominant information and entertainment medium. Its recognition as an object of academic study is even later. Marshall McLuhan's *Understanding Media* may be one of the first books to treat synthetically different forms of communication under the general rubric of 'the media'. (1994: 553)

This new term indicates a new understanding, one that moves beyond the older concept of 'mass communication' and all its accompanying political, social and cultural baggage. McLuhan constantly stressed that his ideas were exploratory, an invitation to think about the social and psychic implications of a very new and contemporary phenomenon. In the late 1950s, television had only just become the dominant medium of communication in Britain and North America. In most of the world, Europe included, its penetration of daily social life was minimal. It was only in the course of the 1960s that television began to be that pervasively familiar, taken-for-granted everyday experience for everyone that it is now. Forty years ago the technology was primitive. Image resolution was poor and in black and white (though the USA had a vividly unstable colour system). The video-recorder did not exist (though McLuhan anticipated it). Satellite links were 20 years away. At the time, most of the discussion about television was about its negative effects. In the UK, the latest parliamentary enquiry into broadcasting, and the first to report on television, was preoccupied with the trivializing effect of TV on British life and culture (Pilkington Report, 1962). Forty years on, in the USA and the UK, we are still talking about the dumbing down effect of television on contemporary life. McLuhan was distinctive in his refusal to moralize about the media. He preferred to try to understand their impact rather than pass judgement.

The electronic global village

Of all the McLuhanisms, the one with most resonance today is that of the global village, first proclaimed in *The Gutenberg Galaxy*: 'The new electronic interdependence recreates the world in the image of a global village' (McLuhan, 1962: 43). The village emblematically represents pre-modern forms of social life. It is the embodiment of 'tribalism', which is oral and dependent on relations of presence and face-to face, direct communicative relationships with a high degree of involvement. In all these ways it differs from the detribalized, detached ways of life in literate, urban environments. Tribalized cultures privilege the society over its members while de-tribalized cultures fragment the social whole and foreground the single, detached individual. Electronic media retribalize (resocialize) the world into a single global village:

> After three thousand years of explosion, by means of fragmentary and mechanical technolgies, the western world is imploding. During the mechanical ages, we had extended our bodies in space. Today, after more than a century of electric technology, we have extended our central nervous system itself in a global embrace, abolishing both space and time as far as our planet is concerned. Rapidly we approach the final phase of the extensions of man – the technological simulation of consciousness, when the creative process of knowing will be collectively and corporately extended to the whole of human society ...
>
> Western man acquired from the technology of literacy the power to act without reacting ... But our detachment was a posture of non involvement. In the electric age, when our whole nervous system is technologically extended to involve us in the whole of mankind and to incorporate the whole of mankind in us, we necessarily participate, in depth, in the consequences of our every action. (McLuhan, 1964: 3, 4)

Electronic media are, in a singularly apt metaphor, like the neural network of the cerebral cortex; an immensely complex, single structure of interlinking nodes that create, for the first time in history, instant, live connectivity between any two points or more on the globe. The worldwide telephone network that has grown and grown as a single global electronic structure since the late nineteenth century quite clearly delivers this, though its significance even today, in the age of the Internet (which links late twentieth-century with late nineteenth-century technology), is still largely overlooked. McLuhan anticipated the rise of the computer and the global spread of television. What was a distant prospect in the 1960s is a reality today. Each one of us has the world in our living room and the whole world watches sporting and ceremonial events and news stories of global significance (Dayan and Katz, 1992). Television today is intimately linked to global politics, business and war. Through television, cultural narratives, images, songs and jokes circulate round the world. Globalized television displays the *world-historical* character of life today (Giddens, 1990).

By the end of the 1960s, McLuhan was a spent rocket and in the next decade he fell sharply out of fashion, overtaken by new marxisms and structuralisms which took a disparaging view of him as the ideologue of corporate, capitalist America. He died in 1980 and since then has gradually, and increasingly, returned to the bookshelves to influence debates about telecommunications and globalization. The most enduringly significant aspect of the work of Innis and McLuhan has turned out to be their linkage of communication and media to the management of time and space, a theme that has received increasing attention in social theory in the past 20 years.[8] Every generation is obliged to rediscover the world afresh, and imagines that what it encounters is new and unprecedented. Some decades, more than others, are preoccupied with the 'shock of the new'. The rate of technological innovation has some bearing on this. The 1960s was such a moment and McLuhan was its guru. In the 1980s and again in the 1990s, technological innovation in communications contributed to revaluations of contemporary cultural life. McLuhan, 'the forgotten prophet' (Giddens, 1984: 262), was resurrected as the first real analyst of a totally mediatized postmodern world.

In 1985, Joshua Meyrowitz published an influential synthesis of the ideas of what was, on the face of it, a very odd Canadian couple: Marshall McLuhan and Erving Goffman. Meyrowitz was impressed by Goffman's pioneering work on face engagements and relations of presence. At the same time he noted McLuhan's prescient interpretations of electronic media, especially television, and changing social attitudes. He sought to combine them in an analysis which linked the study of

---

8 Harvey (1986) (see pp. 201–326) has been particularly influential, along with Giddens (1990).

face-to-face interactions with the approach to media that McLuhan pioneered. Television transforms 'the situational geography of social life' (Meyrowitz, 1985: 6). It has 'no sense of place'. It undermines the traditional relationship between physical setting and social situation. As television becomes a common resource for all social members, it creates new common knowledges and experiences which reconfigure, for instance, the relationships between parents and children, young and old, between politicians and electorates and between the sexes. Meyrowitz's distinction between place and space was elaborated in Anthony Giddens' widely read essay on *The Consequences of Modernity* (1990). A key characteristic of modernity, Giddens argues, is the separation of time and space. This is a necessary condition for the operation of *disembedding* mechanisms that lift social relations out of their local contexts of interaction and restructure them across indefinite spans of time–space (ibid.: 21). The primacy of place is thereby destroyed:

> Place has become phantasmagoric because the structures by means of which it is constituted are no longer locally organised. The local and the global, in other words, have become inextricably intertwined. Feelings of close attachment to or identification with places still persist. But these are themselves disembedded: they do not just express locally based practices and involvements but are shot through with much more distant influences. (ibid.: 108–9)

The role of technologies of communication in this process of 'cultural globalization' has been crucial. 'They form an essential element of the reflexivity of modernity and of the discontinuities which have torn the modern away from the traditional' (ibid.: 77).[9]

The meaning of modernity was under interrogation in the 1980s, in the light of then current arguments that it had been superseded by postmodernity. Postmodernism, in one respect, was yet another attempt by the Left to come to terms with its wily old foe, Capitalism, and its capacity endlessly to reinvent itself. In the 1920s, Lukács and Gramsci had both taken the emergence of scientific management in the workplace (Taylorism) and its application to mass production (Fordism) as indicative of new (and hard) times. In the 1980s, the Left foresaw *New Times* (Hall and Jacques, 1989) in terms of postFordism and the end of the masses. For more than 50 years, the culture industries and the mass production of consumer goods had seemed to shape the form and content of twentieth-century cultural life. In the social relations of mass production, the supply side (production) was dominant. In the 1980s, it seemed as if the reverse was true, with demand (consumption) driving production. The mass production of standardized goods

---

9 For further analyses of communication and modernity (it is sometimes referred to as 'medium theory'), see Crowley and Mitchell (1994), and Thompson (1995).

rolling off the assembly lines (Fordism) had given way to postFordist modes of production, characterized by product diversity, small-scale (rather than mass) production and flexibility (short rather than long production runs). The old joke – that you could have any Ford you liked so long as it was black – no longer rang true. There was a revolution in the high streets and the supermarkets in the 1980s. A much greater range of goods on the shelves, in a wider range of colours, styles, and so on, and with a much shorter shelf life, heralded the arrival of consumer choice. The customer was king. In the analysis of mass production and its attendant mass culture, consumption was treated in largely negative terms. PostFordism required its revaluation. Consumption was no longer the fate of the manipulated, passive masses who had no option but to 'buy' what the supply side ordained. It became a positive act, a means whereby identities were fashioned and individualities were asserted. The rediscovery of 'the active audience' by media studies in the 1980s is one indicator of the revaluation of consumption. Product diversity stimulated cultural diversity.

From the beginnings of broadcast television, channel scarcity had imposed severe limits on the number of different services available to audiences. In the 1980s, a range of technological innovations began to open up the possibility of a much wider range of viewing options. The video-recorder became a standard consumer good in the course of the decade,[10] and renting movies on video to watch at home became a new domestic leisure option. But two other developments – broadband cable and satellite – were the heralds of a new era in telecommunications. Broadband cable could now deliver, down the wires, interference-free, high quality reception of hundreds of channels. Satellite services, in their infancy in the 1980s, could deliver channels services from all over the world to audiences, while offering broadcasters direct live links from almost anywhere for the coverage of world events and for live feeds into news programmes (Peacock Report 1986: 21–7). These technological innovations began to fulfil McLuhan's vision of the new electronic age that he foresaw way back, as it now seems, in the 1960s. But its final fulfilment surely lies in the developments of the past decade or so: the astonishingly rapid rise of the Internet and the world-wide web.

The introduction to the 30th anniversary edition of *Understanding Media* noted that much of what McLuhan had to say made a good deal more sense in 1994 than it did in 1964.[11] *Wired*, a California-based magazine founded in 1993 to celebrate and proselytize on behalf of cyberspace and its emerging on-line culture, took McLuhan as its patron saint. The convergence of different media in

---

10 Even so, by 1986 only 38 per cent of British households had a video-recorder, and this was noted as one of the highest levels of ownership in the world (Peacock Report 1986: 26). The VCR also allowed for time-shifting (the recording of programmes for later viewing); a neat example of the processes of disembedding and re-embedding discussed by Giddens (1990).

11 Most details in this paragraph are taken from Meyrowitz (2003: 206–7).

hypertext – the combination of sound, still and moving images, and print – and its mosaic design and lay-out (multi-windowed click-on options, moving icons, text, etc.) approximated closely to the style of writing that McLuhan sought to achieve as he commented on and sought to break from the linearity of the Gutenberg Galaxy and the age of print. McLuhan, it is now claimed, thought and wrote in hypertext (Morrison, 2000). Paul Levinson's *Digital McLuhan* provides the fullest exploration of McLuhan as the prophet of the Internet. Sub-titled 'A guide to the information millennium', it aims to prove that 'the underlying accuracy of McLuhan's thinking was not available in his lifetime, but vindicated in the 21st century' (Levinson, 1999: 4). He too notes the similarity between McLuhan's aphoristic, 'packaged' writing and the unrestricted movement of hypertext. The on-line world is the incarnation of what McLuhan foresaw as the global village 'whose centers are everywhere and whose margins are nowhere' (ibid.: 2). Summing up on the contemporary revival of interest in McLuhan,[12] Joshua Meyrowitz makes a similar point. The old critiques of centralized media power and control have less force in today's diversified, decentred global media environment. Digital media have been and are used by minorities to organize international resistance to corporate business interests and national governments, 'thereby supporting McLuhan's notions of electronic media fostering participation, decentralisation and the flattening of hierarchies' (Meyrowitz, 2003: 208).

Do technologies make history?

Mass communication research in North America in the 1950s and 1960s was driven by a concern with the effect of media messages on audiences. Innis and McLuhan shifted attention away from the *content* of media (their message) to their form. The material properties of different media disclosed their communicative characteristics that were oriented to the management of time and space. In the many comparative assessments of their work, a number of contrasting themes stand out. Innis, the historian, produced an economic and political analysis that emphasized the macro-social implications of communication technologies. His analyses were oriented to the past and focused on imperial power and conflict. McLuhan, the literary critic, focused on the impact of media in the contexts of daily life and the ways in which they restructured our perception and experience of the world; a micro-cultural analysis.[13] He looked to the future and his view of the world was essentially harmonious and apolitical. A common

---

12 Further recent revaluations include Meyrowitz (1996), Grosswiler (1998), and Carey (1998).

13 Several contributions to Melody et al. (1981) offer comparative evaluations of Innis and McLuhan. See especially those by Theall (1981), and Crowley (1981).

criticism of both, in the literature, is that of *technological determinism* in their writings. Technological determinism argues that machines make history. The printing press produced the Reformation in sixteenth-century Europe, for instance. And this is a common-sense view; 'People often speak of a new world, a new society, a new phase of history being created by this or that technology: the steam-engine, the automobile, the atomic bomb' (Williams, 1974: 9). Is there some direct cause and effect connection between new technologies and social change? Are technologies the direct agents of social change and, if so, how? R.L. Heilbroner advanced a strong argument along such lines in the late 1960s (reprinted in Smith and Marx, 1994). It was obvious, he claimed, that 'in some sense machines make history', but rather more difficult to say exactly how (ibid.: 54). He quoted Marx (*The Poverty of History*): 'The hand-mill gives you society with the feudal lord; the steam-mill, society with the industrial capitalist.' The technology of a society imposes a determinate pattern on the social relations of that society. A more nuanced variation on the same theme was advanced in Friedrich Kittler's historical study, published in 1986, of *Gramophone, Film, Typewriter*. Kittler took up the basic insights (and style) of McLuhan and reworked them in a postmodern, anti-humanist reading of the ways in which 'Media determine our situation' (Kittler 1999: xxxix). He showed how new communication technologies – the gramophone, for instance – change the ways in which we think of ourselves. Today we are all familiar with the *idea* that human brains are rather like computers. This seems a natural idea to us. A hundred years ago it seemed natural to think of the brain as rather like Edison's phonograph (ibid.: 38–45), an idea that to us now seems bizarre.

Raymond Williams' *Television. Technology and Cultural Form* (1974) offers the most thoughtful and balanced discussion of the question of technological determinism in relation to the impact of television. He notes that there is a range of overlapping 'takes' on the social impact of the then new medium and the commonly held view that it has altered our world. The *deterministic* view treats the development of new technologies as an internal process of scientific invention, that creates new societies (the age of television, for instance) and new social relations. The *symptomatic* view regards technological innovation as the product of already existing social processes. A capitalist economy creates a strong demand for continuing product innovation in order to maintain markets and profits. In either case, Williams suggests, the real problem is that what is flattened out of the accounts is any sense or understanding of human intentionality; of technologies as historically situated, sought-for solutions to perceived needs or demands (Williams, 1974: 10–15). He goes on to a brief account of the historical development of broadcasting technologies, emphasizing the slowness and complexity of the interactions between scientific discoveries and their applications and usage. In a general sense, this process was in response to the growing complexity of modern industrial societies and the organizational problems to which it gave rise. The telegraph and telephone provided instant wired connectivity between agents in distant locations. The limitations of wired connectivity prompted the search for wireless connections, leading to the technologies of wireless telephony or radio. Radio was a technical solution to the kinds of problem identified by Innis in his early historical studies of the movements of economic staples (it was used by the fur trade in the early twentieth century). Williams makes two crucial points. First, that it is a characteristic of communication systems that all were foreseen – not in utopian but in technical ways – before the crucial components of the developed systems had been discovered and refined.[14] Second, these developments were, in the first place, conceived as general solutions to the demand – from business, government and the military – for faster and more efficient connections across greater distances. Their general social and cultural applications were unintended by-products of their initial development for more specific uses in business and warfare. Radio, for instance, was conceived of initially and used as an interactive two-way means of communication. It came into its own in the First World War, as a means of maintaining continuous contact between army headquarters and the fronts. In this usage its broadcast characteristics (i.e. that *anyone* could pick up the signals) were a distinct problem, leading to the encryption of messages to avoid giving information to the enemy. It was only after the war, that the implications of the broadcast character of radio transmissions began to be exploited for general social use. The British Broadcasting Company was established, in 1922, in a deal between the early radio and electronics industry and the government, to provide a general broadcasting service for a then non-existent listening public. 'It is not only that the supply of broadcasting facilities preceded the demand; it is that the means of communication preceded their content' (Williams, 1974: 25).

In recent years, sociology has resumed its interest in science and technology, and technological determinism emerges as its *bête noire* (Hutchby, 2001: 15). After a useful review of the literature, Ian Hutchby advances his own position, namely, that technologies have different *communicative affordances*. The concept is borrowed from the psychologist J.J. Gibson who suggested that human beings (and other species) respond to the things they encounter in their world in terms of their affordances; the possibilities that they offer for action. He argues this both for the natural environment (a tree affords safety, shelter, etc. for different creatures) and for human artefacts. Crucially, affordances are the useful, useable properties of natural and man-made things. They are not determined by the subjective needs of the user, but are rather discoverable features of the things themselves. The usefulness of artefacts is always within a finite range of

---

14 Brian Winston's *Media Technology and Society* (1998) offers a detailed account of the lengthy and uneven processes of scientific invention, technological application, market uptake and social acceptance of 'new' communication technologies (most of which, he insists, are much older than we think). Patrice Flichy (1995) offers a fascinating social history of communication technologies from a French perspective.

relevant applications. In other words, as Innis argued, the materiality of paper, papyrus and stone (as surfaces for the inscription of written messages) has some determinate bearing on the appropriate uses to which each can be put. Hutchby takes a similar view. Communication technologies afford particular kinds of general use, without determining the particular uses to which they may be put by individuals. Telephone technology was not invented so that people could chat to each other. The point is, though, that it *affords* this kind of use and today, 100 years after its invention, is used *inter alia*, by everyone as a sociable resource for keeping in touch with distant family and friends the world over. Hutchby, a conversation analyst, is particularly interested in the kind of talk afforded by the telephone as distinct from the kind of talk afforded by relations of presence. Co-conversants on the phone are not visibly present to each other and this has a bearing on the protocols of telephone conversation and the other things they can and cannot do while involved in phone-talk. The form of the technology has a determinate bearing on the possible uses to which it is put. The actual uses to which is put should be studied with this in mind.

To their various admirers neither Innis nor McLuhan is a technological determinist, though Menahem Blondheim (2003) describes Innis as a 'communications determinist'. Perhaps the real point to determine is the relevance or otherwise of their contribution to our understanding of the relationship between communication, technology and society. Their emphasis on the material forms of the various technologies of communication was novel and, in the context of North American mass communication sociology in the 1950s and 1960s, fresh and original. Their ideas generated interest and research in other disciplines. Anthropologists took up the basic distinction between 'oral' societies and those with written or print-based cultures (Goody, 1968). Elizabeth Eisenstein (1979) explored, in careful detail, the historical transition from manuscript to print cultures in Europe. True, their vatic style and a persistent tendency to reduce the history of the world to different epochs of communication have the effect of evacuating human agency out of the workings of history. Williams was right to insist on the crucial role of human intentionality in the processes of technological innovation. The crux of 'The question concerning technology' is, as Heidegger points out (1978), not a technological matter.[15] McLuhan is surely right to think of technologies as 'extensions of man'. We may agree that technologies are instruments that serve instrumental purposes and, moreover, that actualized technologies seem to produce us as their servo-mechanisms. In a machine

---

15 For Heidegger, technology is both dangerous and redemptive. Either way it is disclosive of the 'essence' of humanity. Modern, scientific technologies, which underpin industrialized capitalist societies, express an instrumental and exploitative attitude to the natural world and other creatures. The domination of nature embodies a destructive, careless attitude to life and the world that is peculiar to modern Western culture. On the other hand, we are compelled to confront this and to discover the redemptive power that technology may afford us.

civilization we tend to conceive of ourselves *as* machines. Descartes thought of himself as a clock (the most advanced example of seventeenth-century technology). Today we think of ourselves as computers, our brains as hard-wired with software inputs. We become what we behold, as McLuhan was fond of saying, and thereby lose sight of the fact that the technologized world is expressive of what we are. It is not just that we are like machines but, equally, that machines are like us. We are called upon to try and think not only what we do with them, but what they do with us. The latter question was first raised, in respect of technologies of communication (communication *as* technology), by the two authors under review in this chapter.

References

Barthes, R. (1975) *S/Z*. London: Jonathan Cape.

Barthes, R. (1977) *Image-Music-Text*. London: Fontana.

Blondheim, M. (2003) 'Harold Adams Innis and his bias of communication', in E.Katz et al. (eds), *Canonic Texts in Media Research*. Cambridge: Polity Press, pp. 156–90.

Breisach, E. (1994) *Historiography*. Chicago: University of Chicago Press.

Carey, J. (1992) 'Space, time and communications: a tribute to Harold Innis', in *Communication as Culture*. London: Routledge, pp. 142–72.

Carey, J. (1998) 'Marshall McLuhan: genealogy and legacy', *Canadian Journal of Communication*, 23(3): 293–306.

Crowley, D. (1981) 'Harold Innis and the modern perspective of communication', in W. H. Melody et al. (eds), *Culture, Communication and Dependency: The Tradition of Harold Innis*. New Jersey: Ablex, pp. 235–46.

Crowley, D. and Mitchell, D. (1994) *Communication Theory Today*. Cambridge: Polity Press.

Dahl, H.F. (1994) 'The pursuit of media history', *Media, Culture & Society* 16(4): 551–64.

Dayan, D. and Katz, E. (1992) *Media Events*. Cambridge, MA: Harvard University Press.

Eco, U. (1989) *The Open Work*. Cambridge, MA: Harvard University Press.

Eisenstein, E. (1979) *The Printing Press as an Agent of Change: Communication and Cultural Transformation in Early Modern Europe*, 2 vols. Cambridge: Cambridge University Press.

Flichy, P. (1995) *Dynamics of Modern Communication: The Shaping and Impact of New Communication Technologies*. London: Sage.

Giddens, A. (1984) *The Constitution of Society*. Cambridge: Polity Press.

Giddens, A. (1990) *The Consequences of Modernity*. Cambridge: Polity Press.

Goody, J. (1968) *Literacy in Traditional Societies*. Cambridge: Cambridge University Press.

Gordon, W.T. (1997) *Marshall McLuhan: Escape into Understanding*. New York: Basic Books.

Grosswiler, P. (1998) *The Method is the Message: Rethinking McLuhan through Critical Theory*. Montreal: Black Rose.

Hall, E. (1969) *The Silent Language*. New York: Doubleday.

Hall, S. and Jacques, M. (1989) *New Times*. London: Lawrence & Wishart.

Harvey, D. (1986) *The Condition of Postmodernity*. Cambridge: Polity.

Heidegger, M. ([1949] 1978) 'The question concerning technology' in D.F. Krell (ed.), *Basic Writings,* London: Routledge, pp. 311–41.

Heilbroner, R.L. (1994) 'Do machines make history?', in M.R. Smith and L. Marx (eds), *Does Technology Drive History?: The Dilemmas of Technological Determinism.* Cambridge, MA: MIT Press.

Hutchby, I. (2001) *Conversation and Technology.* Cambridge: Polity Press.

Innis, H. ([1930] 1999) *The Fur Trade in Canada,* with new Introduction by A.J. Ray. Toronto: University of Toronto Press.

Innis, H. (1950) *Empire and Communication.* Oxford: Oxford University Press.

Innis, H. ([1951] 1964) *The Bias of Communication,* with Introduction by M. McLuhan. Toronto: University of Toronto Press.

Kittler, F. ([1986] 1999) *Gramophone, Film, Typewriter.* Stanford, CA: Stanford University Press.

Levinson, P. (1999) *Digital McLuhan: A Guide to the Information Millennium.* New York: Routledge.

Marchand, P. (1998) *Marshall McLuhan: The Medium and the Messenger.* Cambridge, MA: MIT Press.

McLuhan, M. (1962) *The Gutenberg Galaxy: The Making of Typographic Man.* Toronto: University of Toronto Press

McLuhan, M. ([1964] 1995) *Understanding Media: The Extensions of Man.* London: Routledge.

Melody, W.H. et al. (eds) (1981) *Culture, Communication and Dependency: The Tradition of Harold Innis.* New Jersey: Ablex.

Meyrowitz, J. (1985) *No Sense of Place: The Impact of Electronic Media on Social Behaviour.* New York: Oxford University Press.

Meyrowitz, J. (1996) 'Taking McLuhan and "Medium Theory" seriously', in *Technology and the Future of Schooling*, 95th Yearbook, National Society for the Study of Education. Chicago: University of Chicago Press, pp. 73–110.

Meyrowitz, J. (2003) 'Canonic anti-text: Marshall McLuhan's *Understanding Media*', in E. Katz et al. *(eds) Canonic Texts in Media Research.* Cambridge: Polity Press, pp. 156–99.

Morrison, J. (2000) 'No prophet without honour', in *New Dimensions in Communication,* 13: 1–28. Proceedings of the 57th Annual Conference of the New York State Communication Association, Monticello, New York.

Peacock Report (1986) *Report of the Committee on Financing the BBC.* Cmnd. 9284. London: HMSO.

Peters, J.D. (1999) *Speaking into the Air: A History of the Idea of Communication.* Chicago: University of Chicago Press.

Pilkington Report (1962) *Report of the Broadcasting Committee.* Cmnd. 1753. London: HMSO.

Smith, M.R. and Marx, L. (eds) (1994) *Does Technology Drive History? The Dilemmas of Technological Determinism.* Cambridge, MA: MIT Press.

Theall, D.I. (1981) 'Explorations in communication since Innis', in W.H. Melody et al. (eds), *Culture, Communication and Dependency: The Tradition of Harold Innis,* New Jersey: Ablex, pp. 225–34.

Thompson, J.B. (1995) *The Media and Modernity.* Cambridge: Polity Press.

Williams, R. (1974) *Television: Technology and Cultural Form.* London: Fontana.

Communication as interaction

Goffman and Garfinkel
USA, 1950s–1970s

Introduction

Sociology's domain of enquiry is 'the social', but how that was understood has varied since its emergence as a distinct academic discipline in the late nineteenth century. Classic sociology (usually understood in terms of the 'founding fathers' – Marx, Weber and Durkheim) was largely concerned with the social as *society*, and society thought of on a large scale; mass society or society-as-nation differentiated into its economic, political and socio-cultural structures. 'Class', 'the state', 'capitalism' were key concepts. This view of the social permeated the world-view of the Frankfurt School and of American mass communication research. It is sometimes called macro sociology. It emphasizes large-scale impersonal social forces, perceived as structures that impose upon and dominate the lives of individual members. How the social world is perceived, at any time, is always in part the product of the historical pressures of those times which affect academic perceptions as much, and in exactly the same way, as ordinary, common-sense perceptions. It is a striking historical fact that perceptions of the world in the second half of the twentieth century underwent a significant change of focus, a change that appears after the Second World War across a range of separate academic fields of enquiry. In Chapter 4 I reviewed the emergence, in post-war Britain, of a radical reconceptualization of 'culture'; a shift away from a socially exclusive conception of culture as high art, towards a more inclusive understanding of culture as 'ordinary', as a 'whole way of life'. In this chapter, I examine a new kind of sociology that engaged with mundane social life, social actors and their interactions. It developed in America in the 1950s and its two key figures were Erving Goffman and Harold Garfinkel. Although their terms of engagement are very different from the contemporary British pioneers of cultural studies, the core concern, with ordinary social life and ordinary social members, is the same. Goffman and Garfinkel re-specify 'the social' in the same way that Williams and Hoggart re-specify 'the cultural', and at the very same time. For all of them the object of enquiry was what Hoggart called 'the real world of people'.

The interactive order

Erving Goffman

Erving Goffman's work, as many commentators have noted, is difficult to summarize.[1] It is partly to do with his style and method, in part, with a conflicting attitude to his main theme, and in part, to do with a certain fuzziness around some of his key concepts. Goffman's writings are certainly consistent in their subject matter. They represent a continuing engagement, for over 30 years, with the theme announced by his most famous book, *The Presentation of Self in Everyday Life*. His studies of the self in interaction with others appear to be quite concrete and grounded in empirical data. There is little in the way of theoretical discussion and a seeming wealth of descriptive data. The writing is almost always clear and elegant. Goffman is renowned for his laconic style and mordant turn of phrase. Yet on closer inspection the accounts of everyday phenomena turn out to be impressionistic. Data are drawn from diverse sources – from etiquette books, biographies and novels, for instance – but little is provided, in any exact detail, from his own fieldwork.[2] Data are occasionally invented, particularly to provide examples of talk that support the point he wishes to make, a practice that scandalized Emanuel Schegloff (1988). Although there is considerable overlap within the concerns of each of his published books and from one to another, there is little sense of a growing, cumulative understanding or knowledge generated by them. An often voiced objection to his approach to interaction is that it is episodic. There is no sense of temporal depth to his writing, which may account for that 'flatness' and lack of texture detected by Giddens (1987: 138).

---

1 For overviews of Goffman, see Drew and Wootton (1988), Giddens (1986), Manning (1992), Branaman (1997), Lemart (1997). For Atkinson and Housely (2003), Goffmann is a pivotal figure in the sociology of interaction and the Chicago tradition.

2 Goffman did extensive fieldwork, in 1949, in a Shetland Island community (the basis of his unpublished PhD, and often mentioned in *The Presentation of Self in Everyday Life*, which was first published by the Edinburgh University Press). In the mid-1950s he received a grant from the National Institute of Mental Health to do research at St Elizabeth's Hospital in Washington, DC, where he spent some time in 1955 in the assumed role of assistant to the athletic director; a 'front' which allowed him free access to all parts of the hospital without drawing attention to himself (Manning, 1992 106–7). His observations form the basis of *Asylums* – one of his most important works – but it contains no systematic account of the workings of the hospital, nor any first-hand data drawn from any of the inmates, staff or patients.

More problematic is Goffman's view of 'the self', which is a core concern in all his writing. For some, Goffman's attitude is 'machiavellian', 'cynical' or 'amoral'. More sympathetic critics draw attention to Goffman's work on the tact, sympathy and understanding that are shown by others when an individual suffers loss of face in a social gathering. His brilliant observations on the phenomenon of 'civil inattention' are invoked to redress what Garfinkel calls Goffman's 'naughty' view of the self. In fact, there are two versions of the self on offer in Goffman's writings, and the tensions between them remain unresolved. There is, on the one hand, a hidden self that is both defensive and aggressive and, on the other, a precious, sacred self. The former is very much in evidence in *The Presentation of Self in Everyday Life*, whose focal concern is with 'the arts of impression management' (1959: 203–30). Here the individual's concern, in social situations, is with maintaining a front. The underlying, and much discussed, metaphor that runs through the whole book is that of social life as theatre, the dramaturgy of everyday existence. A striking theatrical metaphor deployed to great effect, is that of front stage and backstage regions in daily life; places and occasions in which the individual is or is not 'on display' and subject to the scrutiny and potential criticism of others. Front stage situations call for care in the projection of a managed self-performance. An example might be, for teachers, the classroom. In backstage regions (the school staff room, for instance) an individual can relax. There is no need to maintain a front, and things can be said and done that would be inappropriate in front stage regions. It is one of Goffman's key insights that the self – whatever it might be – is not some innate and given thing (it is not an identity), but rather something that is enacted and performed. What then becomes crucial is the question that immediately arises from this, namely the relation between performer and performance. 'There is no art To find the mind's construction in the face' says Duncan of the treacherous Thane of Cawdor (*Macbeth*, Act 1, Sc. 4). Nor is there in Goffman's presentation of the self–in-everyday-life. The arts of impression management give an account of a possibly hostile or defensive, certainly manipulative, self that hides behind the performed, projected self that it gives out to others. It is this 'two-faced' self that gives rise to accusations of cynicism and amorality (e.g. Macintyre, 1981: 32, 115–17).

A rather different account of the self emerges in *Asylums*. The book is about total institutions – Goffman's striking term for places such as prisons, army barracks or mental hospitals (but also convents, monasteries and boarding schools) – and the fate of their inmates. But in the Introduction he makes clear that 'a chief concern is to develop a sociological version of the *structure* of the self' (1961: 11. Emphasis added). It is a characteristic strategy of Goffman to try to establish the characteristics of the self obliquely, via 'a perspective of incongruity'. Thus what happens to individuals, on entering total institutions, is the systematic destruction of their former 'civilian self'. Goffman calls this the mortification of the self, and he means it literally. Those who enter total institutions undergo 'civil death'. A compelling picture is built up of the ruthless stripping away of the everyday self which we all take so much for granted. Total institutions are so by their total control over the inmates, a point underlined by Michel Foucault's study of the surveillance regime imposed in the modern penal system (Foucault, 1979).[3] Goffman sketches in the methods whereby the supports and territories of the self are removed in total institutions. Names are replaced by numbers; civilian clothing by an institutional uniform; hair may be cropped and the personal possessions and small paraphernalia of the self, that make up an individual's identity kit, are removed. Inmates lead a 'batch' existence in which they are always in a group of some kind and never alone. They sleep in dormitories or shared cells. Bathrooms and toilets are either open or cannot be locked. There are no spaces in which to be alone to be oneself. Total institutions are 'forcing houses for changing persons; each is a natural experiment on what can be done to the self' (1961: 22).[4]

All this amounts to a 'defilement', a 'defacement' – a systematic series of 'abasements, degradations, humiliations, and profanations' – of self (ibid.: 24). It goes to show, via its systematic destruction, whereof the structure of the civilian, everyday self consists. What begins to emerge is a sense of the individual as a sacred object. Sacred objects are entitled to due respect and consideration from others. Only sacred objects can be ritually profaned or desecrated. A sense of the self as sacred, with positive and negative attributes, underpins the ways in which Goffman thinks of *face*: 'one's face ... is a sacred thing, and the expressive order required to sustain it is therefore a ritual one' (Goffman, [1968] 1972: 19). This key concept is derived from Emile Durkheim, for whom 'The human personality is a sacred thing; one dare not violate it nor infringe its bounds,[5] while at the same time the greatest good is in communion with others' (ibid.: 73). When individuals are in the presence of others, they are under solemn and mutually binding obligations to maintain each other's face. In relations of presence, what now begins to come into play is what Goffman means by *the interactive order*, the phrase he used, shortly before his death, to encapsulate his self-understanding of his life's work. I wish to interpret this phrase as implicating a re-specification of the nature and character of human communication; communication as interaction.

---

3 'Reading Goffman on "total institutions" can be more instructive than reading Foucault', in the view of Anthony Giddens. See Giddens (1984: 153–8) for a very useful comparison of them both.

4 For a discussion of the reality programme, *Big Brother*, as a television experiment in batch living, see *Television and the Meaning of 'live'* (Scannell, forthcoming).

5 This is what Goffman means by the 'territories of the self' or '"the circles of the self" which persons draw around themselves' (1963a: 42); a zone of exclusion around the body of the person which none may enter without express permission. These territorial inshore waters are routinely violated by the authorities in total institutions (Goffman, [1961] 1968: 32). The passage quoted here by Goffman is from Durkheim's *Elementary Forms of Religious Life*.

Civil inattention

From start to finish, Goffman's work is about human communication. His doctoral thesis was called 'Communication in an island community' (1953), and his last major work was *Forms of Talk* (1981). How communication works – how people communicate with each other – remained a matter of abiding interest in all his writings. A key perception is of interaction as a determinate and determining structure which, when entered into, must be maintained by all the participants. But what exactly is it that is being maintained? It is the nature of the occasion, the situation itself and its *situational proprieties*. Goffman wrote in his Introduction to *Interaction Rituals*:

> I assume that the proper study of interaction is not the individual and his psychology, but rather the syntactical relations among the acts of different persons mutually present to one another ... Not, then, men and their moments, rather, moments and their men. ([1968] 1972: 2–3).

In public places, whenever others are present, individual behaviours are determinate responses to the requirements of the moment and what it demands of them. One crucial determinant of behaviours is the mutual awareness of being in the presence of others.

This awareness is *always* something that must be communicated. It must be shown to others, somehow or other, in ways that others will recognize as intentional. The phenomenon of 'civil inattention' is exemplary in this respect. The possibility of being in public with others, who we do not know, without anxiety or fear – a central theme of *Behaviour in Public Places* (1963b) – is a long, historical and still incomplete process. It is foundational for the kind of world which we, in fact, inhabit, since our world, of necessity, throws all of us into contact with strangers on a daily basis. If we are to accomplish the myriad small tasks and interactions of daily life we *must* be able to be in the presence of strangers, to deal with them, to interact with them without it being an issue, a problem, a source of anxiety, fear or hostility. This is what Goffman draws our attention to as the phenomenon of civil inattention:

> In performing this courtesy the eyes of the looker may pass over the eyes of the other, but no 'recognition' is typically allowed. Where the courtesy is performed between two persons passing on the street, civil inattention may take the special form of eyeing the other up to approximately eight feet, during which sides of the street are apportioned by gesture, and then casting the eyes down as the other passes – a kind of dimming of lights. In any case, we have here what is perhaps the slightest of interpersonal rituals, yet one that constantly regulates the social intercourse of persons in our society.

By according civil inattention, the individual implies that he has no reason to suspect the intentions of the others present and no reason to fear the others, to be hostile to them, or wish to avoid them. (At the same time, in extending this courtesy he automatically opens himself up to like treatment from others present.) This demonstrates that he has nothing to fear or avoid in being seen and being seen seeing, and that he is not ashamed of himself or of the place and company in which he finds himself. (Goffman, 1963b: 84)

Civil inattention contributes to freeing up the very possibility of a *civil* society in which being in the presence of others in open public spaces without fear or threat is generally and mutually allowed. It presupposes a general equality of being insofar as anyone may expect to be treated with civil inattention by anyone else.

A characteristic procedure of Goffman, as in *Asylums*, is to establish what is 'normal' via apophatic definition (a theological technique for producing a description of God by saying what He is not). Thus, if civil inattention is the norm, the question for Goffman becomes, 'To whom does the norm not extend?' Who gets stared at in public places? Who feels threatened by their being in public? His work on those who, one way or another, experience social stigma indicates clearly that civil inattention is not a universal experience (Goffman, 1963b). He points particularly to 'the "hate stare" that a Southern white sometimes gratuitously gives to Negroes walking past him' (ibid.: 83). At the time he was writing, the civil rights movement in the USA had only recently begun and it was triggered precisely by the demand for the right to civil inattention and thereby to be treated as an ordinary person 'like anyone else'.[6] Civil inattention gives the possibility of being-with-others *in public*. Without it, the ontology of the social (of being with others) collapses, for the world is, first and last, a public matter and it matters that it is, as such, freely and publicly available to all and in the same way.

The sociology of the self

Goffman often stresses that he is concerned with the sociology of the self, not its psychology. A psychology of the self is concerned with what makes an individual tick: with how it sees things (a cognitive psychology of perception) and how it experiences things (a psychology of emotions). The individual has

---

6 The trigger for the civil rights movement is usually taken to be the day that Rosa Parks refused, having been ordered to do so by the driver, to give up her seat to a white passenger on a bus in Montgomery, Alabama, on 1 December 1955. She was arrested and fined for her refusal. Parks was later acclaimed as the inspiration of all that followed and has achieved immortal fame for her simple, yet radical claim to be allowed to be herself in public, like anyone else.

psychological 'needs' which it needs to satisfy. Goffman's starting point is not the psychology of the individual but what is required of individuals for them to be social actors in interaction with one another. At stake is the question as to the necessary conditions, the requirements of social life. How is it possible? What is required of individuals and their actions for there to be such a thing as social interaction? The concept of face is one answer to the question. The psychology of the individual presupposes it as an autonomous, free-standing agent independent of others. But face is not a psychological attribute, since the individual is not the lord and owner of its face. An individual's face is 'on loan' from society and it can be withdrawn (Goffman, 1963b: 10). It may seem, to any individual, as if their face is somehow their own, essential self, but it is not a personal possession. It is something achieved, realized and maintained (or not) in interaction with others. This is what Goffman calls *face work* and he regards it as 'a condition of interaction, not its objective' (ibid.: 12). The mutually binding task of face maintenance in any social situation is the means whereby individual participants display their awareness of others. In so doing, they acknowledge that they are accountable to each other. This accountability is, in essence, a moral matter – a point not emphasized so much by Goffman, but crucial for Garfinkel.

If social interaction were no more than a power struggle in which individuals pursued their own ends to their own advantage, then others would appear to be no more than potential threats or supports in the way of, or on the way to the realization of individual objectives. Something of this view is pervasively present in Goffman's thinking. He frequently draws attention to the stratagems of con-men, tricksters, panhandlers and others out to gull the gullible. Commentators have often pointed to his fascination with gambling (he did fieldwork in the casinos of Las Vegas) and, in 'Where the action is', he attempted to promote 'a casino vocabulary for the analysis of everyday life (Manning, 1992: 66). More specifically, he was interested in game theory as developed by Thomas Schelling in *The Strategy of Conflict* (1960) and applied it in some of his writings, notably *Strategic Interactions* (1969) – the result of a year's sabbatical spent at Harvard with Schelling (Manning, 1992: 61).

The Strategy of Conflict, written at the height of the Cold War, concerns the game of conflict management between the two superpowers. Schelling identifies three different kinds of game. The zero-sum game (pure conflict), whose objective is total victory, has, as its antithesis, co-ordination games in which conflict is to be avoided at all costs. Somewhere between these two extremes are mixed-motive games in which players must reconcile zero-sum ambitions (winner takes all) with the possibility of cooperative actions to achieve advantages (Manning, 1992: 62). Underpinning all variants is strategic (rational) self-interest as the motivation of the players. Two different strategies underpin the play of such games: one of suspicion, the other of trust. In zero-sum games, trust is suicidal and in pursuit of winning, deception and concealment are necessary tactics. For co-ordination games trust is an unavoidable prerequisite. Schelling was grently impressed by Goffman's analysis of face-work (first published in 1955) and declared that it contained 'a rich game-theoretic content' (1960: 128). Likewise there was much for Goffman in Schelling's game-theory since for both of them life appeared to be a mixed-motive game that oscillated between conflict and cooperation, war and peace; one on the grand terrain of international politics, the other on the more mundane stage of daily life.

Face engagements

Nevertheless daily social life, at least in modern middle-class democracies such as mid-century America, requires co-operation as its pre-condition. Perhaps Goffman's most important contribution to our understanding of communication is to treat it always as an occasion, a situation of some kind, into which individuals enter and, in so doing, commit themselves to the nature of the occasion and its situational proprieties (i.e. what the nature of the occasion requires of them). The physical characteristics of the places in which people come in contact with each other mark out the boundaries of the scope of interaction. Elevators, for instance, elicit civil inattention from those who ride in them. There is a strong emphasis on the embodied character of communication. What is communicated in interaction is always much more richly textured than the sum of what is said in it. In 'focused gatherings', wherein individuals are not merely in the presence of others but present to each other for some common, focal purpose, a number of initial transformations are required whereby those entering the situation align themselves to it and its proper concerns. Thus individuals may be required to adjust their *expressive idiom* – the information they give out about themselves through their bodily appearance and dress – if the situation they are entering demands it. In adjusting one's expressive idiom to the situation one indicates a willingness to adopt a demeanour and disposition that are fitting to the situation and which enable one to fit into it. An inappropriate expressive idiom will always be remarkable and may give rise to difficulties, including rejection and expulsion in extreme cases (as children are sometimes sent home for wearing the wrong clothes to school).

This liminal process is a commitment to *involvement*, an engagement with the situation, an obligation to maintain the nature of the occasion. More precisely, Goffman thinks of focused interaction as 'a face engagement or encounter' (Goffman, 1963b: 89). He is extraordinarily perceptive about this process whose very familiarity masks its delicate complexity. In particular, and at all points, he draws our attention to how communication, for it to happen must be communicated. i.e. signalled and recognized as having been signalled. Involvement must be communicated, a willingness to communicate must be communicated (as also of course its opposite, unwillingness), a recognition of the others in the interaction – all this is work of some kind that must not only be done but must be seen to be done and acknowledged as having been done. Thus face engagements begin with an exchange of looks and glances, with the establishment of eye contact. This is the human face, that wonderfully expressive instrument, at work. Eyes, voice and body posture communicate an individual's orientation, positively or negatively, to the situation. In the course of the interaction participants must show and maintain their accessibility to others. They must avoid lapsing into auto-involvements or signs of inattention. Any occasion, for it to be such, must be structured. It must start, it must go on, it must end and all this must be accomplished. There are ritual procedures for engaging with, maintaining and, at some point, disengaging from the situation.

The moral basis of interaction

I have noted how Goffman often seeks to establish the structures of the ordinary self of every life by looking at individuals who have been stripped of their civilian self (prisoners, mental patients, soldiers) or those whose identity is somehow spoiled and for whom the management of 'self' is essentially problematic (*Stigma*, 1963a). Harold Garfinkel proceeds in a similar manner, as we shall see.[7] However, whereas Goffman seems to use a perspective of incongruity as a useful methodological device, for Garfinkel it is much more than this. It is indicative both of the difficulties that arise when investigating mundane existence and, at the same time, disclosive of what it consists of. The focal concern of Garfinkel is not the everyday self, but the everyday *world*:

> In every discipline, humanistic or scientific, the familiar, common-sense world of everyday life is a matter of abiding interest. In the social sciences, and in sociology particularly, it is a matter of essential preoccupation. It makes up sociology's problematic subject matter, enters the very constitution of the sociological attitude, and exercises an odd an obstinated sovereignty over sociologists' claims to an adequate explanation. (Garfinkel, [1967] 1984: 36)

And yet, in spite of its centrality, and although sociologists take socially structured scenes of everyday life as a point of departure, they rarely see, as an object of enquiry in its own right, the fundamental question 'of how any such common sense world is possible' (Garfinkel, 1967: 36). The general blindness to sociology's core question – namely, what are the conditions of the social *as such*? – arises from the difficulty in penetrating the massively obvious and taken-for-granted character of the mundane world in order to discover what it is that produces it *as* the mundane world with such mundane characteristics.

---

7 The best introduction to Garfinkel is Heritage (1984).

Harold Garfinkel

The mundane world is a common world, a world-in-common. This does not at all imply that its members have the same views or opinions about it, for a common world does not depend upon shared value systems, agreements or beliefs. People with quite different, even radically opposed religious or political beliefs can, and indeed do, live in the same world and go about their mundane business and interact with each other. What then are the necessary conditions of such a world, and how might one hope to discover them? Given that the mundane world, for it to be such, must be essentially unproblematic for its members, Garfinkel found ways of rendering the routine character of daily life problematic in his celebrated series of *breaching experiments*. He would ask his students to perform small tasks, in their ordinary encounters with others (family, friends, acquaintances), that appeared innocently to throw a spanner in the works. The best known of these required the students, in the course of an ordinary conversation, to treat a perfectly intelligible remark by the other person as if they did not understand it and to ask for an explanation:

Case 1
The subject (S) tells the experimenter (E) what happened on her way to work.

S: I had a flat tire
E: What do you mean, you had a flat tyre?
S: (stunned) What do you mean 'What do you mean?'?
    A flat tyre is a flat tyre (.) that is what I meant (.) nothing special.
    What a crazy question

Case 3
S and E, husband and wife, are watching television in the evening.

S: I'm tired.
E: How are you tired? Physically, mentally, or just bored?
S: I don't know. I guess physically, mainly
E: You mean your muscles ache, or your bones?
S: I guess so (.) don't be so technical
    (later on)
S: All these old movies have the same kind of old iron bed-stead in them
E: What do you mean? Do you mean all old movies or just the ones you have seen?
S: What's the matter with you (.) you know what I mean
E: I wish you would be more specific

S: You know what I mean. Drop dead.

Case 6
The victim waved his hand cheerily.

S: How are you?
E: How am I in regard to what? My health, my finances, my school work,
      my peace of mind –
S: (*Red in the face and suddenly out of control*) Look! I was just trying
      to be polite. Frankly I don't give a damn how you are!
(Garfinkel, 1967: 42–4. Examples slightly modified)

In these and other cases the responses of the victims to the request to explain themselves are remarkably consistent. First, they do not treat it as reasonable. Nor do they allow that what they said was in any way problematic. They take it be the case that what they said was perfectly clear and understandable. And they are all of them angered by the request, producing – very quickly – hostile responses to the experimenter. What is it that angers them? It is not, we might note, that the requests for clarification are treated by the victims as a threat to their face. It is not Goffman's ritual order that is somehow perceived as threatened. It is rather the conditions of the intelligibility of the world that are being undermined by a threat to the possibility of meaningful interaction. Conversational interaction presupposes common understandings of what is said and meant and these common understandings are not merely embedded features of language, but of the world if it is a world-in-common. If everyday common-sense remarks are challenged in this way, then the common-sense world begins to unravel very quickly. Suppose this procedure were consistently applied, i.e. that perfectly obvious utterances are treated as essentially strange. It is evident that conversation almost immediately becomes impossible, for they can never advance beyond the opening utterance. If it were possible to clarify what one meant by 'how are you?', this would be followed up by requests, for further clarification of the explanations which would be followed by further requests, and so on; a vicious spiral of vanishing meaning from which there is no way back. Thus what is at stake is the possibility of a meaningful world in the face of a radical scepticism that wilfully refuses to acknowledge and accept it as such.

This begins to account for the righteous indignation of the victims. It is righteous because they *know* they are right. A flat tyre *is* a flat tyre in whatever language it is said. 'What do you mean "What do you mean?"?' is the right and proper response to an unwarrantable (unjustifiable) question. It is unwarrantable because it is quite clear what a flat tyre is, hence the force of turning the question back on the questioner: 'What do *you* mean (justify yourself)? It is unaccountable because it is unreasonable – 'are you crazy?'. Why would anyone ask such a question? It might make sense if the questioner was a child or was learning the language and wanted to know what 'flat' or 'tyre' meant (but that is not the case). Maybe they misheard (but that is not implied in the form of the question). The question is strictly without reason or justification.[8] As such, it is irrational or unjust and therefore either mad or malicious or possibly – and one or two of the victims treated it in this way – some weird kind of game.

Implicated in the responses is an anger that is directed against unreasonable and unjustifiable behaviours. Participants in talk – in any kind of interaction – must produce warrantable (justifiable) and accountable (reasonable) behaviours. The pre-condition of a common social world is the accountability (to each other) of social actors. In this fundamental sense, the everyday world is a morality. All of us know and understand this; that we are accountable to others for our actions and others, for their part, are reciprocally accountable to us, as and when necessary. Goffman may think of social life as a game or a play, but Garfinkel finds it to be more serious than this. We have an unavoidable moral commitment to maintain not, in the first place, our own face or those of others, nor even the nature of the occasion and its ritual requirements. Both presuppose the always already existing known and taken for granted world in which all of us find ourselves to be. Social interaction, any time, any place, presupposes and draws upon the existing common human world and each time re-enacts and re-creates it. Something of this essentially awesome fact is disclosed by Garfinkel's breaching experiments.

The biography of the self

'A society's members encounter and know the moral order as perceivedly normal courses of action – familiar scenes of everyday affairs, the world of daily life known in common with others and with others taken for granted' (Garfinkel, 1967: 35). The breaching experiments show that morality is as much a sociological as a religious or philosophical concern. Morality is, in the first place, neither a matter of rules and regulations imposed by external authority, nor a procedure whereby social actors come to agree upon and offer their consent to the rules. It is earlier than any institutionally formulated regulations or any consensual process of establishing agreed social norms. Minimally it is a structural necessity for the possibility of a common world. It presupposes human actors (if they are to be *social* actors) as mutually accountable for the

---

8 Reason and justification are closely linked but not the same. One may have reasons for an action but they may not be good enough (i.e. they lack justification). In other words, justification is the means whereby actions can be defended (justified) as reasonable. Unreasonable behaviours are so because no account can be offered to justify them.

---

conduct of social life which thereby produces and maintains a reasonable (ratio-nal) world. Morality, as accountability, is an embedded feature of the existing world and of social interaction within it. It presupposes *trust*. It is that trust in the ordinary apparent world (the world as it appears, the world *of* appearances) that is violated by the breaching experiments. This world *must* be taken for granted for human interaction to be able to happen. To act as if it could not be so regarded is to put the world in doubt. The force of this revelation is demon-strated again, by Garfinkel, in his celebrated case study of 'Agnes', an inter-sexed person whose sexed status was unsettled and, as such, presented her with fundamental problems in the management of her self.

Agnes appeared at the Los Angeles Department of Psychiatry of the University of California (UCLA) in 1958, referred there by her doctor, as a 19-year-old woman with male genitalia. In her accounts, she was born and grew up as a boy but, around the age of 17 she changed into her real, female self. She wished to convince the medical department of the university that she was, really and truly female, in order to have an operation which would remove her male genitalia and supply her with a vagina, thereby establishing her credentials as a fully and properly sexed female and putting her, as she saw it, to rights. Garfinkel, as a sociologist, was part of the team assembled to examine Agnes' claims in order to decide whether or not to proceed with what she wished, namely a surgical rearrangement of her sexuality. What fascinated Garfinkel was the extent to which what for the vast majority of people is effortlessly accomplished – namely, the management of a sexed identity – was a continuously 'demonic' problem for Agnes. When in the company of those who did not know her secret (i.e. 'normal' sexed persons), she had, continually, to maintain her self-presentation and 'pass' as a young woman. In the presence of the very much smaller group of people who did know her secret (her family, boyfriend, the team at UCLA), she had to persuade them that she was, *really*, female and her male genitalia were a natural (biological) mistake. In either case she had to manage being female, but each called for rather different performances.

Garfinkel's presentation and discussion of Agnes are in part an engaged cri-tique of Goffman's study of the self in everyday life, especially in relation to social stigma. The same terminology is used: 'normals' to describe ordinary social members from the stigmatized person's point of view and 'passing' to describe the task of concealing the discreditable facts of self when in the com-pany of normals (Goffman, [1963a] 1968: 15, 58). Garfinkel agrees that Agnes' dilemma, in relation to those who do and those who don't know her secret, could be considered as a classic case of the art of impression management. 'We would have to agree with Goffman that ... she was a highly accomplished liar and that, as it is in the society produced by Goffman's dissembling members, lying provided for Agnes and her partners conservative effects for the stable features of their socially structured interactions' (Garfinkel, 1967: 174). But, Garfinkel argues, it is not the case that ordinary social members proceed in these ways and Agnes does so only because she has to, in order to make the best of her situation (i.e. in order to be treated as a normal social member):

> Agnes treated with deliberateness, calculation and express management (i.e. in the manner that Goffman would like every one of his informants to confess, if his mode of analysis is to be counted correct) matters that members[9] a) not only take under trust, but b) require of each other, for their mutual judgements of normality, reasonableness, understanding, rationality, and legitimacy, that they treat in a trusting and trusted manner, and c) require of each other that evidences of trust be furnished whenever deliberateness, calculation and express management are used in managing problems of daily life. Agnes would have wanted to act in this trusting fashion *but routine as a condition for the effective, calculated and deliberate management of practical circumstances was, for Agnes, specifically problematic.* (Garfinkel, 1967: 174–5. Emphasis in the original)

Agnes, like the breaching experiments, serves to show yet again that ordinarily and for the most part everyday life is, and must be, taken at face value by ordinary members. The morality of the everyday world is underpinned by a trusting attitude which makes it possible. That trust is not some kind of pious hope, not an optimistic wager. It is not without reason or warrant. It is an effect of the *routine* character of the everyday world. Day in, day out, the normality of the world is renewed by its appearance as the self-same known and familiar, seen but unnoticed, taken-for-granted world that it was yesterday and the day before and will be tomorrow and tomorrow. And so it is with persons. Routinization, as Anthony Giddens has pointed out, is the basis of ontological security for the members of a common world (Giddens, 1984: 60–78), and routine is the one thing Agnes finds that she lacks; not merely routines for her performance 'as a girl' in any particular situation, but a past, a biography that she can routinely draw upon in any set of circumstances. How to do 'being a girl' (or boy) is dependent upon know-how drawn from the accumulated reservoir of past experience which may be relevantly applied in any present circumstances or future course of action. Goffman's 'naughty' view has no grasp of the management of self as something outside a particular situation, as a continuing, unrelenting matter that goes on in time, for a life-time, in fact.

The actors in a drama, or the players in a game, can and do, in the end, walk away from the parts they played. Role distance – the gap between the player

---

9 'Members' and 'membership' are important terms for Garfinkel (and Harvey Sacks). They indicate that individuals do not stand outside of society and somehow negotiate a way in. To the contrary, individuals are always *in* a society of some sort and as such are members, willy-nilly. The terminology represents a particular resolution of the individual/society dichotomy. It avoids thinking of society as an aggregate of individuals.

and their performance – is thrown into relief precisely by this fact. But, and this is Garfinkel's key perception, it is not like this in the continuing ongoing circumstances of everyday life for ordinary social members. There is no 'time out' from the parts we play (except in play). We are all of us called upon to enact, and indeed are committed to, our self-enactments as a case of the real thing. We are called upon to play ourselves 'to the life' – not just now and then or when we feel like it but for as long as we live. Agnes would have liked to be able to do this, and thereby get herself a life, for her peculiar problem was that she had no accumulated life as a girl upon which to draw. She lacked a biography and thus confronted the same existential difficulty as the replicants in *Blade Runner*. Garfinkel documents, with great perceptiveness, Agnes's 'secret apprenticeship', the ways in which she learned how to *be* a young woman (1967: 146–64). A recurring difficulty, for instance, in the company of her room mates and wider circle of girl friends, was knowing how to do girl talk – the usual gossip, analyses of men, parties and dating post-mortems – which crucially depended on a store of past experiences. 'Can you imagine', she said to Garfinkel, 'all the blank years I have to fill in?' (1967: 147–8):

> The troublesome feature encountered over and over again is the cloudy and little-known role that time plays in structuring the biography and prospects of present situations over the course of the action as a function of the action itself. It is not sufficient to say that Agnes' situations are played out over time, nor is it at all sufficient to regard this time as clock time. There is as well the 'inner time' of recollection, remembrance, anticipation, expectancy. Every attempt to handle Agnes' 'management devices' while disregarding this time, does well enough as long as the occasions are episodic in their formal structure; and all of Goffman's analyses either take episodes for illustration, or turn the situations that his scheme analyses into episodic ones. But strategic analyses fail whenever these events are not episodic. (ibid.: 166–7)

Life, in other words, as it stretches out along an individual's time line, is not a game that is susceptible to a strategic analysis, whether that of the individual or the sociologist.

Ethnomethods

Agnes serves, in exemplary fashion, to illustrate the project of *ethnomethodology*, which is a *logos* (discourse) about the methods, the practical courses of action, whereby 'ethnos' (ordinary social members) deal with the world and the circumstances in which they find themselves to be with others. There are two crucial aspects to this process. First, attention is focused on the sense-making skills of social actors, singly, and in interaction with each other. This process of 'making sense' is neither before nor after an action or interaction of some kind. That the world and its circumstances do 'in fact' make sense (for the interactants and any observant third party) is an achieved and accomplished effect of the interaction in action, as it unfolds from moment to moment in any situation. The intelligibility of the everyday world is produced as a self-explicating phenomenon by all those concerned, whether or not as observed by any third party. The third party, in *Studies in Ethnomethodology*, is, of course, the sociologist; the sociologist who set his sociology students the task of making trouble in mundane situations and who taped 36 hours of conversation with Agnes. The second crucial matter for Garfinkel is the nature of the relationship between sociology and its object domain, society. Ethnomethodology presents itself as a new way of doing sociology and, at the same time, as a critique of the 'dominant sociology' of its day.

Harold Garfinkel joined the newly established Department of Social Relations at Harvard in 1946, chaired by Talcott Parsons. Parsons was, by then, one of the most influential sociologists in the United States. Since the 1930s, he had advocated the importance of systematic theory construction in the social sciences when they were, on the whole, concerned with piecemeal empirical research. In *The Structure of Social Action* (1937), Parsons had insisted that theoretical development was the hallmark of science (Heritage, 1984: 5). The establishment of the Department of Social Relations represented a radical departure from the established patterns of research in American sociology. Its recognition and encouragement of theoretical work as a legitimate form of research in its own right proved a powerful attraction to a post-war generation of research students of whom Garfinkel was one.

Any detailed account of the Parsonian theory of action is beyond the scope and concerns of this book,[10] but it was hugely influential. Anthony Giddens, in the introduction to his own major work of social theory, *The Constitution of Society* (1984), begins by acknowledging that *The Structure of Social Action* was 'a key work in the formation of modern sociology ... It set up an approach to social theory of a very definite type, combining a sophisticated version of functionalism and a naturalistic conception of sociology' (Giddens, 1984: xiv). That a modern society such as the USA functions (works) appears self-evident. The question is, how so? A functionalist sociology assumes that social order and stability are the result of the systematic reproduction, through time, of large-scale institutional structures (the state, the economy) whose continued existence requires the adjustment of individuals in ways that are functional for (that reproduce) those

---

10 On Talcott Parsons, see Turner (1999), and Habermas (1987: 199–301). See Heritage (1984: 6–36) for a Parsonian background to Garfinkel.

structures. Structures are privileged over individuals (agents) whose behaviours are functional for the 'needs' of social systems. But how to account for this process of individual adjustment to the system? Parsons' view of the individual is a naturalistic one: it assumes that, in a state of nature, individuals pursue their own interests which bring them into conflict with other individuals who are also in pursuit of their own interests. From such a perspective, the question of social order is essentially problematic. What makes individuals act in ways that uphold rather than undermine a stable social order, that produce peace rather than war? Parsons resolved the problem by proposing that individuals internalize the norms of the system in ways that make their actions functional for its smooth and effective working. The production of 'value consensus' and of 'symbolic order' were key considerations for Parsons and his followers.

Giddens' theory of structuration, introduced in *The Constitution of Society*, is an explicit attempt at 'a radical break' with Parsonian social theory. Structuration theory's core concern is with 'the understanding of agency and of social institutions' (Giddens, 1984: xvii). The key issues are to do with 'the nature of human action and the acting self; with how interaction should be conceptualised and its relation to institutions; and with grasping the practical connotations of social actions' (ibid.: xvi–xvii). The break with Parsons focused on the question of agency, of actors and their actions. The effect of Parsonian theory was to reduce the human actor to being 'a cultural dope'. It privileged society as a mysteriously self-replicating system with socialized social members as its effect. Giddens wishes to stress the active role of human beings as knowledgeable actors in the routine production of the mundane human social world. Goffman and Garfinkel were vital sources of inspiration for his theory of structuration.

Garfinkel, in particular, was concerned with the problems to which academic theorizing gave rise for our understanding of human society, and in particular with the ways in which 'models of man in society portray him as a judgmental dope' ([1967] 1984: 66). The-man-in-the-sociologist's-society is a dope who produces the stable features of society by acting in compliance with pre-established and legitimate alternative courses of action that the common culture provides (ibid.: 68). In such a 'model' there is no acknowledgement by the sociologist of any active, knowledgeable, practical contribution by the individual to the production of those stable features. The constitution of society has nothing to do with the actions of its members. Rather, their behaviours are perceived as standardized responses that are predetermined, within a prescribed range of possibilities, by the culture. Such models of social theory are teleological. In effect, the outcome of social action is known in advance by the sociologist who then uses it as an explanation of the action. An action (a) is explained in terms of its outcome (b), an inversion of causality which normally regards the outcome (b) as the result of the action (a). If sociologists predefine the question of social order as a 'need' or aim of the institutions that make up the social order, then they are likely to interpret individual behaviours as determined in advance by the requirements of the system. There is, of course, the problem as to how such external constraints are internalized by the individual. Hence to the sociological dope produced as the man in the sociologist's society, Garfinkel adds the psychological dope produced by the man in the psychologist's society whose behaviours are determined by 'psychiatric biography, conditioning history and the variables of mental functioning' (ibid.: 68).

A core commitment of ethnomethodology is to the point of view of the laity[11] and a concern with such phenomena as 'social order' (i.e. the orderly character of social life) as the outcome of practical, matter-of-fact, reasonable (account-able) and responsible (justifiable) courses of action and interaction of social members. From this perspective, social order is not some essentially strange external constraint imposed upon individuals by the requirements of the social system. It is rather an outcome, an achieved and accomplished matter of fact that is matter-of-factly produced by individuals in and through their ordinary dealings with one another. How this is achieved is not something to be treated as if known in advance. It precisely states what has to be investigated in order to begin to see *how* it is achieved, how the outcome is eventually arrived at in and through the unfolding course of the interaction itself. One primary site for the investigation of this process came to be the study of talk; ordinary, every-day conversation.

Talk as interaction

The discovery of talk as an object of legitimate enquiry is one of the major achievements of Anglo-American philosophy, sociology and linguistics in the second half of the past century. The so-called 'linguistic turn' in the social sci-ences should, more exactly, be seen as the discovery of talk as an object of enquiry, as something that could, in fact, be analysed. This discovery took place against the prevailing orthodoxies of each discipline from whose perspective talk was an essentially trivial thing. Indeed, the extent to which talk is seen as *seri-ously* interesting, or not, is indicative perhaps of *the* crux at the heart of many of the theories under review, for it is intimately linked to the question of everyday existence. Insofar as talk is found to be a serious and analysable matter, so also, I am tempted to say, is everyday life, and vice versa. If talk seems trivial (a non-question), so too is everyday life. This ambiguity – the unavoidable and essentially enigmatic character of everyday existence and its expressive medium, talk – runs through all the theories under review, and is the fundamental problematic of this

11 As distinct from the point of view of professionals, priests, sociologists, etc.

book to which I will return in the final volume of this trilogy. The immediate task here is to clarify what talk is and is about. What are the concerns of talk and why might it be a matter of academic concern?

Part of the problem, as Garfinkel well understood, are the concerns of academics who, insofar as they conceive of themselves as serious in their professional concerns, feel they must prove themselves by dealing with serious and weighty matters. Parsonian theoretical system-building is a good case of 'doing being seriously academic' and who could doubt the seriousness of Adorno and the Frankfurt School? *Critical* theory is a very good way of being serious, for everyone knows that being critical is a serious matter. Language, when it became an academic matter and transmogrified into linguistics, had to be produced as a serious (scientific) object. Accordingly, it was split into *langue* and *parole*. This distinction produced language as a theoretical object for scientific enquiry. Language (*langue*) was conceived as 'a self-contained whole and a principle of classification' (Saussure, 1974: 9). This was to be the object of enquiry, while *parole* (speech) had to be discarded because it lacked any discoverable unifying principle: 'Taken as a whole, speech is many-sided and heterogeneous; straddling several areas simultaneously – physical, physiological, and psychological – it belongs both to the individual and to society; we cannot put it into any category of human facts, for we cannot discover its unity' (ibid.: 9) The absence of an underlying unity is taken to mean that there is no single, unifying theoretical vantage point from which, *a priori*, one might begin to make sense of speech:

> From whatever direction we approach the question [of how to study speech], nowhere do we find the integral object of linguistics. Everywhere we are confronted with a dilemma: if we fix our attention on only one side of each problem we run the risk of failing to perceive [their] dualities ...; on the other hand, if we study speech from several viewpoints simultaneously, the object of linguistics appears to us as a confused mass of heterogeneous and unrelated things ... Among so many dualities, language [*langue*] alone seems to lend itself to independent definition and provide a fulcrum that satisfies the mind. (ibid.: 9)

The rejection by analytic philosophy of 'ordinary language' was, as we will see, for very similar reasons. It was too vague, ambiguous and imprecise for serious philosophical enquiry. In Chapter 7, I trace the development of the study of ordinary language from philosophy and linguistic pragmatics through to conversation analysis. The analysis of conversation (hereafter, CA) was developed by Harvey Sacks, who did his PhD under the supervision of Goffman and who developed the study of conversation (talk) in close dialogue, initially, with Garfinkel. The discovery of how to analyse talk is a defining achievement of the sociology of interaction and I discuss some of its applications in Chapter 7. Here

I wish to consider some of the difficulties involved in that discovery, difficulties which, along the way, took the form of a quarrel with Goffman about how it should be done.

Goffman's life-long engagement with the interactive order culminated, in his last publication, with the study of *Forms of Talk*. The title makes clear that there is, of course, more than one kind of talk. There is, for instance, radio talk; the talk of DJs, news readers, the weather reporter, etc. There is the lecture, and there is that curious phenomenon of self-righting 'spill cries' such as 'oops' and 'whoops'. On all these matters Goffman has fresh and illuminating things to say. A troublesome matter, discussed in relation to radio talk and the lecture, concerns speaker identity. Who is speaking, and what is their relationship to what they are saying on such occasions? Are they the originators (the authors) of what they say? On whose behalf (their own or others') do they speak?[12] Moreover what kind of talk is produced on such occasions? Is it talk that has already been rehearsed and committed to memory? Is it the reading aloud of a text (as in the case of the newsreader), or is it what Goffman calls 'fresh talk' (unrehearsed and spontaneous)? In a lecture the speaker may move between reading from a text, quoting from memory and producing a flow of fresh talk. Such shifts, along with shifts in speaker identity and alignment, are called changes of *footing*, the title of the book's key chapter.

Changes of footing are a persistent feature of 'natural talk'. They imply 'a change in the alignment we take up to ourselves and the others present as expressed in the way we manage the production or reception of an utterance' (Goffman, 1981: 128). At the heart of the essay is a thoroughgoing deconstruction of those 'primitive notions' of talk as a conversation between two parties, a speaker and a hearer. In each case these two primitives are decomposed into more complex sub-categories. Take the case of the hearer. Who is listening and who is addressed? Are they the same? One might be a 'ratified recipient' of a speaker's utterance (and yet not be listening) or a non-ratified recipient who *is* listening (an eavesdropper), or who may be obliged to, or who cannot avoid listening to, say, someone in conversation on their mobile phone. The relationships between speakers and the addressed and unaddressed recipients of their utterances 'are complicated, significant and not much explored' (ibid.: 133). When one moves beyond the conversational model, the notion of a hearer changes to that of an *audience*, a complex term which also needs deconstructing into some of its component parts: there is the live audience that is present at the occasion and the absent television or radio audience. Moreover, different occasions bespeak different audiences: the audiences for a political speech, a play or a town meeting are in different circumstances which elicit different behaviours (ibid.: 138–9). The upshot of the essay is a demonstration of the

12 For a more detailed discussion of first person speaker identity, see pp. 179–84 below.

structural basis of footing. The primitive categories of speaker and hearer are resolved into more complex formulations, in terms of participation frameworks for hearers and production formats for speakers (ibid.: 153).

It is notable that the kinds of talk to which Goffman mostly attends are speaker monologues of some kind. Although all five essays deal with talk, they deal mainly with the speaker's side of it, as he admits in the Introduction. The only essay to deal with 'conversational dialogue' is the first, on 'replies and responses'. It was this, and a related paper 'Felicity's condition' (1983), that provoked one of his students into open disagreement with him about what exactly the analysis of conversation entails and how it should be done. Emanuel Schegloff was, along with his fellow student and friend, Harvey Sacks, studying towards a doctorate with Goffman. Sacks pioneered the analysis of talk-as-conversation establishing that branch of ethnomethodology that came to be known as Conversation Analysis. In Goffman's later writings on talk, there are little jabs at others engaged in the converging study of ordinary language (at the 'scholastic' efforts of the philosophers, for instance, whose 'whole approach might strike the sociologist as somewhat optimistic if not silly'). The essay on replies and responses, and the closing remarks in 'Felicity's condition' are veiled, but pointed criticisms of some of the discoveries made by Sacks and Schegloff about the structures of conversation. The point of discussing Schegloff's criticisms of Goffman, in return, is that it will to begin to show what is at stake in the analysis of talk-as-interaction. The crux of the matter concerns the extent to which conversation is treated as, and can be shown to be, a social structure.

The notion of structure is basic to human thought. It entails some stable principle or principles of order and regularity between component parts that produce intelligibility and coherence. These begin to 'give' the possibility of meaning (significance), more exactly of a working, workable world of some sort. Sociology's question is, what makes the social possible? Under what conditions can something that is recognizable as meaningful interaction between people take place? It is to Goffman's great credit that he recognized and sought to answer that question. But did he succeed? That is the issue in the quarrel over his approach to the study of conversation. Schegloff recalls approvingly that characteristic Goffmanism, quoted above: 'not men and their moments, but moments and their men'. However, he pointedly goes on to observe, in Goffman's various dealings with social interaction, all too often the men get in the way of their moments. There is an unresolved psychologism running though all Goffman's thinking. The persistent invocation of the concepts of 'face' and 'ritual' implies an emphasis on individuals and their psychology. Interactions are managed so as 'to secure the individual's ritual needs' (Schegloff, 1988: 95–6). Interaction is seldom treated as a phenomenon in its own right and as the starting point of enquiry. More often than not, the starting point is the situation in which individuals find themselves and the various ways in which they deal with the situation. The analysis of footing is probably Goffman's most important contribution to opening up talk as an object of enquiry, yet he often treats it as a problem for the individual rather than a structural feature of talk itself:

> What the speaker is engaged in doing, then, moment to moment through the course of the discourse in which he finds himself, is to meet whatever occurs by sustaining or changing footing. And by and large, it seems he selects that footing which provides him the least self-threatening position in the circumstances, or, differently phrased, the most defensible alignment he can muster. (Goffman, 1981: 325)

In this curiously grim view of talk, changes of footing are understood as defensive moves to protect a vulnerable, hidden self. The value of the concept, however, lies in the ways in which it deconstructs any reductive notion of a self, whether as speaker or hearer.

But the real crux in Goffman's approach is the absence of talk as a displayed and analysable object of enquiry. This was the key innovation made by Harvey Sacks who began to tape-record everyday conversation of various kinds (telephone talk, for instance) and then to work out ways of transcribing it in order to produce it as an analysable object. There are complex methodological issues at stake here but, assuming the validity of the transcription process, the effect is to display talk as data in ways that are robust and reliable and, accordingly, analysable. At last it becomes possible to see how it actually works. In theory, it had been assumed, by the founder of modern linguistics, no less, that speech was strictly unanalysable and therefore of no concern in the scientific investigation of language. In practice, however, via recording technologies, talk became generally available for scrutiny in the minutest detail.

Goffman's habit of making up examples of talk (a habit shared, as we will see, by ordinary language philosophy) scandalized Schegloff precisely because they simply served as examples to illustrate a point that Goffman 'had in mind' (Schegloff, 1988: 102–4). The examples had no independent status. They were not real-world objects. They could not, in principle, be scrutinized and criticized by others. All you could do was to take the point (or not). You might perhaps challenge the point by countering with alternative imagined examples. But that is to reduce the study of talk to academic mind games of interest, no doubt, to academics but hardly to anyone else.

At stake in Schegloff's criticisms of Goffman are some of the foundational concerns that CA shares with ethnomethodology, namely its orientation to social action and what social actors make of it, rather than the sociologist's orientation to social action and what he or she makes of it. It is unobtrusively done, but in Goffman's writings the everyday social world is almost always interpreted in ways that produce it as 'the view from Goffman', with examples produced from a dazzling variety of sources, by way of illustration and support. Whether or not it is proper for sociologists to have world-views that they project onto the world ahead of actually examining it is the crux of the matter in respect of any social theory. The most basic question raised by ethnomethodology and CA is whether it is indeed necessary to theorize the everyday social world. The work of Garfinkel and Sacks is distinctively parsimonious in respect of theory. That is not where they choose to begin. Both prefer to regard the everyday world as an achieved and accomplished fact. It is, as a matter of fact, an orderly world. What needs to be done is not to produce theories as to why this *might* be so, but to begin to explore how it is produced as such, ordinarily and routinely, by the social actions of human beings. The study of talk-as-interaction shows it to possess a quite exquisite order and orderliness which is the outcome of the accountable interchanges between speaker/listener participants who produce it as such. One of CA's most elegant features, as we will see, lies in the convincing ways in which it shows how participants (speakers and listeners) take account of, interpret and respond to what's going on from moment to moment. Unlike Goffman, unlike speech act theory, CA treats the work of listening as equally relevant, if not more so, than the work of speaking. In holding these two roles in tension, in an endlessly dialectical relationship with each other, CA at last begins, really and truly, to produce convincing accounts of talk as a genuinely social, interactive phenomenon.

References

Atkinson, P. and Housely, W. (2003) *Interactionism*. London: Sage.

Branaman, A. (1997) 'Goffman's social theory', in C. Lemert and A. Branaman (eds), *The Goffman Reader*. Oxford: Blackwell, pp. xlv–lxxxii.

Drew, P. and Wootton, A. (eds) (1988) 'Introduction', in *Erving Goffman: Exploring the Interaction Order*. Cambridge: Polity Press, pp. 1–13.

Foucault, M. (1979) *Discipline and Punish*. Harmondsworth: Penguin Books.

Garfinkel, H. ([1967] 1984) *Studies in Ethnomethodology*. Cambridge: Polity Press.

Giddens, A. (1984) *The Constitution of Society*. Cambridge: Polity Press.

Giddens, A. (1987) 'Erving Goffman as a systematic social theorist', in *Social Theory and Modern Sociology*. Cambridge: Polity Press.

Goffman, E. ([1959] 1971) *The Presentation of Self in Everyday Life*. Harmondsworth: Pelican Books.

Goffman, E. ([1961] 1968) *Asylums*. Harmondsworth: Pelican Books.

Goffman, E (1963a/1968) *Stigma: Notes on the Management of Spoiled Identity*. Harmondsworth: Pelican Books.

Goffman, E. (1963b) *Behavior in Public Places*. New York: Macmillan.

Goffman, E. ([1968] 1972) *Interaction Ritual*. Harmondsworth: Penguin Books.

Goffman, E. (1969) *Strategic Interactions*. Philadelphia, PA: University of Pennsylvania Press.

Goffman, E. (1981) *Forms of Talk*. Oxford: Blackwell.

Goffman, E. (1983) 'Felicity's condition', *American Journal of Sociology*, 89(1): 1–53.

Habermas, J. (1987) 'Talcott Parsons: problems in constructing a theory of society', in *The Theory of Communicative Action*, Vol. 2. Cambridge: Polity Press, pp. 199–300.

Heritage, J. (1984) *Garfinkel and Ethnomethodology*. Cambridge: Polity Press.

Lemart, C. (1997) 'Goffman', in C. Lemart and A Branaman, (eds), *The Goffman Reader*. Oxford: Blackwell, pp. ix–xlii.

Manning, P. (1992) *Erving Goffman and Modern Sociology*. Cambridge: Polity Press.

Saussure, F. de (1974) *A Course in General Linguistics*. London: Methuen.

Schegloff, E. (1988) 'Goffman and the analysis of conversation', in P. Drew and A. Wootton (eds), *Erving Goffman. Exploring the Interaction Order*. Cambridge: Polity Press.

Schelling, T. (1960) *The Strategy of Conflict*. Cambridge, MA: Harvard University Press.

Turner, B.S. (1999) *The Talcott Parsons Reader*. Oxford: Blackwell.

PART III

Communicative rationality and irrationality

Communication and language 7

Austin, Grice, Sacks, Levinson
UK/USA, 1950s–1970s

A distinctive aspect of the post-war 'turn' towards the ordinary and the everyday, which I have traced thus far in relation to the study of culture in Britain and of the sociology of interaction in America, shows up again, in new ways of thinking about philosophy and language that crossed the Atlantic in the same period. In the 1950s, a philosophy of ordinary language began to be developed in Oxford by J.L. Austin which proved to be highly influential, particularly in Harvard. His Oxford contemporary, H. Paul Grice, made a fundamental contribution to thinking about language as communication which laid the foundations for a new field of academic enquiry, pragmatics, which has its roots in philosophy, linguistics and sociology. The tributary stream that fed into pragmatics from sociology came from Goffman's work on interaction. A final aspect of the turn to ordinary language that overlaps with pragmatics appeared in the pioneering work of the American sociologist Harvey Sacks who developed the analysis of ordinary talk as a distinctive concern within ethnomethodology. These developments, which began in different places and each with their own agendas and core concerns, nevertheless all bear a striking family resemblance to each other. Taken together, they have produced a major reinterpretation of language which emphasizes its social and communicative functions in the contexts of ordinary daily life.

I will consider in turn the philosophy of ordinary language, pragmatics and conversation analysis before reviewing recent work in the study of talk on radio and television which has come out of these earlier developments. Although there are major methodological and theoretical differences between them, all three have a common focus: language-in-use or language as utterance. This does not so much imply a distinction between the spoken and the written but, rather, between *langue* and *parole*; between language as structure or system and language as action or interaction. Moreover, all three take as their starting point the common language of everyday usage, as distinct from specialist, technical or institutional forms of language-in-use. It is implicit in this that a study of every-day language-in-use will disclose some fundamental and universal features not of 'language' so much as human communication and sociality. The question of language as spoken was initially posed by Austin in relation to a speaker. But it soon became clear – and this was Grice's fundamental contribution – that a speaker's utterance could not be considered apart from a hearer to whom the utterance was addressed. An absolutely basic issue emerged: namely that the design of *any* speaker utterance (in any language) incorporates a hearer for whom the utterance is designed and to whom it is addressed. That is to say, a principle of communicative intentionality appears embedded in the actual design features of ordinary everyday language in use and as used by ordinary lay members in any society. This turn to ordinary language provides powerful insights not only into how social interaction works but also its pre-conditions; that is, it discloses something of what constitutes sociality, the social *as such*.

The philosophy of ordinary language

J.L. Austin

J.L. Austin's most influential work, *How to Do Things with Words*, was originally presented as the William James Lectures at Harvard and published, a year after his early death, in 1961. The book provided the basis of speech act theory (elaborated and formalized by Searle, 1969), whose basic premise is that saying something is doing something. Perhaps this seems unexceptionable, but in the context of mainstream Anglo-American philosophy in the early 1950s, it stood in sharp contrast to the major concerns of analytic philosophy at that time. Logical positivism was then the order of the day. It held that unless a sentence can, at least in principle be *verified* (i.e. tested for its truth or falsity) it was strictly meaningless. It followed, of course, that ordinary talk, not to mention, most ethical, aesthetic or literary discourses, were all (theoretically) meaningless. Ideally, the language of philosophy aspired to the language of mathematics: internally logical, consistent and coherent. The focus of attention was on the correspondence between well-formed sentences which state, assert or propose something and states of affairs in the external world. Thus, 'snow is white' is a well-formed sentence in the English language that is true insofar as there is a correspondence between what is asserted (the 'whiteness' of 'snow') and the stuff that falls from the sky under certain conditions at certain times of the year in certain parts of the world. This 'correspondence theory' of truth regards language as fundamentally fact-stating or descriptive of a reality that is outside, external to, language. The task of analytic philosophy was to discover the irreducible components of truth-as-fact. It aspired to be scientific, objective and clear. What lay outside these parameters was meaningless.

The simple shift from sentences to utterances (the basis of speech act theory) though seemingly slight, entailed a completely different focus on language: meaning and truth. At the heart of the difference is that sentences appear in written texts as context-free (except in relation to other sentences in the text): 'There it is' as a sentence on a page has an general intelligibility (it is grammatically and syntactically coherent) but no particular meaning. 'There it is' as an utterance exists only in some particular situation (or context) as said by someone (usually) to someone else and in reference to some thing (it) which 'is' at the time of the utterance somewhere (there). Who or what these someones, somethings, sometimes and somewheres are is transparent in the moment of the utterance to those implicated in and by the utterance. The circumstance, the situation or the context disclose the performative force of what is said. Utterances are context-bound. Sentences are context-free. The former exist only in a situation, a world of some sort. The latter stand outside the world or any worldly situation. Beyond the unit of the sentence lies the text, the container of sentences. Sentences exist in a world of their own, the text in which they dwell. The study of sentences and the study of utterances are impelled towards different models of reasoning and different understandings of reality.

Austin noted that there was more to sentences than assertion and statement. Ordinary language contained declarations that were not concerned with truth or facts:

- I pronounce you man and wife.
- I name this ship *Titanic.*
- I apologise.
- I promise.
- I sentence you to death.

All these sentences (considered now as utterances, i.e. as said by someone in some situation) do not assert or state something. They *do* something. Austin called them *performatives* as distinct from *constatives* which assert or state something (Austin, 1975: 4–5). He distinguished between performative utterances in three ways:

- *Locutionary acts*: the utterance of a sentence with determinate sense and reference.
- *Illocutionary acts*: the making of a statement, offer, promise, etc. by virtue of the conventional force associated with it.
- *Perlocutionary acts*: that produce effects on others as a consequence of the utterance.

The focus of attention was on the second of these; on their illocutionary force and perlocutionary effect. The force and effect of doing something in saying something does not reside simply in the words themselves. In actual situations such utterances require particular *felicity conditions* for them to succeed. It is not just anyone who can join two people in marriage by saying the words 'I pronounce you man and wife' or sentence another to death (and have that sentence carried out by others).

Austin attempted to set out the felicity conditions of performatives:

- There must be a conventional procedure having a conventional effect.
- The persons and circumstances must be appropriate as set out in the procedure.
- The procedure must be enacted correctly and completely.
- Participants in the procedure must have appropriate intentions and demeanours and, if subsequent conduct is called for, must act accordingly. (Austin, 1975: 14–15, modified)

The perlocutionary effect of the illocutionary force of 'I pronounce you man and wife' is that two erstwhile single individuals are thereby transformed into a married couple. But the effectivity of the utterance depends in the first place on the marriage ceremony (as a conventional procedure), the appropriate status of the person uttering the words (a religious minister, registrar, etc.) and of those to whom it is said (there must be no impediment, according to law and custom, to their entry into marriage). The ceremony must be properly performed and the marriage must be sincerely entered into by both parties at the time and subsequently sustained. Truth/falsehood is not implicated in all this, but rather whether it works or not and that in turn is dependent on the nature of the occasion and the sayings and doings that are proper and appropriate to it. Speech act theory is all about acts. As a way of thinking, it is oriented to the practical and the particular and not the general and the theoretical.

Two key aspects of speech act theory are embedded in its basic premises and concerns. First, that an utterance is essentially a worldly action of some kind. That is, it cannot take place (exist) except in some particular set of circumstances which are themselves situated in a world of some sort or other. Second, any speaker utterance in any situation overwhelmingly presupposes a hearer (or hearers) to whom the utterance is directed. The force of these considerations goes beyond the specific issue of saying something as doing something, and points towards the wider issue of the pragmatic basis and functions of language.

Pragmatics

As a now well-established field of enquiry, pragmatics drew its initial inspiration from speech act theory and, arising from that, the theory of communicative intentionality developed by Paul Grice who took speech act theory beyond its initial focus on the activities of speakers. In the William James lectures on *Language and Logic* which he gave at Harvard several years after Austin's death, Grice drew a crucial distinction between natural and non-natural meaning. If I say, 'It's a lovely day' and 'in fact' the sun is shining, it's warm and windless, then this is a transparent, natural statement about a natural state of affairs. But suppose I say 'It's a lovely day' and it's cold, wet and miserable outside. Either I'm blind or an idiot, or else I'm being ironic. But how is irony understandable by others? The sentence 'It's a lovely day' cannot be read as ironic unless accompanied by further linguistic glosses. '"It's a lovely day" she said, ironically'. However, as an utterance 'It's a lovely day' can be heard as ironic, given shared speaker–hearer knowledge of the situation (it is, in fact, pouring outside). But even granted shared knowledge of the situation, the question still arises as to how hearer can interpret what speaker says as meaning the opposite of what is said.

Paul Grice

What this simple example begins to point up is the cardinal distinction between what is said and what is meant. A speaker can say one thing and mean another. But how could that be? If I am a literal-minded soul (a philosopher, for instance), irony will pass me by and, more generally, I can only ever make sense of what others say in terms of what I take to be their literal meaning or truth content. But a great deal of what goes on in ordinary conversation is not at all like this. Very often there is a discrepancy between what is said and what is meant and it is to the latter that we, in fact, attend in ordinary conversation. So a core concern of pragmatics is with implied or indirect meanings; with how they are understood and with how it is possible for them to be understood. The study of implied meanings (or *implicatures* as Grice called them) is intricately linked to communicative intentionality and cooperativeness. Taken together, these constitute the foundational contribution of Gricean theory to the pragmatic study of language-in-use.

For irony to be understood *as* irony presupposes that an utterance meant as ironic is intended by S (speaker) to be recognized as such by H (hearer). An utterance is communicative insofar as it is meant by its speaker to be understood by its recipient *as* meant and is so recognised. Communicative intentionality is essentially reflexive: an implied meaning is meant to be recognised as meant, and this must be a shared assumption (understanding) between the parties in any speech situation. But how is recognition achieved? Via some basic cooperative principles, as proposed in Grice's famous *conversational maxims*. He suggests that there is a set of over-arching assumptions that guide the conduct of conversation. These arise from basic rational considerations that serve as guidelines for the efficient and effective use of language in conversation for cooperative ends. Grice identifies four basic maxims, or general conversational principles, which together amount to a general cooperative principle:

The cooperative principle:

- Make your contribution such as is required, at the stage at which it occurs, by the accepted purpose or direction of the talk exchange in which you engaged (Grice, 1989: 26).

And in particular

Maxim of quality: try to make your contribution one that is true.

- Do not say what you believe to be false.
- Do not say that for which you lack sufficient evidence.

Maxim of quantity: say as much as is necessary.

- Do not say more than you need.
- Do not say less than you need.

Maxim of relation:

- Be relevant.

Maxim of manner: make your contribution clear and to the point.

- Do not be obscure.
- Do not be ambiguous.
- Be brief (avoid unnecessary prolixity).
- Be orderly.

(Grice, 1989: 26–7, slightly modified)

The maxims specify what participants have to do in order to converse in a maximally efficient, rational, effective and cooperative way. They should be truthful, informative, relevant and clear. Conversation, for it to be conversation, entails a cooperative communicative intentionality as the shared basis of interaction. There is no implication, in this, that conversation is normatively oriented to consensus, or to coming to agreement. Arguments, disagreements and rows presuppose collaborative, communicative intentionality for them to be what they are – it takes two to make an argument, as they say. The common ground that is presupposed in communicative behaviour is not to do with shared norms, values or world-views.

Collectively the maxims provide a powerful and far-reaching explanation of the gap between what is said and what is meant. To study this is to engage not only with what language means but with how it works. Insofar as, in a general sense, pragmatics engages with language-in-use, it deals not simply with the analysis of instances of usage, but also with what gives the possibility of such usage. Fundamentally, pragmatics explores the conditions of the useability (or workability) of language. It is ultimately concerned with what makes it possible to *have* a conversation. Communicative intentionality and cooperativeness (including the maxims) are not social or linguistic conventions. They are their pre-conditions. Moreover, they may apply not simply to conversation but to social life in general.

Grice felt the maxims had a wider explanatory power and suggested that they held good in all kinds of non-linguistic interactions in ordinary daily life.[1] If, for instance, I'm fixing something and I ask for four screws, I expect whoever's helping to give me that number, not two or six – the maxim of quantity applies (Grice, 1989: 28). The maxims derive from general considerations of rationality applicable to all kinds of cooperative exchanges and, as such may have universal application within culture-specific constraints (Levinson, 1983: 103).

Politeness

Grice had, in passing, identified 'Be polite' as a maxim normally observed by participants in talk, though he did not clarify what kind of a maxim it was (Grice, 1989: 28). Penelope Brown and Stephen Levinson made a seminal extension of Gricean concerns in their groundbreaking study of politeness as a universal feature of language usage (Brown and Levinson, 1987). Politeness was not to be considered as etiquette (as a social convention or norm) but rather as a basic component of the moral order if by that is meant something like a reciprocal principle of accountability as a pre-condition of social life. Brown and Levinson's project was underpinned by Goffman's concept of face. Human beings are sacred objects and one's face is a sacred thing (Goffman, 1972). Sacred things can be desecrated and face is thus something to be protected and maintained against possible threats to, or loss of, face. In face-to-face encounters with others (most typically, in conversation) participants are necessarily committed to face maintenance in a double sense (their own and others). As we have seen, Goffman regards face maintenance as a condition of

Penelope Brown

interaction, not its objective or outcome (Goffman, 1972: 12). Politeness is a prerequisite of interaction. It makes the social sociable.

Many social situations are potentially face-threatening. The social order is maintained by a double commitment on the part of interactants to maintaining their own face and that of others. Individuals have *positive* and *negative* face. My positive face confirms me as that social member and worthwhile person in my own right that I take my self to be. As such, it is entitled to respect from others

---

1 I will explore this hypothesis in Vol. 3 (*Love and Communication*) where I will argue that the communicative logic of ordinary things is the same as that of ordinary conversation, i.e. that how we understand what to do with things depends on the same logic as that of talk.

who are called upon to anoint my face when they address me. My negative face protects me from the impositions and demands of others. My self is not unconditionally available to others. It has its own requirements and inviolable territories. 'The human personality is a sacred thing; one dare not violate it nor infringe its bounds, while at the same time the greatest good is in communion with others' (Durkheim, quoted in Brown and Levinson, 1987: 44).

Stephen Levinson

Brown and Levinson posit a 'model person' with positive and negative face requirements. They study the ways in which these are attended to in relation to potential 'face threatening actions' (FTAs) in conversational situations. Their 'tongue-in-cheek' model person is rational in a particular sense: s/he is given to means–ends reasoning and deploys strategies to preserve face against potential FTAs. Obvious examples of conversational threats to positive face include criticisms and refusals. I ask whether you like this poem I've just written. How do you deal with the fact that it's not very good? I invite you to have a meal or to go to a movie with me. How do you say no? How, in each case, do you avoid hurting my feelings (and thereby preserve my positive face)? Threats to negative face include that large and importunate class of requests, demands and claims upon our attention. Whenever someone begins with 'Would you mind awfully if ...', I know I'm in a conversational fix. They want me to do something, or to borrow something, or to intrude in some way on what I am at that moment doing.

It is evident that, in these cases, an FTA is intrinsic to the situation and that since they have to be done, they had better be done in such ways as to reduce and soften their impact. If I have to make a criticism, it must be done circumspectly. If I have to make a refusal, I must show hesitations and offer apologies and explanations: 'Uh ..., I'm sorry, I'd love to, but unfortunately I'm doing something else'. It is a familiar experience to accept an invitation of some sort because one cannot think fast enough of a reason to refuse. If I want to borrow something, then how I go about the request will be commensurate to the value of what it is that I want to borrow. To borrow a dollar or a pound from someone is less of an FTA than to borrow their new car. A cardinal feature of FTAs is that they must be done indirectly, in ways that both acknowledge that a threat is somehow involved and at the same time display a commitment to mitigate it. The management of FTAs is a prime site for the study of conversational implicatures and the Gricean cooperative maxims.

The Gricean maxims presuppose conversational efficiency or effectiveness. You should say what you mean and do so sincerely, succinctly, relevantly and directly. However, direct and efficient utterances in many cases violate politeness considerations and pose a potential threat to one's own face and that of others.

At lunch, I want the salt. I do not, however, say 'I want the salt' or 'Hey, you, pass the salt' (both of which are direct, clear and to the point). I say 'Could you pass the salt, *please*' or '*Would you mind* passing the salt, *please*' (the latter being more polite than the former since it makes a double admission of the FTA implicated in the request). A literal soul (or someone from another planet) would treat these utterances as questions and produce a yes or no response. But any normal person will hear them as requests and produce the appropriate response, which is to pass the salt. The indirect request violates the maxim of manner (it is less than perspicuous), but has greater chances of success than a direct request which may provoke a direct refusal.

Indirect utterances have great advantages for speakers (and hearers). If you adhere to the maxims – if what you say is what you mean and it is said directly and clearly – then you are 'on record'. That *is* what you said and meant and you will be held accountable. However, if you apparently flout the maxims, if you are indirect and circumspect, then (1) you cannot be held directly to account (you can deny the implication – it's not what you meant); and (2) hearers can also ignore or avoid the implication of what you said, if it suits them, nor can they be held accountable if they so choose. Hints are an obvious case in point. We're in the car and I say, 'Gosh, it's stuffy'. The driver opens the sun-roof, and I say 'Thanks.' The hint has been taken. But the driver could ignore it if s/he's cross with me, or cold or whatever. If I want to press the point, I will have to make a direct request. But I know my hint has been ignored (assuming it was heard), so the driver apparently doesn't want to open the window. If I make a direct request it's a double FTA. I'm asking someone to do something it seems they don't want to do (threatening their face), and I run the risk of a refusal if I ask (threatening my face) ... maybe it's best to say nothing. Although hints apparently violate the maxim of manner (be clear, say what you mean), they adhere to the underlying force of the maxims which are geared to efficient, effective conversation for, if my objective is to get some air into the car, a hint can be a safer and more successful means to that particular end. And if it doesn't work, at least I'm not out of countenance. Hints protect both speaker and addressee from possible threats to face.

Brown and Levinson produce an elaborate model of politeness strategies that attend to negative and positive face via direct (on record) and indirect (off record) means. They build some important variables into the model, of which differences in social power between participants is one key factor, social distance is another (requiring more formal procedures than the informal procedures of intimates) and the 'weight' of the FTA is another. Their highly ambitious study argues for the universal significance of politeness as a socio-linguistic phenomenon by a detailed demonstration of the same conversational strategies in three separate and unrelated languages: English, Tzeltal (a Mayan language spoken in a district of Mexico) and South Indian Tamil. Since they are able to show, in fine detail, the same phenomena in three quite different languages, it is at least a strongly warrantable assumption that politeness is fundamental to social interaction.

Deixis

Another basic concern of pragmatics is with words whose point of reference is not determined by the linguistic form or content of the utterance but by the situation and circumstances in which they are said and upon which they depend for their referential meaning to be clear. In sociology and philosophy such terms are dealt with as *indexical* expressions and in linguistics as *deictic* expressions. The former is derived from the root of the Latin verb and the latter from the Greek verb 'to point' (the index finger is so called because we use it to point or indicate). Deixis is typically concerned with the use of demonstratives ('this', 'that'), pronouns, tense, adverbs of time and place and a variety of grammatical features whose meaning is determined by the circumstances of utterance (Levinson, 1983: 54):

There it is
Here it is

I put it there
Can't *you* see it there

It *was* there *yesterday*
It *was* there a *minute ago*

The italicised words in each paired case are the deictic terms. 'Here' and 'there' are adverbs of place and, along with similar words whose force is determined by their context (near, far, high, low, etc.), are examined as instances of *spatial deixis*. The second pair, in which who is speaking and who is addressed is indeterminate in the sentence structures but transparent *in situ*, are considered as *personal* or *social deixis*, while the third pair highlights examples of *temporal deixis*. Time, place and person – the irreducible components of any human situation – are the central concerns of the pragmatic study of deixis and underline, yet again, the intrinsic importance and relevance of the immediate environment in which any social interaction is embedded. The environment is not just some kind of passive, or inconsequential backdrop before which things happen. It is in all sorts of unnoticed ways constitutive of what happens. It contributes to determining the nature of the occasion whatever it may be. The environment is a resource that is drawn upon by speakers in the taken-for-granted knowledge that it is known, shared and understood by others *as* the common ground of the interaction. Thus, I say 'There it is!' where 'I' am a father and the addressee is my daughter and 'it' is her school bag and 'there' is behind the door of the kitchen where we both are and it *is* time we were out of the house and on our way to school. The deictic components of a language remind us, yet again, of its essentially practical worldly character. If they seem (in written sentences) vague, abstract and general, the apparent referential indeterminacy of deictic terms on the page becomes transparent in any actual worldly situation.

A brief consideration of personal deixis should begin to indicate the relevance of this topic for any consideration of *mediated* communication and how it works. Two things have thus far been unproblematically assumed; that ordinary talk is *immediate* (that participants are face-to-face and in each other's presence) and typically consists of a twosome; an 'I' and a 'you', a speaker and hearer. In many cases, however, talk takes place between participants who are not in each other's presence (phone talk has been extensively studied in this respect: Hutchby, 2001), or within groups or for a third party (an audience) of some sort. Broadcasting combines both these features. It is designed for an absent third party, namely listeners or viewers. To point this out is to begin to indicate the specific communicative problems that must be addressed by radio and television broadcasters.

Consider the following as a conversational exchange:

D.   Now sir you to to identify you are
     Dr Geoffrey Francis Fisher
     the ninety ninth Archbishop of Canterbury
F.   That is correct (.)

The first speaker begins by doing an identification; telling the person to whom he is speaking who he, in fact, is in some detail. This, on the surface, is a deeply uninformative conversational gambit (a tautology that violates the maxim of quantity, *inter alia*) for clearly speaker knows who he's talking to and presumably the person he's addressing knows that too. There is surely a rule of the sort 'don't tell people what they already know' (Levinson, 1983: 180, and cf. Levinson, 1986). So how could this be a reasonable, informative conversational exchange unless this identification is an introduction performed on behalf of a third party, such as a television audience, which does not know what is common knowledge between the two speakers. It only makes sense in some such circumstances and, indeed, this brief exchange is taken from a live television programme, *At Home*, broadcast in 1956. The exchange serves further to illustrate issues relating to speaker identities. In ordinary talk we assume that people speak 'as themselves' and on their own behalf. But clearly Richard Dimbleby, who puts the question to the Archbishop, is not speaking 'as' the person Richard Dimbleby (a role he inhabits in his private life), but as 'Richard Dimbleby', broadcaster and interviewer. And what he says is not on his own behalf but in the interests of viewers of the programme. It is they, not the Archbishop, who are informed by his utterance.

Goffman identifies three different positions or roles that a speaker may assume:

1.   *Animator*: saying something but not necessarily 'owning' what is said.
2.   *Author*: saying and owning what is said
3.   *Principal*: speaking, as a representative, on behalf of others (Goffman, 1982: 226)

He identifies these three speaker positions in the course of a discussion of 'radio talk', to which they are evidently applicable. In broadcast news on radio or television, the newscaster is evidently the animator of the news but not its author (as everyone knows he is reading a script prepared by the news-team). He can be thought of though as a principal, for in reading the news he does so not on his own behalf, but as the appointed spokesperson of the broadcasting institution which he fronts. His is an institutional voice that animates the news text. In many interviews, phone-ins and other broadcast situations lay-speakers can and do claim to speak not as themselves but as representative members of a social group of some kind. Thus, in radio phone-ins, where the topic is 'pensions', participants may seek to legitimize their contribution by identifying themselves as pensioners:

> **I'm a pensioner myself** of seventy-two
> Now if every working person, and even **every pensioner of which I am one**, was deducted 10p per week. (Hutchby, 2001: 486)

Speaker identity is thus not fixed or transparent in broadcasting, and can change from moment to moment in the course of an utterance or interaction. In a study of DJ talk by one of my students, it was found that a single radio presenter, Tony Blackburn, moved in and out of a number of different speaker-identities (professional broadcaster; radio expert and authority; joker; chat-up artist; transvestite and camp comedian) as he addressed his radio audience or engaged in conversation with audience members who had phoned in to the programme. To understand these 'changes of footing' (Goffman, 1982), which were accomplished by changes of voice depends, in part, on fore-knowledge of the 'world' of the programme that is routinely talked into being by its host-presenter (Brand and Scannell, in Scannell, 1991).

The I-that-speaks (the deictic first person) is not always some fixed or clearly identifiable position. It is determined by the situation and its circumstances and may change its footing from moment to moment within it. Nor is the you-that-is-addressed (the deictic second person) fixed or transparent. The intended recipient of an utterance is clear perhaps only in one-to-one situations in which both participants are in each other's presence. But in the case of broadcasting, the question of who is addressed by an utterance is always more complex since, insofar as any programme is *for* an audience of some kind, a third party is necessarily implicated in any communicative situation on radio and television. Consider, as a familiar kind of thing, any programme that makes use of a studio audience (talk shows, quizzes, game shows and people programmes). What exactly is the performative and communicative role of the audience in the studio? Is the talk, the game or whatever is performed *before* them, performed *for* them? Or are they part of the performance? In other words, who is the programme for – the audience in the studio or the absent audience of viewers?

If a programme is for an audience, this must show up in various ways in the programme itself; that is, it must be available for a listener or viewer to find that the programme is somehow for them. The direct address of the newscaster (and, on television, the direct look-to-camera) or a talk-show host presupposes absent listeners or viewers as the recipients of what is being said. The overall design of the broadcast interview (a genre invented by and for radio and television) implicates an absent third party – the audience – for whom the interaction is being staged. But what also needs to be considered are the invisible ways in which broadcast productions are managed with the absent audience in mind. In this respect the role of the audience-in-the-studio is illuminating. Suppose this audience is part of the overall intended effect of the programme for absent listeners or viewers. Then their behaviours must be managed as part of the overall way in which the programme is produced. And of course, it is common knowledge that this is what happens if you take part in a show as an audience member. First, studio audiences are 'warmed up' before the actual recording or transmission of the programme, in order to get them into producing the appropriate participatory responses that the programme seeks to elicit (laughter, cheering, applause, etc.). At the same time they are rehearsed in the production of their responses – they are advised when and when not to applaud, or they are given guidance on how to ask their question from the floor in a discussion programme. During the show itself they may be prompted either to be more or less enthusiastic in their responses by floor-managers or monitors visible to the studio audience but not to viewers. All this begins to indicate that the studio audience is part of the overall communicative effect that the programme seeks to achieve. More exactly, properly managed, it is an important contributory factor to the *mood* of the programme.

Why bother with a studio audience if the programme is not for them so much as the broadcast audience? Is the studio audience redundant? By no means. It is there to create the appropriate mood. First, the presence of the audience-in-the-studio establishes what is taking place as a public event and it serves to draw listeners into the event, whatever it may be. The communicative relationship between a broadcast production and its audience can work in one of two directions: the programme may seek, in various ways, to enter into the spaces of reception, the situations and circumstances of listening or viewing. Or it may seek to create its own space and to bring its absent audience into that space. These two alternatives, in a general way, implicate different dimensions of the communicative character of radio and television, which is both public and private. It is public in that any transmitted programme is meant to be available for a public of some sort (the audience that is implicated in its form and content). It is private in that the reception of any transmitted programme is by individuals listening or watching in the ordinary contexts of their own daily private lives. In a basic way the studio audience constitutes the programme of which it is a part as a public event, and their behaviours help to establish its communicative character and mood. If fun is the object of the occasion, then an atmosphere of fun is powerfully established (or not) by the reactions and interactions of the live studio audience who, in manifold ways, are doing being-an-audience not only on their own behalf (they chose to be there) but also on behalf of others who are not there. When examined in detail, shows that use live and present audiences have a number of communicative interactions in play at any moment: between programme host and participants on the platform, between host and studio audience, between host and listeners or viewers, between platform participants and studio audience, between platform participants and viewers and listeners. Thus, the question of who is speaking to whom (the first and second persons) in such programmes is a complex, shifting phenomenon that calls for careful, close analysis.

Conversation analysis

The study of the history of technologies tends to show that things invented in the first place for particular strategic purposes may turn out to have different applications and unanticipated possibilities. Radio broadcasting, or wireless telephony as it was initially conceived and implemented, is an obvious case in point. The *broadcast* character of radio (originally, and in principle, a two-way system of transmission and reception, like the telephone) was at first perceived as a problem and only gradually discovered to be its greatest asset when it was put to use not for one-to-one conversational interactions but for one-to-many transmissions of organized programme material that was informative or entertaining. All broadcasting was, perforce, live at first. Technologies to record and capture live talk and events came later in the development of radio and subsequently television. The lightweight magnetic audio-tape recorder came into general use in the mid-1950s, and the portable television camcorder a decade later. Their availability for general social use, in each case, came some time after their professional use in broadcasting. One felicitous affordance of the tape-recorder, for academic purposes, was discovered by the Californian sociologist Harvey Sacks who, in the 1960s, began to record people talking to each other in ordinary daily situations of one sort or another, with a view to exploring how such talk 'worked' (Sacks, 1995). Thus began the now well-established sociological sub-division called Conversation Analysis (hereafter CA).

Harvey Sacks

The tape-recorder does something astonishing. It captures the liveness of talk as it unfolds and preserves and makes it available and editable in ways that were hitherto impossible. It had long been assumed that language-in-use could not be systematically examined because actual talk is such a fleeting, transitory thing that lives and dies in the moment of speaking. Moreover, it was generally assumed to be incoherent and clumsy, full of hesitations, mumbles and repetitions in comparison with the tidy, orderly appearance of words in sentences on pages. Grice defended his own concern with ordinary language as a fit object of enquiry against the prevailing scepticism of Oxford philosophy which regarded it as 'unfit for conceptual analysis' on account of its 'ambiguity, misleadingness, vagueness and the incorporation of mistakes and absurd assumptions'. He, and Austin, to the contrary, regarded 'ordinary language as a wonderfully subtle and well-conceived instrument which is fashioned not for idle display but for serious (and non-serious) *use* (Grice, 1989: 178–9; 384. Emphasis added). However, in speech act theory, ordinary language remains something theorized and imagined. It is notable that all the examples of conversational utterances offered in discussion by Austin and Grice are, in fact, made up by them and the reader is invited to recognize them as standing for the sort of thing that might get said in actual talk.

CA for the first time, courtesy of the tape-recorder, produced language-in-use as an observable, analysable, empirical object of enquiry. There are two stages to this process. There is, first, the actual recording of the data in which the sociologist-recorder claims to do no more than start and end the recording (with the consent of the speakers) whose status is taken as the record of a naturally occurring social phenomenon uninfected by the sociologist or the equipment (for a discussion of this point, cf Hutchby, 2001). There then comes the crucial business of transcribing the data in ways that preserve, as far as, possible what exactly was said (and not said) in the recorded interaction. Thus the transcript must capture the silences, the hesitations, the stutters and repetitions, the overlaps when two or more people are speaking at the same time, the stress on words and how they are pronounced, the inhalations and exhalations of breath, the volume and intensity of utterance. And when this is done, something extraordinary begins to emerge: namely that *all* these things are, in fact, relevant aspects of the overall communicative design and effect of what is going on. The things that seem apparently meaningless – the mms and uhuhs; the pauses and momentary silences – all have precise meanings for the participants in the ongoing context of the interaction. Nothing escapes notice in talk, including the conversational equivalent of nothing, namely silence. The meaningful character of momentary silences in conversation was one of CA's early discoveries and is an elegant demonstration of its powerful and innovative contribution to our understanding of how human interaction does, in fact and matter of factly, work. To hesitate is to *communicate* hesitation and that, in turn, is likely to preface a negative response of some kind:

```
A:    So I was wondering would you be in your office
      on Monday (.) by any chance?
>>    (2.0)
      probably not
(Heritage, 1984b: 320)
```

In this fragment from a phone conversation the caller's initial question is met with a micro-hesitation (.) and then a 2-second silence from the person B who's answered the call. The question is completed at 'on Monday' at which point it is appropriate for B to speak. A momentary silence (.) at that point leads caller to wonder further whether B – by any chance – will be in her office. The longer 2-second pause following this hedge leads speaker to conclude that B will probably not be available. Thus two pauses – the first one fractional, the second longer and confirming that the first *was* a hesitation – are treated as meaningful (as indicating hesitation) and generate inferences; the first weaker and the second, stronger. The silences are both taken by caller to mean that the answer to her question is probably 'no'. The general implication is that a positive answer to a question should be immediately forthcoming. If it is not, then it will be assumed that the question is in some way problematic for the recipient of the question:

```
A:   What about coming here on the way?
>>   (.)
     or doesn't that give you enough time?
B:   Well no I'm supervising here
(Heritage, 1984a: 274)
```

Thus, in this second example, the micro-pause from B following A's initial invitation is immediately taken to imply that B may have some difficulty in accepting it and a possible explanation (not enough time) is anticipated as a reason for a momentary hesitation.

In both these cases, the first point to note is that the interpretation here being attended to is *not* that of the analyst of the data, but of the speaker-participant in the interaction. CA has the same basic concern of ethnomethodology with the methods employed by ordinary social members to make sense of, figure out and deal with what's going on rather than with the methods used by sociologists to figure out their behaviour. This is one of the most distinctive features of this kind of sociology. It expresses, as noted in the previous chapter, a dissatisfaction with the tendency of social theory to impose its own agenda on actually existing social phenomena rather than attending to the agendas of those involved in the phenomenon under consideration.

Second, the data are always phenomenally complex. There are many things going on simultaneously in ordinary talk and even the smallest scraps of transcribed talk have multiple layers of meaning:

```
D.   Now sir you to to identify you are
     Dr Geoffrey Francis Fisher
     the ninety ninth Archbishop of Canterbury
F.   That is correct (.)
```

This conversational fragment from an old television programme was earlier cited to show how the absent audience is implicated in Dimbleby's utterance. If, however, we focus on Dr Fisher's response, a quite different set of issues emerges. Dimbleby's introduction provides three fact-claims about the person to whom his utterance is addressed: that his name is Dr Geoffrey Francis Fisher, that he is the Archbishop of Canterbury, and that he is the ninety-ninth incumbent of this office. To which of these three facts about himself does Fisher respond?:

F. That is correct (.)
   you've been doing some mathematics
D. I have
F. I've been called everything
   from the ninety seventh to the hundred and third (.)
   ..hhh but I am the ninety ninth(.)
   Saint Augustine being the first

Dimbleby's opener furnishes the addressee with immediate possibilities in terms of developing the topic as to who *exactly* he is. Of the three facts stated about him, one is more vulnerable than the others. Fisher's own name and current status as head of the Anglican Church are pretty incontrovertible facts about him, but that he is, in fact, the 99th holder of the office is more challengeable, as Fisher himself goes on to make clear. It is, in this respect a more noticeable and thereby more 'talkable-about' datum than the other two items of information. Dimbleby's *sotto voce* overlapping acknowledgement that he has, indeed, been doing some maths implies that he has done some preparatory work before this conversation. That, of course, is part of his job as a broadcaster and Dimbleby was famously diligent in his pre-broadcast preparations (Dimbleby, 1975). While name and occupational status are the commonplace facts about certain kinds of broadcast interviewees (those who are being interviewed by virtue of what they do) that are established immediately by interviewers, the extra datum is strictly surplus to the situational requirements of the broadcast interview (it violates the maxim of quantity). So its motivated inclusion may be meant to serve as a conversational offering. It furnishes a topical resource – it is remarkable and thereby talkable-about – and is immediately treated as such by the person to whom it is offered. Topic management in relation to the sequential turn-taking unfolding structure of talk is a prime consideration for CA. As this conversation unfolds, the preliminary 'fact' that Fisher is the 99th Archbishop serves as a basis upon which to explore the function of the Anglican arch-episcopacy of Canterbury within the long tradition and history of British church and state relations. This tiny speech fragment sets the direction and tone for the whole of what follows.[2]

2 An account of what follows can be found in a fuller discussion of the programme in the companion volume to this book, *Television and the Meaning of 'Live'*.

Third, we should note the manifold and detailed significance of what is happening from moment to moment in talk; the slightest hesitation, for instance, may be noted and treated as a meaningful and accountable matter. Conversation is a self-explicating phenomenon that unfolds, moment by moment, in real time. What emerges from the empirical study of the ways in which invitations are offered by speakers and accepted or declined by those to whom they are addressed are some generalizable rules of conversational sociability. If you are going to accept an offer, do so immediately and without qualification. If you are going to refuse an offer, do so with apologies and explanations. The following are canonical instances:

```
(1)
A:   Why don't you come and see me some  ⎡times
B:                                        ⎣I would like to
(2)
A:   I mean can we do any shopping for her or something
     Like tha:t?
>>   (0.7)
B:   Well that's most kind Hetherton .hhh at the moment no:.
     Because we've still got two boys at home
(Heritage, 1984b: 272–3)
```

Thus, in (1) the acceptance is unqualified and immediate, overlapping with first speaker's utterance, whereas in (2) the declination is preceded by marked hesitation plus an appreciation (most kind) and followed by an explanation (two boys at home). These ways of doing accepting and declining show up in a large body of recorded conversations. Together they should be regarded as strongly indicating the existence of tacit pragmatic rules embedded in the conduct of ordinary social life rather than prescriptive, conventional and explicit rules that are taught and learnt. It is not difficult to see that politeness considerations in respect of negative and positive face underpin the ways of doing accepting and declining. CA takes a rather austere view of such theorizing. It is willing to extrapolate from its data generalizable formats for conversational performatives of one kind or another. It is reluctant, however, to follow the step taken by Brown and Levinson of hypothesizing a model social actor to whom they attribute face needs and a capacity for instrumental (means–ends oriented) rationality. CA sticks to its task, which is to show how participants in interactions interpret and deal with what is going on. If the followers of CA are, in the end, a bit po-faced about what they do, they are nevertheless on the side of the angels (at least in my view) in their reluctance to impose their own opinions and ideas on their objects of enquiry. Such respectful reticence treats the thing under consideration as worthy of study and thought in its own and proper terms. It allows conversation itself to appear, at last, as a *serious* object of enquiry, showing it indeed to be that 'wonderfully subtle and well-conceived instrument' that Austin and Grice thought it was, against the grain of philosophic opinion in their day.

Broadcast talk

In the past 20 years or so, the concepts and methods of pragmatics and conversation analysis have been applied to talk on radio and television. The pioneering work of John Heritage and his doctoral student, David Greatbatch, on the broadcast political interview undoubtedly served to establish the focal issues for the study of broadcast talk. Their initial concern was with the organization of *institutional talk*. CA had begun with the study of talk as it occurred in the interpersonal contexts of daily life. It subsequently turned to examine talk in institutional contexts, in the first place in order to see how it differed from non-institutional talk. One systemic difference that quickly emerged was that, in institutional settings the responsibility for the management of talk is allocated in advance according to pre-assigned social roles and their institutionally appropriate performative behaviours. Thus, it turns out that in the classroom, the surgery, the law court or the television studio, one class of speakers is mainly responsible for asking questions (the teacher, the doctor, the lawyer, the interviewer) and another class of speakers (pupils, patients, witnesses and defendants, interviewees) is mainly responsible for answering them. While in some of these settings there is some degree of flexibility in terms of who asks/answers questions, in others there is very little, as Heritage and Greatbatch found in the case of the political news interview (Heritage, 1985; Heritage and Greatbatch, 1991).

The institutions of broadcasting are subject to two major external constraints that impinge on them from opposite directions. Historically broadcasters have been, from the start to the present day, subject to varying degrees of regulation by the political authority of the nation–state. In the case of Britain and the USA (until the early 1990s), broadcasters were required to exercise 'due impartiality' in the handling of news and politics. This requirement is a cardinal consideration in the management of all kinds of broadcast political news, talk and discussion. The other constraint is the audience which, in various ways, must be taken into account in the design of any radio or television broadcast. Consideration of these two factors – the absent audience and the requirement of institutional impartiality – combine to constitute the distinctive characteristics of the political interview. These show up as, in various ways, departures from the norms of non-institutional forms of talk, and particularly, Heritage and Greatbatch claim, in the systemic absence of *continuers* (mmhm, uhuh, yes, etc.) and *response tokens* (oh, really, Ok, etc.).

Such interjections have been carefully studied by CA and are fascinating in a number of ways (Schegloff, 1982; Jefferson, 1984; Heritage, 1984b). In the first instance they show, yet again, the essentially *interactive* character of talk. A hearer (the deictic second person) is not there in some background role as audience to a speaker holding forth but rather is, from moment to moment, jointly responsible, as a co-participant, for the management of the ongoing production of the interaction. It is a nice question, to which CA typically attends, as to how participants *know* when opportunities for a change of turn occur. It is demonstrably not the case that when A has finished his or her 'turn' there follows a perceptible pause or silence before B (or whoever) takes up the next conversational turn. Nor is it the case that the transitional points of turn-taking are on the whole marked by overlapping talk between A and B before the former gives way to the latter and relinquishes 'the floor'. Rather, what is typically displayed in the data is an instant transition from A to B when a change of turn occurs. It is a non-trivial question as to how such precise and accurate transitions are routinely accomplished by participants in talk. Does speaker, by some means, indicate an up-coming turn-completion in such a way as to be recognizable by the other co-participant(s)? In attending to this question CA discovered other phenomena that occur at potential points of conversational transition, including the presence of continuers and response tokens. In attending to such seemingly trivial (indeed, 'meaningless') speech particles, CA furnishes significant evidence yet again of the fine-grained interactive and meaningful character of talk. And as always, its interpretation of these phenomena is oriented to the practices and interpretations of the participants and not those of the sociologist investigating them.

Continuers and response tokens have a number of functions. They furnish evidence, for speakers, that co-participants are doing listening and providing proof of this. Listeners display, in the selection of their response, not only that they are attending to what is being said, but also their particular orientation to what is being said. So that being interested (Really? No!) or surprised (Oh!) may be indicated by the selected response. Continuers have a different function. They acknowledge the occurrence of a potential change of turn and indicate, in an appropriately low-key manner, a 'pass', thereby allowing (encouraging) speaker to continue. Overall, response tokens and continuers neatly indicate a curious reversal of personal deixis. A speaker does not always or only speak *as* a speaker but, on occasion and on cue, as a listener (the first person has become the second person). Now what Heritage and Greatbatch found as an overwhelming fact about their data was the systematic absence of continuers and response tokens in all the broadcast interviews they examined. They demonstrate that interviewees (IEs) are permitted and expected by interviewers (IRs) to produce lengthy 'multi-unit' turns at talk. A multi-unit turn has a number of potential junctions at which, in ordinary talk, a change of turn might take place or, if not, a response token or continuer might be produced. However, IRs invariably refrain from such interpolations when IE is speaking. A generalizable feature of response tokens is that 'their producers thereby show their understanding of themselves as the recipients of what is being said. Thus to withhold them is a means whereby IRs decline the role of primary addressee of IE's remarks in favour of the absent broadcast audience' (Heritage and Greatbatch, 1991: 110).

To produce response tokens is, *inter alia*, to indicate (negatively or positively) particular alignments with what speaker is saying. In ordinary conversation, addressees are not expected to be neutral or non-committal, in their orientation to what's being said. To withhold response tokens indicates not so much neutrality as boredom or indifference or, in the case of phone-talk, suspicion in caller's mind as to whether there is anyone there on the other end of the line. But neutrality is a primary external constraint that is laid upon the broadcasters. IRs must not express opinions when they ask questions. Nor must they align themselves, negatively or positively, with IEs' expressed statements or opinions. Thus the systemic absence of response tokens displays attentiveness both to the imposed requirements of political broadcasting and to the audiences for such broadcasts. The institutional character of the broadcast interview is achieved in various ways, especially in opening and closing routines, wherein the viewing or listening public is directly addressed. But a news interview is not only intermittently hearable as such. It is so from start to finish and throughout as Heritage and Greatbatch conclusively establish.

This sociological work on the institutional features of the political interview began to disclose the specifically *broadcast* features of broadcasting, and its implications were taken up and explored in the study of broadcast talk (Scannell, 1986, 1991). The issue of power is central to media and cultural studies yet it is something usually assumed but seldom proved. The study of how institutional authority and control are maintained in the interview, in phone-ins and other familiar broadcast situations began to show precisely how power routinely worked and how, routinely, it might be resisted. Institutional control is exercised through 'first-speaker hegemony' (Hutchby, 2001) which concedes control over the whole interactive, communicative set-up to the interviewer or programme host. The ways in which participants challenge, evade or (occasionally) refuse first-speaker hegemony shows how conflict and disagreement are routinely and jointly negotiated within the institutional frames of broadcast talk (Harris, 1991; Hutchby, 1991).

The study of political talk focuses on its informative and conflictive dimensions. But not all talk on radio and television is political. Much of it has a relational, sociable character, in which the object of the talk is no more than the pleasure of talk itself (Scannell, 1996: 22–57). The study of DJ talk began to explore these aspects of broadcasting. DJ talk is distinctive in a number of ways. First, it typically is a monologue addressed to an absent audience. Thus turn-taking – the focal concern of CA – is not a consideration. What comes to the fore is a different issue, raised by Goffman (1982: 325); how does a DJ bring off a fluent, coherent flow of talk through the course of a two- or three-hour live-to-air show? At the same time, how is the audience constructed in this talk? Montgomery's seminal study of social and spatial deixis in DJ talk began to show how 'intimacy at a distance' is achieved through the ways in which listeners are spoken to and the links are established and maintained between where the programme is (the studio) and where the listeners are (Montgomery, 1986).

All this work began to point up two fundamental aspects of the communicative character of radio and television for further consideration: *performance* and *liveness*. In non-institutional talk, participants are usually taken to be speaking as themselves. They may be, as Garfinkel will have it, 'doing' being themselves, but this performance is, as he showed, in the vast majority of cases brought off naturally and effortlessly as a case of 'the real thing', the one-and-only genuine 'me' (Garfinkel, 1984). However, on radio and television the performed character of all interactions becomes apparent. In news and documentaries, ordinary people perform 'being ordinary' as witnesses or representatives, while experts and authorities enact their punditry in various ways. In entertainment programmes the playful character of broadcasting is highlighted through what Tolson calls the 'synthetic personality' – the 'made-for-television' celebrity, of whom Dame Edna Everage (played by Barrie Humphreys) is a classic British example (Tolson, 1991). In the study of television talk shows that followed on from this, the issue of fakery (cf. Nelson and Robinson, 1994) emerged as a crucial issue: faked identities, faked spontaneity, faked emotions and responses, in shows such as *Vanessa* in the UK and, most notoriously, the *Jerry Springer Show* from the USA. The new genre of 'people programmes' in the 1990s emphasized the role of ordinary people in them, rather than experts and authorities whose status was undermined in such shows (Livingstone and Lunt, 1992, 1994). They were widely criticized (by lay and academic opinion) as vulgar and tasteless, as phoney, insincere and sexist (Tolson, 2001).

Such responses all, in one way or another, criticize interactions which appear to be, one way or another, constructed, manufactured and manipulated (in short, performed) from an implicit normative preference for immediate, spontaneous and genuine interactions. The problem of *authenticity* (and the related issue of *sincerity*) is raised by the public and performed character of broadcast interactions in contrast with the apparently spontaneous character of conversation and interactions in ordinary, private life. It is a crux for the understanding of the communicative character of talk and of the differences between mediated and unmediated interaction. The academic study of the media has, on the whole, displayed a hermeneutics of suspicion towards its objects of enquiry. It has shown a vague but powerful mistrust of the media as unreliable, as somehow neither genuine nor truthful. Insofar as the latter depends on the former, then mediated performances will of necessity raise the question of the relationship between actors and their actions.

'Authentic talk', as Montgomery points out, is not an analytic term like 'adjacency pair', 'noun', 'presupposition' or 'implicature'. It is not a term that occurs very often in CA texts, yet some undeclared and unexamined notion of it underpins CA's preference for 'ordinary talk' as 'the benchmark' against which all other forms of talk are measured (and underpinning this preference is the sometimes explicit belief that, in engaging with ordinary talk, CA is doing real and genuine – in short, authentic – sociology, unlike some other sociologies and their sociologists). Authenticity is a term which , like 'sincerity', captures something of the ordinary evaluations made by ordinary social members of talk-as-performance especially in public contexts such as television (Montgomery, 2001: 398–402). The complexities of sincerity, and the extent to which it is applicable or appropriate to mediated interactions, may serve to indicate the even more complex issues that the notion of authenticity raises. On the one hand, sincerity – that seemingly natural and spontaneous thing – has, somehow or other, to be done, enacted, performed (Scannell, 1996: 58–74). It has to be done in such a way as to *be* natural, spontaneous, genuine, etc. If it does not succeed in this, then the hermeneutics of suspicion – the charges of 'trying too hard', of fake or inauthentic sincerity – may kick in. Such issues routinely arise, in our kind of society, in terms of the evaluation of the performances in public of political leaders or of media celebrities for whom 'being oneself' is a more self-conscious and problematic issue than for ordinary social members (Tolson, 2001).

The politics of sincerity was dramatically highlighted in the aftermath of the death of Diana, Princess of Wales (Montgomery, 1999). Among the many issues in the public domain in the eventful week between her death and funeral, one stood out at the time. Why did it seem to matter so much? What could she possibly have meant to so many millions that they should weep for her? This question was extensively discussed in the media as they reflected on their own role in producing Diana as *the* global media celebrity, the most famous woman in the world. Why should ordinary people care when she was not really part of their lives? When asked this question by television interviewers, members of the public ('ordinary people') produced replies that demonstrated sophisticated understandings of their own responses, of the role of the media and of public opinion:

> In looking at vox pop interviews we see one way in which the public is taken up and represented in the event. 'Public response' is not just waiting there to be photographed and interviewed, but has to be constructed with the collaboration

of the interviewees, and in terms of what they expect of broadcast forms. The public we see in these interviews is reflexive about their own experience of media, self-monitoring in their justification of their own performances and implicitly aware of challenges to what they say and how they say it. (Myers, 2000: 183).

The general viewing and listening public had become the *publicum in fabula*, the public as an interactive part of the event itself. 'I was very shocked and I was shocked at how shocked I was' (ibid.: 180). Sincerity is no longer just a case of genuinely feeling something. It is rather something that is proved by a critical awareness and self-evaluation of that feeling. And why should shock at being shocked be the authenticating component that confirms, not just for speaker but for others too, the sincerity of this response? The question points to the complexities of *entitlements to experience* in which routinely all social members have access to events in the world through the mediations of television. Experience is no longer something tied to presence, to being there, to first-hand witnessing (Scannell, 2001). The perception of the media as inauthentic depends upon unexamined assumptions of the primacy, the authenticity, of relations of presence, 'face engagements', 'ordinary conversation', all of whose privileged claims to truth and authenticity are undermined by radio and television.

The study of broadcast talk has, at its heart, a concern with the mediated and performed character of what goes out on radio and television. It has developed from pragmatics and CA. It has, necessarily, had to engage not only with how interactions are managed by, and work for, participants in programmes, but also with how they are managed and work (or not) for absent audiences. Nor can it ignore the evaluations of those for whom these interactions are managed. Issues to do with authenticity and sincerity are relevant not because they seem so to academics, but because they appear so to audience members, because they are part and parcel of the ways in which mediated performances are ordinarily thought about, discussed and assessed in private life, in newspapers and on radio and television too. In other words, the object of enquiry for the study of broadcast talk must include talk about talk on radio and television (Livingstone, 1994).

Talk has been thought of, thus far as a speech act, and as an interaction. To begin to think of it in relation to *events* opens up another fruitful line of enquiry that begins to engage with perhaps the most fundamental and most neglected aspect of broadcasting, namely its *liveness*. A prevalent kind of talk on radio and television is *commentary* on events, 'live and as they happen'. What are the functions of such commentaries and how do they work for absent listeners and viewers? The deictic components of any occasion are time, place and person. Broadcasting's most fundamental task is the management of liveness, which has a specific temporality: the phenomenal now, the unfolding now of the event, the now of being there, the now of concern: *this* now in which we are caught up, which confronts and engages us, with which we must deal, wherein we are involved. It is to this now, and on behalf of absent viewers, that broadcast commentaries speak. In a ground-breaking linguistic study of temporal deixis, Stephanie Marriott examined the now-and-then of televised sporting events (Marriott, 1996). Again the real complexities of mediated occasions becomes apparent. In ordinary daily life, a face-engagement has its 'here' and 'now' as a shared resource for those who are in it. But in live broadcast coverage of events it is obvious that 'here' and 'there' have a more complex referentiality. For television producers the here of the event is managed with an eye to the there of viewers, on whose behalf the event is shown from multi-dimensional points of view that are far greater than the restricted individual point of view that is available to any present participant viewer there in the event itself. It is not so obvious that, at certain moments, a multi-dimensional temporality appears in such coverage, and particularly in the commentaries on 'instant re-plays' which was the focal issue of Marriott's study.

In such moments the commentary attends to a moment just past (when a goal, say, was scored) that is repeated, often from several different angles. The commentary, which is in present, real time is dealing with a moment of past time which is magically restored to the present for further scrutiny. What is replayed, however, is only the visual track without its accompanying live commentary, so that the commentators do not have to speak over themselves speaking. It restores something to sight in order to be talked over afresh. In dealing afresh with the replay, the commentators are momentarily ignoring the continuing event, which is hearable as the ambient background 'live' sound over which their commentary is spoken. Thus there are two times in the same moment: that of the ongoing event in the auditory background and that of the moment just past in the visual foreground to which television attends. The 'then' has entered into the 'now' to produce, via television, a new kind of temporality, a simultaneous now-and-then. These two times can, and sometimes do collide with each other, if something significant should happen off-screen while the commentary is attending to the replay:

> Here's a replay. Now you see Fittipaldi go out of the picture there and spinning – *Oh! and that's Gerhard Berger.* Well this this this is in effect is Grand Prix that we have seen in these conditions before and I don't know what the answer is but it proves to me that it's a farcical situation. (Marriott, 1996: 75)

The commentator is attending to a replay *here* (on screen) of a Formula One driver (Fittipaldi) spinning out of control. His surprised and excited *Oh!*, responds to another crash (Berger) which he sees happening live out on the track even as he speaks with one eye on the television monitor screening the replay. It takes a second or so before the production gallery abruptly cuts away from the replay and back to the live event in order to catch up with what's going on 'now' in the race.

Marriott's paper begins to disclose something of the phenomenal spatial and temporal complexity of live television. It opens up new lines of enquiry into the ways in which involvements and effects of being there are created for absent viewing audiences. Everyone knows that watching something on television is not the same as being there live 'and in the flesh'. This kind of close, careful analysis of television coverage of live events helps us understand, in sometimes surprising ways, wherein the difference lies. It shows, moreover, that television does not just 'show' things live and as they happen. It produces and narrates the occasion, re-working it as a television event. The relationship between the event-in-itself and the event-as-televised raises yet again the question of the authenticity (or not) of the mediations of television. I will resume these issues in the companion volume to this book in which I investigate the meaning of 'live' in relation to radio and television broadcasting.

References

Austin, J.L. (1975) *How to Do Things with Words*. Oxford: Oxford University Press.

Brown, P. and Levinson, S. (1987) *Politeness: Some Universals in Language Use*. Cambridge: Cambridge University Press.

Dimbleby, J. (1975) *Richard Dimbleby*. London: Hodder and Stoughton.

Goffman, E. (1972) *Interaction Ritual*. London: Penguin Books.

Goffman, E. (1982) *Forms of Talk*. Oxford: Blackwell.

Grice, H.P. (1989) *Studies in the Ways of Words*. Cambridge, MA: Harvard University Press.

Harris, S. (1991) 'Evasive action: how politicians respond to questions in political interviews', in P. Scannell (ed.), *Broadcast Talk*. London: Sage.

Heritage, J. (1984a) *Garfinkel and Ethnomethodology*. Cambridge: Polity

Heritage, J. (1984b) 'A change-of-state token and aspects of its sequential placement', in J.M. Atkinson and J. Heritage (eds), *Structures of Social Action*. Cambridge: Cambridge University Press, pp. 299–345.

Heritage, J. (1985) 'Analysing news interviews: aspects of the production of talk for an overhearing audience', in T. van Dijk (ed.), *Handbook of Discourse Analysis*, Vol. 3. New York: Academic Press.

Heritage, J. and Greatbatch, D. (1991) 'On the institutional character of institutional talk; the case of news interviews', in D. Boden and D. Zimmerman (eds), *Talk and Social Structure*. Cambridge: Polity Press.

Hutchby, I. (1991) 'The organisation of talk on talk radio', in P. Scannell (ed.), *Broadcast Talk*. London: Sage.

Hutchby, I. (2001) *Conversation and Technology*. Cambridge: Polity Press.

Jefferson, G. (1984) 'Notes on a systematic deployment of the acknowledgement tokens "yeah" and "mm hm"'. *Tilburg Papers in Language and Literature*, 30: 21–53.

Levinson, S. (1983) *Pragmatics*. Cambridge: Cambridge University Press.

Levinson, S. (1986) 'Putting linguistics on a proper footing: explorations in Goffman's concept of participation', in P. Drew and A. Wootton (eds), *Erving Goffman: Exploring the Interaction Order*. Cambridge: Polity Press. pp. 161–227.

Livingstone, S. (1994) 'Watching talk: gender and engagement in the viewing of audience discussion programmes'. *Media, Culture & Society*, 16(3): 428–48.

Livingstone, S. and Lunt, P. (1992) *Talk on Television*. London: Routledge.

Marriott, S. (1996) 'Time and time again: "live" television commentary and the construction of replay talk', *Media, Culture & Society*, 18(1): 69–86.

Montgomery, M. (1986) 'DJ talk', *Media, Culture & Society*, 8(4): 401–22.

Montgomery, M. (1999) 'Speaking sincerely: public reactions to the death of Diana', *Language and Literature*, 8(1): 5–33.

Montgomery, M. (2001) 'Defining authentic talk', *Discourse Studies*, 3(4): 397–405.

Myers, G. (2000) 'Entitlement and sincerity in broadcast interviews about Princess Diana', *Media, Culture & Society*, 22(2): 167–86.

Nelson, E. and Robinson, E. (1994) 'Reality talk or telling tales? The social construction of sexual and gender deviance on a television talk show', *Journal of Contemporary Ethnography*, 23(1): 26–51.

Sacks, H. (1995) *Lectures on Conversation*. Oxford: Blackwell.

Scannell, P. (1986) 'Editorial', *Media, Culture & Society*, 8(4): 387–90.

Scannell, P. (1991) 'Introduction', in *Broadcast Talk*. London: Sage.

Scannell, P. (1996) *Radio Television and Modern Life*. Oxford: Blackwell.

Scannell, P. (2001) 'Authenticity and experience', *Discourse Studies*, 3(4): 405–11.

Schegloff, E. (1982) 'Discourse as an interactional achievement: some uses of "uh huh" and other things that come between sentences', in D. Tannen (ed.), *Analysing Discourse: Text and Talk*. Washington, DC: Georgetown University Press, pp. 71–93.

Searle, J. (1969) *Speech Acts: An Essay in the Philosophy of Language*. Cambridge: Cambridge University Press.

Tolson, A. (1991) 'Televised chat and the synthetic personality', in P. Scannell (ed.) *Broadcast Talk*. London: Sage.

Tolson, A. (2001) *Television Talk Shows*. Mahwah, NJ: Lawrence Erlbaum Associates.

Communication as ideology 8

Hall

UK, 1960s and 1970s

Media studies

In the past 30 years the academic study of communication and media has been established in many parts of the world. Universities offer programmes in Communications Studies and, more commonly, in Media Studies at undergraduate and graduate levels. PhD programmes in these and related fields (telecommunications; digital media, the Internet) continue to grow. Taught programmes need a body of research and literature upon which they can draw and to which they can refer students for further reading. They need not only an available pool of data and knowledge, but frameworks within which to begin to think about 'communication' and 'media', particular issues and questions through which to focus thinking and discussion. None of this existed before the 1970s. I began my working life as an academic in 1967, when I was appointed as a Lecturer in Communication at the then Regent Street Polytechnic, with a brief to contribute to developing a Diploma in Communication Studies as a mix of practice-based courses on radio, television and journalism with a range of add-on 'liberal studies' options in languages, history and literature. In 1975, after polytechnics were allowed to offer honours degree programmes, we began teaching a BA in Media Studies which remained for a number of years the first and only degree on this new academic subject in the UK. I vividly remember sitting at my desk in my first week at work and wondering what on earth my job title meant and, more exactly, what on earth I should read in answer to my perplexity. Three books remain etched in my memory: Colin Cherry's *Human Communication*, Konrad Lorenz's *On Aggression*, and Marshall McLuhan's *Understanding Media*. From the first, I learnt little since I could not understand it, from the second, I learned something about the non-verbal communicative behaviour of grey-lag geese, and from the third I learnt that the electric light-bulb was pure information and a great deal more besides. McLuhan was the first great stimulant to my thinking about 'media'. The second was Stuart Hall whose weekly general theory seminars for his graduate students at Birmingham I attended for a year in 1974 in preparation for the launch of our new degree the following year.

It is a rare distinction to have put a new academic field of study on the map, but this is what Hall achieved as Director of the Centre for Contemporary Cultural Studies (CCCS) at Birmingham from 1968 to 1979. Of course this was not achieved single-handedly. It was built on the foundational work of Raymond Williams and Richard Hoggart in particular who founded the Centre. But undoubtedly Hall's charismatic brilliance as a teacher, combined with his voracious appetite for new ideas culled from disparate disciplines, enthused and energized a generation of students. They became his disciples going forth to spread the word and establish the academic credentials of something that, 30 years ago, was yet to be recognized as 'cultural studies'. It is beyond the scope of this chapter to sketch the intellectual trajectory of Stuart Hall's academic life.[1] I will focus only on one strand within the development of Cultural Studies in its 'heroic decade', namely the formation of something called 'media studies' which was a key aspect of the activities of the Centre throughout the 1970s. Hoggart and Williams each made important and innovative contributions to thinking about the press and broadcasting in the 1950s and 1960s. But neither spoke of 'the media' in the taken for granted way that Hall and CCCS did in the 1970s. It was Marshall McLuhan, as we have seen, who established this usage through his seminal *Understanding Media* which, in the early 1960s, foresaw the new electronic media age. Work in the Centre explored the press, radio and television, but the last of this trio received most attention, because it had become, in the 1960s, the most popular everyday source of entertainment and political information and debate for most British people.[2]

Re-thinking the study of culture

Television then, in the 1970s, was at the heart of contemporary culture and thus a fit object of concern for a graduate centre set up for its study. Hall's engagement with television was at two levels. There was first of all the question of the impact of television on contemporary life. Beyond that, there was the wider question of the approach to the study of culture itself. Hall was, at that time,

---

1 For the first full-length study of Hall's intellectual career, see Rojek (2003).

2 On the press, see Smith et al. (1975). Dorothy Hobson's study of the domestic routines of working-class housewives attends to their use of both radio and television (Hobson, 1980).

engaged in a thorough-going re-think of that question most clearly summarized in his well-known essay on the two paradigms of cultural studies in which he explored the differences between himself and the founding fathers of Cultural Studies (Hall, 1980b).[3] The terrain upon which they – Edward Thompson, Richard Hoggart and Raymond Williams – had located their concerns was culture as a 'common' and 'ordinary' and 'everyday' thing. It was rooted in everyday practice and experience both of which were indicative (for Williams) of human 'energy' and 'creativity'. In essence, such positions were 'humanist' and 'voluntarist' (Hall, 1980b: 63). They side-stepped the question of determination, of those social forces that structured, determined and constrained the scope of human praxis[4] and creativity. The 'structuralist' paradigm[5] was a critique of the culturalist notion of the centrality of 'experience' and its categories:

> Whereas, in 'culturalism', experience was the ground – the terrain of the lived – where consciousness and conditions intersected, structuralism insisted that 'experience' could not, by definition, be the ground of anything, since one could only 'live' and experience one's conditions in and through the categories, classifications and frameworks of culture. These categories, however, did not arise in or from experience: rather experience was their 'effect'. (Hall, 1980b: 66)

---

3 I'm quite proud of the fact that this article appeared in the first issue of *Media, Culture & Society* that I put together and edited. It is followed by John Corner's much-cited critique of 'codes and cultural analysis', the earliest and still the best criticism of Hall's application of encoding to the analysis of television (Corner, 1980). See my editorial comments (*MCS*, 1980, 2(1): 2–3).

4 The preferred term, at the time, in Marxist discourse, for the unity of theory and practice.

5 Structuralism was a term that, by 1980 when it was still in fashion, had come to cover a multitude of rather different positions. Originally it was applied to a new approach to the study of language opened up by the Swiss linguist Ferdinand de Saussure at the beginning of the twentieth century. Saussure's theory and method for the study of language were taken up and applied to other disciplines, especially in France. In the late 1950s Claude Lévi-Strauss established what he called Structural Anthropology, based on Saussure. From there structuralism rapidly took off in a number of directions, influencing the study of literature (Roland Barthes), psychoanalysis (Jacques Lacan) and philosophy (Jacques Derrida). At the heart of the structuralist project was an attempt to simplify the bewildering diversity and difference of surface social phenomena (e.g. spoken language, what Saussure called *parole*) by identifying the underlying structures that produced and determined such apparent diversity. Structuralism is reductionist and determinist. In the 1970s, both Freud and Marx were read as structuralist thinkers; Freud for his theory of the unconscious, and Marx for identifying the economy as the structural determinant of the whole social formation in its manifest economic, political and cultural forms. Louis Althusser was widely recognized at the time as *the* Marxist structuralist.

Experience does not validate (authenticate) lived existence. It does not give us access to the *real* conditions of existence, but rather mystifies them. In reality, the authenticity of experience is an effect of ideology wherein and whereby 'men' live in an imaginary relation to the real. 'In the last instance', Hall claims, this 'imaginary relationship' serves 'the expanded reproduction of the [capitalist] mode of production itself' (ibid.: 42).

The great strength of the 'structuralisms', in Hall's view, was their stress 'on "determinate conditions"' (ibid.: 43). Experience cannot presume itself as a self-validating category, since what determines it is and elsewhere and otherwise than what it (experience) thinks it is. The concept of ideology serves to account for how the real (material, economic) conditions are hidden from us in ordinary everyday experience. It is precisely through the crucial concept of ideology that a materialist (Marxist) theory sought to account for the *real* material conditions of a capitalist society which remained obscured in (and by) the lived experience of such a society. It is the task of thought that thinks outside of 'lived experience' to reveal it for what it is: 'Ideologies are ... the sphere of the *lived* – the sphere of *experiencing* rather than of "thinking"' (Hall, 1977). A culturalist perspective, with its emphasis on 'experience', cannot really mobilize the concept of ideology: 'The authenticating power and reference of "experience" imposes a barrier between culturalism and a proper conception of "ideology". Yet, without it, the effectivity of "culture" for the reproduction of a particular mode of production cannot be grasped' (ibid.: 45).

Williams et al. locate the question of culture in relation to ordinary, everyday existence, and this is captured by the category of 'lived experience'. But for Hall, it is this that is the problem. In a capitalist society the 'real' conditions of existence are obscured and hidden. And how does this take place? Where is the veil drawn? It is in that everyday existence wherein we are immersed, in which we 'live' unthinkingly. Lived experience operates through 'common sense' which is 'at one and the same time, "spontaneous", ideological and *unconscious*' (Hall, 1977: 325. Original emphasis). Common sense is unconscious in two ways: in its spontaneous immediacy it shows the absence of reflective, conscious thought (rationality, theory) and as that 'space' wherein the 'real conditions of existence' are repressed, it functions as the social unconscious.

Hall wanted to hang on to the determinacy of 'the relations of production', as must any properly orthodox Marxism. However, he wished at the same time to avoid the obvious problem of economic reductionism whereby all other social phenomena are regarded as having no independent existence and impact but are treated as mere 'effects' of the determining economic relations of production. Althusser addressed this problem, notably in his 'famous' (Hall, 1980b: 45), 'important and influential' (Hall, 1977: 335) *Ideological State Apparatuses* essay where, in the first part, he asked what it is that 'gives' the social relations of production (Althusser, 1971). It is not that *in the first place* there are the relations of production and everything else can be explained or inferred as arising from them. To such a view the obvious retort is, 'But what produces the relations of production? They don't come from nowhere.' What Hall tries to grasp is 'the effectivity of "culture" for the reproduction of capitalism as a particular mode of production'. Following Althusser, he thinks of the social institutions for a capitalist society – the family, education, the media – as the primary sites for the reproduction of a complex set of social relationships, attitudes and beliefs that separately and together work to sustain the existing dominant economic mode of production. In common-sense ways we inhabit and live our social structures and the ways of life and the common-sense views of the world which they embody and express. This is the terrain of lived experience. This is the social unconscious that functions to reproduce unquestioningly the material 'base'. It is the task (the duty and obligation) of thought precisely to put all this *in* question.

The relevance of ideology

If there is one idea that Stuart Hall has bequeathed to the study of culture and the media in particular, it is the concept of ideology. 'It is difficult', he writes, 'to conceive of a Cultural Studies thought within a Marxist paradigm which is innocent of the category of "ideology"' (Hall, 1977: 45). Ideology is not a central term in Marx's writings and it is usually derived from one of two sources: either from *Capital*, and the concept of commodity fetishism (the starting point, as we have seen, for the Frankfurt School) or from the much earlier *German Ideology* (1845). The latter is Hall's primary reference point. It does make a difference which of the two is chosen, since they generate quite different perspectives on the ways in which the ideological veil is drawn over social life. As we have seen, starting from *Capital* and commodity fetishism, what emerged, for Critical Theory in the 1930s, were the key concepts of alienation and reification as terms to capture the false consciousness of an emerging capitalist consumer culture. This perspective is absent in Hall's appropriation of the concept of ideology partly because it is over-deterministic and partly because of its cultural pessimism about the fate of the masses. Neither the first, nor the second generation of cultural studies was inclined to speak of 'mass' culture. Hall did not want to use such a term, as the Frankfurt School had done, to explain the stupefaction of the masses by mass culture but rather as a potential site of struggle and contestation, something challenged and resisted not merely 'in theory' but by ordinary social members in the contexts of daily life.

Hall's starting point is *The German Ideology* and 'ruling ideas':

> The ideas of the ruling class are in every epoch the ruling ideas; i.e. the class which
> is the ruling material force of society is, at the same time, its ruling intellectual

force. The class which has the means of material production at its disposal, has control at the same time over the means of mental production, so that thereby, generally speaking, the ideas of those who lack the means of mental production are subject to it. The ruling ideas are nothing more than the ideal expression of the dominant material relationships, the dominant relationships grasped as ideas; hence of the relationships which make the one class the ruling one, therefore, the ideas of its dominance. The individuals composing the ruling class possess among other things consciousness, and therefore think. Insofar, therefore, as they rule as a class and determine the extent and compass of an epoch, it is self-evident that they do this in its whole range, hence among other things rule as thinkers, as producers of ideas, and regulate the production and distribution of the ideas of their age: thus their ideas are the ruling ideas of the epoch. (Marx and Engels, [1845–6] 1970: 64–5)

This, in a nutshell, is 'the dominant ideology thesis'. Those who, in any age, control the means of material production also control the means of mental production and, through them, circulate ideas, values and opinions that are broadly favourable to their continuing, material (i.e. economic and political) dominance. Subordinate classes, who lack the means of production, are unable to disseminate competing versions of social and political reality that might challenge the rulings' ideas. Left-wing readings of British press history argue this very point (Curran, 1977, 1981). Though 'the media' as we know them did not exist in the mid-nineteenth century, there is no doubt that its roots were already established in the formation of the modern newspaper industry. Marx himself was a jobbing journalist in order to provide for his family. It was but a short step to apply this famous passage to the media landscape of the late twentieth century.[6]

However, while it remains the case to this day that the ownership of the means of mental production continues, on the whole, to be in the hand of private capital and while it is true that the ideas that circulate in them do not, to put it minimally, pose a threat to their material interests, there yet remains the question (not dealt with by Marx) as to how the ruling ideas actually get into the heads of individuals and, once there, how effective they might be in securing their acceptance. This is the crux of the matter for Stuart Hall. As we will see, in attempting to set up a model for analysing the social relations of cultural production which seeks to explain how television 'works', he begins by rejecting the then prevalent social scientific approach to the media which was heavily influenced by the American sociology of mass communication. It too had started from a heavily deterministic model of powerful media which injected passive

---

6 It was notably applied to the role of the media and the social production of news in relation to the 'moral panic' about mugging in the early 1970s (Hall et al., 1978: 53–77).

media consumers with their messages. Hall wanted to account for the production of media output, its transmission and its reception, a model, in short, of the social relations of cultural production: producers, programmes, audiences. His solution was the encoding/decoding model which served as the basis for the development of the study of the media at Birmingham in the 1970s.

Encoding/decoding

'Encoding/Decoding' was published in *Culture, Media, Language* in 1980. It appeared in the book's third sub-section, called 'Media Studies'. A footnote at the start of the article tells us that, as published, it is an edited extract from a longer piece called 'Encoding and Decoding in the Television Discourse', CCCS Stencilled Paper No. 7, produced at the Centre in 1974. The paper was originally presented by Stuart Hall to a colloquium at the Centre for Mass Communication Research at the University of Leicester in 1973; for the benefit of CCCS students, some notes on its reception at the colloquium and points for further consideration were subsequently added at the end. The paper received another airing a year later, when it was presented as 'Encoding and Decoding' in a symposium on Broadcasters and the Audience held in Venice as part of the Prix Italia. Throughout the 1970s, CCCS produced and published its work in progress. Individual work was circulated in the stencilled papers series, available on application, from the Centre. Group work on particular themes was self-published in the aptly named series, 'Working Papers in Cultural Studies' (WPCS). At the end of the decade Hutchinson contracted to publish the material hitherto produced and disseminated by the Centre, along with unpublished work in progress and future projects. *Culture, Media, Language* is subtitled 'Working Papers in Cultural Studies, 1972–1979'. Thus the appearance of 'Encoding/Decoding' in a published book marks both an end and a beginning – the end of a samizdat culture of dissemination and circulation, and its entry into mainstream academic literature.

At first sight, the published version of 'Encoding/Decoding' (hereafter E/D) is a slight piece. It is only ten pages long, and is not overburdened with footnotes and references. It has a provisional, unfinished air about it. It is a 'work in progress' that might be further reworked. Its title proposes a topic that needs no further elaboration than two words separated by a slash. It has by now contracted to an internal shorthand reference understood by all concerned. At the same time it indicates an external reference point, *S/Z* (Barthes, 1975), which elaborated a model for analysing the various codes that constitute the literary text. In itself, E/D is a text without aspirations to an afterlife. Its importance lies not just in what it is about but also in what lies outside it: the issues, concerns, and commitments that called it into existence and that prompted its changes of direction and revisions. These concerns were not static, but evolved over the eight or so years that preceded its emergence in published form. To clarify those concerns is not to furnish a historical backdrop to the text (its 'context'), it is to begin to account for the textual features of the published article itself in its provisional and unfinished character. If the text-as-published does not seem to propose itself as something that was conceived in the first place as written-to-be-published, we might reasonably seek its *raison d'être* as residing elsewhere. To illuminate the text in this way, then, is to recover the concerns to which it was a crucial contribution. That means invoking the working life of the Centre in the 1970s and its samizdat culture of writing as work-in-progress, *working* papers that contribute to the unfolding project of cultural studies, the study of contemporary culture.

The period between the first presentation of E/D (1973) and its publication (1980) was one of astonishing productivity for Hall himself. The 'working bibliography' of his writings at the end of a book produced in his honour by David Morley and Kuan-Hsing Chen (1996: 504–14) reveals a continuing flow, in these years, of written contributions to an extraordinarily wide range of issues. For all the tensions generated by the Centre – and doubtless, in part, because of them – the 1970s was the high point of Hall's work in terms of teaching and writing, and the encoding/decoding model was at the centre of both. Colin Sparks describes it as 'one of Hall's major intellectual achievements during [this] period' (Sparks, 1996: 86).[7] By the time *Media, Culture, Language* was published in 1980, Hall had left Birmingham to take up a chair in sociology at the Open University. He had been in CCCS since 1964, and its director since 1968. After 15 years, he was exhausted:

> I felt I'd been through the internal crises of each cultural studies year once too often ... Then the question of feminism was very difficult to take ... if I'd been opposed to feminism, that would have been a different thing, but I was for it. So, being targeted as 'the enemy', as the senior patriarchal figure, placed me in an impossible position ... In the early days of the Centre we were like the Alternative University. There was little separation between staff and students. What I saw emerging was that separation between generations, between statuses – students and teachers – and I didn't want that ... So I wanted to leave, because of all these reasons. (Morley and Chen, 1996: 500)

Now none of this – the life of the Centre in the 1970s, its 'lived reality' – is necessarily relevant to its written output. There is no necessary correspondence

---

7 And in Rojek's account, Hall's 'most important methodological contribution to Cultural Studies was arguably the famous paper on encoding and decoding which is now regarded as a key paper in narrative analysis' (2003: 14).

between life and works, either in the case of individuals or institutions. However, the rows, the banging doors, the angry silences, the bruised egos were provoked not, as in soap operas, by the grittiness of interpersonal life and family relations, but by passionate commitments to particular political and theoretical positions (Brunsdon, 1996). To hear in the texts produced and published by the Centre the echoes of 'the noise of theory', of things hotly and loudly contested, is to begin to see how they once mattered and what they meant at a time which, though only 30 or so years ago, now seems infinitely remote. But why should that matter now? It matters not at all if texts are proposed as autonomous objects of inquiry, uncoupled from their historical conditions of production, palimpsests upon which later readers inscribe their own concerns. That, however, is not the position E/D argued for.

A model in opposition

'Encoding/Decoding' can be seen as a response to what was regarded as the dominant paradigm in media scholarship at the time, associated primarily with the American tradition of media effects research. American mass communication sociology was read, if at all, in Britain in the 1960s and 1970s, as defined by social-scientific positivism and preoccupied with quantitative, empirically-oriented studies of the mass media. The foundational studies of the 1940s, which combined critical and administrative research, were no longer an inspiration on either side of the Atlantic. Intellectual sclerosis had set in. American mass communication research, from the mid-1950s onwards, had lost that critical, questioning edge which characterized the work of Lazarsfeld, Merton, Riesmann and their contemporaries. It was a tree that was ready for shaking. At the same time, as we have seen, there was no indigenous tradition of critical sociology in Britain. American sociology was no help in the search for a *critical* approach to the study of contemporary British society and culture. Hall's critique of mass communication research was aimed, however, not at American scholars but a target closer at hand:

> The piece has a number of different contexts … The first, in a sense, is a kind of methodological/theoretical context, because the paper was delivered to a colloquium, which was organised by the Centre for Mass Communication Research at the University of Leicester. Now the Centre for Mass Communication Research was a traditional centre, using traditional empirical positivistic models of content analysis, audience-effects survey research, etc. So the paper … has a slightly polemical thrust. It's positioned against some of those positions and it's positioned, therefore, against a particular notion of content as a performed and fixed meaning or message.

... The encoding/decoding model was not a grand model. I had in my sights the Centre for Mass Communication Research – that was who I was trying to blow out of the water. (Cruz and Lewis, 1994: 253, 255)

The colloquium for which the paper was written was organized by James Halloran, then director of the Centre for Mass Communication Research in Leicester. Hall acknowledges Halloran's contribution to the proceedings as properly raising the question of studying 'the whole mass communication process', from the structure of the production message at one end to audience perception and use at the other. However, the key difference between Hall and Halloran (and, more generally, between Birmingham and Leicester) is that the former came out of literary studies (initially concerned with texts, language and meaning), whereas the latter came out of sociology, more particularly American mass communication sociology. Furthermore, the concerns of Hall and of CCCS were beginning to be situated within a specifically Marxist framework, whereas Leicester had no such clear theoretical/political agenda.

The key point of difference, for Hall, is that the communication process, through all its various stages, is not neutral. Mass communication sociology regards communicative failures as kinks in the system, 'technical faults in transmission' (1973: 19). Through the interventions of professionals in sociology and education, cultural policies might be directed towards 'helping the audiences to receive the television communication better, more effectively' (ibid.: 1). As Hall saw it, such a position does not begin to address, does not even see, what the problem really is: namely that 'in societies like ours, communication between the production elites in broadcasting and their audiences is necessarily a form of "systematically distorted communication"' (ibid.: 19). The presumed neutrality of both the communicative process and the interventions of academics contributes to that systemic distortion and is, albeit unconsciously, a political choice even if not seen as such:

To 'misread' a political choice as a technical one represents a type of unconscious collusion to which social science researchers are all too prone. Though the sources of such mystification are both social and structural, the actual process is greatly facilitated by the operation of discrepant codes. It would not be the first time that scientific researchers had 'unconsciously' played a part in the reproduction of hegemony, not only by openly submitting to it, but by simply operating the 'professional bracket'. (Hall, 1973: 19)

These are the concluding sentences to Hall's 1973 paper, which clearly fire a broadside at a rival research centre in the same field. They were excised in the 1980 published version, however, for the focus of attention had by then changed.

A text in transition

Let us consider, then, which parts of the earlier draft disappear in the later, revised version that gets into print. The focal topic of the Leicester colloquium – television as discourse – in part determined the paper's address, while its location in part determined the 'take' on the topic: what the paper was setting itself against as much as what it was for. What it was arguing for was a semiotic decoding of elements of popular culture, which are variously treated as texts, messages, and practices of signification. To decode the text is not simply to produce a 'reading' of the message as if it were in any way transparent. Rather, it invokes a 'hermeneutics of suspicion' that regards the forms of popular culture (cinema and television, in particular) as 'systematically distorted forms of communication'. This phrase, introduced in quotes in the first paragraph of the paper but not attributed until much later (Hall, 1973: 16, n. 23), is from an essay of that title by Jürgen Habermas, which treats Freudian psychoanalysis as a 'scientific' resource for unravelling the systematic distortions of the unconscious as manifested in the discourses of patients in the therapeutic situation. If the texts of popular culture are like dreams 'that express in "disguised" form the repressed content of a culture' (ibid.: 11), then the critical analytical task is akin to Freudian decodings of the 'condensation and displacement [that take place] in the encoding of latent materials and meanings through manifest symbolizations' (ibid.: 10). If 'depth analysis' gets through to the latent meanings concealed by the 'phenomenal forms' of popular culture, then decoding is the means of cracking open what is hidden (disguised) in their codes. The emerging field of semiotics, most closely associated in the essay with the work of Umberto Eco and Roland Barthes, is used to move between the surface structures of popular texts and their deep, mythic structures. These ideas are developed in a lengthy discussion of the Western as a genre in cinema and, later, television (ibid.: 5–11), no traces of which remain in the published version of the paper.

David Morley and Charlotte Brunsdon, in their engaging account of the working life of the Centre in those years, note that '[t]here were many boxes of something labelled "The Western" in Birmingham in the 1970s, the uncompleted labour of yet another CCCS project' (Morley and Brunsdon, 1999: 3). This was doubtless the trace of a much earlier engagement with cinema on Hall's part. In 1961, he began teaching media, film, and popular culture at Chelsea College, University of London. Through the education department of the British Film Institute, he worked on film and television with Paddy Whannel between 1962 and 1964, which resulted in their joint publication, *The Popular Arts* (1964). But the concern with cinema (a key popular art) and television fiction genres, which was the substantive heart of E/D in 1973, had vanished seven years later. E/D is thus a text in transition. Present in the first version, but on its way out, is the residual trace of a complex of concerns with the textual analysis of the forms of popular culture. There, but not yet central to the model, is the break into a complex Marxism that would become the defining characteristic of Hall's work through the 1970s. For this, the concept of ideology would be central. Althusser's essay on 'Ideological State Apparatuses' and Gramsci's more historical concept of hegemony drawn from *The Prison Notebooks* both take a bow towards the end of the paper. Each had become available in English only a year or so earlier. But neither had yet been fully assimilated into a reworked Marxist analysis of culture, which would become Hall's most significant contribution to a field of study that he, more than any other individual, helped to establish.

The 1980 text

The main difference between the stencilled paper and the text as published is the excision of the semiotics of the Western, which reduces the overall length by a third. It has, moreover, been topped and tailed. Gone are the references to the topic of the colloquium to which it contributed, and the overt polemics against the sociology of mass communication and behaviourist psychology have been much toned down. Whereas the earlier paper read like a contribution to the deconstruction of texts via semiotics, the published version reads like a contribution to the interpretation of texts by audiences within a Marxist/class-based problematic, with the 'dominant ideology' as the master concept underpinning the piece. The emphasis in the model and its theoretical base has shifted.

For those reared in the American tradition of mass communication research, an initial reading of the essay may first trigger a sense of *déjà vu*.[8] The terms 'encoding' and 'decoding' have been familiar since Claude Shannon's (1949) essay, 'Mathematical Theory of Communication', in which Shannon, an electrical engineer, sought to enhance the integrity of the communication process by protecting messages from being garbled and distorted by 'noise'. His model of communication and information processing consisted of

source → encoder → message → decoder → destination

This outline was picked up by Wilbur Schramm, who elaborated the model of the communication process between two people as shown in Figure 8.1 overleaf. Schramm thus introduced notions of feedback into the model, and then further contextualized it within the general framework of social relationship and a sociocultural environment.

---

8 This and the following two paragraphs were written by Michael Gurevitch in our jointly authored chapter on 'Encoding/Decoding', in Katz et al. (2003).

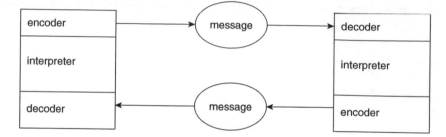

Figure 8.1 Schramm's model of the communication process

Hall's use of the terminology of encoding and decoding looks superficially like a throwback to the Shannon and Schramm models. But that impression is misleading. Hall begins his essay by referring to the 'traditional' model of sender–message–receiver. He then criticizes the linearity of this model with its focus on message exchanges, and offers an alternative model of communication based on Marx's model of commodity production, comprising the stages of production, circulation, distribution/consumption, and reproduction. Thus, Hall incorporates the notion of production, essential to an analysis of the mass media as content-producing organizations, into the encoding/decoding framework.

Hall then highlights the institutional structures of the production of media messages, in terms analogous to Marx's 'labour process', and uses the encoding/decoding labels to identify what he calls 'meaning structure 1', referring to the encoding side of the equation, and 'meaning structure 2', referring to the decoding side. The two meaning structures are not necessarily symmetrical. In fact, Hall assumes that they rarely, if ever, overlap. Unlike Shannon, however, Hall is not concerned about this absence of symmetry. On the contrary, he views it as essential to the argument that the decoding process may be independent of the encoded meaning, with a life and power of its own. Thus, while his theoretical framework draws on the basic principles of structuralism and semiology, it also challenges the semiological claim about the power of the encoded text and the notion that meanings are firmly embedded in the text. The receivers of messages are not obliged, in this view, to accept or decode messages as encoded, and can resist the ideological power and influence of the text by applying divergent or oppositional readings.

The model can therefore be applied in at least two ways, depending on whether the emphasis is placed on the moment of encoding or that of decoding. More exactly, what is obscured in entitling the piece 'Encoding/Decoding' is the crucial question of what is encoded in the first moment and decoded in the second, namely, 'the television discourse'. To flesh it out more fully: the first moment is 'encoding → program(text)-as-discourse', and the second moment is 'program(text)-as-discourse → decoding'. While the stencilled paper focuses more on the moment of encoding, the published version moved towards the moment of decoding.

This leads to another significant contribution of the essay, namely the introduction of the notion of different modes of decoding. This discussion is adapted from a three-fold typology of value systems proposed by Frank Parkin (1971) in *Class Inequality and Political Order*: (1) a dominant value system, which results in deferential or aspirational orientation among people in a class system; (2) a subordinate value system, leading to accommodative response; and (3) a radical value system, which promotes oppositional interpretation of class inequalities. Hall's typology is, by and large, similar. He labels the first the 'dominant-hegemonic position', in which the message is decoded 'in terms of the reference code in which it has been encoded'. Located within this position is the professional code, 'which the professional broadcasters assume when encoding a message which has already been signified in a hegemonic manner'. The second he labels the 'negotiated code', which 'contains a mixture of adaptive and oppositional elements'. Finally, the 'oppositional code' refers to decoding in a 'globally contrary way' (1980a: 136–8). Despite the similarities between Parkin's and Hall's typologies, however, there is a basic and significant difference between them. Whereas Parkin's typology of value systems is essentially a *sociological* one, relating different value systems to class differences, Hall's typology is *semiological*, deploying the typology to identify different modes of decoding and meaning-making.

The moment of encoding

Hall's 1973 text had a largely internal reference point, produced for the students at CCCS, and the Media Studies Group in particular, as a kind of diagnostic model and tool-kit for their work in progress. This largely accounts for the provisional feel of the text and its 'incompleteness'. What completes the piece, what validates it (or not), is its application in concrete instances. This is a text whose autonomy is indeed relative – relative, that is, to the work it inspired and supported. In his note on responses to the paper as presented at Leicester, written as an addendum 'for Centre Members Only' (note the strong sense of an exclusive in-group), Hall remarked, 'The paper was quite well received, many of the questions being directed to discover whether the centre had begun to make the schema outlined at the end of the paper [i.e., the different ways in which the television message might be decoded] "empirical and operational"!' (1973: 21). The exclamation mark signals that Centre members already know the answer to that question. The whole point of the schema was to make it operational, that is, to apply it to television programmes and to test empirically whether 'real' viewers decode the programmes in the ways predicted by the model.

The work of two students in the group, Charlotte Brunsdon and David Morley, was developed precisely to test aspects of the model: namely, the codes of television as inscribed in a particular programme, *Nationwide*, and in a separate exercise, how actual viewers made sense of the programme's encoded 'ideological problematic' as they had analysed it. Did viewers 'buy' its message unproblematically? Did they adopt a more nuanced ('negotiated') interpretation of it? Or did they refuse to buy the programme's (ideological) world-view and possibly come up with an oppositional decoding that 'saw through' and unmasked the programme's ideological discourse (a highly specific framing of the meaning of 'nationhood')? Morley and Brunsdon hoped to run a full check on the model – the moment of encoding, the programme as encoded, and the programme as decoded by selected viewers – but succeeded in dealing only with the last two. They wanted to study the production process, the internal operational practices, the professional culture of broadcasting, and the 'moment of encoding' that yielded the programme-as-broadcast (David Morley, personal communication). But that was virtually impossible – with a few exceptions, access to the BBC for academics was very hard to come by in the 1970s. The model had proposed a tripartite structure whose three 'moments' were integrally connected, so that the 'proof' of the schema lay in examining all three aspects of it. But it was the model's subsequent fate to be read with such an emphasis on the moment of decoding that the other two moments were gradually effaced.

Largely overlooked now, but very important at the time, was the Media Group's detailed study of one *Panorama* programme (Hall et al., 1976), the third and final of three programmes broadcast during the run-up to the election. It was transmitted on Monday, 7 October 1974, three days prior to polling day, and was called 'What Kind of Unity?' – a title that questioned the theme of national unity against a background of resurgent nationalisms in Wales, Scotland, and Northern Ireland and pressures for political devolution. The paper is a careful analysis of the operations of ideology, understood as the struggle over meanings within an accepted, unquestioned consensus (the legitimacy of parliamentary politics). It is a brilliant exploration of the ways in which preferred meanings are inflected through television discourse which, in this programme, was controlled partly by the BBC and partly by representatives of the political parties. What is programmatically sketched in E/D is thus put to work here in a detailed case study of the moment of encoding:

> In relation to the messages available through Television we shall suggest that they
> never deliver one meaning: they are, rather, the site of a plurality of meanings, in

which one is preferred and offered to viewers, over the others, as the most appropriate ... The broadcasters' encoding practices ... aim at establishing a transparency between the presentation of the topic, as embodied in the program, and the view which the audiences 'take' of it. The broadcaster tries, by all the technical and communicative competences at his command, to bring the encoding and decoding moments into alignment: it is an attempt to realise a certain kind of ideological closure, and thereby to establish a *preferred reading* of the topic ... However, it is in the nature of all linguistic systems which employ codes, that more than one reading can potentially be produced ... It follows, in our view, that different audiences ... can make more than one reading of what has been encoded. (Hall et al., 1976: 53, 67. Emphasis added)

The concept of the preferred reading[9] makes clear the central point that E/D programmatically established, namely that there was no necessary correspondence between the two moments of encoding and decoding. There was no guarantee that the ideological message encoded in the television programme would be 'bought' by all those who viewed it. This position was in sharp contrast with the theoretical model of the film viewer elaborated at exactly the same time (over the early 1970s) by the then influential journal, *Screen*. It was also at odds with some of the more advanced Althusserians at Birmingham, in particular, Rosalind Coward and John Ellis, as we will shortly see.

I have suggested that E/D functioned as a methodological tool-kit for the study of contemporary media, especially television. In its first incarnation, in the early 1970s, the emphasis was on the moment of encoding; the focal concern was with a semiotic analysis of the narrative structures of popular genres (the Western, for instance). In the course of the decade the emphasis moved towards the moment of decoding, as understood within a fiercely contested 'Marxist problematic' – a favourite phrase in what came to be known as 'Centre-speak' – concerning the ways in which ideology operated on individuals-as-subjects. If E/D was a text in transition, it was accompanied on its way by a travelling theoretical apparatus designed to justify and validate it. This apparatus was, as Colin Sparks has noted, baroque and intrinsically unstable (1996: 88). It was a complicated bricolage of theoretical bits and pieces culled from

---

9 Chris Rojek calls this a vexatious concept because it is not easy to distinguish whose preferred reading is up for discussion; that of the critical analyst or that of the subject under analysis (Rojek, 2003: 96). But as used in the study of current affairs television, it clearly refers to neither of these. Rather it identifies the hidden labour of television production as a process in which taken-for-granted social, political and cultural values are inflected into the ways in which the programme is itself framed and, within that framing, itself frames the issues. The concept of the preferred reading or meaning is very helpful for dealing with the vexed question of how 'bias' works in broadcasting and elsewhere.

anthropology, linguistics, sociology, literary theory, Marxism, psychoanalysis and other sources. As new concepts were added to it, others were discarded or simply fell off. Keeping up with Theory in the Centre in the 1970s was no easy matter since it was always on the move. The preface to *Culture, Media, Language* disarmingly declared that 'Readers must not expect to find here a consistent theoretical position, unfolding from the beginning to its appointed conclusion: nor even a unified set of findings' (Hall et al., 1980: 10). To explain the shifting focus of the encoding/decoding model and the instability of its accompanying theoretical underpinnings, we must attend to the changes of direction that were taking place in the Centre in the 1970s.

Changing the subject

The account offered so far of the concept of ideology as mobilized at the Centre remains one-sided. The dominant ideology thesis addressed a key issue that Marx posed; those who control the means of material production also control the means of mental production. The media, as Benjamin had put it, were 'in the hands of the enemy'. They were instruments for the dissemination of ruling ideas and to be critiqued as such. Marx made his case specifically against the owners of the means of production, the capitalist bourgeoisie. In the febrile climate of the Centre in the 1970s, the struggle over 'ruling ideas' became detached from its umbilical link with the capitalist economy. It was partly that, in Britain, class had always been as much a social as an economic concept. The 'ruling class' was thought of more as an unholy mix of monarchy, church, state and the landed aristocracy rather than those vulgar bourgeois economic upstarts, the self-made men of business and manufacturing. But, more importantly, the new social movements of the late 1950s identified new and different enemies. The women's movement pointed the finger at men. The American civil rights movement pointed the finger at whites. Both had a powerful and destabilizing impact on the work of the Centre in the 1970s.

The original project for Cultural Studies at Birmingham came from Richard Hoggart and was concerned with British class and culture. An important strand of the Centre's work engaged with 'the problem' of working-class youth in Britain. The problem was emblematically deposited in *The Uses of Literacy* in the figure of 'the juke-box boys' who used to sit around in milk-bars mainly to play the latest hits on the nickelodeon: 'Compared even with the pub around the corner, this is all a peculiarly thin and pallid form of dissipation, a sort of spiritual dry rot amid the odour of boiled milk' (Hoggart, 1992: 248). Hoggart's dismissive evaluation was much criticized by later Centre students, but working-class youth culture remained a continuing focus of attention through the 1970s and produced important work, gathered and published in *Resistance through Rituals* (Jefferson and Hall, 1975). However, it was subject to a surprise ambush from the female students who noted that youth, class and culture were being treated quite unproblematically, by the male students engaged on the topic, as a boyzone thing. Never mind the juke-box boys and their heirs – bike boys, for instance (Cohen), or the factory 'lads' (Willis), or mods, rockers and punks (Hebdige) – what about girls, class and culture? Lucy Bland, Charlotte Brunsdon, Rosalind Coward, Dorothy Hobson, Angela McRobbie, Janice Winship and others had been recruited to Birmingham to do graduate research on gendered topics that included women's magazines, girls' subcultures, romantic love, girls' comics and the culture of working-class women. However, they seemed to spend most of their time, as Brunsdon recalls, trying to figure out what feminist intellectual work should be and how it related to the dominant definition of cultural studies already in place at the Centre (Brunsdon, 1996: 276). Feminism broke into cultural studies 'like a thief in the night; interrupted, made an unseemly noise, seized the time [and] crapped on the table', Stuart Hall later declared in some less than tranquil recollections of his time at Birmingham (Hall, 1996: 269).

The question of race and racism appeared on Birmingham's agenda at about the same time and marked a decisive turn in Hall's own theoretical and public intellectual work[10] as well as the Centre's (ibid.: 270). Again the politics of race undermined the normative assumptions of the original concern with class and culture. Feminism attacked it for ignoring gender-related issues. To this were added criticisms of its unexamined assumptions about Britishness. The English working class was now found to be male and white and chauvinist and racist; a very different picture from Hoggart's idealized account and Thompson's heroic narrative. Getting race and racism onto the agenda of cultural studies, in the late 1970s, was accomplished only through

a long and sometimes bitter – certainly bitterly contested – internal struggle against a resounding but unconscious silence. A struggle which continued in what has since become known, but only in the re-written history, as one of the great seminal books of the Centre for Cultural Studies, *The Empire Strikes Back*. In actuality, Paul Gilroy and the group of people who produced the book found it extremely difficult to create the necessary theoretical and political space in the Centre in which to work on the project. (ibid.: 270)

---

10 Hall has always been critically aware of the relationship between his academic (theoretical) work and his wider social role as a public intellectual and spokesperson of the Left.

'Movements provoke theoretical moments' (ibid.). The new social movements called for new theoretical approaches to questions of power, domination and ideology. Neither could easily be assimilated within orthodox Marxism's preoccupations with class, economy and the state. The question of ideology, as the mechanism whereby social inequality and conflict were papered over and normalized, had now to account for gendered and ethnic subjectivities as well. The question of 'the subject' was foregrounded by the new social movements and called for yet another 'theoretical detour' at Birmingham. What further dislocated and decentred the original settled path of CCCS was its 'linguistic turn'; 'the discovery of discursivity, of textuality' (ibid.).

Language and ideology

I have sketched, in the previous chapter, some major developments in the study of language and communication that took place in the United States and Britain from the 1950s onwards and which were taken up and applied to the study of the media, and especially television, from the 1980s onwards. Birmingham's linguistic turn was in a very different direction. Developments in the philosophy of ordinary language, pragmatics and the analysis of conversation were almost completely overlooked. Instead, and in tune with the structuralist predilections that ruled at the Centre, the engagement with language morphed into an engagement with semiotics or semiology as it was named by its only begetter, the Swiss linguist, Ferdinand de Saussure:

> Language is a system of signs that express ideas, and is therefore comparable to a system of writing ... *A science that studies the life of signs within society* is conceivable; it would be a part of social psychology and consequently of general psychology; I shall call it *semiology* from Greek *semeiôn* 'sign'). Semiology would show what constitutes signs, what laws govern them ... The task of the linguist is to find out what makes language a special system within the mass of semiological data. (Saussure, 1979: 16. Original emphases)

The starting point for the consideration of language, in the last chapter, was as a speech act and, arising from this, as a communicative interaction whose expressive medium was talk. Speech (*parole*) as we saw, was specifically ruled out by Saussure as an impossible object of enquiry. It was 'a confused mass of heterogeneous and unrelated things' lacking in any perceivable unity. Saussure thought of language (*langue*) as a theoretical system that underpinned the possibility of spoken and written languages (*parole*). It is a difference between language 'as *structure* and *event*, that is to say between abstract systems of rules and the concrete, individual happenings produced within that system' (Sturrock,

1979: 8). The basic components of the system were linguistic *signs*. The sign has two components: the signifier (the sound-image) and the signified (the concept). 'Tree' as signifier is the spoken/written sound/image of the concept 'tree' which identifies a (leafy) real-world object. The signifier is reducible to its 'atomic' parts: the individual, different sounds/letters that combine to produce the sound/image or 'word' that *represents* the concept that indicates a worldly thing. Language is analysed by Saussure as a system of signification constituted by difference.

The structuralist 'moment' in Birmingham, while ultimately derived from Saussurean liguistics, was mediated through his latter-day French disciples of whom the first and most influential was Roland Barthes. In *Elements of Semiology* (1967) and *Mythologies* (1972), Barthes took up Saussure's challenge to apply semiology, the study of signs, beyond language itself. In *Mythologies*, Barthes made a basic distinction between denotative and connotative levels of meaning which was taken up and built into the encoding/decoding model.[11] In his essay on 'The rhetoric of the image', Barthes extended his semiological principles to the analysis of visual images in magazines and advertisements. The essay was translated and published in the very first *Working Papers in Cultural Studies* (1971) produced at the Centre and remains to this day a 'key text' for the analysis of media texts in Media Studies. It was natural for everyone at Birmingham to think of media output as *texts*. It was partly that they spent a lot of their time reading and discussing the latest academic texts from France, and partly the natural consequence of the Centre's intellectual origins in the study of Literature and literary texts. So texts, their textuality and intertextuality were part of the basic vocabulary of the Media and the Language groups. Grafted onto them were 'discourse' and 'discursivity', terms appropriated from yet another *maître penseur* across the channel whose ideas were thrown into the bubbling theoretical cauldron. Michel Foucault's theory of discursive practices and formations, as set out in *The Archeology of Knowledge* (1974), was assimilated into the Centre's growing engagement with language and subjectivity (Weedon, et al., 1980: 209).

The question of the subject can be deferred no longer. Perhaps it is best raised in relation to 'power', yet another keyword in the emerging theoretical vocabulary of Cultural Studies. Foucault identified three ways in which power operated upon individual human beings as exploitation, domination and subjection. The first he defined in economic terms and the struggle over the means of subsistence; the second, in political and religious terms (ideologies as domination), and the third as the suppression or denial of individual identity and the right to

---

11 See Hall (1980a: 132–3).

be one's self (Foucault, 1982: 212). It was the suppression of one's own individual identity *as* a women and/or black American that the new social movements identified and challenged. The 'politics of recognition', as it later became known,[12] asserted the rights of marginalized social groups to be themselves and to be accepted as such by others. The theoretical question of the subject, at the Centre, concerned the ways in which individuals internalized their subjection to power. Orthodox Marxism provided no answer and so solutions were sought elsewhere, starting with Althusser 'who first emphasised the term subject within a theory of ideology' (Coward and Ellis, 1977: 76). In the first part of his ISAs essay, Althusser raised the orthodox question as to how the capitalist relations of production were themselves re-produced. His answer, still quite orthodox, was that they were secured by the State through its repressive and ideological apparatuses. The state had the monopoly of legitimate violence and could enforce compliance through its use of the police and the army (its repressive state apparatuses), both of which, in moments of political crisis, have always been used by governments to quell social unrest. But in normal times the democratic capitalist state operates through the negotiation of social consensus which is achieved (never completely and seldom smoothly) through its ideological apparatuses which, for Althusser, included the family, the churches, education and the media.

So far so good. But there remained the question as to how those ideologies were secured at the level of individual social members. How did ruling ideas get inside their heads in such ways as to secure their acquiescence? The second half of the ISA essay attempts to answer that question and proceeds to do so by quietly abandoning Marx and turning instead to psychoanalysis. Marxian theory had little to say about the formation of individual subjects (individualism was regarded, after all, as perhaps *the* bourgeois ideology) and concentrated its attentions on the formation of class subjects, and particularly the working class as 'the subject and object of history'. So Althusser was out there on his own in attempting to account for the formation of individuals-as-subjects. He had distinguished between ideology-in-general and particular ideologies. The latter included class ideologies, nationalism, religious beliefs, 'family values', etc. These all had histories and were historical. But ideology-in-general which underpinned them all had no history because it was outside and beyond the time-bound historical process. It was eternal, like the Freudian Unconscious. The individual becomes an individual-as-subject and the subject-of-ideology at the point of socialization or, in other words, at the point of entry into language; the moment in which we are constituted as speaking subjects. We are all of us, Althusser famously

12 See Taylor's influential essay on 'The politics of recognition' (Taylor, 1994).

argued, interpellated[13] as subjects through our entry into language. Marx had thought that the contradictions in the relations of production produced ideology to rationalize and smooth over those contradictions. But this was much more radical. Language itself was *the* ideological mechanism from which there was no escape because there was no escape from language; no meta-language, nothing outside language that could give us a purchase on language-as-ideology. The idea of overcoming ideology was a dream, a fantasy. There was no escape from 'the prison house' of language/ideology.

The implications of this were worked through by the Centre's most rigorous Althusserians, Rosalind Coward and John Ellis whose *Language and Materialism* is subtitled 'Developments in Semiology and the Theory of the Subject'. It attempted a synthesis of semiology, Marxist theory and psychoanalysis, the latter as inflected through the writings of Jaques Lacan who, drawing on Saussure, had re-interpreted Freudian theories of the socialization process as the entry into language. Freud's Oedipal moment was re-interpreted as the mirror phase, the moment in which the still speechless child sees itself reflected in a mirror and begins to form an awareness of its self. This Narcissus-like moment, in which the child sees itself as an Other, is one of mis-recognition in which the ego (the 'I' of language) is formed as irredeemably split between subjective Self and objective Other: 'the notion of the Other [is] the locus of the deployment of the Word ... it must be posited as a facet of man as an animal at the mercy of Language' (Coward and Ellis, 1977: 120). Lacan's work was read as proposing 'a way of understanding language and discourse which denied every vestige of the notion of the "wholeness" of identity and consciousness. Man can never be the "total personality" while ever the play of displacement and condensation in which he is doomed to exercise his functions, marks his relation as subject to the signifier' (ibid.: 121). Human beings are *constructed* as subjects in and by language which, in ordinary usage, works to conceal itself as a construction. If we are indeed at the mercy of language as its irreparably fractured subjects, then at best we can make this visible by 'shaking the Sign', by de-constructing it and thereby exposing it *as* a construction. Hence the turn in the end, by Coward and Ellis, to the European *avant-garde* and their de(con)structive practices.

I have discussed, in Chapter 2, some of the elements in Bertolt Brecht's critique of bourgeois theatre and his alternative theory and practice of drama that at one and the same time sought to destroy the illusions of theatrical realism and to establish an alternative theatre that was both critical and popular. His

---

13 Fr. *interpeller* to call out to, to hail or summon. Also to be taken in for questioning (by the police). Interpellation is 'a hailing mechanism'. In Althusser's much cited example, we recognize and acknowledge ourselves as subjects when we respond to someone (a cop, maybe) shouting 'Hey, you!'

concepts, as we saw, contributed to a set of hotly contested debates in the 1930s about art, politics and the masses. Brecht was resurrected in Britain as these issues reignited three decades later but, in his second coming, as a split personality: Bert Brecht the advocate of a popular political theatre or Bertolt Brecht, exemplar of an avant-garde art-as-political-theory-and-practice. Both Brechts were reactivated in contemporary debates about theatre, film and television in the 1960s and 1970s.[14] For Coward and Ellis, Brechtian theatre 'consists of putting into crisis the normal forms of thinking and representation in bourgeois society' (1977: 36). *Épater la bourgeosie* had always between the shock-objective of the European artistic avant-garde. The critiques of 'realism' and 'naturalism' made by Barthes and others in the 1970s, keyed in with Brecht's idea of alienation as a device to shake the complacencies of bourgeois theatre, thereby engendering a new and critical theatrical engagement with contemporary reality. Coward and Ellis endorsed Brecht as an avant-garde revolutionary political practice that could destabilize the linguistic sign and the human subject and thereby reactivate the historical possibilities of individual and social change. This was the logical solution to their view of human beings as trapped in a contradictory subjectivity formed by language-as-ideology and from which, ordinarily, there was no escape.

Viewing subjects

After this lengthy but 'necessary theoretical detour' (as Hall would say) we can return to the moment of decoding and the question of the 'positionality' of the viewing subject which it addresses. As noted above, the E/D model argues for a non-correspondence between the moments of encoding and decoding. The broadcasters, for instance, may encode the programme 'message' in ways that

---

14 John McGrath was the exemplary practitioner/advocate of a Brechtian popular theatre. He was the founder/director of the 7:84 Theatre Company, the most outstanding product of the counter-theatre movement that developed in the late 1960s. It was committed – as was the agit-prop theatre of the 1930s from which it was descended (Goorney and MacColl, 1986) – to taking theatre to the people, and depended on a dedicated repertory company of actors willing to go on the road and perform all over the country in village halls, clubs and pubs (McGrath, 1981). In stark contrast, *Screen* and the British Film Institute advocated an avante-garde Brechtian 'filmic practice' that would destroy the naturalistic illusion of the regime of Hollywood cinema and its uncritical pleasures. It would do so by reminding viewers of the materiality of the filmic process. The most advanced advocate of this position at the time was Colin McCabe: see especially, 'Realism and the Cinema: Notes on some Brechtian Theses' in a special Brechtian issue of *Screen* (15: 2). For an overview of the whole Brechtian debate, as applied to contemporary narrative film and television drama, see Bennett et al. (1981).

favour the dominant ideology, but their 'preferred meaning' would not necessarily be so read and accepted by viewers in the decoding process. The model allowed for three different reading positions: dominant, negotiated and oppositional. As such, it represented a challenge to a powerful rival interpretation of the moment of decoding. If one function of E/D was to see off Leicester's uncritical endorsement of effects studies, another of its functions was to deal with *Screen*, the journal of the British Film Institute and, at the time, as committed as Birmingham to radical, political theories of culture inflected through the study of cinema. *Screen*, like many at Birmingham, was very much under the influence of contemporary French avant-garde theories. It took a strong Althusserian line on the filmic moment of decoding, arguing that the film-goer was interpellated as the viewing subject of the filmic process. The viewer was fixed in position with his or her 'gaze' (or way of seeing) always already given by the film camera's point-of-view, from which there was no escape. *Screen*-theory drew heavily on Lacan's re-reading of Freud, and on French semiotics as applied to film by Christian Metz. It was endorsed, at Birmingham, by the Language and Ideology group and rejected by the Media Studies group.

In *Culture, Media, Language,* the work of the two groups is presented one after the other with 'Media Studies' (Hall et al., 1980: 117–76) immediately preceding 'Language' (ibid.: 177–226). Hall's personal stake in the work of the Media group is evident throughout. He wrote the introduction, two of the five contributions included in that section, and heavily revised David Morley's piece on 'Texts, readers, subjects'. He is conspicuous by his absence in the work of the Language Group, introduced by Chris Weedon, Andrew Tolson and Frank Mort and with a heavily edited lead-piece by John Ellis. One of Hall's two contributions to the Media Studies section is, of course, E/D. The other is 'a critical note' on 'Recent developments in theories of language and ideology' (ibid.: 157–62), which directs its fire at *Screen*, theories of the avant-garde and, much closer to home, the recently formed Language and Ideology group which had started in October 1975 (ibid.: 178). Its activities had provoked the Media group to spend most of 1977–78 attempting 'to identify the central thesis and premises of the 'Screen theory' problematic' (ibid.: 162). For Hall, the most unacceptable aspect of the whole complicated language-subject-ideology theory construct was its denial of human agency and, hence, the possibility of resistance to imposed subjectivities and ideologies. It was, he argued, 'conceptually impossible to construct from this [*Screen's*] position an adequate concept of "struggle" in ideology' (ibid.: 61).[15]

---

15 It would take another lengthy detour to set out Hall's position on ideology-as-struggle. It is much indebted to Antonio Gramsci – whom Rojek identifies as 'the principal intellectual influence on Hall – and his concept of hegemony. For a discussion, see Rojek (2003: 108–16).

Resistance and struggle were core articles of faith for Hall and were linked to his most cherished beliefs about his own role as an intellectual and teacher. *Screen* theory and the work of the Language and Ideology group effectively eliminated the possibility of overcoming ideology except through avant-garde artistic practices, which Hall dismissed as simplistic. The three different decoding positions built into the E/D model should be seen, in part, as a rebuttal of the theoretical positions of *Screen* and the Language and Ideology group. Hall's model allows for partial and full resistance to the dominant value system inscribed in, for instance, the BBC's *Nationwide* programme as analysed by Brunsdon and Morley. Hall's rejection of avant-gardism is in tune with his consistent liking for 'the popular arts' and a refusal to dismiss television out of hand as a form of mass deception. The position of *Screen* and of Ellis and Coward had the effect, yet again, of reducing ordinary mortals to cultural dopes, but it was more consistent than Hall's. They, having bought into Althusser's take on ideology, saw it through to its terminal position. Hall's attitude to ideology – at least in relation to media – slipped back and forth between the culturalist and structuralist paradigms outlined in his 1980 article. It is tempting to interpret this tension in Hall's position in terms of Althusser's distinction between ideology-in-general (which has no history) and particular ideologies which do have histories. Coward and Ellis sign up to Althusser's ideology-in-general and work out the logic of its implications. Hall prefers to deal with ideologies and their histories and this allows him to combine Althusserian ideology with Gramsci's core concept of hegemonic struggle between social classes. The two are melded in his most considered discussion of the media and their ideological effect (Hall, 1977).

In this heroic essay Hall produces his most thought-out synthesis of the various positions outlined above – on language, semiology, Marxism and ideology – in relation to the media in general and television in particular. In a fine passage, he argues that the media operate on the terrain of common sense in a double sense: they work with it and are themselves worked by it. Common sense stands for the taken for granted, normalized, normative take on the 'real world' that is held in place at any time by any society (Hall, 1977: 325). Hall treats common sense as 'unconscious' in two senses. It is that which is inaccessible to consciousness and it is that which is unreflective and uncritical (unselfconscious). The slippage between these two meanings allows Hall movement between his structuralist and culturalist paradigms. The first is an orthodox Freudian definition and is used by Althusser to define ideology in general. The second is much closer to Gramsci's definition of common sense as the sedimented depository of ideologies that once had to be fought for but have now been naturalized as what anyone thinks. As such, they can of course be excavated, exposed and criticized (that is what the women's movement did in digging up and exposing 'patriarchy' as oppression). Hall sets out his theoretical stall in orthodox fashion starting from Marx and working through to Althusser and from there to semiology and language (a structuralist position), finally turning to Williams and Gramsci (a culturalist position). Althusser, in the first part of his ISA essay, had developed the distinction between repressive and ideological state apparatuses. In this he was deeply indebted to Gramsci (acknowledged in a footnote) and Hall re-reads Althusser via Gramscian hegemony; the struggle between classes, played out through the state, to secure the dominance of their world-view.

Classes rule, in normal times, not by force and oppression but by securing general consent to their version of reality. This process is played out as class politics in capitalist, democratic societies and in contemporary Britain it is, to a considerable extent, staged on television. The Media Group's analysis of the 'unity' of current affairs television had shown how the moment of encoding worked to secure a preferred reading that favoured the dominant definitions of political and social reality in Britain, by working to hold in place the unity of Britain-as-nation in the face of an upsurge in Welsh and Scottish nationalism. The struggle to secure consent entails the possibility of dissent which Hall's concept of decoding allowed for. Thus, for Hall, the media work to secure social consensus 'within the mode of reality of the state'. The democratic state as a whole (parties, governments, state departments) is the legitimate site of the power struggle for dominance between different classes and ideologies. 'The media serve, in societies like ours, ceaselessly to perform the critical ideological work of "classifying out the world" within the discourse of the dominant **ideologies**. This is neither simply, nor **conscious**, "work": it is *contradictory work*'. (Hall, 1977: 346. Emphases as in the original.) Ideologies then (not ideology-in-general) and work that is not conscious (self-aware, self-critical) but contradictory: this is Gramsci's view of ideologies as common sense, the elements of hegemonic struggle, as played out in the discursive practices of television.[16]

---

16 However, in the later essay on 'The rediscovery of "ideology": return of the repressed in media studies', the media are read in a distinctly Althusserian light. 'The media can be said (with plausibility – though the terms continue to be confusing) to be "ideological state apparatuses"' (Hall, 1982: 88). This essay is just about Hall's last word on the media for he wrote very little about them thereafter and he concludes on a rigorously Althusserian note:

> In the critical paradigm, ideology is a function of the discourse and of the logic of social process, rather than an intention of the agent. The broadcaster's consciousness of what he is doing … is indeed an interesting and an important question. But it does not substantially affect the theoretical issue. The ideology has 'worked' in such a case because the discourse has spoken itself through him/her. Unwittingly, unconsciously, the broadcaster has served as the support for the reproduction of a dominant ideological discursive field. (Hall, 1982: 88)

A preliminary assessment

This has not been an easy chapter to write due, in part, to the instability of the theoretical underpinnings of the encoding–decoding model and in part to the intellectually restless figure of Hall himself who warns against expecting to find, in the work of the Centre, any consistent theoretical position.[17] Theory, at Birmingham in the 1970s, was always on the move. But what was the heat and noise of Theory all about? Why did it matter so much? It seemed to be the answer to everything, but what was its question?

> To think about or to analyse *the complexity of the real*,[18] the act of [or?] practice of thinking is required; and this necessitates the use of the power of abstraction and analysis, the formation of concepts with which to cut into the complexity of the real, in order to precisely reveal and bring to light relationships and structures which cannot be visible to the naïve naked eye, and which can neither present nor authenticate themselves. (Hall 1980b: 67. Emphasis added)

This, for Hall is what privileges structuralism over culturalism. The latter remains stuck within the real-as-experience. But that can only be grasped by a process of abstraction, analysis and concept formation which is the work of theory making. Structuralism is a method, but it should never operate as pure abstraction – Theory with a capital T – as both judge and jury of the real. Structuralism is a method for dealing with, and moving between, different levels of abstraction that are closer and further from the empirical 'real'. In this way structuralism as a theoretical method avoids the 'absolutism of Theoretical Practice' and 'the anti-abstraction "Poverty of Theory" position[19] into which, in

---

17 There is also the problem of Centrespeak. An arcane theoretical vocabulary developed at Birmingham, cobbled together from the many different authors consulted in the long march through Theory, and even ordinary words (like 'real') acquired extra-ordinary meanings. I have tried to decode most of the terms that became part of CCCS's lexicon.

18 'The real' is one of those 'snakes in the linguistic grass' that Austin endeavours to scotch in *Sense and Sensibilia* (Austin, 1964). As used by Hall, and the Centre generally, it needs scare-quotes to indicate that it is a deeply problematic term for both Marxist and psychoanalytic theory and was much debated at the time. Was Marxism a realism? (see Lovell, 1980: 9–17, for an affirmative answer to that question). In Lacanian theory, the Real is that which is left behind (like Eden) at the point of entry into the Symbolic via language.

19 *The Poverty of Theory* was a lengthy, passionate attack by Edward Thompson on Althusser who was denounced, at great length, for his idealist irrationalism and the denial of history (Thompson, 1978: 193–397). For a discussion of this intervention, see Kaye (1984: 203–15).

---

reaction, culturalism appears to have been driven or driven itself' (Hall, 1980b: 68). Hall hoped to avoid the barren polarities between Theoreticism and Empiricism 'which have both marked and disfigured the structuralism/culturalism encounter to date' (ibid.).

I have referred to the 1970s as Cultural Studies' 'heroic' period and I have applied the same term to Hall's own writings at this time. In recent interviews Hall describes himself as having wrestled with angels in trying to clarify his thinking. What seems to me genuinely heroic was the decade-long wrestling match that took place at Birmingham in which Hall and his students, calling for help from the Angel of Theory, tried to pin the Angel of Reality to the ground and win a submission from it. A key word in the Birmingham lexicon was 'struggle', which took place on a number of fronts and with a number of opponents but always coming down to the effort to produce an adequate theoretical account of contemporary social reality. Yet they could never pin Reality's shoulders to the floor long enough for a submission. Whenever they thought they had it locked in their theoretical embrace, Reality slipped their grasp and stood up again to challenge them. Class and culture? Marxian theory would do for that. But then what about gender? Or race? And what about language? And so on. Theory was perpetually on the move at Birmingham in the 1970s because reality was always on the move and try as it might Theory could never stop it in its tracks long enough to pin it down. I do not mean to mock. Looking back on it all, with the detachment that comes with the passing of the years, it now seems to me both comical (though it was then all in deadly earnest) *and* heroic. It would be hard to find a more sustained effort of thinking, reading, discussing and writing over a decade, by a brilliant teacher and an outstanding group of students, in any other British university in the last century. At the end of it, Hall was, by his own admission, exhausted, and so he moved on. The effort to produce an adequate Theory of the Real at Birmingham did not outlast his departure. And yet his valiant efforts in that direction serve to highlight one of the most fundamental themes of this book; the relationship between thought and reality and the role of intellectuals – matters to which I will return in the final volume of this trilogy.

Hall himself wrote little of importance on the media after leaving Birmingham as his interests turned elsewhere, towards the impact and consequences of Thatcherite neo-conservatism in the 1980s, and the politics of race. But the version of Cultural Studies that he hammered out at Birmingham has had a huge impact on the humanities and social sciences not just in Britain but throughout the world. Today one can speak, without exaggeration, of a globalized field of Cultural Studies within which the study of the media, though still important, is not as pivotal as it was in the 1970s. Cultural Studies has moved on, but the study of the media has not advanced significantly beyond the theoretical work outlined in this chapter. It remains for me to indicate something of the continuation of that work, in two distinct lines of development in the 1980s – feminism and audience studies.[20]

Feminist media studies

The women students at Birmingham included Dorothy Hobson who went there to study the ways young mothers at home with their children used radio and television in their daily routines (Brunsdon et al., 1997: 6). An excerpt from her unpublished MA thesis on the topic ('Working class women at home: femininity, domesticity and maternity') was published in the Ethnography section of *Culture, Media, Language* (Hobson, 1980). Perhaps it was not theoretical enough for inclusion in the work of the Media group. Be that as it may, it established one important line of enquiry that would be taken up and explored in the expanding field of television studies. Hobson began to build up a picture, through interviews and participant observation with her subjects, of the kinds of things that women did and did not like watching. From this a morality of viewing emerged. There are some things you apologize for because you don't like watching them (news, documentaries, etc. – all boring, serious and masculine) and some things you apologize for because you do like watching them (soaps and light entertainment – all fun, trivial and feminine). Hobson went on to produce a full-length study of a much-derided British television soap, *Crossroads* (Hobson, 1982), which remains to this day one of the best and most sympathetic studies of the production and reception of television serial drama.

At the same time Film Studies was beginning to add the study of television to its territory and an important collection of papers on *Coronation Street* was published by the British Film Institute in 1980. 'Corrie', as it is affectionately known by its multitude of fans, was then rather more intellectually acceptable

---

20 These two developments are not, of course, the only consequences of the work at Birmingham in the 1970s on the media. It had an important impact on Linguistics and Literature. The combination of Marxism and semiotics was taken up by linguists at East Anglia and Lancaster, and used to analyse the ideological workings of language in the press (Fowler, 1990) and the media more generally (Fairclough, 1989). Kress and his colleagues extended a Marxist-based semiotics to the general study of culture (Hodge and Kress, 1988). Literary Studies were deeply infected by theoretical critique in the 1970s and all sorts of genres and many famous authors of both sexes were found to be riddled with the death-watch beetle of ideology. British film, media and cultural studies all have their roots in the study of English Literature; the parent discipline for Hoggart, Williams, Hall and many others (myself included). Terry Eagleton was the doyen of literary ideology critique (Eagleton, 1990). All the humanities and social sciences of the 1970s were shaken by ideology critique, as class, gender, race and generational relations stirred and shifted, producing shock waves in British society.

than *Crossroads*. The introduction links the moment of the programme's inception (Granada Television, 1960) and its social milieu – a working-class street of back-to-back terraced houses in Manchester – with Hoggart's classic study of the everyday life of the northern English working class. It was a good object for cultural studies and 'the politics of the representation of class and gender' (Dyer et al., 1981: 15) along with the question of the programme's realism were examined by Marion Jordan and Terry Lovell. Christine Geraghty's introductory essay – 'The continuous serial: a definition' – remains a classic analysis of the time-based structure of a genre specific to radio and television, the never-ending fictional narrative serial.

Work in the United States and Europe at around the same time, and notably that of Tania Modleski and Ien Ang, widened the study of this kind of television fiction and the study of soap opera soon became a global academic enterprise (Allen, 1995). Gradually the political readings of soaps (in terms of gender and class, representation and ideology) gave way to questions of the pleasure and enjoyment to which they gave rise for viewers and even (though tinged with guilt) for critical academic viewers. Charlotte Brundson, Julie D'Acci and Lynn Spigel's edited collection, *Feminist Television Criticism* (1997) effectively covers the major trends in Anglo-American research in the last two decades of the twenteith century, which are reviewed in its authoritative introduction. Frances Bonner's (2003) recent study of *Ordinary Television* in Britain and Australia insists on the significance of the ordinary and the everyday in relation to television, themes that feminist television studies had, from the beginning, struggled to redeem from the blight of triviality and irrelevance. Outside television there was innovative work on magazines for girls and women, and on romantic fiction and its women readers. All this and kindred work has enormously enriched the study of popular culture, while remaining largely within the theoretical framework established at Birmingham in the 1970s. *Feminist Media Studies* by Lisbet van Zoonen (1994) offers a critical introduction to the relations between gender, media and culture that begins with Hall's encoding/decoding model because 'it serves as a framework to order the different subjects and themes covered by feminist media theory and research' (ibid.: 8).

Audience studies

Through the 1980s and well into the 1990s, E/D was ritually invoked as the ur-text of a reincarnate audience studies, kick-started by David Morley's work on *Nationwide*. The whole point of E/D was to run an empirical check on what theory had predicted about reality. Brunsdon and Morley's textual analysis of *Nationwide* had shown how it mobilized the ideology of 'nation' encoded as common sense. But how would actual viewers decode it? Morley's study of the

Nationwide audience is almost as canonical a text for Cultural Studies as E/D itself and has generated almost as much discussion. The methods used to study audience responses to the programme were closely scrutinized and criticized as was the interpretative frame deployed by Morley (carried over from the earlier analysis of the ideological work of *Nationwide*) for the analysis of their responses (Moores, 1993). James Curran protested that what Morley started was no more than a new revisionism in audience studies that appeared to rediscover the wheel first invented by American effects studies many years earlier. Morley, who had begun by defining his study as a break with that tradition, replied in defence and an exchange of views ensued (Curran et al., 1996). Whether or not it was old wine in new bottles, Morley's study defined the work of a new generation of audience studies. It made a key distinction, in opposition to *Screen*, between the implied and actual viewers of filmic/television texts.

This distinction was elaborated in Janice Radway's superb study of American women readers of romantic fiction in which she showed the primary importance for her Smithton women of the act and circumstances of reading itself as a way of creating a space and time for themselves (of caring for themselves) irrespective of what book they were reading (Radway, 1984). This turn towards the situated circumstances of reception was also explored in Herman Bausinger's anthropological account of a typical German family's weekend use of radio, television and newspapers (Bausinger, 1984). It was taken further in Morley's next major study of audience behaviours, based on participant observation in 18 London households, of families and how they watched television (Morley, 1986). This study of domestic television usage and control – Who has access to the remote? Who does/not know how to operate the VCR? – opened up a rich seam of ethnographic enquiry into the questions of family power in relation to everyday technologies of communication (Silverstone and Hirsch, 1992). Such sociological work stimulated similar historical research on domestic viewing in many countries from the 1950s onwards.

Valuable though all this was, what disappeared from sight was the question of encoding. Far less work has been done on the production culture of television, whether in terms of genres or particular programmes, than on its reception. The usefulness of E/D was precisely that it proposed an integrated study of the relations of production and consumption. If the television programmes were bearers of ideology they had nevertheless to be produced as such. There was real human labour inscribed in them. But little research was ever done on this.[21] Likewise the analysis of television programmes themselves – their form and content – remains under-examined to this day. Why was the moment of

---

21 There are some notable exceptions: Elliott (1972), Schlesinger (1978), Alvarado and Buscombe (1978), Feuer et al. (1984), Alvarado and Stewart (1985), D'Acci (1994).

---

decoding so over-determined as to suppress its own moment of origin? One answer might be that it represented part of a wider re-adjustment to the historical imbalance in the study of the relations of cultural production and consumption. Hitherto it had appeared that supply determined demand. The production side of the relationship was powerful and determining; the consumption side was vulnerable and exploited. So it had seemed to an earlier generation. Left Puritanism had always been suspicious of the (false) pleasures of consumption. In rescuing viewers from their Althusserian over-determination by *Screen* as always already subjects, Centre theory opened the way for a revaluation of consumption in a positive light. The question of ideology was gradually shed as the old view of passive cultural consumption (re-affirmed in *Screen* theory) gave way to a recognition of active audiences who enjoyed television. Feminist work on television confronted this from the start – although the researchers might think of the things that ordinary women enjoyed (romantic fiction, soaps, and light entertainment) as ideological, they were compelled to re-think their own position since they could scarcely regard the women they studied as, yet again, cultural dupes. Not all ordinary pleasures, it was found, were necessarily political or ideological or suspect.

This revaluation of cultural consumption was part of the post-modern moment of the 1980s, briefly considered in the next chapter. It opened up the study of television *in situ*, as part of the ordinary daily life and the domestic routines of societies today, and this was invaluable. But what was lost in the process was the meaning (the significance) of the output of television. Within the Cultural Studies frame, the question of the labour of cultural production virtually disappeared and with it, the question of ideology itself. I do not think the media are ideological in the way that that Hall and CCCS thought they were, but the issue posed by ideology critique remains a crux for the study of culture. At the heart of its problematic, clearly identified in Hall's two paradigms, is the status of human experience and the enigmatic character of ordinary daily life.

References

Allen, R.C. (1995) *To be Continued … Soap Operas Around the World*. London: Routledge.

Althusser, L. (1971) 'Ideology and ideological state apparatuses', in *Lenin and Philosophy and Other Essays*. London: New Left Books.

Alvarado, M. and Buscombe, E. (1978) *Hazell: The Making of a TV Series*. London: BFI and Latimer.

Alvarado, M. and Stewart, J. (1985) *Made for Television: Euston Films Ltd*. London: BFI.

Ang, I. (1985) *Watching Dallas: Soap Opera and the Melodramatic Imagination*. London: Methuen.

Austin, J. (1964) *Sense and Sensibilia*. Oxford: Oxford University Press.

Barthes, R. (1975) *S/Z*. London: Jonathan Cape.

Bausinger, H. (1984) 'Media, technology and daily life', *Media, Culture & Society*, 6(4): 343–52.

Bennett, T. et al. (eds) (1981) *Popular Television and Film*. London: BFI Publishing and the Open University.

Bonner, F. (2003) *Ordinary Television*. London: Sage.

Brunsdon, C. (1996) 'A thief in the night: stories of feminism in the 1970s at CCCS', in D. Morley and H-K. Chen (eds), *Stuart Hall: Critical Dialogues*. London: Routledge, pp. 276–86.

Brunsdon, C., D'Acci, J. and Spigel, L. (1997) *Feminist Television Criticism*. Oxford: Oxford University Press.

Burns, T. (1977) *The BBC: Public Institution and Private World*. London: Macmillan.

Chambers, I. and Curti, L. (1996) *The Post-Colonial Question*. London: Routledge.

Corner, J. (1980) 'Codes and cultural analysis', *Media, Culture & Society*, 2(1): 73–86.

Coward, R. and Ellis, J. (1977) *Language and Materialism*. London: Routledge and Kegan Paul.

Cruz, J. and Lewis, J. (1994) *Viewing, Reading, Listening: Audiences and Cultural Reception*. Boulder, CO: Westview Press.

Curran, J. (1977) 'Capitalism and control of the press, 1800–1975', in J. Curran et al. (eds), *Mass Communication and Society*. London: Edward Arnold, pp. 195–230.

Curran, J. (1981) 'Press history', in J. Curran and J. Seaton (eds), *Power Without Responsibility: The Press and Broadcasting in Britain*. London: Routledge, pp. 5–114.

Curran, J. (2002) *Media and Power*. London: Routledge.

Curran, J., Morley, D. and Walkerdine, V. (1996) *Cultural Studies and Communications*. London: Arnold.

D'Acci, J. (1994) *Defining Women: Television and the Case of Cagney and Lacey*. Chapel Hill, NC: University of North Carolina Press.

Dyer, R., Geraghty, C., Jordan, M., Lovell, T., Paterson, R. and Stewart, J. (1981) *Coronation Street*. BFI Monograph 13, London: British Film Institute.

Eagleton, T. (1990) *The Ideology of the Aesthetic*. Oxford: Blackwell.

Elliott, P. (1972) *The Making of a Television Series: A Case Study in the Sociology of Culture*. London: Constable.

Fairclough, N. (1989) *Language and Power*. London: Longman.

Feuer, J., Kerr, P. and Vahimagi, T. (1984) *MTM: 'Quality Television'*. London: BFI.

Foucault, M. (1982) 'The subject and power: an afterword', in H. Dreyfus and P. Rabinow (eds), *Michel Foucault: Beyond Structuralism and Hermeneutics*. Brighton: Harvester Press, pp. 209–26.

Fowler, A. (1990) *Language in the News: Discourse and Ideology in the Press*. London: Routledge.

Goorney, H. and MacColl, E. (1986) *Agit-Prop to Theatre Workshop*. Manchester: Manchester University Press.

Habermas, J. (1970) 'Systematically distorted communication', in P. Dretzel (ed.), *Recent Sociology, 2*. London: Collier-Macmillan.

Hall, S. (1973) 'Encoding and decoding in the television discourse', Stencilled Paper 7. Birmingham: University of Birmingham, CCCS.

Hall, S. (1977) 'Culture, the media and the "Ideological Effect"', in J. Curran et al. (eds), *Mass Communication and Society*. London: Edward Arnold, pp. 315–48.

Hall, S. (1980a) 'Encoding/Decoding', in *Culture, Media, Language: Working Papers in Cultural Studies, 1972–1979*. London: Hutchinson, pp. 128–38.

Hall, S. (1980b) 'Cultural studies: two paradigms', *Media, Culture & Society*, 2(1): 57–72.

Hall, S. (1982) 'The rediscovery of "ideology": return of the repressed in media studies', in M. Gurevitch et al. (eds), *Culture, Society and the Media*. London: Methuen, pp. 56–90.

Hall, S. (1996) 'Cultural Studies and its theoretical legacies', in D. Morley and K-H. Chen (eds), *Stuart Hall: Critical Dialogues in Cultural Studies*. London: Routledge, pp. 262–75.

Hall, S., Connell, I. and Curti, L. (1976) 'The "unity" of current affairs television', in *Working Papers in Cultural Studies 9*. Birmingham University: Centre for Contemporary Cultural Studies, pp. 51–94.

Hall, S., Critcher, C., Jefferson, T., Clarke, J. and Roberts, B. (1978) *Policing the Crisis: Mugging, the State and Law and Order*. London: Macmillan.

Hall, S. and Whannel, P. (1967) *The Popular Arts*. Boston: Beacon Press.

Hall, S. et al. (eds) (1980) *Culture, Media, Language*. London: Hutchinson.

Hobson, D. (1980) 'Housewives and the mass media', in S. Hall et al. (eds), *Culture, Media, Language*. London: Hutchinson, pp. 105–14.

Hobson, D. (1982) *Crossroads: The Drama of a Soap Opera*. London: Methuen.

Hodge, R. and Kress, G. (1988) *Social Semiotics*. Cambridge: Polity Press.

Hoggart, R. (1992) *The Uses of Literacy*. Harmondsworth: Penguin.

Jefferson, T. and Hall, S. (eds) (1975) *Resistance through Rituals*. London: Hutchinson.

Katz, E. et al. (2003) *Canonic Texts in Media Research*. Cambridge: Polity Press.

Kaye, H.J. (1984) *The British Marxist Historians*. Cambridge: Polity Press.

Liebes, T. and Katz, E. (1990) *The Export of Meaning: Cross-cultural Readings of Dallas*. New York: Oxford University Press.

Lovell, T. (1980) *Pictures of Reality: Aesthetics, Politics and Pleasure*. London: BFI.

Marx, K. and Engels, F. (1970) *The German Ideology*. London: Lawrence and Wishart.

Modleski, T. (1984) *Loving with a Vengeance. Mass-Produced Fantasies for Women*. London: Methuen.

McGrath, J. (1981) *A Good Night Out: Popular Theatre: Audience, Class and Form*. London: Eyre Methuen.

Moores, S. (1993) *Interpreting Audiences*. London: Sage.

Morley, D. (1980) *The* Nationwide *Audience: Structure and Decoding*. BFI Monograph 11. London: British Film Institute.

Morley, D. (1986) *Family Television: Cultural Power and Domestic Leisure*. London: Comedia.

Morley, D. and Brunsdon, C. (1999) 'The Nationwide project: long ago and far away...', in *The Nationwide Television Studies*. London: Routledge.

Morley, D. and Chen, K-H. (1996) *Stuart Hall: Critical Dialogues*. London: Routledge.

Parkin, F. (1971) *Class Inequality and Political Order*. New York: Praeger.

Radway, J. (1984) *Reading the Romance*. Chapel Hill, NC: University of North Carolina Press.

Rojek, C. (2003) *Stuart Hall*. Cambridge: Polity Press.

Saussure, F. de (1979) *Course in General Linguistics*. London: Methuen.

Schlesinger, P. (1978) *Putting 'Reality' Together: BBC News*. London: Constable.

Silverstone, R. and Hirsch, E. (1992) *Consuming Technologies: Media and Information in Domestic Spaces*. London: Routledge.

Smith, A.C.H., Immirzi, E. and Blackwell, T. (1975) *Paper Voices*. London: Chatto and Windus.

Sparks, C. (1996) 'Stuart Hall, Cultural Studies and Marxism', in D. Morley and K-H Chen (eds) *Stuart Hall: Critical Dialogues*. London: Routledge, pp. 71–101.

Sturrock, J. (1979) *Structuralism and Since: From Lévi-Strauss to Derrida*. Oxford: Oxford University Press.

Taylor, C. (1994) *Multiculturalism*. Princeton, NJ: Princeton University Press.

Thompson, E.P. (1978) *The Poverty of Theory*. London: Merlin Press.

Weedon, C. et al. (1980) 'Theories of language and subjectivity', in S. Hall et al. (eds), *Culture, Media, Language*. London: Hutchinson.

Zoonen, van L. (1994) *Feminist Media Studies*. London: Sage.

Communication and publicness

Habermas
Germany (USA/UK), 1950s–1990s

Introduction

Strukturwandel der Öffentlichkeit by Jürgen Habermas was published in Germany in 1962. In 1989, it was translated into English as *The Structural Transformation of the Public Sphere*, hereafter referred to as *STPS*. The book is about changing historical forms of public life in Europe from pre-modern times to the present. It is essentially concerned with the emerging role of public opinion and the media in modern, democratic politics. It also raises wider political and philosophical issues to do with modernity, Enlightenment and the rational basis of public discussion. *STPS* was Habermas's *Habilitation* thesis and his first major publication in Germany, where it had an immediate impact. When it appeared in English, it prompted considerable debate in the very different political climate of the early 1990s, a sure sign that the book's central concerns had not lost their relevance. In the intervening period, Habermas had become an internationally renowned social theorist who maintained his abiding engagement with politics through an intensive study of philosophy, language and law. The historical analysis, so distinctive a feature of *STPS*, gave way to a prolonged attempt to theorize the rational basis of communication, culminating in the two-volume *Theory of Communicative Action* (1981/1989). Ten years later, Habermas published *Between Facts and Norms* ([1992] 1996) in which he returned to the

Jürgen Habermas

original concerns of *STPS* in a further attempt to ground the legitimacy and practice of democratic politics in constitutional law and reasoned, critical public discourse. To examine Habermas's concern with communication and politics, spread over five decades, I will first outline the thesis set out in *STPS* and briefly discuss it in terms of the current political situation in Germany in the late 1950s. Next I will outline the main features of the turn to pragmatics and the theory of communicative action. Finally, I will review the impact of *STPS* after its appearance in English, nearly 30 years after its original publication in Germany.

Historical forms of publicness

STPS is a drama in three acts. It begins with a brief account of pre-modern forms of public life. The second and central part of the story concerns the emergence of the European bourgeoisie, in their private and public parts, in the course of the eighteenth century. This new, revolutionary class creates the classic, bourgeois public sphere. In the course of the nineteenth century the public sphere is put under increasing strain from the contradictions of a class-based society. In the third and final act – from the early twentieth century through to the present (the 1950s) – the rise of consumer capitalism and the mass media combine with new forms of political management to suborn public life, which regresses to its earlier, pre-modern forms. It is a morality tale of the rise and fall of rational, critical public opinion.

In pre-modern Europe, public life did not exist as an acknowledged, independent social space into which each and all could enter. It was rather a status attribute of certain persons – monarchs and the lords spiritual and temporal. The king embodied publicness in his person – *L'État, c'est moi*. Public life was a theatre in which the authorities periodically displayed themselves on ceremonial occasions in stage-managed representations of their power: 'They represented their lordliness not for but "before" the people' (Habermas, 1989: 8). The common people did not constitute 'a public', as we now understand that term, for the distinction between public and private life – so familiar and fundamental for us – did not then exist. The emergence of publics and, especially, *the* public, was the culmination of a long and complex historical process that was, and remains, intimately tied to the formation in Europe, over centuries, of capitalist economies and democratic political systems. A number of strands in this process are lightly sketched in. The rise of long-distance trade and mercantile capitalism was linked to the growing importance and power of towns and cities not as local centres but as networks through which commodities and news circulated. The slow emergence of the mail and of newspapers, not fully in place until the eighteenth century, grew out of the requirements for the management of long-distance business interests. Correspondingly the lineaments of nation–states begin to appear in that long dance with the modern forms of economic life upon which they depend and which they exist, in part, to support and protect. In particular, Habermas notes that power ceases to reside in *the person* of the ruler and becomes a defining attribute of a depersonalized state apparatus which assumes continuing, objective existence through a permanent administration backed up by a permanent military force (ibid.: 18). The state begins to appear as a permanent *public authority* that increasingly intrudes upon the lives of the majority. Linked to these historic processes is the emergence of *society*.

We are today so familiar with the idea of 'society' – we hold it to be the case that we live in societies; that societies exist and can be discussed as such – that it requires some effort of imagination to acknowledge its appearance as a distinctive strand in the formation of our modern world and in our understanding of it. Habermas develops an account of the emergence of society, drawing on Hannah Arendt's then recently published magnum opus, *The Human Condition*, in which she traces 'the rise of the social' (Arendt, [1958] 1989: 38–49). From the Greeks onwards, the household had been regarded as essentially private (deprived of any public significance). It was the sphere of the *oekonomia*, of economics, the withdrawn space in which reproduction and daily subsistence needs were managed and met by household members, in various roles, on their own behalf. Private, domestic life begins to be *publicly relevant* as economic life moves more and more beyond the scope of households (Habermas, 1989: 19). The complex restructuring of economic and political life over many generations begins to knit together hitherto separate, self-sustaining, above all, *local* units into that transcendent thing we recognize today *as* 'society', a phenomenon whose essential characteristics are public.

One of the most suggestive, and overlooked aspects of Habermas's account is that the emerging bourgeois 'public sphere' was, in the first place (and necessarily) a literary and cultural, not a political phenomenon. The terms 'culture' and 'society' (Habermas had read Williams) are structurally interdependent. The emergence of the European bourgeoisie, as an historical phenomenon, is manifest in the ways in which it expressed its own understanding of itself through the creation of its own and particular culture in the form of a reading *public* (ibid.: 23).[1] Print created new forms of publicness and new publics. What was implicated from the beginning in the printing press – the transformation of written texts into books and their valorization as marketable, circulating commodities – came to fruition in the eighteenth century. The development of newspapers, magazines and literature (as we now know it, in the rise of the novel: Watt, 1957), was the means whereby a new social class articulated and explored its own self-understanding. The then new medium, the periodical

---

1 The concept of 'the reading public' is derived from Altick (1957).

magazine, most clearly shows this process. *The Spectator* and *The Tatler*[2] were concerned, one might say, with the arts of impression management in new social situations. They gave advice and guidance to their readers on manners and taste, on the conduct of their social encounters with unfamiliar others. The novel, that essentially bourgeois form, explored relations between men and women, parents and children – inter-personal life as we now call it – in ways that opened up and went public on hitherto private matters. The novel was the classic site wherein the new social class examined its own conditions and concerns; families, sex and money and their circuits of power. To be a player in this new bourgeois society one had to have opinions on matters of fashion and taste. What clothes to wear, what books to read were not private choices. They became advertisements to others about one's self. To have opinions (to be able to express and defend them) was to engage with, to be part of, 'society'. Opinions were formed in the interactions between texts and their readers and the conversations and debates to which they gave rise. Opinion, in a general sense, became socially and publicly relevant as an arbiter of taste.

The formation of taste publics was a critical process of 'self-clarification by private people focusing on the genuine experiences of their novel privateness'. They, and their experiences, were private because they were excluded from existing political public life. 'The line between state and society, divided the public sphere from the private realms' (ibid.: 30). Private persons, although they had novel forms of public social and cultural life, had not yet become enfranchised in the political public realm. The public sphere, as Habermas conceives it, is a particular kind of political publicness that ultimately becomes the normative underpinning of twentieth-century mass democracies. In its classic form, it first arose in Great Britain at the turn of the eighteenth century (ibid.: 57), forged in the ongoing confrontation between the government and the press which came to a climax in the fevered political climate engendered by the American and French Revolutions (ibid.: 60). If magazines and novels were instrumental in the formation of new cultural *taste publics*,[3] newspapers played a key role in the formation of new political *opinion publics*.

---

2 The significance of the titles of these two leading English magazines should be noted. The spectator is one who gazes on the social scene. The new reading public is interpellated as an audience for new forms of social life. Today we think of ourselves as spectators of television. Luc Boltanski derives the origins of the television news viewer, confronted by distant suffering, from the 'moral spectator' of the eighteenth century (Boltanski, 1999). Tatler is the older spelling of 'tattler', one who tattles. Idle chat, or gossip (such an absorbing feature of contemporary mediatised social life) finds its modern origins here. The magazine was aimed at the 'worthy citizens who live more in a coffeehouse than in their shops' (Habermas, 1989: 260, n.36).

3 I have adopted this term from William Weber's path-breaking study of *Music and the Middle Class*. He coined it in order to capture the new social phenomenon of paying concert-going publics that formed around contemporary currents of musical taste in Berlin, London, Paris and Vienna in the early nineteenth century (Weber, 1975: 10).

Opinions, political or otherwise, are neither here nor there unless they somehow matter. Private opinion is, precisely, privative; deprived of any public relevance or effectivity. The political opinions of private persons began to matter as and when those in power began to feel obliged to take them into account. When the opinions of 'the public' impact upon the exercise of political power then, indeed, it has become historically relevant. Here, in 1792 (three years into the revolution across the channel, in France), is Charles Fox, in the House of Commons, speaking against the government:

> It is certainly right and prudent to consult the public opinion … If the public opinion did not square with mine; if, after pointing out to them the danger, they did not see it in the same light with me, or if they conceived that another remedy was preferable to mine, I should consider it as my due to my king, due to my Country, due to my honour to retire, that they might persue the plan which they thought better, by a fit instrument, that is by a man who thought with them … but one thing is most clear, that I ought to give the public the means of forming an opinion. (ibid.: 65–6)

This remarkable speech, as Habermas notes, is a clear indication that Parliament was no longer an exclusive forum of oligarchic rule. It acknowledged that, in their deliberations, members must be sensitive and responsive to the voice(s) of public opinion. As the state increasingly imposed taxes on the population to support its wars, so the demand for a say in the matter – 'no taxation without representation' – became increasingly difficult to resist.

For Habermas, critical public opinion in the eighteenth century was an historical phenomenon with strongly normative underpinnings. It was the moment of a general demand (or will) for the rational regulation of politics. Political rule could no longer continue as the arbitrary exercise of power over the majority by unaccountable elites. A new legitimacy (validity) for the short- and long-term management of whole populations was called for, based on the universal rule of law. 'The bourgeois idea of the law-based state, namely, the binding of all state activity to a system of norms legitimated by public opinion, aimed at abolishing the state as an instrument of domination' (ibid.: 82). The constitutional state was the embodiment and expression of this radically new commitment to the management of the affairs of nation–states in the interests of all. Written constitutions (as in the United States) are formal expressions of the general will. As such, they constitute the legitimacy of the new form of political governance that they bring into being. By definition, public, constitutional documents set out the commitments and principles of the political public sphere, expressed as rights. These include:

- Rights of the public engaged in rational-critical debate, backed up by freedom of the press, freedom of opinion and speech and freedom of assembly and association. These are underpinned by basic political rights, crucially concerned with voting equality.

- Rights concerning the status of the individual as a free human being, grounded in theintimate sphere of the patriarchal, conjugal family (personal freedom, inviolability of the home, etc.).
- Rights of property in the sphere of civil society, including equality before the law, protection of private property, etc.

These guaranteed both the public and the private realms, with the family at its core. They recognized and protected the institutions and instruments of the public sphere (political parties, the press) and the private autonomy of families and their property. Individuals had political rights as citizens, economic rights as property owners, and human rights as private individuals.[4]

Now it becomes clear why the book's subtitle is 'an enquiry into a category of bourgeois society' for the new legal, political and economic rights contained a basic contradiction. On the one hand, they were claimed as universal political principles: 'We hold these truths to be self-evident: that *all* men are created equal, that they are endowed by their Creator with certain inalienable rights ...', At the same time they entrenched social and economic inequalities. The eighteenth-century critical public sphere was restricted to bourgeois, propertied men. The rights of the propertyless and the wrongs of women were not countenanced. Nevertheless, for a moment at least, a self-interested party (the patriarchal bourgeoisie of Europe and North America) claimed to act in the interests of all those excluded from the polity in order to wrest power from unaccountable minorities. The legitimacy of such claims *had* to be represented as a universal interest, the general will. The power of such claims to inalienable rights, for all their inner contradictions, lay precisely in their publicness. In the open light of publicity there could, ultimately, be no going back on them. As public statements of the will of the public, the new rights of man could be claimed by all those *de facto* and *de jure* excluded from them. That long historic struggle remains with us to this day.

The refeudalization of public life

Marx had regarded the bourgeois state as pure ideology, an illusory realm of freedom.[5] Habermas took a more nuanced view. The formation of the modern state, with its commitment to universal rights, was precisely the moment that ideology came into existence, born in the tensions between the genuinely utopian longings for universal equality and freedom and the harsh unfreedoms and inequalities of the actually existing world (ibid.: 88). But bourgeois culture was not merely ideological (ibid.: 160), at least in its formative period. The

---

4 This paragraph is a summary of *STPS*: 82–3.

5 See especially 'On the Jewish Question' (Marx, [1843] 1992). Habermas provides an extensive critical review of early nineteenth century theories of rights, politics etc, including Kant, Hegel, and Marx and the English Utilitarians from Bentham to Mill (*STPS*: 89–140).

coffee-houses, clubs, philosophical and debating societies of the late eighteenth and early nineteenth centuries had a genuine commitment to knowledge, enquiry and criticism that could not be dismissed as mere self-interest. However, Habermas argues, in the course of the nineteenth century this culture of critical discussion unravelled, to be replaced by a culture of consumption.

The transformation of publicness, in Habermas's accounts, first begins in the restructuring of domestic and social life in the nineteenth century and is completed in twentieth-century reconfigurations of the state and the culture of politics. One of the more difficult aspects of this overall thesis concerns the refeudalization of society (ibid.: 42). At the heart of Habermas's idealization of a deliberative politics is the involvement of ordinary private social members in an ongoing critical discussion of matters of general interest. The public sphere arose in the larger private realm of 'society' from whence it spoke to the narrower public realm of politics. It was thus an intermediary space held in tension between state and society. For the Greeks, private economic life – the household, the family – was simply privative. It was the realm of necessity, deprived of the collective pleasures and excitements of life in the *polis*, 'the great and glorious public realm' (Arendt, [1958] 1989). The rise of 'the social' reversed this relationship. It revalued and universalized the small, private family as its basic unit and made public its hitherto private concerns (reproduction and subsistence). The corresponding formation of that other modern phenomenon, the 'nation–state', appeared as an instrument of power and domination over and above 'society'. From the late nineteenth century onwards, the separation of state and society began to erode, and so too the public sphere. From this period on, Habermas notes the rise of state intervention in the affairs of social and family life culminating in the contemporary 'welfare state' of the 1950s. Politics is 'societalized', society is politicized; the distinction between public and private begins to collapse and the classic bourgeois public sphere begins to lose its function (Habermas, 1989: 142).

A key Weberian theme in *STPS* is the increasing administration of society,[6] through the intervention of the state in what had previously been the responsibilities of the family unit. The functions of the patriarchal, self-sustaining household are more and more hollowed out. The home becomes detached from work which developed its own separate culture and ethos. The household is deprived of many of its educative and caring functions. Paternal authority is dismantled. The private sphere shrinks to 'a conjugal family largely relieved of function and weakened in authority – the quiet bliss of homeyness' (ibid.: 159). The bourgeois culture of the eighteenth century looked outwards from the intimacy of the patriarchal household to a public space of discussion. In the nineteenth century, it retreated into a shell of domesticity and of marginal leisure time in the residue left over after the demands of the working week.

---

6 For a more detailed discussion of this theme, see Keane (1984: 70–110).

That residue of 'free time' was increasingly oriented to consumption. Earlier forms of sociability – literature, newspapers, drinking and conversation in clubs, pubs and coffee houses – gave way to more sober domestic pleasures. By the mid-twentieth-century, we had all become home lovers. There we listened to the radio, watched television and consumed. In an increasingly mediatized world, even conversation began to lose its spontaneity:

> Put bluntly: you had [formerly] to pay for books, theatre, concert and museum, but not for conversation about what you had read, heard, and seen and what you might completely absorb only through this conversation. Today the conversation itself is administered. Professional dialogues from the podium, panel discussions, and round table shows – the rational debate of private people becomes one of the production numbers of the stars in radio and television, a saleable package ready for the box office; it assumes commodity form even at 'conferences' where anyone can 'participate'. Discussion, now a 'business', becomes formalised. (Habermas, 1989: 164)

Public discussion (including that of academics!) has regressed to the form of a commodity. It is managed, manipulated and packaged. 'The world fashioned by the mass media is a public sphere in appearance only' (ibid.: 171). The culture of the mass media is a culture of integration that functions to obtain the consent or, at least, acquiescence of a mediatized, manipulated public (ibid.: 175, 177).

The packaging of public discourse finally comes to penetrate the state and politics. The refeudalization of politics shows in its regression to pre-modern forms of staged publicness; politics as a theatre of display enacted before the people.[7] Publicness transmogrifies into publicity. In the course of the nineteenth century, magazines and newspapers lost their initial literary and political functions as they became increasingly market-oriented, a process completed when, as mass-circulation businesses, they became dependent on advertising to keep prices down for growing mass readerships. In this process, the periodical and daily press lost their original function as the organs of literary and political discussing publics. Their public functions receded as they came increasingly to serve the private interests of their owners. At first, the role of the editor – whose function was established at the beginning of the nineteenth century – was crucial. He was often the owner of his publication which he produced not, in the first place, for profit but 'as a dealer in public opinion' (ibid.: 182). By the end of the century, the editor had become a hireling: 'The publisher appoints editors in the expectation that they will do as they are told in the private interest of a

---

7 A tendency noted by the English political journalist, Walter Bagehot, in the late nineteenth century. The monarchy, as the 'dignified part' of the English Constitution, functioned as a theatre to distract attention from the activities of its 'efficient parts', namely the activities of governments and ministries. The monarchy provided a public spectacle for the masses, more interested in royal weddings than the actual politics of state (Bagehot, [1867] 1963).

profit-oriented enterprise' (ibid.: 186). The irresistible rise of advertising as the economic base of magazines and newspapers in pursuit of larger and larger readerships contributed to the collapse of the multitude of non-profit oriented publications that spoke for and to their many taste and opinion publics. Advertising developed as an industry that transformed the meaning of publicity which now became a means of managing and manipulating consumers rather than informing and educating publics. It began with the commodification of taste and moved on to the commodification of opinion as its techniques were transferred from the marketing of products to the marketing of politics.

Opinion management began in the early twentieth century with the innovative practice of *public relations*. By the end of the 1930s, in Great Britain, for example, all major departments of state and the Prime Minister's office had appointed press officers whose function was to manage publicity, negatively and positively, in the interests of the department and government. On the one hand, they stage-managed events (with press hand-outs and photo-opportunities) designed to place the department and, particularly, the minister in a good light. Damage limitation, the management of discreditable revelations, 'leaks', etc., were the flipside of their novel task of media-management into which the press and broadcasting were not unwillingly co-opted (Scannell and Cardiff, 1991: 39–56). The black arts of spin are a familiar feature of media-saturated politics at the start of the third millennium. Forty years ago Habermas was remarkably prescient in foreseeing the consequences of then recent techniques for the management of publicness. Politics was re-personalized. It became less concerned with issues, more with appearances: 'Public relations do not genuinely concern public opinion but opinion in the sense of reputation. The public sphere becomes the court *before* whose public prestige can be displayed – rather than *in* which public critical debate is carried out' (Habermas, 1989: 201). The circle is complete. Modern public life is refeudalized. It has regressed to its pre-modern form in which power represented itself in public, 'not for but "before" the people' (ibid.: 8).

However, this process is not, nor can be, one of complete closure, for the democratic nation–state has an unavoidable commitment to publicness and accountability enforced by the vote and strictly limited periods of office and underwritten by its normative, constitutional foundations. Post-war welfare states have a principled commitment to rights, reaffirmed by the United Declaration of Human Rights in December 1948. As against manipulative publicity, welfare states must also recognize and deal with, if not encourage, rational, critical publicity. Critical publicity is generated by 'a public of organized private people'. The opposition to atomic weapons was a notable example of its time: 'the potential for self-annihilation on a global scale has called forth risks so total that its specific negation articulates the universal interest with great precision' (ibid.: 235). The effectiveness of such movements depends in part upon the extent to which they achieve publicity through the media. Protest movements and lobby groups harness the same techniques of 'news management' but for different ends. In sum:

> The outcome of the struggle between a critical publicity and one that is merely staged for manipulative purposes remains open; the ascendancy of publicity regarding the exercise and balance of political power mandated by the social-welfare state over publicity merely staged for the purpose of acclamation is by no means certain. (ibid.: 235)

Which of the two – manipulated or critical publicity – would characterize the relationship between state and society remains a crucial issue for democratic politics to this day.

A preliminary assessment

Habermas was in his teens when Germany surrendered to the allied forces in May 1945. He was profoundly shocked by the unfolding horrors of the Nazi regime:

> At the age of 15 or 16 I sat before the radio and experienced what was being discussed before the Nuremberg tribunal; when others, instead of being struck silent by the ghastliness, began to dispute the justice of the trial, procedural questions and questions of jurisdiction, there was that first rupture, which still gapes [between the older and younger generation in Germany]. Certainly it is only because I was still sensitive and easily offended that I did not close myself to the fact of a collectively realised inhumanity in the same manner as the majority of my elders. (Bernstein, 1985: 2)

The calamity of Nazism remains a defining experience underlying his life's work. When Habermas took the theatre of power as his historical starting point in *STPS*, he was not just thinking of the High Middle Ages. Nazism, as Benjamin had noted at the time, transformed politics into a stage-managed mass spectacle performed *before* the masses. The manipulation of broadcasting and of cultural life in general enforced from above the ideology of a regime which had brutally stamped out all opposition from the moment it seized power. Public opinion did not exist, for it had, like the lambs, been silenced. A politics grounded in law and reason stood in starkest contrast to a regime that was the negation of both. In its own time and place, *STPS* was part of the effort by Habermas and his generation to reconstitute the validity of public life and politics in Germany in the aftermath of their complete and catastrophic collapse.

Habermas has always been a public intellectual in Germany, engaged in politics, writing in newspapers and magazines, and involved in polemical debate.[8] The contemporary relevance of *STPS* shows up clearly when seen in conjunction with his other concerns at the time of its writing, notably the co-authored *Students and Politics*, 'a sociological inquiry into the political awareness of Frankfurt students'.[9] Habermas had joined the Institute for Social Research, as an associate and a research assistant to Adorno in 1956. In the following year, with two other colleagues, he undertook an empirical survey of student opinion in the university, combining quantitative analysis with qualitative research methods, notably a series of carefully structured in-depth interviews that lasted, on average, two and a half hours. The introduction, written entirely by Habermas, sketched in the current situation of democracy in Germany and the problem of student participation (more exactly, the lack of it) in politics. It noted the growth of an administrative state system, beyond public control, that increasingly intervened in social and private life. Germany was at a crossroads between manipulative and genuine politicization, between an authoritarian welfare state and substantive democracy (Wiggershaus, [1986] 1994: 549). The depoliticization of the masses corresponded with an increase in the politicisation of society itself – precisely the theme of the refeudalization of society in *STPS*.

The criteria by which political participation was assessed were strict. The introduction stated that the only opportunity for political participation lay in extra-parliamentary actions led by mass organizations (trade unions or political parties) or through the functional elites in lobbying organizations and, on the whole, students belonged to neither. However, even as *Students and Politics* was being written, the first mass protests took place against the government's proposal to purchase atomic weapons for the armed forces. On 20 May 1957, there were demonstrations by 20,000 university teachers and students in Frankfurt and elsewhere against this proposal. Habermas wrote a piece in the Frankfurt student newspaper, *diskus* [sic], against a simultaneously published article by one of the university's professors, and a CDU member of the Bundestag, Franz Böhm. Böhm denounced the protests as class rabble-rousing and a brutalization of discussion that paved the way for the return of Nazism. These were the clichés of authoritarian thinking, and Habermas defended the protests against 'the statesmen ruling in our name'. He supported demands for a referendum (rejected by the Constitutional Court, 30 July 1958) on the grounds that the Federal republic was not yet 'a representative democracy in the classical sense'.

---

8 See Ryan (2003) for a review of Habermas as a public intellectual in Germany over the past 40 years.

9 The following account is summarized from Wiggershaus ([1986] 1994: 547–55).

When Horkheimer read the draft of Habermas's introduction, he was appalled. Its author was too left-wing and its publication would do the Institute no good. He refused to allow it to be included in the Institute's own series, 'Frankfurt Contributions to Sociology' and it was published elsewhere. By now Habermas's study of the bourgeois public sphere was well under way and he wanted to present it as his *Habilitation* thesis as an associate of the Institute, but Horkheimer, 'like the king in the fairytale who does not want to give away his daughter in marriage', imposed impossible conditions.

> Habermas gave in his notice – and Horkheimer had achieved what he wanted: to get rid of someone who in his opinion had incited the Institute's staff into a kind of class struggle in a teacup, and about whom he had remarked, 'He probably has a good, or even brilliant, career as a writer in front of him, but he would only cause the Institute immense damage'. (Wiggershaus, [1986] 1994: 555)

Habermas transferred to Marburg to complete his thesis under the supervision of Wolfgang Abendroth, a professor of politics and 'perhaps the only openly and staunchly socialist professor at any university in the Federal Republic' (ibid.: 556). *The Structural Transformation of the Public Sphere* had 'an exceptional impact' on the younger academic generation when it was published in Germany (Hohendahl, 1992: 99). Reviewers noted its gloomy diagnosis of the current state of politics and public life but accepted that the post-war European democracies were in practice far from the ideals to which they were in principle committed. *STPS* was read as a critique of *Dialectic of Enlightenment* and, in particular, as attempting to rescue Enlightenment and the claims of reason for the practice of contemporary politics.

In this it was and remains a major contribution to our understanding of communication and politics. Its core concerns would be carried forward as enduring commitments in Habermas's intellectual development. At the heart of the book is the theme of modernity as a political project: the establishment of politics on a legally and normatively valid basis. Most simply this means politics in the interests of all, not just a few. What could constitute the justifiable basis for such a politics? How could it come about? Or, rather, *who* would bring it about? At least part of the novelty of Habermas's thesis lies in the answer to that last question. The validity basis of modern politics in its institutional form, the nation-state, can only rest with ordinary people, the general public and their deliberate opinions. Not then, politicians, administrators, experts, or academics, all of whom are part of the institutional apparatuses of modern societies, what Habermas will later call the system world. If the social itself is part of the modern world, formed outside of the traditional instruments of power as exercised by church and state, then it is out of society (the life-world) that the demand for a politics grounded in reason is formed and articulated. And how could that be achieved other than through the processes of open, critical discussion and debate, the formation by a public of its publicly achieved and expressed opinions?

Modernity versus postmodernity

The distinction between system and life-world and their different communicative rationalities is at the heart of Habermas's next major publication, *The Theory of Communicative Action (TCA)* published in 1981 and quickly translated into English (1985). It brings together a number of strands that Habermas had pursued in the years since the publication of *STPS*. A crucial concern was with the theoretical basis of rationality and its historical medium, modernity. In the 1970s, both had come under fire in French postmodern theory. Jean-François Lyotard provided an influential and elegant definition of postmodernism as 'incredulity to grand narratives' ([1979] 1984). The grand narrative of modernity was that of history-as-progress, the political project of the eighteenth century, the age of Enlightenment. Enlightened thought conceived itself as emerging into the sunlight of true human self-understanding out of the dark cave of superstition and tradition. It rejected the old authority and the absolute claims to power and truth of kingship and Catholicism. The Christian grand narrative conceived of history as beginning with humanity's estrangement from its Creator and ending in reunification with Him. The eighteenth century rewrote this narrative, dispensing with God and placing Man at the centre of it, in a secular narrative of progress towards a truly human society based on reason. The religious struggle for salvation and redemption in a heavenly hereafter was replaced by a political struggle for freedom and equality on earth below. In Hegel's *Phenomenology of Mind (Geist)*, history is understood as the progressive development of humanity's self-conscious understanding of itself through the dialectical rise and fall of civilizations. In the nineteenth century, Marx and Engels rewrote this narrative as the struggle to achieve world communism which, when realized, would bring history as we know it to an end.

Postmodern thought was deeply suspicious of all this, particularly since the communist dream (which many of the European left had thought of as achieving its earthly incarnation in Russia) was at that very moment beginning to fall apart. A critique of the political project of Enlightenment (the modernization of society on rational grounds) was, more radically, a critique of reason as the basis of its validity and legitimacy. This was not, in itself, new. It was at the heart of the tradition of Critical Theory. But Critical Theory never rejected the transcendental claims of reason. That rejection *was* new. For Habermas, who has always understood himself as positioned within critical theory and the German intellectual tradition, modernity was and remained 'an unfinished project', the title of a speech he gave in September 1980 on the occasion of his acceptance of the Adorno Prize, bestowed on him by the city of Frankfurt. It was a theme that never lost its hold on him (Habermas [1985a] 1987: xx).[10] He has steadfastly insisted that in a post-metaphysical world (a world without God or *Geist* to legitimate it), the only basis for the legitimacy of human action is human reason. If that is rejected, all that remains is the ceaseless grinding of power, a concept which, as Hayden White observes, had the status in late twentieth-century thought that *Geist* had enjoyed in an earlier, humanist dispensation (White, 1975: 113). Such was the vision of Michel Foucault's analysis of modernity expressed in his most influential work, *Discipline and Punish: The Birth of the Prison*. Power plus knowledge equals truth. This grim equation reduces truth to an effect of power. Reason is reduced to its instrumental form, the calculation of means to ends in pursuit of power or profit. It has no transcendental validity and confers no legitimacy beyond an affirmation of the effectivity of power itself (Foucault, 1978, 1983). For Habermas, it became a matter of urgency to rescue reason from the onslaught of such postmetaphysical thinking (Habermas, [1988] 1992). If reason is no more than the pragmatics of power, and truth no more than its effect, then what could gainsay the old adage that might is right? The politics of postmodernism afford no principled resistance to the pursuit and exercise of power as an end in itself, which had, after all, found its most complete and recent realization in the lawless tyranny of the Nazi era.

To redeem reason, Habermas proceeded on two fronts. First, he examined the tradition of modern philosophy to see what could be retrieved from it. Then he attempted to reconstruct a difference basis for its legitimating, validating basis in human life and affairs. In essence, this involved a shift from a subject-centred rationality to one grounded in social interaction; from reason as a conversation with oneself to reason as the condition and outcome of communication between one's self and other selves. *The Philosophical Discourses of Modernity*, published in Germany in 1985, was based on a series of lectures on the topic that Habermas had given in the early 1980s in Germany, France and the United States. It was conceived as a response to the postmodern critique of reason signalled by Lyotard and elaborated by Foucault. Since Descartes, modern philosophy had developed as a practice of introspection whereby the philosopher explored the contents and the workings of his own mind as the starting point for knowledge of the inner self and from thence of others and the outer (external)

---

10 Habermas gave the speech again as a James Lecture at New York University in March 1981. It was published as 'Modernity versus Postmodernity', in *New German Critique* 22 (Winter 1981) and again as 'Modernity – an unfinished project', in Habermas (1985b).

world. *Cogito ergo sum.* I think therefore I am. The self (the *sum*) is grounded in knowledge or consciousness (the *cogito*): the mind moves from the inner subjective self to the outer objective world, from subject to object. Starting from the radical subjectivity of the self-reflecting subject, the problem was to establish the conditions of knowledge of everything outside of the transcendental self. Nothing could be taken as certain, beyond the certainty of thinking available to itself in and as thinking. The philosophy of the subject, or the philosophy of consciousness as it was alternatively called, was the dominant intellectual trajectory of modern European thought, with epistemology (knowledge) as its object and deductive reason to supply its method.

By the 1980s, three centuries down the line, the philosophy of consciousness, after exhaustive self-analysis, was itself exhausted. Habermas agreed, with its critics, that it was a burnt-out case. Reason could no longer be validated as the self-reflection of a thinking subject. Yet it had been a genuinely heroic project that needed a radical reconstruction rather than outright rejection. Modern scepticism represented a principled refusal of the dogmatic certainties of absolute truth that demanded uncritical faith and belief in the name of religion and politics, God and the king. The basis of Enlightenment was that very modern faith in the individual who, through his own unaided efforts, through the exercise of his own subjective rational faculties, could come through to a valid knowledge of the natural and human world. The aim of self-consciousness was self-emancipation – to liberate oneself from the chains of dogma and become a free and independent, thinking, self-critical agent on one's own behalf. When Kant asked himself 'What is Enlightenment?' he replied that it was nothing other than the reasoning human mind reflecting upon the conditions of its employment. Enlightenment's motto was *Sapere aude!* Have the courage to think for yourself![11] Foucault came to think of the subject not as the basis of reason, but as an effect of power (Foucault, 1983). Habermas wished to preserve reason as the valid and legitimate basis of human action. To do so he proposed to shift from a subject-centred to an *inter*subjective conception of reason that emphasized the role of communication.[12] Reason was to be grounded not in self-consciousness but in social interaction with language as its universal medium of expression.

---

11 This famous short essay, written in 1784, is reprinted in *The Portable Enlightenment Reader* (Kant, [1784] 1995: 1–7).

12 For a penetrating, slightly tongue-in-cheek critique of Habermas's 'broad theory of collective rationality', see Elster (1985: 35–42). He notes the slogan from the German student movement: *Diskussion ist Repression!* (p. 37).

Communicative rationality

Since *STPS*, Habermas has been preoccupied with working out this problem. His thinking on the matter is complex and, in detail, hard to follow. The ways in which he deals with it have changed over the years. But the overall aim is clear enough; to redeem the moral basis of reason whose normative foundation, he wants to claim, resides in the ideal speech situation or, in another formulation he favoured in the early 1970s, in 'undistorted communication'. Crucially, and against the corrosive relativism of postmodern thinking, Habermas wants to claim that reason, as undistorted communication, has a universal, unconditional basis. Only as such can it serve as a valid, legitimate guide and clue to lead us through the maze of difficulties that we encounter in our ordinary, everyday efforts to come to agreement and understanding with one another. If he can do this, he will have preserved the original emancipatory project of European Enlightenment for whom human reason was the only valid and legitimate basis of human action when freed from the force of tradition and the irrationality of religious belief. Thus Habermas is the pre-eminent defender of modernity against the irrationalities of premodern and postmodern thinking. He faced two crucial difficulties. First, as Critical Theory had so clearly shown, reason split in two when enlightened *self*-interest began to displace the general interest or, as Weber put it, when instrumental rationality came to dominate substantive reason in the triumph of means over ends. Reason becomes practical, utilitarian and technical, concerned above all with the most efficient means of obtaining the greatest output for the least input. This was more or less inevitable, Weber thought, because there was no longer any general agreement, in substance, nor could there be, as to what the general good might consist of. The interests of labour and capital were simply irreconcilable. Later, radical feminists would reach similar conclusions about the interests of women and men. Habermas accepts Weber's bleak analysis of the deformation of right reason, but thinks he can rescue it in two ways. First, by moving from the individual to the social and, second, by moving from a substantive to a procedural rationality. The first move is intended to solve the problem of reason as subjective self-interest. The second move is meant to solve the problem of the collapse of substantive reason as articulated in the grand narratives of modernity which postmodernism rejected.

Both these moves are pre-figured in the historical account of the classic public sphere. It is first and last a public whose medium is discussion and whose end is coming to agreement about the general interest. What are the normative foundations of discussion oriented to agreement? In an ideal speech situation, all voices in any way relevant are entitled to be heard; the best available arguments are brought to bear on the matter under discussion and only the gentle, uncoercive force of the best argument in the circumstances will determine the final collective 'yes' or 'no' as the expression of the general will (Habermas, 1995: 163). There must be no internal or external constraints on this process. Participants are entitled to all relevant information that may assist them in coming to their collective resolution. The model is intended to indicate the conditions under which 'the general interest' can be achieved since it can no longer be either assumed as known and shared, nor can it be prescribed in advance by experts:

> Under modern conditions philosophy can no longer stand in judgement over the multiplicity of individual life projects and collective forms of life, and how one lives one's life becomes the sole responsibility of socialised individuals themselves and must be judged from the participant perspective. Hence, what is capable of commanding universal assent becomes restricted to the *procedures* of rational will formation. (Habermas, 1995: 150)

Philosophy has no longer any prescriptive function; no legislative or legitimizing role in the formation of world-views, ideologies, values or belief systems. In a pluralistic society the members themselves have that responsibility in their deliberations with each other. The task of philosophy is to clarify the normative basis of the procedures of rational will formation, thereby guaranteeing their validity by making them visible. Habermas attempted this in his programmatic statement of a 'universal pragmatics' in which he argued that every communicative speech act raises universal validity claims. A *communicative* speech act is oriented towards coming to an understanding with others. As such a speaker claims to do the following:

- Say something *intelligibly.*
- Give the hearer *something* to understand.
- Make *herself* thereby understandable,
- And thereby come to an understanding with *another person.*
  (Habermas, [1979] 2002: 22. Slightly modified. Emphases as in the original)[13]

The four validity claims implicated in this process are comprehensibility, factual truth, truthfulness (sincerity) and rightness (appropriateness). Together they ground the intersubjective process 'of reaching understanding from the dynamic perspective of *bringing about* an agreement' (ibid.: 23). This specific kind of *communicative action* is distinguished from *strategic action* that is oriented

---

13 These are similar to Grice's four conversational maxims (pp. 175–9 above) but they do not address Grice's fundamental issue, namely the intelligibility of non-natural meanings in which what is meant does not correspond with what is said (as in irony). Habermas is an unrelenting literalist who always says what he means (and means what he says), usually at considerable length.

to success. At a conscious level, strategic action entails a concealment of motives and introduces an element of deception and manipulation of the communicative process. It thereby distorts the transparency of communicative action oriented to agreement through mutual understanding.

In *STPS*, Habermas dealt with the historical emergence of 'state' and 'society' as two separate but interdependent formations. These terms, in *TCA*, are displaced by 'system' and 'life-world', each driven by a different kind of rationality: the former by strategic rationality, the latter by communicative rationality. The historical analysis of *STPS* has morphed into a social theoretical analysis. Society is *both* system and life-world, but they have become separated out so that the life-world stands outside of and dominated by the system. The system world – economic and political life in its organised, institutional forms – is strategically oriented to technical and administrative efficiency whose 'steering media' are power and money. In *STPS*, Habermas had argued that society was refeudalized by the administrative welfare state that removed from families many of their former responsibilities, thereby politicizing (and at the same time depoliticizing) everyday life through the management of health, education and welfare. In *TCA*, the same theme is explored as 'the colonization' of the life-world by the system. The communicative structures of the system, mediated by power and money, are thereby distorted. Undistorted communicative rationality is preserved in the life-world of individuals in their everyday dealings with each other. But this is increasingly threatened by the system's invasive strategic rationality.

STPS revisited

In 1989, *STPS* was published, at last, in English. Nearly 30 years had passed since it was written and the world was a very different place. The Cold War was ending with the collapse of the Soviet system as a historically viable alternative to the western economic and political system. Back in the 1950s, democracy in Germany, born in the rubble of war, was still in its infancy;[14] so too, the media-saturated society of today. The academic study of 'the media' had not yet begun since the concept itself did not then exist. Habermas's original thesis was well ahead of its time in its analysis of the role of the press and broadcasting in contemporary political life. But above all what has become clearer with the passing of time is the success of the original analysis as an interdisciplinary analysis of

---

14 Habermas takes 1968, the year of student revolution, as a breakpoint 'that made it possible for democracy and the constitutional state to take political and cultural root in German soil for the first time' (Habermas, 1994: 148).

modernity. Habermas managed to bring together history, sociology, and politics, supported by philosophy and a dash of nomology (legal theory), in a fresh and convincing thesis that, for all its complexity, held together throughout and in the end. The underlying tension in the work is between its historical and normative aspects. On the one hand, it describes the formation of public opinion as an actual, real-world historical process. On the other, the original public sphere is conceived as an ideal-type of non-dominative, non-manipulative communication. It stands as a yet unrealized norm for deliberative politics. It provides a model of what, ideally, public discussion of matters in the general interest should be. But a crucial question, at the end of the twentieth century, concerned the validity of that underlying concern for a single, unitary model of public life. Was there ever such a thing as *the* public sphere? If so, was it still desirable or even plausible?

In the intervening years since its first publication the character of democratic politics had changed, not so much in its institutional forms but within civil society whose historic formation was mapped in *STPS*. The new social movements of the 1960s and 1970s indicated that civil society was alive and kicking. It had not turned into a television couch potato. These movements put in question the universalizing implications of Habermasian notions of public, communicative rationality. The women's movement and the civil rights movement in the USA have had a powerful and still unfolding impact on how we think of and seek to implement democracy-as-a-practice today. A class-based analysis of societal formation was enriched by analyses that draw attention to sex and race (in their socio-cultural articulations as 'gender' and 'ethnicity') as crucial fault-lines in the unequal distribution of rights and power and access to social resources.

In 1989, Habermas was invited to the University of North Carolina at Chapel Hill to take part in a conference devoted to the discussion of *STPS*. The participants, almost all of whom worked in American universities, represented a wide range of interests from politics, history, sociology, philosophy, women's studies, literature and communication studies. The historical aspects of the thesis were closely scrutinized by a number of participants, with Michael Schudson wondering whether there had ever been a political public sphere as described by Habermas. In nineteenth-century America, the politically-oriented riot was a more familiar form of political activity than learned discussion of political principles (Schudson, 1992: 160).[15] From the perspective of a feminist-oriented political theory, Nancy Fraser opened up an incisive critique of a number of unanalysed assumptions in the original model of the male, bourgeois public sphere. Perhaps her crucial objection was to the privileging of a single, unitary public sphere

---

15 Schudson has subsequently produced an absorbing history of American civic life (Schudson, 1998) which is an extended engagement with the underlying themes of *STPS*.

which presumed that social inequalities might be set aside and that, at least in discussion, all participants enjoyed equal discursive rights and entitlements. *The* public sphere also presupposed that what was appropriate to talk about (the topics taken and accepted as matters of general public concern) were not essentially problematic. The things that concern women, however, are not what concern men. Or rather, it is men and their concerns that are the problem. Women have found, through long experience, that it is preferable to constitute their own separate public spheres in which to address the wrongs done to their sex. Fraser called them *subaltern counter-publics*:

> Perhaps the most striking example is the late-twentieth-century US feminist subaltern counter-public, with its variegated array of journals, bookstores, publishing companies, film and video distribution networks, lecture series, research centers, academic programs, conferences, conventions, festivals, and local meeting places. In this public sphere, feminist women have invented new terms for describing social reality, including 'sexism', 'the double shift', 'sexual harassment', and 'marital, date and acquaintance rape'. Armed with such language, we have recast our needs and identities, thereby reducing, although not eliminating, the extent of our disadvantage in official public spheres. (Fraser, 1992: 123)

Fraser by no means idealizes these counter-publics, some of which are inegalitarian and antidemocratic. Radical variants tend to constitute themselves as separate from and exclusive of 'the mainstream' which they despise. However, the politics of separatism is complicated. It was the product, in the first place, of the careless exclusionary practices of the mainstream, which did not, could not and would not see that there was an issue. Even though organized as separate and sometimes closed discussion groups, the counter-publics had a necessarily outward-looking, public character that aspired to disseminate their newly won understandings to ever widening arenas, 'the public at large' (ibid.: 124). They thus had a dual character, functioning not only as spaces of retreat wherein they formed their own self-understanding, but also as launch-pads for agitational activities directed towards wider publics.[16]

This kind of public was not anticipated by *STPS* in which, as Habermas conceded, he could not imagine any vehicles for critical publicity other than

---

16 For further discussion of Fraser's contribution to the discussion of feminism, politics and the public sphere, see McLaughlin (1993). Habermas did not engage directly with multiculturalism in his response to the issues posed by the conference. However, he did deal with it in response to an influential paper, by the Canadian philosopher, Charles Taylor, on 'The Politics of Recognition'. See his contribution 'Struggles for Recognition in the Constitutional State' (Habermas, 1994, and Taylor, 1994).

internally democratized associations (e.g. trade unions) and political parties, leavened by occasional single-issue street protest. The new counter-publics bespeak the multicultural societies of the last decades of the twentieth century which are characterized by increasing social and cultural diversity. The politics of multiculturalism is much concerned with identity formation. Habermas has consistently assumed that these were set aside in a common, discursive public sphere that was blind to social and cultural differences. Moreover, the public sphere presupposed some notion of coming to agreement about the common public good. Fraser questioned all this. Public spheres, she claimed, were spaces for the articulation and expression of identities and private issues and interests. If violence against women is treated as a private matter, if it is labelled a 'personal' or a 'domestic' issue, and if discussion about it is channelled into administrative apparatuses – family law, social work, the social and psychological discourse of 'deviance' – then the abuse of women by men remains publicly unacknowledged and unaddressed (ibid.: 132). Before the question of the common good about which 'we' might come to agree, there are those concerning the still outstanding wrongs of violated social groups. Here coming to agreement or consensus is beside the point. What is called for is something more like publicly owning up to and acknowledging injustice. The politics of truth and reconciliation, for instance, in the wake of the apartheid state in South Africa, implies a new kind of critical public sphere with a different moral validity (injustice) and a different ethical aim (forgiveness). The classic male bourgeois public sphere turns out to have a normalizing force (in a Foucauldian sense) rather than the normative force of the best argument. In the face of manifest injustice, there is not much to argue about anyway. The difficult thing is to establish the truth. The even more difficult thing is to forgive, not in order to forget, but in order to free the present from the chains of past enormities in the name of a better future. Consensus and forgiveness are not equivalent since the former is between equals and the latter is between the oppressed and their oppressors.[17]

In response to the robust, critical discussion at the conference, Habermas undertook a vigorous review of the original thesis which, he concluded, had stood up well over the years. He acknowledged the strong influence of Adorno's theory of mass culture. That and the depressing results of the study of *Students and Politics* contributed to the somewhat gloomy conclusions of the original thesis: 'At the time I was too pessimistic about the resisting power and above all the critical potential of a pluralistic, internally much differentiated mass public whose cultural usages have begun to shake off the constraints of class'

---

17 On the politics of forgiveness in the light of the Truth and Reconciliation Commission, see Derrida (2001: 27–60).

(Habermas, 1992: 438). He noted the crucial development, since the 1950s, of the sociological analysis of the politics of 'civil society'. The new social movements of the 1960s and 1970s emerged from civil society, or what Habermas prefers to call the life-world, as constituted in voluntary unions outside the realm of the state and the economy and ranging from churches, cultural associations, and academies to independent media, sport and leisure clubs, debating societies, groups of concerned citizens, and grass-roots petitioning drives all the way to occupational associations, political parties, labour unions and 'alternative associations' (ibid.: 453–4). John Keane, a leading theorist of civil society, saw its task as that of redefining the boundaries between itself and the state with the twin aims of expanding social equality and liberty and of restructuring and democratising the state (Keane, 1988: 14). The concern with civil society in the 1980s was, as Habermas notes, invigorated by the collapse of state socialism in Russia and the emergence of *glasnost*. State socialism had liquidated the distinction between state and society and, hence, the public sphere, through terror and the secret police. As it began to crumble, new citizen movements, formed in the hitherto invisible private realm, applied increasing pressure that led quickly to the final collapse of state socialism in the Soviet Union.

The collapse of the soviet system is finally linked to the crux of the original thesis, namely the role of the media in public life. To what extent, Habermas asks, can

> a public sphere dominated by mass media provide a realistic chance for members of civil society, in their competition with the political and economic invaders' media power, to bring about changes in the spectrum of values, topics, and reasons channelled by external influences, to open it up in an innovative way, and to screen it critically. (ibid.: 454)

He goes on to note the thesis of Meyrowitz's *No Sense of Place*, that television restructures the social geography of the life-world and, indeed, the world itself. The revolutionary events of 1989 in East Germany, Czechoslovakia and Romania formed a chain of events

> not merely as a historical process that happened to be shown on television but one whose very *mode of occurrence* was televisual. The mass media's worldwide diffusion had not only a decisive infectious effect. In contrast to the nineteenth and early twentieth centuries, the physical presence of the masses demonstrating in the squares and on the streets was able to generate revolutionary power only to the degree to which television made its presence ubiquitous. (ibid.: 456)

So Habermas ends with a riddle. On the one hand, the mass media are part of the system whose invasive power still dominates civil society or the life-world.

Yet in spite of this, contemporary television played a decisive part in the revolutions, generated from within the life-worlds of member states of the former soviet system, that precipitated the dramatic overthrow of totalitarian state socialism. The media, central to his theory of public life, remains enigmatic in his analysis of their mediating role between system and life-world.

The media, politics and publicness

The publication of *STPS* in English stimulated a vigorous debate about the role of the media in public life, more so in Europe than the United States because the latter had no strong tradition of public service broadcasting (PSB) whereas in many European countries and, pre-eminently Britain, PSB was from the start, through to the present day, the dominant institutional form of national radio and television broadcast services.[18] At Chapel Hill, Nicholas Garnham, the only British representative, was the one participant to engage directly with the media and the public sphere. Garnham was one of the first to link the Habermasian public sphere with debates about the role of public service broadcasting (PSB) at the moment when it seemed threatened by technological innovations in cable and direct satellite broadcasting and Thatcherite neo-conservatism. The former promised an end to channel scarcity. The latter wanted the market to regulate the new multi-channel broadcasting environment. Faced with economic and political arguments in the mid-1980s that PSB had had its day, Garnham led a vigorous defence on its behalf (Garnham, 1986). PSB, he pointed out, occupies an autonomous space between state and civil society – precisely that claimed by Habermas for the classic public sphere. My own historical work on the BBC showed how it created a quite new *general* public, equivalent to the whole of society, on whose behalf and in whose interests it developed a number of mixed programme services available throughout the country and catering for a wide range of educative, informational and entertainment needs. Doubtless it was, like its classic forebear, a bourgeois broadcast public sphere. Yet it was and remains defensible as resisting the profit-oriented rationality of markets and the manipulation of public opinion by parties and governments. I argued that PSB created new communicative entitlements for listeners and viewers. It asserted, on behalf of its new public, a right of access to public life from which the majority had hitherto been excluded. It brought previously unheard voices into the studios and gave their opinions and experiences a

---

18 For a review of the literature at the time see Curran (1992). See also Keane (1991), Syversten (1992), Bono and Bondebjerg (1994), Dahlgren (1995).

public airing. It asserted the right, on behalf of its audiences, to hold politicians accountable for their actions through the political news interview, a new forum for political discussion created by broadcasting (Scannell, 1989). In all these ways PSB could be seen as providing realistic and valid solutions to the problem at the heart of representative mass democracy, namely the representation of the public interest in the political process.

At Chapel Hill, Garnham drew attention to the ways in which current thinking still remains trapped within a paradigm of face-to-face communication, and thus the problem of representation and mass democracy remains unaddressed (Garnham, 1992: 357). This issue was taken up by John Durham Peters (1993) who addressed Habermas's two-fold 'distrust of representation'. It is in part a deep-rooted suspicion of politics as a theatre on whose stage the powers that be represent their authority. At the same time it is a rejection of representative democracy in favour of direct, participatory democracy. In the former, the people are represented by those they elect to the national debating chamber to discuss politics on their behalf. In the latter the people themselves form the discussing public. But here we encounter the problem of scale, as both Garnham and Peters point out. Face-to-face discussing publics are necessarily small: 'STPS does not address "natural" limits on the size of the public' (Peters, 1993: 564). 'Are we to conceive of ourselves', asks Garnham, 'as citizens of the world, or of a nation-state or of a community or of what?' (Garnham, 1992: 368). Garnham was an early advocate of an international public sphere for, if there is a 'universal interest', its reach today must be global in scale not simply, as is often tacitly assumed, coterminous with the interests of the members of a nation-state. (1986, 1992).

In his most recent major work on law and democracy, Habermas returns to the issues concerning civil society and the political public sphere (Habermas, 1996: 329–87). It contains little new in that respect, beyond the introduction of the concept of communicative power, taken from Hannah Arendt for whom power was the potential of a common will formed in non-coercive communication. Power, in this formulation, stands opposed to violence. It corresponds to the human ability not just to act, but to act in concert. A communicative power of this kind can develop only in undeformed public spheres (ibid.: 147–8). Thus, four decades after the original thesis, Habermas remains convinced of its validity and is still attempting to reformulate it with greater clarity and exactness. The thesis itself, the ways in which its author attempted to rethink it, the discussions and criticism it generated, have been the themes of this chapter. Yet in all the criticism it generated on this or that aspect of the theory, no-one has questioned its centrality to the understanding of politics and communication in modern societies. Craig Calhoun, the convenor of the Chapel Hill conference, sums it up well:

The most important destiny of Habermas's first book may prove to be this; not to stand as an authoritative statement but to be an immensely fruitful generator of new research, analysis and theory ... Perhaps this is not only because of its theme but also because of the way in which it weaves economic, social-organizational, communicational, social-psychological and cultural dimensions of its problem together in a historically specific analysis. This multidimensional, interdisciplinary account is central to enabling Habermas to offer the richest, best developed conceptualisation available of the social nature and foundations of public life. (Calhoun, 1992: 41)

The discussion that *STPS* generated on its first publication, and ever since, serves to underscore its own most basic premise; that in modern societies there is no single, substantive rationality that binds us together. The communicative power of people in open, critical engaged discussion with each other is the only valid procedure that can generate general agreement and consent on matters that concern us all. *How* that is achieved was and remains precisely the matter under discussion.

References

Altick, R.D. (1957) *The English Common Reader: A Social History of the Mass Reading Public*. Chicago: University of Chicago Press.

Arendt, H. ([1958] 1989) *The Human Condition*. Chicago: University of Chicago Press.

Bagehot, W. ([1867] 1963) *The English Constitution*. Oxford: Oxford University Press.

Bernstein, R.J. (1985) *Habermas and Modernity*. Cambridge: Polity Press.

Boltanski, L. (1999) *Distant Suffering: Morality, Media and Politics*. Cambridge: Cambridge University Press.

Bono, F. and Bondebjerg, I. (1994) *Nordic Television: History, Politics and Aesthetics*. Copenhagen: University of Copenhagen.

Calhoun, C. (1992) *Habermas and the Public Sphere*. Cambridge: Polity Press.

Curran, J. (1992) 'Mass media and democracy revisited', in J. Curran and M. Gurevitch (eds), *Mass Media and Society*. London: Arnold, pp. 81–119.

Dahlgren, P. (1995) *Television and the Public Sphere: Citizenship, Democracy and the Media*. London: Sage.

Derrida, J. (2001) *On Cosmopolitanism and Forgiveness*. London: Routledge.

Elster, J. (1985) *Sour Grapes: Studies in the Subversion of Rationality*. Cambridge: Cambridge University Press.

Foucault, M. (1978) *Discipline and Punish: The Birth of the Prison*. Harmonsdworth: Penguin Press.

Foucault, M. (1982) 'The subject and power', in H. Dreyfus and P. Rainbow (eds), *Michel Foucault: Beyond Structuralism and Hermeneutics*. Brighton: Harvester Press, pp. 208–26.

Foucault, M. (1983) *Power/Knowledge*. London: Routledge.

Fraser, N. (1992) 'Rethinking the public sphere: a contribution to the critique of actually existing democracy', in C. Calhoun (ed.), *Habermas and the Public Sphere*. Cambridge: Polity Press, pp. 109–42.

Garnham, N. (1986) 'The media and the public sphere', in P. Golding et al. (eds) *Communicating Politics*. Leicester: Leicester University Press, pp. 37–54.

Garnham, N. (1992) 'The media and the public sphere',[19] in C. Calhoun (ed.) *Habermas and the Public Sphere*. Cambridge: Polity Press, pp. 359–76.

Habermas, J. ([1962] 1989) *The Structural Transformation of the Public Sphere*. Cambridge: Polity Press.

Habermas, J. ([1979] 2002) *On the Pragmatics of Communication*. Cambridge: Polity Press.

Habermas, J. ([1981] 1985) *The Theory of Communicative Action*, 2 vols. Cambridge: Polity Press.

Habermas, J. (1985/9) *The Philosophical Discourses of Modernity*. Cambridge: Polity Press.

Habermas, J. (1985b) 'Modernity – an unfinished project', in H. Foster (ed.), *Postmodern Culture*. London: Pluto Press, pp. 3–15.

Habermas, J. ([1988] 1992) *Postmetaphysical Thinking*. Cambridge: Polity Press.

Habermas, J. ([1992] 1996) *Between Facts and Norms*. Cambridge: Polity Press.

Habermas, J. (1994) 'Struggles for recognition in the democratic constitutional state', in A. Guttmann (ed.), *Multiculturalism*. Princeton, NJ: Princeton University Press, pp. 107–41.

Habermas, J. (1995) *Justification and Application*. Cambridge: Polity Press.

Hohendahl, P. (1992) 'The public sphere; models and boundaries', in C. Calhoun (ed.), *Habermas and the Public Sphere*. Cambridge: Polity Press, pp. 99–108.

Kant, E. ([1784] 1995) 'What is Enlightenment?' in I. Kramnick (ed.), *Enlightenment Reader*. Harmondsworth: Penguin Books, pp. 1–7.

Keane, J. (1984) *Public Life and Late Capitalism*. Cambridge: Cambridge University Press.

Keane, J. (1988) *Democracy and Civil Society*. Cambridge: Polity Press.

Keane, J. (1991) *The Media and Democracy*. Cambridge: Polity Press.

Lyotard, J-F. ([1979] 1984) *The Postmodern Condition: A Report on Knowledge*. Manchester: Manchester University Press.

Marx, K. ([1843] 1992) 'On the Jewish question', in *Early Writings*. Harmondsworth: Penguin Classics, pp. 211–47.

McLaughlin, L. (1993) 'Feminism, the public sphere, media and democracy', *Media Culture & Society*, 15(4): 599–620.

Nieminen, H. (1997) *Communication and Democracy: Habermas, Williams and the British Case*. Helsinki: The Finnish Academy of Science and Letters.

Peters, J.D. (1993) 'Distrust of representation: Habermas on the public sphere', *Media, Culture & Society*, 15(4): 541–71.

Ryan, A. (2003) 'Habermas: the power of positive thinking', *New York Review of Books*, 50(1): 43–6.

Scannell, P. (1989) 'Public service broadcasting and modern public life', *Media Culture & Society*, 11(2): 135–66.

Scannell, P. and Cardiff, D. (1991) *A Social History of British Broadcasting. 1923–1939*. Oxford: Blackwell.

---

19 A completely different article to the one above.

Schudson, M. (1992) 'Was there ever a public sphere? If so, when? Reflections on the American case', *Habermas and the Public Sphere*. Cambridge: Polity Press, pp. 143–63.

Schudson, M. (1998) *The Good Citizen: A History of American Civic Life*. New York: The Free Press.

Syvertsen, T. (1992) *Public Television in Transition: A Comparative and Historical Analysis of the BBC and the NRK*. Oslo: NAVF/KULT.

Taylor, C. (1994) 'The politics of recognition', in A. Guttmann (ed.), *Multiculturalism*. Princeton: Princeton University Press, pp. 25–74.

Watt, I. (1957) *The Rise of the Novel*. London: Peregrine Books.

Weber, W. (1975) *Music and the Middle Class*. London: Croom Helm.

White, H. (1975) 'Michel Foucault', in J. Sturrock (ed.), *Structuralism and Since*. Oxford: Oxford University Press, pp. 81–115.

Wiggershaus, R. ([1986] 1994) *The Frankfurt School*. Cambridge: Polity Press.

Conclusion

The historiography of academic fields

In the foregoing chapters I have attempted to reconstruct the beginnings of the academic study of what we have come to think of as 'the media' at different times and in different places in the course of the twentieth century. I have also threaded in another narrative about the emergence of the question of communication as it began to develop in a number of different disciplines – philosophy, sociology, history and literary studies – in the second half of the past century. I turn now to a review and critique of these histories, beginning with media before turning to communication, because the former constitutes the book's point of departure. It is the first term under consideration here: media *and* communication, and not the other way round. Had I undertaken the study of Communication and Media, I would have begun elsewhere: not with the developments at Columbia in the 1930s, but the attention given to the question of communication somewhat earlier at Chicago or perhaps, even, the beginnings of structural linguistics in the work of Ferdinand de Saussure. So the question of the media is what anchors and defines the overall project of this book and the question of communication stands in a secondary, supplementary relationship to it, as we shall see.

I have been concerned with the formation of intellectual fields, more exactly, of academic disciplines as taught in universities, and especially those in which I work – media and cultural studies. Academic disciplines are what Foucault called 'discursive formations'; they are *institutional* discourses with the nominative power to produce that of which they speak (Foucault, 1974). There is no such thing as 'English (or any other) Literature'. I mean there is no such worldly, non-academic thing. 'Literature' is a purely academic creation, the end product of an institutional process of selection that has nominated certain things as worthy of study and ruled out others as not. It begins by defining its field of study as a canon of carefully chosen texts which become, by definition, Literature, while everything outside the canon becomes, by definitional exclusion, unworthy of that name. Thus, English Literature is the product and effect of self-validating, self-legitimating institutional discourses with the power to nominate, define and objectify a field of enquiry as worthy to be taught and studied in universities. New disciplines seldom have an uncontested rite of passage into the already existing university curriculum. Sociology to this day is regarded with suspicion at Oxford and undergraduates are kept away from it. The study of English Literature, now well established there with a large faculty and undergraduate intake, was regarded for many years as an inferior version of Greats (the study, in their original languages, of ancient classical literatures) and English Literature graduates (when I was there) were not accepted as candidates worthy to compete for that rarest prize, a fellowship at All Souls. The odium in which Media Studies is held today is not unlike that which attached to English as it sought academic recognition a century ago. In each case, the new candidate for admission to the university was championed in some quarters and regarded with contempt in others. For its supporters, the new subject was a breath of fresh air, recognition of changing historical realities and an attempt at contemporary relevance. For its opponents, it meant not only a lowering of standards, but thereby the entry of new kinds of students from the lower orders with lower levels of educational attainment. It undermined the elite status of the university itself.

Each new discipline has its own internal history, although the narrative content and structure turn out to be pretty much the same in all cases. In every instance the discipline will first take root and achieve recognition in a particular place and time (Sociology at Chicago in the 1890s, English Literature at Cambridge in the 1920s). Naturally one starts with the concrete and the particular. Thus I tell the tale of how Paul Lazarsfeld ended up at Columbia and pioneered a social scientific approach to the study of the effects of new media on individuals; how the Institute for Social Research at Frankfurt also ended up there, its somewhat fraught relationship with Lazarsfeld and its own distinctive 'critical' take on mass entertainment. We have seen how Stuart Hall theorized the study of television in a small, pioneering research centre that Richard Hoggart had initiated at Birmingham. The accounts of such developments have a familiar narrative structure. There is a host institution; there are founding fathers, an emerging agenda, key texts, turf wars perhaps within the founding institution or against others that arise to challenge it. All this is the usual stuff of historical accounts of developing academic fields. But what they do not account for are the historical circumstances that summoned them into existence in the first place and that, I gradually came to think, was the crucial question with which the historiography of intellectual fields must engage.

It is never simply a question of why things happened as and when and where they did. These are partly a matter of chance. The Centre for Contemporary Cultural Studies was established at Birmingham because that happened to be the place where Hoggart got a chair in Literature in the early 1960s. But the emergence of intellectual fields of enquiry themselves is never a matter of chance. They are a determinate effect of the historical process; responses, I will argue, to the pathologies (the disorders) of modernity. They show up, in particular times and places, as one response to contemporary anxieties about the world. The form that such responses take is an effect of history in the first place, not of the founding institutions and their founders. Thus, if the two key moments in the academic study of the media in the twentieth century are at Columbia from the 1930s to the 1950s and Birmingham in the 1960s and 1970s, then what must be accounted for, in the first place, is why each moment took the form that it did: why did it appear as a *social* question in 1930s America and as a *cultural* question in 1970s Britain and why in that order (i.e. why does the social question appear, historically, before the cultural)? An immanent account of these developments cannot answer the question in either case. Thus there are two quite distinct and separate historiographies to the formation of intellectual fields: the *endogenous histories* of particular developments and the *exogenous history* to which they are a response.

If there is one book that clarified my thinking on this matter, it is *The Lonely Crowd* by David Riesman, a work which addressed a change taking place in contemporary America on the cusp of the mid-century and interpreted it historically. It was a most unusual text within American sociology of that time precisely because of the long historical frame it deployed to account for the contemporary social phenomena with which it was concerned. From it, I learned to see the doubled narrative in the histories I was attempting to write; their own and particular internal histories *and* those histories as responses to the play of external historical processes. Riesman argued that a structural transformation of the American soul was taking place in the late 1940s; a transition from the inner-directed to the other-directed individual. This restructuring of the self was not an endogenous reorganization of the American psyche but was brought about by exogenous historical forces working through contemporary American society, most fundamentally and pervasively the transformation of the economy from the production of primary heavy industrial goods to the manufacture of secondary, light domestic products. It was the then accelerating transition from an economy of scarcity to an economy of abundance that forged a new kind of individual in its own image and likeness. The life-circumstances of individuals were changing from work-defined patterns of existence to new leisure-defined ways of living. The coercive time of work and the workplace no longer dominated individual life and experience which now were oriented towards free time. The pendulum was swinging from production to consumption. It was a decisive change of gear in the long, still continuing world-historical process of societal modernization in which subsistence economies, and the forms of life developed in adjustment to them, gave way to unprecedented surplus economies of abundance and new forms of life defined, for the first time, by economic choice and freedom.

The crucial thing I learnt from this was the historical specificity of the moment in which the book was written, the moment that produced it as its symptom and diagnosis. From Riesman, I came to see the 1940s as the pivot of the last century. The world going into that decade and the world coming out of it was different. One has only to compare Britain and the USA in the 1930s and the 1950s, as I suggested in Chapter 4, to see the general force of this claim. In both countries, poverty defined the decade before the Second World War, whereas increasing prosperity for the majority of the population defined the decade that followed it. In Britain, the Conservatives won an election in 1959 with the campaign slogan 'You've never had it so good!' The Second World War was the historical hinge of the last century. It is a bitter historical irony that a war in which 50 million people perished resolved the politics of poverty that had precipitated it. In Britain and America, the outbreak of war brought about full employment within months and the working population experienced a real rise in its general standard of living which continued through the next decade and has been sustained ever since. The world we inhabit today is the product of the last world war whose lineaments began to appear in the 1950s. If it was, as we now can see, a victory for capitalism and democracy, it must now be remembered that neither had, up to that moment, seemed particularly compelling, necessary or even desirable in most if not all European countries (Dunn, 2005). Now it seems 'there is no alternative' to either.

Taking this as my template – the structural transformation of the world taking place across a pivotal 30-year span in the mid-twentieth century – I will try to account for the formation of the sociology of mass communication in 1930s America and of media studies in 1970s England as, in each case, a contemporary response to this fundamental historical process. I will try to show how and why it should be that America before the war produces a sociological response to what is happening and why it should be that England going into the 1970s produces a cultural response to contemporary social change. I will interpret each of these two historical moments in which the question of the media becomes the focus of academic attention as effects of the sea-change taking place in the world brought about by movement in the tectonic plates of the world economy as it shifted from an economy of scarcity to an economy of abundance. The basis of the argument is pretty orthodox. I do take the economy – *the* economy as a world-historical, world-defining phenomenon – as having a determinate effect on contemporary forms of social, political and cultural life everywhere.[1] Thus, as the economy changes gear from scarcity to abundance,

---

1 This of course, is the interpretative frame developed by Marx in his later life as he moved 'towards a more and more profound attempt to grasp the logic of the process of global economic change which he had already long decided to be the fulcrum of the history of the modern world and which the history of the world ever since has increasingly confirmed to be indeed such' (Dunn, 1993: 87. See pp. 82–120 for a magisterial review of Marx's economic and political thought.)

it gives rise to new kinds of politics, new ways of life and a new kind of individual, as Riesman argued. These interlocking historical changes show up in and as the contemporary world for those who live in it, and all must come to terms with it somehow or other and manage and cope with it as best they can – at individual and institutional levels. At an individual level, for instance, we have seen how intellectuals from the old world of Europe managed and dealt with their experience of the new world when they arrived as political or ethnic refugees in America of the 1930s. Lazarsfeld and Adorno are exemplary in their individual differences. At an institutional level we have seen the same individuals, working in the same university that took them in and gave them shelter, produce markedly divergent ways of engaging with and accounting for the same contemporary social phenomena – the rise of mass communication and entertainment: radio, cinema and music.

In what follows I try to interpret from our own and present times the politics of the present[2] in the past as played out in two historical moments which each produced an academic engagement with then very new media of communication; radio in America of the 1930s and 1940s, and television in Britain of the 1960s and 1970s. The focus throughout the book has been on formative moments, the time-spans within which a new domain of academic enquiry comes into existence and defines itself. Thus it is of some importance as to where the line is drawn between the innovation of a field and its subsequent routinization and normalization. In line with the preceding narratives I will take the formative moment of the sociology of mass communication to be located in Columbia and defined by the formation of the Bureau of Applied Social Research and Lazarsfeld's commitment to the investigation of the effects and uses of the media. The work that is the culmination of this moment and at the same time brings a degree of closure to it is, I have already argued, *Personal Influence* published in 1955 by Katz and Lazarsfeld. Thereafter, the field settles down to the work mostly of consolidation and diffusion. Likewise the formative moment of Media Studies is located in Birmingham, defined by the establishment of the Centre for Contemporary Cultural Studies (CCCS) and Hall's work on ideology and television. That ends with his departure for the Open University in 1980 and the then emerging field of Media Studies, again, settles down to consolidation and diffusion; the normalization of an agenda worked out in the 1970s at CCCS. I turn now to a consideration of what shaped and defined the working agendas of these two formative moments.

---

2 The term is from Boltanski (1999). It is a core concept in my own thinking and the meaning and significance of the politics of the present is discussed in detail in *Television and the Meaning of 'Live'* (Scannell, 2007, forthcoming).

The rise of 'the social'

In respect of developments in Columbia before the Second World War, the question must be *why* sociology in the first place and, within that, why a sociology of mass communication? If sociology came into being to deal with the question of the social, then what *is* that question and how did it arise, and where and when? An answer to such questions is provided in yet another key text from the 1950s, *The Human Condition*, by Hannah Arendt. This wonderful book should be read in conjunction with those by Riesman, Williams and Habermas (who was directly influenced by it) as one more contemporary attempt, in the aftermath of the war, at a critical analysis of the meaning of modernity and its historical formation. Arendt was yet another European political and ethnic refugee from the horrors of

Hannah Arendt

Nazism who found a new life in the United States. She was a contemporary of Adorno (whom she disliked) and of Walter Benjamin whom she liked and admired. Her intellectual formation was shaped by the study of Greek and Roman civilizations, their politics and literature. She was Martin Heidegger's most gifted student (and lover) at the University of Marburg in the 1920s. She settled well into the life of an East Coast intellectual, living in New York and moving between university life and the milieu of the metropolitan literary intelligentsia, writing regularly for the *New Yorker*. Her thinking, a kind of political phenomenology that fuses her deep love and understanding of the ancient world with Heidegger's contemporary *Existenz* philosophy, is quite distinctive and original. It enables us to see and understand the historical formation of sociology's object domain, *society*.

For Arendt, 'the rise of the social' is a key to understanding the modern world (Arendt, [1958] 1989: 38–49). It is a complex argument that has generated much critical debate and hinges on a reading of the structure of Greek life in the era of Athenian democracy over 2000 years ago. Arendt reads the everyday life of free men (the male citizens of Athens) as split between the private life of the household and the public life of the *polis*. The former is for them the realm of necessity, the latter the realm of freedom. The household, as the space of privacy, is privative – a place of deprivation from which men escape as they enter the 'great and glorious public realm' to participate in the political life of the city – state. This, for us today, is an extraordinarily counter-intuitive reading of the relationship between the private and the public. We take private life as the realm of freedom, of intimacy and authenticity and leave the management of public life to the professionals – politicians and the permanent bureaucracy – while occasionally performing our civic duties in turning out to vote. We value the former and despise the latter. But Arendt thinks it is (or should be) quite the reverse.

The household is the realm of necessity in a double sense. It is the locus of sexual reproduction and the sheltering provider for the bodily subsistence, maintenance and care of its members. Domestic life is in this double sense concerned with meeting and managing basic material human needs. Our modern word economy has two Greek roots; *oikos* (the household) and *nomos* (law) and once meant the management of the household, domestic economy. The 'law of the household' (its *oikonomia*, or economy) did not only refer to patriarchal authority and the regulation of household affairs. It meant more fundamentally that all household members were subject to its implacable law, the law of sexual and bodily necessity and need:

> [Today we] see the body of peoples and political communities in the image of a family whose everyday affairs have to be taken care of by a gigantic, nation-wide administration of housekeeping … The collective of families economically organised into the facsimile of one super-human family is what we call 'society', and its political form of organisation is called 'nation'. We therefore find it difficult to realise that according to ancient thought on these matters, the very term 'political economy' would have been a contradiction in terms: whatever was 'economic', related to the life of the individual and the survival of the species, was a non-political, household affair by definition. (Arendt, [1958] 1989: 28–9)

For Arendt, the rise of the social realm is 'a relatively new phenomenon whose origin coincides with the emergence of the modern age' (ibid.). It was an effect, as Habermas argued in developing her thesis, of the long historic process whereby, in Europe, the modern capitalist economy was gradually formed as the management of subsistence needs (the provision of food, shelter, clothing, etc.) passed out of the immediate, private environment of individual households and slowly fused, over centuries, into larger 'economic' units of production that came to supply the material needs of households. Modern societies are inextricably linked with the formation of the modern economy which, from the start, has operated within while always transcending the bounded authority of modern nation–states. The tensions generated by the economy in modern societies were what hailed or summoned into existence the modern academic discipline of sociology to engage with the question of the social.

Those tensions were the central theme of Arendt's next book, a comparative study of the American and French Revolutions and the birth of modern politics. Here she analysed the emergence of 'the social question' in the nineteenth century as formed by the politics of poverty and the rise of the masses (Arendt, [1963] 1990: 59–114). There is a tendency nowadays to claim that the masses never existed. In his robustly enjoyable broadside against *The Intellectuals and the Masses, 1875–1939*, John Carey begins by briskly dismissing 'the masses' of the late nineteenth and early twentieth century as a fiction; the product of the rancid, class-ridden snobbery of the European bourgeois literary intelligentsia of that time who nearly all, to a man and a women, despised the uneducated, unwashed urban working classes (Carey, 1992: 1). But, while I have some sympathy with Carey's knockabout treatment of the intellectuals, it has to be said that the masses were no fiction.[3] They were the defining political and economic reality of those times, in Europe and North America. The question of 'the masses' became *the* social question ever since the French Revolution; it was more exactly to do with the politicization of poverty.

That, Arendt argued, was the conclusion that Karl Marx drew from it:

> He interpreted the compelling needs of mass poverty in political terms as an uprising not only for the sake of bread or wealth, but for the sake of freedom as well. What he learned from the French Revolution was that poverty could be a political force of the first order. (Arendt, 1963/1990: 62)

It ceased to be a natural fact and became an historical fact that entered into, indeed determined, the politics of Europe and North America from the nineteenth century through to the mid-twentieth century. It was the driver of history because the labour of an immiserized urban working class was the essential wealth creator

---

3 What provokes Carey's wrath was a widespread view amongst the European literary intelligentsia of the masses as sub-human vermin, fit to be exterminated – an attitude which, he argues, found definitive expression in Hitler's *Mein Kampf*. Carey has no difficulty in showing the vileness of the views of many very well-known authors, but fails to acknowledge that the conditions of life for millions were, in fact, vile. I have shown how the BBC documented the widespread poverty in inter-war Britain and the impact of unemployment and bad housing on individuals and their families (Scannell and Cardiff, 1991: 57–71, 333–55). When slum-dwellers and the unemployed spoke at the microphone or on film of what their life was like, they appeared naturally as ordinary, decent people and not the members of some sub-human race of Morlocks. But they were people forced, through brute poverty, to lead an undifferentiated existence in which they had no access to the ordinary luxuries of daily life which others took for granted (and they knew this of course). To speak of 'the masses' is to acknowledge the *undifferentiated* life to which millions were condemned: a life of 'mere' subsistence, of constant struggle and anxiety to meet basic everyday needs, of wretched housing, meagre diet, gnawing hunger, ragged clothing (shoes an unaffordable luxury), ill health (itself an effect of poor diet and housing) and a shortened life-span. Such misery was endured by many millions in Europe and North America throughout the nineteenth century and the first half of the last century. Such an existence has, in the course of the second half of the twentieth century, receded. To be sure, poverty stubbornly persists in the advanced economies of Europe and North America, but not so pervasively and not at such a brutal, primary level. It is no longer a defining political issue as it was throughout the classic era of urban, industrial capitalism which lasted from the early nineteenth to the mid-twentieth century. Primary poverty now presents itself to 'us' as existing in other parts of the world, most notably and visibly on our television screens, in Africa.

for the mass-produced goods of factory capitalism. The structural economic antagonism between capital and labour, so clearly and presciently analysed by Marx, gave rise to continuing industrial unrest and conflict whose resolution required the increasing intervention of the state: the length of the working day and week, the appalling abuse of child labour, health and safety in the work-place, wage bargaining, the unionization of labour and the rights of unions ... a host of issues requiring continuous political management in order to keep the economy going and defuse the fear (always in the background) of insurrection from below. All this *was* 'the social question', as Raymond Williams understood and showed so clearly in the exemplary case of British 'society' from the late eighteenth to the mid-twentieth century. And in all this the nature of the state itself was gradually reformed and redefined in the long revolution towards mass representative democracy, a new kind of politics that only came to fruition in Europe in the early twentieth century.

The question of the masses, then, defined and determined economic and political life in the first decades of the last century. It acquired new significance and urgency in two key moments: the Bolshevik Revolution in Russia in 1918 which coincided with fierce industrial unrest in all the advanced economies, and the Wall Street crash of 1929 whose consequences defined the next decade. This – the inter-war period – was the moment of 'mass communication' and 'mass culture'. In the writings of those years 'mass' and 'masses' were taken for granted, unmarked terms, used as natural descriptors of natural facts. To be sure, the words meant different things in Europe and North America. The masses in Europe were the urban proletariat. In America, they were the atomized individual components of the lonely urban crowd. But in neither case could they be regarded as the imaginary constructs of contemporary intellectuals looking at social phenomena through the wrong end of a telescope. They were real, insistent social facts. The politics of poverty returned to haunt the 1930s and to drive the world into war. It was called, lest we forget, the *hungry* 1930s.

The sociology of mass communication

This then is the world-historical frame within which to consider the formation of a sociology of *mass* communication in the USA in the 1930s. It enables us to understand why the emphasis fell on the first and not the second term. The concern at the time was not with the communicative character of the new technologies of communication but their impact and effect on the mass of the population. The inter-war sociology of mass communication was hailed into existence by current concerns of the elite with the vulnerability of the urban masses to manipulation by advertising, newspapers and radio. But the inter-war period was also the moment when new, modern forms of entertainment that would define the rest of the century (radio, cinema, television and the music industry) were established. While millions endured hunger, unemployment and squalid living conditions in Europe and North America, millions more were beginning to enjoy a marginal surplus of disposable time and money which they spent on the newly emerging culture of consumption and entertainment. The post-war culture of everyday life was formed in the inter-war period. The new mass media showed the consequences of poverty to contemporary audiences but were themselves part of a new culture of leisure and consumption under-pinned by the rapidly developing economy of abundance. The sociology of mass communication across a 20-year span from the mid-1930s to the mid-1950s tracks this transition taking place in American society.

It was driven initially not so much by fear of the revolutionary potential of the masses as anxiety about their well-being. What was the effect of powerful new communication technologies on the ordinary man? Was he not vulnerable to manipulation because he was ill-informed through lack of education and psy-chologically suggestible through economic insecurity? Such were the underly-ing assumptions of the first important case-study of the impact of the first great and then very new technology of broadcast communication, radio. Hadley Cantril's study of *The Invasion from Mars* was sub-titled 'A study in the psychol-ogy of panic'. The fact that large numbers of people were so frightened by a spoof scary play for Halloween – an adaptation of *The War of the Worlds* by H.G. Wells – that they fled their homes and took to the road seemed to confirm the power of radio and the vulnerability of 'the common man'. It was the task of intellectuals 'to spread knowledge and scepticism more widely among common men' so that they might be 'less harassed by the emotional insecurities which stem from underprivileged environments' (Cantril et al., 1940: 205). That important task was addressed in Paul Lazarsfeld's key study of *Radio and the Printed Page*, published in the same year, whose aim was to answer the ques-tion 'uppermost in the minds of many citizens: what will radio do to society?' and to provide those concerned with mass education with an analysis of the conditions in which the 'masses' would or would not expose themselves to edu-cation by radio (Lazarsfeld, 1940: 133). The theme of *Mass Persuasion* was addressed a little later, in Robert Merton's elegant study of audience responses to Kate Smith's marathon radio broadcast to promote the purchase of govern-ment war bonds (Merton [1946] 2004).

All these studies of the impact of radio in the late 1930s and early 1940s presupposed its direct and powerful impact on powerless masses. It *did* make people flee in fear. It *did* make them buy $40 million worth of war bonds in a single day. But at the same time this concern with the top-down impact of radio on individuals starts to change. On closer inspection the question begins to transform from what the media do to individuals into what individuals do with the media. Herta Herzog's study in the late 1930s of what women got from listening to daytime radio serials opened up what came to be called 'uses and gratifications' studies. It began as an attempt to study the influence of radio on women's lives but became a study of what it meant to them. Two contrasting themes are threaded through the study: the loneliness of many listeners and the compensatory 'use' of radio as a source of company and friendship – isolated individuals warmed by the sociable aura of the new mass medium of radio (Herzog, 1941). The same picture emerges in studies of newspapers and, a little later, of television. Bernard Berelson's charming investigation of what 'missing the newspaper' meant to New Yorkers during a two-week strike in 1945 was another early, classic 'uses and gratifications' study. Like Herzog's study it deployed psychoanalytic concepts to get below the surface and find what missing the daily paper 'really' meant for individuals (Berelson, [1949] 2004). Its findings were similar: the newspaper was a small daily life-support system that gave meaning and structure to otherwise empty days and lives. Without it people did not know what to do with themselves. They felt lonely and isolated. With it they had access to a fuller, richer and more exciting social world. The enduringly influential study of early television by Donald Horton and Richard Wohl is the fullest exploration of the sociable character of television output and 'the bond of intimacy' ('the 'para-social' relationship) it created especially with 'the socially isolated, the socially inept, the aged and invalid, the timid and rejected' (Horton and Wohl, [1956] 2004: 380).

We must acknowledge the truth of these testimonies to the alienated experience of contemporary American life for city dwellers, particularly those whose lives were economically and emotionally insecure. The findings of Herzog and Berelson capture an authentic 'structure of feeling', as does the title of Riesman's book (chosen by his publisher) – the loneliness of the isolated members of the lonely crowd.[4] In pre-war Britain, Leavis saw both the traditional and the new mass arts as substitutes for real life and experience. Contemporary American social science research also saw radio, movies and newspapers as offering a kind of inauthentic, pseudo-social substitute for authentic existence. Shorn of value judgements about 'the masses', the data point to the loss of the very possibility of experience for the mass of the population condemned by economic deprivation to an undifferentiated existence. That is, the meaning of mass society and mass culture. For the masses under the yoke of dull economic compulsion, music, film, radio and the morning newspaper might indeed offer a momentary respite from daily care. If desire and longing spring from lack, then escapism as their (in)authentic promptings may be the realest expression of the experience of

---

4 *Nighthawks,* by Edward Hopper (1942), is the iconic American painting that captures this structure of feeling to which the pulp fiction and movies of the period also bear eloquent witness.

modernity in mass society. The fundamental ambiguity at the heart of this experience (real or not; authentic or not?) is the enigmatic critical question in any assessment of the role of the new culture industries. The uses and gratifications literature suggests that the mass media had (as interpreted by the researchers) an uneasy compensatory function; they filled a gap in daily lives shorn of meaningful experience. They created a culture of dependency for lonely individuals. This is a deeply equivocal picture which is partly true to historical reality and partly a misreading of it, for in *all* the literature the audience is treated as an aggregated mass of isolated individuals. This is a sociology that has yet to discover the meaning of sociality. It is partly an effect of the premises and the methodology of a sociology under the sway of positivism; partly of the social position of intellectuals and their distance from the lives of 'the masses'; partly an effect, as Lukács argued, of the reification of modern thought, but ultimately of the experience of the world itself for those who lived in those times – not only the subjects of research but also their researchers.

And yet a different picture peeps through the data. Almost all the women who listen to radio soaps talk about them with others and 41 per cent discuss their favourite programme with friends. Herzog tells of one woman who phones her friend in New Jersey every day to talk about what she's just heard in the latest episode.[5] Berelson's data also show how newspapers function as a sociable resource for conversations with others, and Horton and Wohl's analysis, stripped of its emphasis on vulnerable, isolated viewers, in fact emphasizes the sociability of television as interacting with viewers' own sociable existence. An alternative reading becomes possible. The sociable character of social life is about to be discovered in the sociology of mass communication. This discovery is latent in the long gestation and manifest in the published findings and analysis of *Personal Influence* by Katz and Lazarsfeld. The inner and outer history of this book exemplifies the historical transformation taking place in America from the 1930s to the 1950s as diagnosed by David Riesman: the transition from the pre-war to the post-war world, from scarcity to abundance, from the time of the masses to the time of everyday life.

The book, it will be recalled, is a fusion of two different fields of enquiry: an investigation of the 'two-step flow' hypothesis formulated by Lazarsfeld from a study of voting behaviours in 1940 and, welded onto this, the later doctoral research of Katz into small group dynamics. It should be emphasized that the Decatur data had been on the shelves for some time until Katz came along. This was due in particular to ructions between C. Wright Mills and Lazarsfeld, but more generally it was because mass communication sociology could not make

---

5 'In a world which offers so few chances for real experiences any happening must be made immediately into something owned', Herzog comments. Her famous study of women listening to radio serial dramas is tellingly entitled 'On borrowed experience'.

sense of it. It needed someone from outside the field to unlock its significance. Mass communication sociology, as Katz points out, regarded interpersonal communication either as non-existent or irrelevant to its concerns (Katz and Lazarsfeld, 1955: 34). But Lazarsfeld saw that it might help to explain the role of what he thought of as 'opinion leaders' in his two-step flow hypothesis and so he recruited Katz's aid in another attempt to make something of the Decatur material. Katz begins with a robust criticism of 'the traditional image of the mass persuasion process'. It took no account of 'people'. It was no use thinking of 'opinion leaders' as if they were a group apart and as if leadership was a trait that some possessed but others did not. It was essential to begin to think of opinion leaders as 'an integral part of the give-and-take of *everyday interpersonal relationships*' (ibid.: 33. Emphasis added). The new field of interpersonal communication, if we consider it exogenously, can be seen as a precise response to the historicization of everyday life which, so to speak, summoned it into existence as its sociological interlocutor. I do not mean, of course, to suggest that everyday life did not exist until this moment – that would be absurd – but rather that hitherto it lacked any historical and sociological significance. Previously it was *beneath* history and *below* the radar of sociology. Now, in 1950s America and elsewhere in Europe as we shall see, everyday life begins to achieve visibility and recognition as something distinctive and meaningful in its own terms and for its own sake.

This is the emerging world explored by *Personal Influence* which, in this exogenous reading, is a pioneering study of the *sociable* character of everyday life in mid-twentieth-century America. A richly patterned network of relations within and between younger and older, married and unmarried women of differing socioeconomic status emerges from the data. The role of personal influence in the formation of tastes, attitudes, opinions, shopping choices and media usage is convincingly established: it is an 'almost invisible, certainly inconspicuous, form of leadership at the person-to-person level of ordinary, intimate, informal, everyday contact' (ibid.: 138). It is 'casually exercised, sometimes unwittingly and unbeknown, within the smallest grouping of friends, family members and neighbours' (ibid.). This is a very different picture to that described and analysed in the earlier classic study of *Mass Persuasion* in which urban Americans are seen as living in a climate of reciprocal distrust. In *Personal Influence* everyday life is an end in itself. In *Mass Persuasion*, it had a marginalized role in the work-defined lives of the masses under the dull economic compulsion of factory capitalism.

The war, I have argued, resolved the prolonged economic crisis of the 1930s. In America and Britain unemployment disappeared overnight. More and more people were recruited to the labour force. All those in work achieved an absolute rise in their standard of living and, for the first time, blue-collar workers saw theirs rise faster than that of white-collar workers. For women, especially, it was a moment when they were massively recruited into work and, as *Rosie the*

Riveter showed so charmingly and poignantly, ordinary working-class American women (black and white) briefly achieved a new economic independence and greater purchasing power than had ever previously been possible for them (Frank et al., 1982). It did not last. When the war ended, they were told to get back home and breed while the men, returning from the far-flung fighting fronts, replaced them in the workplace. This was the moment of the Decatur study, undertaken in the final stages of the war. Coming out of the war the American economy entered into a long period of continuous growth and expansion, in which life for many if not most Americans was better than ever before and the hungry 1930s became no more than a rapidly receding trace memory.

The transition to an economy of abundance, increasingly evident in the inter-war period, is decisively established by the mid-1950s and is everywhere apparent. That is why, to grasp the full significance of *Personal Influence* we must attend to the inner history of its long gestation. If we attend only to the text-as-published, we will miss its real crux: the fact that the sociology of mass communication could not, in its own terms, make sense of the question it had raised and the data it had gathered. It was a sociology without a conception of what connected people to each other. It is precisely across this period, from the mid-1930s to the mid-1950s, that the sociality of the social manifested itself as a historical phenomenon. A new sub-branch of sociology in America was formed in response to this – the first recorded instance of the usage of 'inter-personal' is in 1938.[6] The fusion of the two sub-branches resolves a riddle within the field and that is why *Personal Influence*, on publication, was recognized as a key text that had an immediate and lasting significance within sociology.

The exogenous historical reading that I have essayed necessarily starts from the internal history of the text and its position (at the time and since) within the field, both of which are crucial to its understanding. But moving outwards from this we must think of it as embedded in the economic, political, social and cultural determinants of its own and present times as these impinged upon and shaped the concerns of sociological work-in-progress. In attending to the historical gestation of *Personal Influence*, I have offered a symptomatic reading of it as a response to a profound sea-change in the world with which it engages – the passing of the time of the politics and culture of the masses and the emergence of the politics and culture of everyday life. Thus what the book discloses both in its internal history *and* as a response to the historical process of its own time (its inner and outer dialectic, so to speak) is the passage from modernity to postmodernity, if by that is meant the structural transformation of the global economy from scarcity to abundance and the corresponding reconfiguration of contemporary political, social and cultural forms of life.

---

6 I am indebted to John Durham Peters who told me this.

The culture of everyday life

Thus far I have been concerned with the question of 'the social' and the discipline to which it gave rise, sociology. I turn now to the question of 'the cultural' and the discipline it summoned into existence. The when and where of this development are central to the understanding of its formation. It will also shed light on the historically emerging relationship between 'culture' and 'society'. The academic discipline created in response to both those historical pressures is the study of literature and, paradigmatically, English Literature (hereafter Eng Lit). The 'literature' addressed by this new academic field of study is itself a significant element in the long historic process that elicited it, for it is modern, not ancient, literature that is the focal object of study in the new discipline. Its two object domains were poetry and the novel. The study of poetry established one continuing strand in Eng Lit's approach to its subject matter: a hermeneutics that treated the poem as a thing-in-itself, a *text* to be read as if nothing existed outside of it. The close reading of texts for their immanent meaning was part of the tradition from the start, but the unasked question was what warranted (justified) the readings produced. Where *was* the meaning of the object: in the mind of its creator, in the poetic text itself or in the mind of the reader? These questions returned to haunt later generations. The other object of study, the novel, more insistently posed questions outside itself for its formal realism posed unavoidable questions about the relationship between fictional narrative and the actual world in which and about which it appeared to have been written.

The question of literature and society appears as a focal concern in three key academic texts of the 1950s: one published in America, one in Britain and one in Germany. The first two have a common source in the Leavises and Cambridge and both informed the historical narrative of the third and last. They are, in order of appearance, *The Rise of the Novel* by Ian Watt (Stanford University Press, 1956), *Culture and Society* by Raymond Williams (Chatto and Windus, 1958) and *The Structural Transformation of the Public Sphere* by Jürgen Habermas (Hermann Luchterhand Verlag, 1962).[7] Between them, they provide an engaging account of the historical formation of the literary culture of modernity that gives rise eventually to an academic field of enquiry inhabited by two of them (Watt and Williams). It is not for nothing that these texts are essentially products of the 1950s though all have their roots in the two preceding decades, for the 1950s is the historic 'moment' in which the question of culture achieves renewed historical salience and recognition and is found to be inseparable from 'literature' and 'everyday life'.

---

7 In the end references, the most recent edition of each of these three works is cited, not the original. Habermas had read Watt and Williams and his concept of the 'literary public sphere' is a synthesis of their work and that of Altick (1957). Adorno is acknowledged (along with Talcott Parsons) by Watt in his introduction.

I have thus far discussed 'the social' in relation to the rise of the urban masses in the nineteenth century, the problem of poverty and its politics. But the rise of 'society' preceded these convulsive developments. Industrialization accelerated the global development of the transport and communications infrastructure and commodity production and in so doing universalised the material basis of modern societies upon which their way of life depends. The universalization of this 'way of life' (its extension through *all* sectors of society) was finally accomplished in the advanced economies only in the 1950s. But the essential characteristics of modernity's 'way of life' were created long beforehand: the *culture* of everyday life as we know and experience it today was in all essentials set in place and worked through in the eighteenth century. That historic development was masked by the enormous convulsions of factory capitalism and the immiseration of the workforce it created, and only recovered in the mid-twentieth century when continuing economic growth made a way of life created by the eighteenth-century bourgeoisie finally available to the majority of the peoples of North America and Northern Europe.

It was a way of life focused on the home and family in which the relations between household members had been radically transformed. As the household's *oekonomia* was no longer driven by necessity, relations between men, women and children gradually became less impersonal and instrumental. The new relationships, no longer determined by the needs of survival, now became substantive ends and goods in themselves. Lawrence Stone, the great historian of the family, sex and marriage, has traced with remarkable diligence and subtlety the emergence in England between 1500 and 1800 of this basic social unit of modernity. He calls it the 'companionate marriage' based on love and affection between the sexes, in which children too are objects of affection, loved in themselves and no longer small unruly brutes to be whipped into submission (Stone, 1979). Sociologists call this the nuclear [two-generation] family. It is the fundamental social unit, the bedrock of modern societies everywhere. The companionate marriage presupposes real equality between the sexes, the domestification of feral males and the reigning in of masculine violence that the older 'honour' code had demanded. As distinct from the older dispensation, which it gradually replaced across all social classes, modern marriage was based on a *relationship* between the sexes rather than on pre-assigned duties and responsibilities hitherto determined by the immemorial sexual division of labour when Adam delved and Eve span and they and their offspring, throughout the life-course, led largely unconnected lives within their separate gendered communities. The new relationship was grounded, so Stone argues, on the rise of 'affective individualism': not the isolated, inner-directed individualism of *homo economicus*[8] but an other-directed individualism in which women and men acknowledged each other in their difference but recognized common emotional

---

8 See Watt ([1956] 2000: 60–92), for a discussion of Daniel Defoe's *Robinson Crusoe* as *Homo Economicus*, the prototype of modern economic individualism.

needs, desired each other's continued presence as a comfort, support and pleasure and treated the marriage as a life-long developing, shared and negotiated relationship between them. This is the ideal-typical ethical foundation of the modern family in which the goodness of the relationship is confirmed by the couple's discovery of the good in each other. It is based on the politics of *eros*, incarnate human love dependent on reciprocity and mutuality. Its communicative medium is continuing, life-long dialogue. All problems can be solved in modern relationships so long as the partners continue to communicate with each other. In American movies and television series about family life and relationships today the moment of crisis will inevitably come in which someone says – usually the woman (or Frasier) – 'We need to talk'.

It is evident that such a relationship presupposes a dwelling-place fit to live in, and hence the long historic development, across all sectors of society, of 'the home' as something more than a mere shelter from the elements and otherwise to be escaped from, but as a place capable of sustaining non-instrumental relationships, to which one would turn and return for relaxation, leisure, ease and enjoyment, a *comfortable* place in which parents and children would wish to spend their time together. This development was greatly accelerated in the early twentieth century after the First World War with renewed programmes of slum clearance, the provision of council housing by local authorities, and the rise of suburbia and affordable privately owned small dwellings with inner sanitation, cooking and washing facilities and separate bedrooms.[9] The universalization of

---

9 This transformation is charted in Seebohm Rowntree's two pioneering social surveys of working-class life in York: *Poverty: A Study of Town Life* (1901) and *Poverty and Progress* (1941). It is a unique, meticulous longitudinal study of social change by a Quaker pioneer of the ethnography of daily life. By the end of the 1930s the old slums had begun to be replaced by council housing and affordable private homes, described in detail by Rowntree and based on his own observations. He notes a decline in drinking across this 40-year period which he attributes to the new attractions of the home itself, of 'staying in' and, for instance, listening to the radio rather than, as in the 1890s, thronging the streets, brawling and filling the public houses. Both surveys are powerful, detailed, closely observed accounts of (1) the prevalence of 'primary poverty' in an old English city at the end of the nineteenth century, and (2) of the emergence of a new culture of daily life as a result of rising wages and better housing and hence better health and an incremental increase in the marginal surplus of time and money for leisure and relaxation. Introducing his final conclusions on 'leisure time activities' in the late 1930s, Rowntree observes:

> A community ill-fed and worn out with hard work will have little time or energy for anything except 'work and bed'. But with a growth in the amount of leisure and an improvement in economic conditions not only will people have more time in which to express themselves through their leisure pursuits, but they will have more energy to indulge in forms of recreation which would make no appeal to tired and ill-fed men. (1941: 468)

This may stand as a succinct and vivid summary of the passage from the politics of poverty to an emergent culture and politics of everyday life. Note that his final study of post-war Britain is called *English Life and Leisure* (Rowntree and Lavers, 1951): thus over a 50-year span the shift from poverty to leisure is tracked in three case studies.

---

these developments was not finally sealed until the 1950s when the wired home and a whole clutch of electrically powered domestic appliances at last established the material and technological basis of the way of life first enjoyed in the advanced economies of Europe and North America and, in the past 20 years or so, now rapidly spreading through almost all parts of the world except Africa. The fundamental importance of the new labour-saving domestic appliances of the mid-twentieth century can scarcely be exaggerated. Before the Second World War, the largest single source of employment in Britain was domestic service. The middle and upper classes sustained a (more or less) leisured life-style because they employed other human beings to cook and clean and wash and iron and wait on them hand and foot. Servants were the wage-slaves of the better off. After the war, domestic service noiselessly faded while the new domestic appliances – electric cookers, clothes and dish wash-and-drying machines, fridge-freezers and vacuum-cleaners – took the manual toil out of basic domestic tasks.[10] This culture of everyday life, based on the companionate marriage and the small self-sustaining domestic household goes back several centuries but is finally available to the majority of whole populations only after the Second World War. It *was* a long, uneven revolution, this transformation of the day-to-day conditions of existence for whole populations. Only when such circumstances were generally achieved could the culture of everyday life appear as the common culture of post-modernity, as it did at last in the 1950s. That is why the reconnection with the emerging bourgeois culture of the eighteenth century is made in this decade.

Literature, culture and politics

A culture of everyday life presupposes that people have time, money and health for its enjoyment. That is why the question of culture comes *after* the question of the social. To say that the masses lack culture is not to wag a finger at them but to identify a primary lack; the lack of the very conditions that make possible the enjoyments of what we have come to think of as 'culture'. In modernity culture requires money and leisure, a surplus (however small) of

---

10 'I do not know', E. P. Thompson wrote in the 1950s, 'what moral and cultural values are attached to the kitchen sink, a washboard and the week's wash for a family of five. But if we are getting more washing machines, we should recognize in that fact at least the potential of greater emancipation for working women' (quoted in Woodhams, 2001: 179). Diaries kept by working-class women in York for Rowntree's second social survey show that the family wash took four days in the 1930s. Clothes were washed, rinsed and rung dry by hand on Mondays, hung out to dry indoors on Tuesdays and ironed on Wednesdays and Thursdays (Rowntree, 1941: 441). See Arendt [1958] 1989: 79–93) on 'The labour of our body and the work of our hands'.

disposable income and time freed from unavoidable and necessary concerns. That surplus is the tantalizing gift of the modern economy, the creation of the modern bourgeoisie who first experienced its benefits in a new home-and-family-centred way of life and the new forms of leisure and enjoyment that accompany it. This is the modern culture of everyday life that finally becomes generally available through all sectors of society in the post-war world of the last century. It is what the enormities of the 'industrial revolution' finally delivered. Having at last begun to surpass the politics of poverty – the legacy of the nineteenth century – it became possible to see that what mass production promised, when applied to the manufacture of domestic appliances, was in fact the universalization of the way of life created by the eighteenth-century bourgeoisie. That is, the re-connection made in the historically informed work of Watt, Williams and Habermas, all of whom take eighteenth-century England as the classic site of this historic socio-cultural formation.

Watt's indispensable study makes clear the new economic and social conditions in the early eighteenth century that make possible 'the rise of the novel' as a novel and popular genre of entertainment especially for women. The novel is, after all, the first truly modern cultural commodity that presupposes a surplus of individual disposable money and time for its purchase and consumption. It is a key consumable for a new 'taste public' that reads not for spiritual edification nor for information and knowledge, but for pleasure and enjoyment. The novel bespeaks a new leisured class for whom reading is an agreeable pastime. Its readers are mainly the female members of the new mercantile bourgeoisie. Its concerns are with families, power, sex and money for these are the concerns of the new social class whose self-understanding is explored in the new genre of writing.[11] Notably the novel, in its classic formation, overlooks the public world of politics. It is pre-occupied by the

---

11 These concerns, in their final, purest form, are the subject matter of the novels of Ivy Compton-Burnett. *A Family and a Fortune, A House and its Head, Parents and Children, Brothers and Sisters* – these and other similar titles are indicative of Compton-Burnett's subject matter. Their deliberate blandness belies the merciless and occasionally hilarious relationships between husbands and wives, sons and daughters, aunts and uncles, maid-servants and men-servants all trapped in a strange, timeless and utterly inescapable small world that is her unique fictional creation. Her novels, written in the mid-twentieth century (between 1929 and 1963) are usually set in the late nineteenth century and take place in an eighteenth-century country house (*A House and its Head* is exemplary). They are quite astonishing to read and expose the latent violence, masked by wit and civility, generated by male sexuality and unbridled patriarchal power in the closed relations of the nuclear family. They are a dark counterpoint to the novels of Jane Austen, read over and over again by Compton-Burnett (Spurlingm, 1984), which stand as definitive explorations of the new feminine culture of everyday life that comes into being in the eighteenth century. The enormous popularity of Jane Austen's works, in umpteen film and television versions, testifies to the continuing power and vitality of her world for us today.

intense intimate politics of love and sexuality, of the power relations between men, women and children as played out in families. The novel was the first genre of writing that women could produce and consume and literature became, as Watt remarks, 'a primarily feminine pursuit' ([1956] 2000: 45).

Ian Watt

The Rise of the Novel stands out as a classic in the sociology of literature, a study in the relationships between a particular historical society and the culture it created and through which it articulated its own understanding of itself. *Culture and Society* is a longer study in the politics of a process stretched over three centuries in which those two words – 'culture' and 'society' – entered into the historical consciousness of modernity as crucial interpretative terms for the long revolution taking place in the world. That it was indeed not *a* revolution but *the* long revolution was the claim made explicit by the volume that immediately followed on from *Culture and Society* as an extended gloss on its central concerns. *The Long Revolution* goes over the same period and deepens and enriches the historical analysis; its final chapter, 'Britain in the 1960s', makes explicit that it was a slow, uneven journey, with set-backs and checks at every point, in the direction of a democratic society, whose human energy springs 'from a conviction that men can direct their own lives by breaking through the pressures and restrictions of older forms of society and by discovering new common institutions' (Williams, [1961] 1965: 375). Both books read as a study of social change in a single country but it is not difficult today to read the analysis as a case study in the world-historical process of societal modernization driven by factory capitalism and the mass-production of commodities. Our strong sense today of the world-as-a-whole, a knowable common world that all of us inhabit, is an effect of the extraordinary rate of technical innovation in the transport and communications infrastructure, driven as ever by economic globalization, that was as yet over the hills and far away in the 1950s. There was then no mass air travel; no colour television; no satellite technologies in place to provide instant global link-ups for live television feeds; no video cameras or recorders, no digital technologies, no computers, no Internet, no mobile phones, pod-casts, blogospheres and the rest. The world, in the experience of people everywhere 50 years ago, was much more immediately defined. The 'local' now is thought in relation to the global; then it was thought in relation to the national as the natural horizon of experience for most people. It is part of the enduring power of Williams' historical analysis that it remains robustly serviceable in terms of its narrative sweep and the conceptual analytical framework within which it was developed. *Culture and Society* is this book's inspiration and model and its author is its 'hidden king'.

Jürgen Habermas had read Watts and Williams and his historical analysis is in part a synthesis of theirs, although he treats the structural transformation of publicness as a European phenomenon taking place in Germany and France as well as England. Still the British case is taken as the classic site of the working through of the struggle for public opinion as the normative basis of democratic politics. Habermas's analysis of this development appears to differ significantly from that advanced by Williams who has been criticized for his gradualist account of seemingly inevitable progress towards a democratic society. There is no such progression in Habermas's account. The moment of democratic awakening is taken as the late eighteenth century; by the mid-twentieth century politics is regressing to premodern forms of publicness in which critical discussion is suborned and public life is stage-managed through the media as a theatre of power. Williams and Habermas repay the most careful critical comparison (Nieminen, 1997) since they remain the two most important authors on the historical development of the interlocking connections between politics, democracy and communication. Hannu Nieminen's judiciously balanced study tends to favour Habermas's analysis of these developments. I share his view of the fundamental similarity of their concerns but for my part I swerve more toward Williams in the end. It is a question, as Williams would say, of where the emphasis falls. For me, as for him, it falls on the ordinary culture of everyday life. The original and primary public sphere was not the political public sphere of the late eighteenth and early nineteenth century, but the literary public sphere that took shape earlier in the first half of the eighteenth century. Habermas's overriding concern with politics means that he fails to give due recognition to the enduring significance of the new reading public of the early eighteenth century which he acknowledges as the precursor of the political public sphere. That was formed in response to a gathering and prolonged moment of political crisis which Habermas takes as a rule rather than the exception and thereby overlooks the fact that in normal times the literary public sphere is the norm.

We are all political in critical political moments. But in normal times we are not. One reason for this misrecognition of the significance of the two public spheres has to do with enduring male prejudices and presumptions (in and out of academia) about what is important, weighty and serious and what is not. The lineaments of our world-wide public culture of entertainment today first took shape in the popular fictions and life-style magazines of a new reading public three centuries ago. It was then, and remains to this day, a gendered culture. In the eighteenth century as now, it was focused on the sphere of privacy and its immediate concerns – family life, sex, gossip, everyday matters. It was not solemn or serious, earnest or demanding. It bespoke a comfortable existence of leisure and relaxation, enjoyment and entertainment. If there is (as it now appears) no alternative to capitalism and democracy, we must also add that there is no apparent alternative to the 'way of life' that the economic and political determinants of modernity created as their *raison d'être*. It is all we have and, perhaps, all we deserve. It is certainly a deeply enigmatic legacy – a blessing and a curse, as educated, white middle-class American women began to realize in the 1950s.

The politics of everyday life

The academic discovery of everyday life is one indication of its quite new importance in post-war North America and Europe. It first appears from the rubble of war-torn France in Henri Lefebvre's quite remarkable *Critique of Everyday Life* ([1947] 1992). In America it achieves definitive recognition in Erving Goffman's *The Presentation of Self in Everyday Life* (1959) which takes for granted that the self in question is indeed the new 'other-directed' type identified by Riesman. In Britain, along with the work of Hoggart and Williams, I want to emphasize the quite different, but no less important work of J.L. Austin and H.P. Grice who pioneered the philosophy of ordinary language on the stony soil of Oxford philosophy in the 1950s. Their work was fundamental to establishing ordinary language and its everyday (non-academic) usage as a valid object of academic enquiry, thereby making possible the beginnings of an adequate understanding of human communication. Finally at the end of the decade Jürgen Habermas published in Germany *The Structural Transformation of the Public Sphere* – a key work which argued for the political opinions of ordinary people and the ways in which these were arrived at as the historical and normative basis of modern democracy.

All these works and more testify to the renewed significance of a culture of everyday life across all social classes. But it shows up in all sorts of ways in the 1950s. It is there in the theatre, novels and films of the decade but nowhere more than television, which now becomes the new looking-glass of everyday life. And most significantly of all it begins to show up as a new kind of politics, as the politics of the masses gives way to the politics of everyday life. The first stirrings of the new politics show up in the United States: the civil rights movement, the women's movement and, a little later, the student movement. This was not a politics produced or led by established organizations and their representatives or delegates. It came from ordinary people and what they wanted was something other than what traditional mass politics offered. Foucault has distinguished between three forms of oppression: exploitation, domination and subjection. The first is economic and concerns the struggle over the means of subsistence; the second is ideological and concerns the struggles over imposed political and religious authority, and the third is social and cultural and concerns the struggle to be allowed to be oneself (Foucault, 1982). The new social movements, as they began to articulate their own self-understanding, were concerned with this third claim. The politics of recognition, as it was aptly called by Charles Taylor (1994), has grown in global significance in the past half century. In many ways its defining moment was the refusal of Rosa Parks to give up her seat to a white passenger on a bus in Montgomery, Alabama on 1 December 1955: an act which in itself perfectly encapsulates the then new politics of everyday life.

This politics is no longer concerned with distributive justice (the politics of poverty) and its demand for freedom from want. The riddle of post-modernity and the politics of plenty concerns what comes after that. As the corrosive fear of poverty fades and as most people find they have some control over their life choices and circumstances, the question of freedom ceases to be about freedom *from* something (from the five giants of want, disease, ignorance, squalor and idleness, for instance, that the Beveridge Report of 1942 was designed to overcome)[12] and poses a new, quite different question – freedom *for* something ... but *what?* Amartya Sen has posed this issue most forcefully. The greatest of the evils of poverty is its denial of the right of individuals to discover and develop their human capabilities; their entitlement to a full, fulfilled existence (Sen, 2000). That is, the new condition of existence established in the advanced economies in the past 60 years. Working through what it means has been, and remains a core concern in post-modern democracies. It is the essence of the politics of culture and it hailed into existence a new academic field of enquiry to try and get to grips with it: Cultural Studies.

The politics of culture

Cultural Studies takes the ordinary and the everyday as its object of enquiry. It began, in orthodox fashion, with the everyday life and culture of the English working class in the 1950s and developed in response to the new cultural politics of the 1960s. Its task was to identify and account for the significance of these developments, initially in terms of their impact on working-class life. Its difficulty, from the start, lay in recognizing and adjusting to what was happening. Cultural Studies was, from the start, concerned with *contemporary* culture and therein is the essence of its own internal 'problematic', for how are we – any of us – to make sense of the unfolding present? The play of the politics of the present – its meaning and significance – is what forever eludes the actors in the present even as they seek to grasp it. None of us can jump over our own shadow. It is our destiny and fate that we must act in our own here and now without any assurance of the success of our actions for none of us can foresee the future. Only as time goes by and the present recedes into the past does its

---

12 Named after Sir William Beveridge, who wrote it, the Report on Social Security, published in November 1942, was a key war-time document that set out the terms for social security for all 'from the cradle to the grave'. Its mantra was 'Freedom from Want' and was designed to prevent the recurrence of the conditions of primary poverty to which millions were reduced by unemployment in the preceding decade. It laid the foundations for the creation of the 'Welfare State' by a newly elected Labour Government in the aftermath of the war.

once futural horizon begin to appear and we, in later generations, may be able to see what simply could not be seen at the time by those caught up in the play of the politics of their own and present times. The wisdom of hindsight means precisely that it *can* only come in retrospect. It does not mean that actors in the present are foolish and unwise but rather underscores the real heroism and courage of action; for all actions are a leap of faith and all contemporary efforts, in good faith, to interpret those actions are as historically contingent as what they seek to account for and justify. It is only now that the historical lineaments of the world as it was 30 or 40 years ago have begun to appear for only now has it begun to fade from the noisy present into the silent past. It is not history that is relative but we the living, who stand in an always contingent and relative relationship to it. The world endures. Those who dwell in it at any time do not.

Hannah Arendt has noted the occasional occurrence of what she calls an 'odd in-between period' which sometimes inserts itself into historical time. In such moments

> Not only the later historians but the actors and witnesses, the living them-selves, become aware of an interval in time which is altogether determined by things that are no longer and by things that are not yet. In history these inter-vals have shown more than once that they may contain the moment of truth. (Arendt, [1961] 1993: 9)

The 1950s – her time of writing – was, Arendt implies, just such an interval in historical time and I think she was right. There was a palpable sense, in the intellectual engagements of that decade, of the world in a moment of transition which I have tried to capture as the passage from modernity and its politics of poverty to a postmodern world and a politics of plenty. The meaning of this transition, how it played out at the time, was what those who lived those times sought to grasp. On the one hand, there was the recognition of the 'things that are no longer' which was manifest in the fading of 'the masses' and the redis-covery of 'people'. It was well understood in North America and Northern Europe that the 1950s was a period of unprecedented affluence across whole societies, as America's most distinguished economist made plain at the time (Galbraith, 1958). Almost everyone felt better off. There was, indeed, no return to the pre-war hungry 1930s. But 'the things that are not yet' were naturally the hardest to see and speak of. The difficulty of articulating what was truly felt but somehow then beyond the reach of words was most clearly expressed in the founding text of what came to be the Women's Liberation movement. In *The Feminine Mystique*, Betty Friedan began with 'the problem that has no name' – the obscure but very real sense of the oppressive character of post-war everyday domestic life for educated, comfortably off American women (Friedan, 1963).

The gendered character of academic life in the 1950s, completely dominated by men and in which women were, at every level, marginalized and exploited would only become apparent in the decades that followed.[13] Similarly the great fault-line of racial injustice exploded into life in this decade with the civil rights movement. And finally 'the young' appeared both as a new socio-economic category and a newly self-aware politicized social stratum as students became disenchanted with their 'parent culture'. This was the new politics of everyday life and it nowadays hardly needs saying that middle-aged middle-class white male academics were not best placed to make much sense of any of this. But they of course were in charge of the academy. It was they who controlled and defined the discourse and they of course did not 'see' these things or, insofar as they did, saw them only as subsidiary aspects of the ways in which they sought to account for what was going on in the world. In the light of the later colonization of the politics of everyday life by Cultural Studies it bears emphasizing that the new social movements in their formative moments had little or no connection with academics or academia.[14] The student movement is the exception that proves the rule for, from the perspective of student protest, it was the professors and what they taught that was their problem, not their answer.

It is crucial to acknowledge the simple fact that the politics of everyday life did in fact arise from everyday life and experience itself – from the experience of being treated as less than human if you were black, from a sense of the futility of the American dream if you were a woman trapped in the role of housewife and mother,[15] from a sense of the pointlessness and irrelevance of what the older generation offered as culture and education if you were young. The politics of everyday life that emerged in 1950s America was global in its implications and reach from the start: the abuses of race, the oppression of women, the condescension of the older generation towards the young all had a common experiential basis for those on the receiving end – the palpable denial of what it was *to be* black or female or young. The demand to be recognized and valued *as* what indeed you were, to be allowed to be expressively yourself in public – this was and remains the essence of the new politics. It was a demand for the realization of the promise of democracy – the right and entitlement, the freedom to be and

---

13 See the devastating report on *The Status of Women in Sociology* edited by Helen McGill Hughes for the American Sociological Association in 1973. Hughes produced what for me was one of the most original and exciting individual pieces of mass communication research that I came across in the pre-war literature (Hughes, 1937, 1940) on the newspaper human interest story. Yet she never held a full-time post in an American university. She was part-time editor, for many years of the *American Journal of Sociology*, while her husband, whom she met in graduate school at Chicago, went on to become a professor.

14 See especially Francesca Polletta's excellent study of the mid-century social movements in the USA (Polletta, 2004).

15 For a ferociously funny assault on 'The mommy myth', see Douglas and Michaels (2004).

---

to become your self. Such demands could only arise in societies where the majorities were freed from primary poverty and the pressing exigencies of immediate want and need.

We are today still working through the meaning and significance of the politics of everyday life. The present moment feels, to me, like another of Arendt's 'intervals in time'. At the start of the twenty-first century we begin to able to see something of the overall historic impact and significance of the receding preceding century. We can now begin to glimpse its overall shape and structure. It was not so in the decades that succeeded the 1950s. From the mid-1960s to the end of the 1980s the fog banks rolled in on the politics of the present. They were fractious and ill-tempered times inside and outside academia in which the impact of historical change was deeply felt but obscurely and divisively understood. I have tried, in my account of the moment of 'media studies' at Birmingham in the 1970s, to do justice to its real difficulties and complexities. The initial project of CCCS – the heritage of Richard Hoggart – was to grapple with the impact of the new culture of affluence on the historic urban working class of the North of England. It was thrown off balance almost immediately by the new social movements – not only feminism and race but the student revolution of the late 1960s as well, which all combined to produce a peculiarly intense and prickly working environment in the fractious decade of the 1970s. None of these things was easily accommodated. Feminism, in Hall's memorable phrase, crapped on the table. Race was, again in his retrospective accounts, even more difficult to assimilate into the working life of the Centre. As for the student revolution, the Centre itself was conceived as an attempt – in its organization and day-to-day practices – to overcome the limitations of bourgeois university education. There was therefore much emphasis on collective work (the famous working groups) and collective writing. Individualism was a petty bourgeois notion and so not many individual PhDs got done during the long march through Theory. And in all this the English Working Class as a normative political ideal unravelled. The traditional EWC so affectionately remembered by Hoggart, and whose origins had been heroically rescued from the neglect of History by Thompson, turned out to be, under the scrutiny of race and gender studies, white and racist and male and chauvinist. Its death rattle was the ugly, futile miners strike of 1983 which finally put paid to the National Union of Miners, one of the oldest, greatest unions of workers, whose dirty dangerous industry was the very cornerstone of nineteenth-century industrial capitalism and the spearhead of organized labour politics for much of the twentieth century. Coal by the 1980s was an energy source in terminal decline and mining, as a way of life, was dead.[16]

---

16 On mining as a way of life, see the classic study by Dennis, Henriques and Slaughter (1956).

Stuart Hall's cogent analysis of the two paradigms in Cultural Studies classified them as their culturalist and the structuralist moments (Hall, 1980). The first generation of the 1950s and 1960s (Hoggart, Williams and Thompson) had privileged 'lived experience' as the authenticating, validating category of everyday existence. The new structuralisms of the 1970s undermined that claim. Lived experience could not be claimed as validating anything since what determined it was quite simply beyond its grasp. Lived experience was an effect of ideological forces that reconciled individuals to their immediate circumstances and thereby to the economic and political forces which determined those circumstances. Hall's ideology critique, with which I do not agree, nevertheless clearly and accurately identified the fundamental 'problematic' of the politics of the everyday; the status of human experience and the enigmatic character of daily life. That enigma, in the 1970s, showed up most clearly in the dominant communicative medium of everyday life, television, whose seeming immediacy and transparency appeared to validate the facticity (the matter-of-factness) of ordinary lived experience while mystifying the hidden forces of economic and political domination that produced it as such. The key text produced by the Media Studies group was a study of how everyday television did precisely that. *Everyday Television: 'Nationwide'* by Charlotte Brunsdon and David Morley (1978) is today quite unjustly ignored in preference for the subsequent study of the programme's audience that Morley (1980) produced. It provided a detailed, persuasive analysis of the ideological work performed by the programme, the ways in which it interpelled its audience as a nation of families with a shared set of unexamined commonsense values and assumptions about Englishness and the English way of life. It served to demonstrate the force of Hall's ideology critique of lived experience, its evasions and concealments.

Media, society and culture

If we now compare the two moments of 'media studies' we can see in what ways they were like and unlike each other. Both presume the power of the media and both are concerned with its social and cultural effects on those on their receiving end. James Curran has argued that the revived concern with audiences studies in the 1980s was, in effect, a revival of the agenda of American effects studies 30 or more years earlier (Curran et al., 1996). There is more truth in this than the defenders of new reception and ethnographic studies will allow, yet the differences are striking. In the 1930s, the question of media effects was a pre-conception for the new social science of mass communication and, as such, was treated as empirically provable or disprovable. The discovery of the two-step flow of media influence challenged and revised the initial working hypothesis which fell into abeyance for a time after the publication in 1955 of *Personal Influence*. The question of media power needed to be re-thought and the theory of ideology revived it. This time though, the assumed power of television was not an open question. That was foreclosed from the start, for its ideological effect was not a hypothesis to be tested but a theoretical *a priori*. The concrete task of ideology critique was to show how it worked and with what effects for media audiences. It too faded as the discovery of 'active audiences' begin to show (yet again) that individuals were not merely the bearers of ideological effects but used the media as aspects of their lifestyles and self-definitions. There were different premises in each case but similar outcomes in the turn to audiences and reception studies. But the politics of these two moments were different. The politics of poverty and the question of the masses which defined the 1930s have a different basis to the politics of plenty and the question of everyday life which defined the 1950s and since. Each was a response to the state of the world in its own time. The difference between them is an effect of the slow structural transformation of the world in transition from an economy of scarcity to one of abundance.

I would like to suggest, by way of tentative conclusion, that the crucial difference between these two politics can be thought of in moral and ethical terms; more exactly, that the politics of poverty is a moral question, whereas the politics of plenty raises ethical questions. Morality is concerned with the conditions of social existence; with how we live with each other. It is *the* normative social question. It is about the basis of a just and fair society. Poverty is an affront to any such notion and modern theories of positive justice (Rawls, [1971] 1999 and Sen, 2000) are about social fairness. Ethics is a refinement of basic moral questions. It concerns the good life and only becomes salient, as the question of *how* to live, for individuals and societies that have risen above the realm of necessity. That poverty is a basic social injustice to be remedied by political action is a distinctively modern concept (Fleischacker, 2005), and its elimination from the lives of the majority of its citizens is a real achievement of advanced capitalist democracies since the end of the Second World War. What these societies now face are a whole series of ethical questions that have arisen only as the earlier pandemic disease of poverty has faded. Fat is indeed a political and ethical issue today. It was not in the lean 1930s. The characteristic dilemmas of postmodernity arise from our difficulties in finding common ground about what a good and meaningful life might consist of in unprecedented conditions of economic abundance.

If we ask what the politics of plenty is about, we might agree with John Dunn's analysis of the story of democracy as the triumph of the party of egotism over the party of equality. We have settled for security and comfort, ease and amusement. That, in Dunn's view, is what contemporary democracies deliver for the majority of its citizens (Dunn, 2005). Is the good life no more than this – shopping, eating out, holidays abroad and the continuing banquet dished up daily and weekly by the contemporary entertainment industries? Should we not take seriously those who warn that we are amusing ourselves to death? Such questions indicate something of the ethical dilemmas we face today. They also point to our difficulties in knowing how to begin to answer them if it is the case, as Alisdair MacIntyre has so vigorously argued, that we no longer know the meaning of the virtues (MacIntyre, 1985). The critics of modernity had a clear moral basis from which to denounce the evils of poverty. We have no clear perspective on the goods and evils that prosperity has brought us. This, our postmodern dilemma, shows up in postmodern thinking which lacks any normative basis and is simply uncomfortable with moral categories (Bauman, 1993).

The original sociology of mass communication had a clear normative basis in both its key academic articulations; Lazarsfeld and Merton just as much as Adorno and Horkheimer. Merton in particular was concerned with the condition of the masses in a society characterized by cynicism and anomie. Critical Theory's devastating critique of Enlightenment was intended somehow to salvage its original emancipatory promise, but how that might happen was beyond the reach of Horkheimer and Adorno's thinking in the early 1940s. For them the Second World War was indeed the end of reason. There is a similar clear moral basis to the thought of the first generation of cultural criticism in Britain. Both Williams and Thompson write in the name of social justice and on behalf of the underprivileged. But when we get to the 1970s, the study of culture and the media has lost any normative grounding. There is no moral basis that I can see in ideology critique. One can see what is being criticized (power) but *why* it is being criticized and in the name of what remains quite opaque. In Foucault's grim equation (power plus knowledge equals truth), truth has lost any normative or moral basis and amounts to no more than the old saying that might is right. This lack of moral clarity is an effect of the exogenous world historical process in play at that time. One of the most striking features of Birmingham in the 1970s was the frantic pursuit of Theory in order to get some compass bearings on what the world was about and where it was heading. That pursuit led to a pervasive cultural relativism and the loss of confidence in the possibility of normative critique and judgement, for any such attempt was immediately torpedoed by the charge of Western phallogocentrism. The moral confusions of postmodernity are the effects of an economy of abundance which has brought about an increasingly diverse and pluralized world celebrated as such in multicultural identity politics. This world, our world, has no acknowledged moral basis to it and no shared ethical concerns. And it is precisely this that presses on us with increasing urgency at the start of the twenty-first century.

Media and communication

In the late 1970s a group of colleagues at the Polytechnic of Central London (I was one of them) decided to establish a new journal for the new field of Media Studies. We called it *Media, Culture & Society*. There was no big debate about the name. It simply served to acknowledge the core concerns of the study of the media as we then saw them in terms of their social and cultural impact. The journal's name confirms the historical thesis outlined above: that what started as a social critique of mass communication in the 1930s had morphed into a cultural critique of the media by the time of the journal's foundation. It is, of course, interesting to examine the play of contemporary social and cultural processes in radio and television, but they can equally well be examined in other institutions and were in the 1970s with similar results. Althusser's little shopping list of ISAs included education, religion and the family and they too were examined and found to be, like the media, ideological state apparatuses. And that is my key criticism of both moments. Neither tells us anything specific about the media. In both historical moments a special case was initially made for the special effectiveness of media on contemporary attitudes and behaviours but in each case the claim, when empirically examined, began to fade. It is certainly true that (to take notable instances) the politics of class, gender and race are pervasively implicated both in the institutional workings of the media and in their output. They are indeed important matters and worthy of serious academic attention but such studies are invariably more about the questions of race, class and gender than they are about the question of the media. The historically determined economic, political and cultural processes that play through the media at any time are not in any way particular to them. They are in play at any time (as Raymond Williams made especially clear) through *all* social institutions and practices.

The title of this book has, for me at least, more than a hint of irony. When you pair words together you suggest that they have some natural affinity to each other, like 'love' and 'marriage' or 'culture' and 'society'. No such natural affinity between 'media' and 'communication' has yet been established in Media Studies. If we are to consider radio and television (the two media under consideration in the 1930s and the 1970s) in their own terms then I think we are bound to ask 'What is *their* question?' I take it to be the question of communication. If radio and television are properly to be thought of as new technologies of broadcast communication with a general social application – if communication is their general business – then what do we mean by that and how does it work? How do, in fact, radio and television communicate with their audiences? There was, of course, a model of communication put forward for the study of radio in the 1930s and for television in the 1970s. In the effects tradition it was posed as the question of 'Who says what to whom with what effect?' – a one-way transmission model of communication. Stuart Hall's encoding/decoding model significantly revised the earlier direct transmission model and envisaged the encoding (transmission) and decoding (reception) of the television 'message' as a complex, related social process. But neither historical moment focused on the question of communication for in neither case was communication a focal matter of concern.

I have not attempted here (for it is quite beyond me) anything like a full account of academic developments in the study of communication in the past century. It is a vast topic that is, in my view, pretty thoroughly confused and confusing now and in the course of its historical career as an object of academic concern.[17] Instead I have offered a selective account of post-war developments in the study of communication in different academic fields; history, literature, sociology and philosophy. I have dealt with the historical work of Harold Innis on the question of communication and technology and its further exploration by Marshal McLuhan; the sociology of interaction as pioneered by Erving Goffman and Harold Garfinkel; culture and communication as explored by Raymond Williams; the ordinary language philosophy of John Austin and Paul Grice; the analysis of conversation by Harvey Sacks; and the theory of communicative rationality developed by Jürgen Habermas. There are strong thematic links and narrative connections in all this work and there is a fascinating historical thesis to be developed about it since it all began in the quite pivotal decade of the 1950s.[18] It was pivotal because it was the decade in which the

---

17 The *Journal of Communication* recently produced a survey of the 'State of the art in communication theory and research' (December 2004, September 2005). The journal is a publication of the ICA (the International Communication Association) and the editors invited overview articles on 17 of the ICA's current divisions and special interest groups: the philosophy of communication, visual communication, public relations, mass communication, popular communication, organizational communication, health communication, language and social interaction, interpersonal communication, feminist scholarship, political communication, GLBT (gay, lesbian, bisexual and transgender) studies, information systems, intercultural and development communication, instructional/development communication, communication law and policy, and communication and technology. All contributions bar one (on organizational communication) are by authors at universities in the United States. Every contribution is written as a purely endogenous narrative with no recognition of anything outside its immediate concerns. The editors make no attempt (how could they) to indicate any connection between any of the parts for there is none. Their special issue stands as an awesome confirmation of Lukács's critique of technical rationality, the reification of consciousness and the loss of any possible sense of the whole.

18 The thinking of the 1950s in North America and Europe registered a sharp break with the modernist thinking of the pre-war period. The key moment of post modernity was not in the 1970s and 1980s when it was belatedly grasped by modernist thought but in the immediate post-war decade when all the conditions of the world we now inhabit first became apparent. In the final volume of this trilogy I will return to a revaluation of the structure of postmodern thinking that emerged in Europe and North America in the 1950s and a critique of the regressive late modernist thinking that rolled over it in the 1970s and 1980s.

---

conditions and character of the world we inhabit today were decisively established in the aftermath of a global war. It was a mundane world of unprecedented affluence for the majority of people. It was a newly sociable, talkative, communicative world as *Personal Influence* found. And this was made visible at the time by the rise of television as it took over from its pre-war parent, radio, as the pre-eminent broadcast medium of everyday life.

In this book's companion I begin with two chapters on the discovery of new formats for broadcast talk – unscripted, sociable talk designed as public entertainment for others – on British wartime radio and on television in the mid-1950s. The thinking that underpins both chapters and throughout is informed by the authors of the 1950s discussed above and their pioneering work on the sociable, interactive, character of daily life and on the moral foundations and communicative logic of ordinary language and the ordinary world. And thus the final purpose of this book is disclosed as the basis of the next. Between them, I hope, they unite the torn halves of an integral whole – the question of communication as it bears upon the question of the media.

References

Altick, R.D. (1957) *The English Common Reader: A Social History of the Mass Reading Public.* Chicago: University of Chicago Press.

Arendt, H. ([1958] 1989) *The Human Condition.* Chicago: University of Chicago Press.

Arendt, H. ([1961] 1993) *Between Past and Future.* Harmondsworth: Penguin Books.

Arendt, H. ([1963] 1990) *On Revolution.* Harmondsworth: Penguin Books.

Bauman, Z. (1993) *Postmodern Ethics.* Cambridge: Polity Press.

Berelson, B. ([1949] 2004) 'What missing the newspaper means', in J.D. Peters and P. Simonson (eds), *Mass Communication and American Social Thought, 1919–1968.* Lanham, MD: Rowman and Littlefield, pp. 254–62.

Boltanski, L. (1999) *Distant Suffering: Morality, Media and Politics.* Cambridge: Cambridge University Press.

Brunsdon, C. and Morley, D. (1978) *Everyday Television: 'Nationwide'.* BFI Television Monograph 10. London: British Film Institute.

Cantril, H., Gaudet, H. and Herzog, H. (1940) *The Invasion from Mars: A Study in the Psychology of Panic.* Princeton, NJ: Princeton University Press.

Carey, J. (1992) *The Intellectuals and the Masses, 1880–1939.* London: Faber and Faber.

Curran, J. et al. (eds) (1996) *Cultural Studies and Communications.* London: Arnold.

Dennis, N., Henriques, F. and Slaughter, C. (1956) *Coal is Our Life.* London: Eyre and Spottiswoode.

Douglas, S.J. and Michaels, M.W. (2004) *The Mommy Myth: The Idealization of Motherhood and How it Has Undermined All Women.* New York: Free Press.

Dunn, J. (1993) *Western Political Theory in the Face of the Future.* Cambridge: Cambridge University Press.

Dunn, J. (2005) *Setting the People Free: The Story of Democracy.* London: Atlantic Books.

Fleischacker, S. (2005) *A Short History of Distributive Justice*. Cambridge, MA: Harvard University Press.

Foucault, M. (1974) *The Archaeology of Knowledge*. London: Tavistock Publications.

Foucault, M. (1982) 'The subject and power', in H. Dreyfus and P. Rabinow (eds), *Michel Foucault. Beyond Structuralism and Hermeneutics*. Brighton: Harvester Press, pp. 208–26.

Frank, M., Ziebarth, M. and Field, C. (1982) *The Life and Times of Rosie the Riveter*. Emeryville, CA: Clarity Educational Productions.

Friedan, B. (1963) *The Feminine Mystique*. London: Gollancz.

Galbraith, J.K. (1958) *The Affluent Society*. London: Hamish Hamilton.

Goffman, E. ([1959] 1962) *The Presentation of Self in Everyday Life*. Harmondsworth: Penguin Press.

Habermas, J. ([1962] 1989) *The Structural Transformation of the Public Sphere*. Cambridge: Polity Press.

Hall, S. (1980) 'Cultural studies: two paradigms', *Media, Culture & Society*, 2(1): 57–72.

Herzog, H. (1941) 'On borrowed experience: an analysis of listening to daytime sketches', *Studies in Philosophy and Social Science*, IX(1): 65–95.

Horton, D. and Wohl, R.W. ([1956] 2004) 'Mass communication and para-social interaction: Observations on intimacy at a distance', in J.D. Peters and P. Simonson (eds), *Mass Communication and American Social Thought, 1919–1968*. Lanham, MD: Rowman and Littlefield, pp. 373–86.

Hughes, H.M. (1937) 'Human interest stories and democracy', in J.D. Peters and P. Simonson (eds), *Mass Communication and American Social Thought, 1919–1968*. Lanham, MD: Rowman and Littlefield, pp. 118–28.

Hughes, H.M. (1940) *News and the Human Interest Story*. Chicago: University of Chicago Press.

Hughes, H.M. (ed.) (1973) *The Status of Women in Sociology 1968–1972*. Washington, DC: The American Sociological Association.

Katz. E. and Lazarsfeld, P. (1955) *Personal Influence: The Part Played by People in the Flow of Mass Communications*. Glencoe, IL: The Free Press.

Lazarsfeld, P. (1940) *Radio and the Printed Page*. New York: Duell, Sloan and Pearce.

Lefebvre, H. ([1947] 1992) *Critique of Everyday Life*. London: Verso.

MacIntyre, A. (1985) *After Virtue: A Study in Moral Theory*. London: Duckworth.

Merton, R.K. ([1946] 2004) *Mass Persuasion*, edited and with an Introduction by P. Simonson. New York: Howard Fertig.

Morley, D. (1980) *The Nationwide Audience: Structure and Decoding*. BFI Television Monograph 11. London: British Film Institute.

Niemenen, H. (1997) *Communication and Democracy: Habermas, Williams and the British Case*. Helsinki: Annales Academiae Scientiarum Fennicae.

Polletta, F. (2004) *Freedom is an Endless Meeting: Democracy in American Social Movements*. Chicago: University of Chicago Press.

Rawls, J. ([1971] 1999) *A Theory of Justice*. Oxford: Oxford University Press.

Riesman, D. ([1950] 1976) *The Lonely Crowd*. New Haven, CT: Yale University Press.

Rowntree, B. Seebohm (1901) *Poverty: A Study of Town Life*. London: Macmillan.

Rowntree, B. Seebohm (1941) *Poverty: and Progress*. London: Longmans, Green and Co.

Rowntree, B. Seebohm and Lavers, G.R. (1951) *English Life and Leisure*. London: Longmans, Green and Co.

Sen, A. (2000) *Development as Freedom*. New York: Anchor Books.

Spurling, H. (1984) *Ivy: The Life of Ivy Compton-Burnett*. New York: Knopf.

Stone, L. (1979) *The Family, Sex and Marriage in England, 1500–1800*. Harmondsworth: Penguin Books.

Taylor, C. (1994) *Multiculturalism*. Princeton, NJ: Princeton University Press.

Watt, I. ([1956] 2000) *The Rise of the Novel*. London: Pimlico Edition.

Williams, R. ([1958] 1965) *Culture and Society*. Harmondsworth: Penguin Books.

Williams, R. ([1961] 1965) *The Long Revolution*. Harmondsworth: Penguin Books.

Woodhams, S. (2001) *History in the Making: Raymond Williams, Edward Thompson and Radical Intellectuals, 1936–1956*. London: Merlin Press.

Index

Entries in *italics* denote publications, television and radio programmes

Bonner, Frances 227
bourgeois culture 238
bourgeois intelligentsia 94
breaching experiments 154
Brecht, Bertolt 55, 56, 219
Britain
    bourgeois intelligentsia 94
    Centre for Contemporary Cultural
        Studies 95, 199
    class 104, 109, 214
    class boundaries 110–11
    culture 111, 113–17, 279
    education 96–8
    English Association 97
    English literature 96–8, 99, 111,
        112, 260, 274
    English Working Class 104, 285
    feminism 215
    nationalism 223
    politics 52
    radio 81
    sociology 93
    television 135
    Workers Educational Association 104, 105
British Broadcasting Corporation (BBC) 26, 81,
    119, 141, 212, 255, 267
British Film Institute 221, 226
broadband cable 138
broadcast audience 183
broadcast talk 189–96, 213
Brown, Penelope 177, 178
Brunsdon, Charlotte 208, 212, 227, 286
Bryson, Lyndon 70
bureaucracy 41–2

CA see conversation analysis
Calhoun, Craig 256–7
Canada 123–4
canalization 72
Cantril, Hadley 22, 269
capitalism 137
    see also factory capitalism
Carey, James 2, 124–5
Carey, John 266–7
causality 161
Centre for Contemporary Cultural
    Studies 95, 199
Centrespeak 224
Cherry, Colin 198
Chicago School 9–10, 33, 146
children 107
cinema 48, 53, 80, 208, 221
civil death 147–8
civil inattention 147, 149–50
civil rights movement 150, 214, 251, 281
civil society 254, 256

civilization 128
class 104, 109, 215, 223
class boundaries 110–11
Class Inequality and Political Order 211
Cold War 151
Coleridge, Samuel Taylor 112
comics 79
commodification 43
commodity fetishism 37–40, 202
common sense 201, 222
communication
    academic study 198, 260
    bias 126–9
    civil inattention 149
    culture 117–21
    electronic 130
    face engagements 152–3
    face-to-face 256
    global village 135–9
    institutions 119
    interpersonal 272
    model 209–10
    noncoercive 256
    radio 141
    social psychology 10
    speech act theory 172–4
    talk as interaction 162–7
    technology 142
    two-step flow 84
    value systems 211
    writing 127, 132
communication theory 290
communicative affordances 141
communicative intentionality 175, 176
communicative rationality 248–50
Communism 56
community study 12
companionate marriage 275
comprehensibility 249
Compton-Burnett, Ivy 278
computers 119
conformity 78
connectivity 140–1
consciousness 43–5
constatives 173
The Constitution of Society 160
constitutional life 237
consumer capitalism 36
consumption 58, 137, 238
content analysis 65
context 173
continuers 190
conversation analysis (CA) 142, 165–7, 184–9
conversational dialogue 165
conversational maxims 175–6
co-operation 152, 175

MacIntyre, Alisdair 288
McLuhan, Marshall 123, 129–33, 136,
  139, 198
magazines 240
male domination 50
male rationality 49
Marcuse, Herbert 45, 100
market research 10, 11, 13, 17
marketing analysis 85
Marriott, Stephanie 195
Marxism 15, 32, 37–40, 113, 218, 226
mass civilization 100
mass communication 9–29, 70–4, 117, 268
  audience response 17
  Chicago School 10
  effects tradition 21
  Institute of Social Research 13–21
  media 134
  morality 288
  research 86, 139
  sociology 1, 2, 89, 142, 207, 263, 268–73
mass consumption 48
mass culture 31–61, 99, 277
  art 51–7
  critical theory 34–7
  happiness 49
  instrumental reason 40–3
  Marxist theory 37–40
  reification of consciousness 43–5
mass democracy 256
mass entertainment 36
mass media 71, 73
mass panic 22, 82
mass persuasion 64–70, 71, 82, 272
mass production 33, 35, 48, 101,
  123, 137, 278
mass reproduction 54
meaning 155, 165, 172, 217
media
  analysis 134
  cultural impact 289
  development 1, 260
  digital 139
  electronic 135–6
  encoding/decoding 204–6
  intervening variables 86
  McLuhan 129–34
  mass communication 134
  ownership 74
  political news interview 189, 191
  power 286
  public life 254, 255
  ruling ideas 202
  social role 72
  writing 127, 142
media education 25, 27

media events 82
media exposure 88–9
media imperialism 125
media studies 1, 198–9, 226–7, 261
Media Technology and Society 141
media texts 217
membership 158
Merton, Robert 63, 66, 68, 70, 72, 269
methodology, quantitative/qualitative 26
Metz, Christian 221
Meyrowitz, Joshua 136–7, 139, 254
Middletown 12, 101
migration 31
Mills, C. Wright 85, 89, 271
mixed-motive games 151
modern literature 103
modernity 137, 245, 251, 262
  America 32
  economic relations 35, 42
  family 275
modernization 76
modes of conformity 76
Modleski, Tania 227
monopolization 72
monopoly capitalism 45–6
morality 156, 287
Moreno, Jacob 87
Morley, David 208, 212, 227, 286
mosaic technique 132
motivation 152
movies 49
multiculturalism 253
music 19–20, 51, 57–61
mutual awareness 149
Mythologies 217

narrative analysis 205
narrative excess 68
nation-state 239
National Curriculum 96
national unity 212
nationalism 223
Nationwide 212, 222, 227, 286
natural talk 164
naturalism 220
Nazism 72, 242
negative face 177
New Deal 52
Newbolt, Sir Henry 97
news programs 138
newspapers 48, 54, 240, 270, 284
Niemenen, Hannu 280
noise 209
non-literate cultures 129
novels 115, 278
nuclear family 275

radio *cont.*
   program analysis 17
   public service broadcasting 255
   serious listening 26
   service programs 27
   soap operas 27, 73, 270
   social progress 19
   technological determinism 141
Radio and the Printed Page 25-6, 269
Radway, Janice 228
rationality 40, 45, 49, 245
reading public 235
realism 220
reason 156
records 49
reference 179
regressive listening 60
reification 43-5, 58, 202
religious power 129
Renaissance painting 132
Resistance through Rituals 215
response tokens 190
Riesman, David 74-82, 262
The Rise of the Novel 274, 279
Rojek, Chris 213
romantic fiction 228
Rossi, Peter 85
routinization 158
Rowntree, Seebohm 276
ruling ideas 202, 214, 218

Sacks, Harvey 158, 163, 166, 171, 184
Sade, Marquis de 50
Sampson, George 98
satellite services 138
Saussure, Ferdinand de 200, 216
scepticism 81, 155
Schegloff, Emanuel 146, 165
Schelling, Thomas 151
Schramm, Wilbur 21, 89, 209
Schudson, Michael 251
science 141, 160
scientific management 44
screen-theory 221
self 146, 147, 148
   America 262
   biography 156-9
   sociology 150-2
self-expression 54, 119-20
self-interest 151
semiology 216, 219, 226
Sen, Amartya 282
Sense and Sensibilia 224
sentences 173
service programs 27

sexuality 157
Shannon, Claude 209
shopping 85
significance 165
signifiers 217
signs 217
Simonson, Peter 65, 72
sincerity 80, 192-4, 249
situational proprieties 149
Smith, Kate 64, 65, 66, 67, 269
soap operas *see* radio serials; television
sociability 78, 81, 239, 272
   see also gregariousness
social 9
social action 72
social actors 156, 159
social attitudes 73
social control 71
social deixis 180
social environment 87
social injustice 287
social interaction 151
social life 147, 152, 271
social movements 214-16, 218, 251, 285
social order 75, 177
social progress 19
social psychology 10, 23
social relations 33
social theory 161
social units 275
socialist realism 52
sociality 271
society
   administration 239
   culture 109-13, 120, 235, 239
   emergence 234, 265-6
   individual 75
   literature 274
   membership 158
   politeness 177-9
sociology 145
   Britain 93, 261
   ethnomethodology 159-62
   functionalism 160
   linguistics 162
   literature 279
   man as judgemental dope 161
   mass communication 1, 2, 89, 142,
      207, 263, 268-73
   methodology 13
   self 150-2
   structuration 161
   talk 171
   technological determinism 141
sociometrics 87